Hegel and German Public Law

Europe's Legacy in the Modern World

Series Editors: Martti Koskenniemi (University of Helsinki, Finland) and Annabel Brett (University of Cambridge, UK)

The 19th century is often described as Europe's century. This series aims to explore the truth of this claim. It views Europe as a global actor and offers insights into its role in ordering the world, creating community and providing welfare in the 19th century and beyond. Volumes in the series investigate tensions between the national and the global, welfare and warfare, property and poverty. They look at how notions like democracy, populism and totalitarianism came to be intertwined and how this legacy persists in the present day world.

The series emphasizes the entanglements between the legal, the political and the economic and employs techniques and methodologies from the history of legal, political and economic thought, the history of events, and structural history. The result is a collection of works that shed new light on the role that Europe's intellectual history has played in the development of the modern world.

Published:

Historical Teleologies in the Modern World, Henning Trüper, Dipesh Chakrabarty and Sanjay Subrahmanyam

Europe's Utopias of Peace, Bo Stråth

Political Reform in the Ottoman and Russian Empires, Adrian Brisku

European Modernity: A Global Approach, Bo Stråth and Peter Wagner

The Contested History of Autonomy, Gerard Rosich

Caesarism in the Post-Revolutionary Age: Crisis, Populace and Leadership, Markus J. Prutsch

Orientalism, Philology, and the Illegibility of the Modern World, Henning Trueper

Roman Law and the Idea of Europe, Ed. Kaius Tuori and Heta Björklund

The History and Politics of Free Movement within the European Union: European Borders of Justice, Saila Heinikoski

Hegel and German Public Law, Nathaniel Boyd

Forthcoming:

Social Difference in Nineteenth-Century Spanish America: An Intellectual History, Francisco A. Ortega

Hegel and German Public Law

Nathaniel Boyd

BLOOMSBURY ACADEMIC
LONDON • NEW YORK • OXFORD • NEW DELHI • SYDNEY

BLOOMSBURY ACADEMIC
Bloomsbury Publishing Plc, 50 Bedford Square, London, WC1B 3DP, UK
Bloomsbury Publishing Inc, 1359 Broadway, New York, NY 10018, USA
Bloomsbury Publishing Ireland, 29 Earlsfort Terrace, Dublin 2, D02 AY28, Ireland

BLOOMSBURY, BLOOMSBURY ACADEMIC and the Diana logo are trademarks of Bloomsbury Publishing Plc

First published in Great Britain 2026

A catalogue record for this book is available from the British Library.

A catalog record for this book is available from the Library of Congress.

ISBN: HB: 978-1-3505-8417-4
ePDF: 978-1-3505-8419-8
eBook: 978-1-3505-8420-4

Series: Europe's Legacy in the Modern World

Typeset by Newgen KnowledgeWorks Pvt. Ltd., Chennai, India

For product safety related questions contact productsafety@bloomsbury.com.

To find out more about our authors and books visit www.bloomsbury.com and sign up for our newsletters.

Hegel and German Public Law

Nathaniel Boyd

BLOOMSBURY ACADEMIC
LONDON • NEW YORK • OXFORD • NEW DELHI • SYDNEY

BLOOMSBURY ACADEMIC
Bloomsbury Publishing Plc, 50 Bedford Square, London, WC1B 3DP, UK
Bloomsbury Publishing Inc, 1359 Broadway, New York, NY 10018, USA
Bloomsbury Publishing Ireland, 29 Earlsfort Terrace, Dublin 2, D02 AY28, Ireland

BLOOMSBURY, BLOOMSBURY ACADEMIC and the Diana logo are trademarks of Bloomsbury Publishing Plc

First published in Great Britain 2026

A catalogue record for this book is available from the British Library.

A catalog record for this book is available from the Library of Congress.

ISBN: HB: 978-1-3505-8417-4
ePDF: 978-1-3505-8419-8
eBook: 978-1-3505-8420-4

Series: Europe's Legacy in the Modern World

Typeset by Newgen KnowledgeWorks Pvt. Ltd., Chennai, India

For product safety related questions contact productsafety@bloomsbury.com.

To find out more about our authors and books visit www.bloomsbury.com and sign up for our newsletters.

For my daughter Isa

But seek ye first the kingdom of God,
and his righteousness; and
all these things shall be added unto you

(Matthew 6:33)

Contents

Foreword xi
Acknowledgements xiii
Note on the text and translations xiv
List of abbreviations xv

Introduction 1

1 Imperial public law in *statu cadentis imperii*: Johann Jacob Moser 9
1.0 Prologue 9
1.0.1 Moser and Hegel 9
1.0.2 The dismissal of the *forma Reipublicae* 10
1.0.3 Historical context: The body politic and the results of an empirical methodology 12
1.0.4 Outline 13
1.1 Moser's methodological empiricism 15
1.1.1 Statelessness and statistics 15
1.1.2 The futility of *politica* 17
1.2 The question of sovereignty: Territorial supremacy 18
1.2.1 The *ratio status* and sovereignty 18
1.2.2 *Landeshoheit* 19
1.2.3 Constitutionalization: Origin and custom 21
1.2.4 A centrifugal structure without concept 22
1.2.5 The emergence of territorial sovereignty 24
1.3 A definitive description of the Empire: The head and members 25
1.3.1 A metaphor from imperial public law 25
1.3.2 The conceptual language of Jean Bodin 27
1.3.3 The supreme head and sovereignty 28
1.3.4 Moser and the *Hippolythus* 30
1.3.5 Hegel and the *Hippolythus* 32
1.4 Hegel's Aristotelianism and the Germanic World 33
1.4.1 The impossibility of form: Transition to legal culture 33
1.4.2 From the constitution of fiefs to the *simulacra imperii* 35
1.4.3 Historical continuity 36

1.4.4 The philosophy of world history and the *forma Reipublicae* 37
1.5 Epilogue 40
1.5.1 Eclecticism 40
1.5.2 The unity of Moser's public law with the imperial constitution 41

2 The Empire as the impersonal legal connection of the composite state: Johann Stephan Pütter 43
2.0 Prologue 43
2.0.1 An epoch of imperial public law 43
2.0.2 Hegel and Pütter 43
2.0.3 Doctrine and impact 44
2.0.4 Outline 47
2.1 *Diversae reipublicae formae* and the Empire as a composite state 48
2.1.1 From the simple to the complex 48
2.1.2 Hegel's eclecticism 49
2.1.3 The taxonomy of the *civitas composita* 50
2.1.4 Critique 52
2.2 Defining elements of sovereignty: Electoral monarchy and the *status mixtus* 52
2.2.1 Decomposition: The *civitas composita* and *forma Reipublicae* 52
2.2.2 Centrifugal political evolution and the Imperial Diet 55
2.2.3 Contract law, the capitulations and the imperial state 57
2.2.4 The objective legal connection of the state 59
2.2.5 The *societas herilis*: Despotism and a kingship bound by laws 60
2.2.6 The *status mixtus* and the composite state 61
2.3 Aristocratic despotism 62
2.3.1 Slavery, corporate inequality and the *cives imperii* 62
2.3.2 The Roman legal concept of ownership: *Dominium* 65
2.3.3 The *Hippolythus* and the rejection of Roman law 67
2.3.4 Hermann Conring and Germanic legal history 68
2.3.5 The return of Roman law 70
2.3.6 Hegel and Roman law 71
2.4 Epilogue 72
2.4.1 Pütter's imperial *forma Reipublicae* 72
2.4.2 The restrictive typology: Electoral monarchy 73
2.4.3 The critique of Roman law 74

3 The twilight of German imperial public law: Johann Christian von Majer 75
3.0 Prologue 75
3.0.1 Majer's modernity and Hegel 75

3.0.2 The shift towards law in Tübingen and the religious question 77
3.0.3 State of the art and *forma Reipublicae* 78
3.0.4 Hegel's first *Ständeschrift*, Majer and Württemberg *Landtagspublizistik* 81
3.0.5 Outline 83
3.1 Assessments and doctrine 83
3.1.1 Critique 83
3.1.2 Parallel, analogy and the nameless form 84
3.1.3 Classification and the turn to contemporary history 86
3.1.4 The exception to the rule: Monarchy and the aristocratic body politic 87
3.1.5 The interpretation of Mevius's formula: A final assessment of Majer 91
3.2 Justus Möser and Tacitus: Agriculturalism and the ancient constitution 94
3.2.1 Obscure antiquities 94
3.2.2 The genealogy of the composite state 96
3.2.3 Novel principles for territorial law: Primitive private land acquisition 97
3.2.4 Tacitus and the ancient constitution 98
3.2.5 Private law as public law 101
3.3 The predial principle: Historical sociology, patrimonial and freeholder states 104
3.3.1 New political foundations 104
3.3.2 Ulpian's dichotomy 106
3.3.3 The distinction between *dominium* and *imperium* 107
3.3.4 Private princely law 110
3.3.5 Positive freedoms: Germanic law versus Roman law and natural jurisprudence 111
3.3.6 Lordship and bondage 114
3.4 The concept of the state 117
3.4.1 On the necessity of the state and the *adiaphora* 117
3.4.2 The essential criteria and the return of the *Hippolythus* 121
3.4.3 Disintegration of the state 125
3.5 Epilogue 128
3.5.1 Singularity 128
3.5.2 Majer and Max Weber 129
3.5.3 A definitive connection between Majer and Hegel 130
3.5.4 Public law and *Privatfürstenrecht* 131

4 The empire of ethical life: Georg Wilhelm Friedrich Hegel 133
4.0 Prologue 133
4.0.1 Early biography and imperial dissolution 133
4.0.2 Crisis as concept 134
4.0.3 Constitution 135
4.0.4 Crisis in the philosophy of nature 135
4.0.5 The turning point of world history 136
4.0.6 Outline 138
4.1 The machinery of enlightened revolution 140
4.1.1 Roman law and revolution 140
4.1.2 The minimal state 140
4.1.3 Form against formlessness 142
4.1.4 Robespierre's despotism of liberty 147
4.1.5 The Roman World and political modernity 149
4.1.6 From Kant's separation of powers to Fichte's Ephorate and the constituent power of the French revolutionary state 151
4.2 The division between constitutional law and government law: Political metaphysics and the structured monism of the state 153
4.2.1 Leibniz and Spinoza in Hegel's early absolute idealism 153
4.2.2 Irreducible simple substances in contrast to composite parts 157
4.2.3 The doctrine of organism within the single substance of the state 159
4.2.4 The philosophy of union 161
4.2.5 The eclecticism of *System der Sittlichkeit* 163
4.2.6 The historical context of late imperial patriotism 164
4.3 Toleration and religion: From the imperial constitutional context to the philosophical eschatology of world history 167
4.3.1 The integration of the *ius internum* into the *ius externum* 167
4.3.2 Law as a doctrine of the state 170
4.3.3 The *Aufklärung*, conscience and religion 172
4.3.4 Philosophical eschatology: The theodicy of world history 177
4.4 Epilogue 182
4.4.1 Codification, the universal estate and civil society 182
4.4.2 Consciousness and revolution 186

Conclusion 189

Notes 193
Bibliography 253
Index 269

Foreword

Hegel is one of the most sophisticated and challenging philosophers. Few philosophers have inspired those thinkers writing after them to such an extent that Hegel managed to do. It is therefore no surprise that the scholarship on Hegel is immense. Hardly any other philosopher succeeded in having such an impact on later philosophy. His thought was used and misused in many – often diametrically contradicting – ways and thus put to work for very different purposes. Marx infamously claimed to reorient Hegel's dialectic: 'With him it is standing on its head. It must be inverted, in order to discover the rational kernel within the mystical shell.'[1]

This notorious rhetorical claim certainly does not capture the complex relationship between Hegel and Marx. Perhaps more importantly, it distorts Hegel's philosophy. Exploring the roots of a thinker aims at understanding how his thought is anchored within the archaeology of the history of philosophical thought. This study offers an original and innovative approach to Hegel's early political writings. What is therefore surprising is the fact that this is indeed the first time that the complex relationship between the works by Moser, Pütter and Majer are discussed in relation to Hegel's own system in the scholarship. If we want to understand where Hegel's feet are resting, we need to understand the ground on which they are standing. This study offers a truly remarkable overview of this territory.

It is thus in this regard that this study takes a different approach and opens up a different route for understanding Hegel. It is concerned with the young Hegel and his grappling with the political situation, if not survival of Germany in the post-revolutionary age of Napoleonic expansion. Nathaniel Boyd's meticulous analysis shows how Hegel arrived at his positions. Already in the earliest fragments of the *Verfassungsschrift* we can perceive that Moser was the principal figure for Hegel's description of modern German public law. Ever since Pufendorf's assertion that the constitution of the Holy Roman Empire was 'monstro simile', the discussion of the *forma imperii* defied categorization in the classical Aristotelian terms. The question remained how such an often-conflicting multitude of rights and claims to sovereignty could establish unity. Boyd draws out what was at stake here and how Hegel fits into and draws on this earlier tradition. Moser as much as Pufendorf argued for a specific approach to understand and defend the German legal and political arrangement as found in the fundamental laws that composed the constitution of the Holy Roman Empire.[2] As far as Hegel was concerned, it was impossible to transform such a collection of rights into a viable political system. This was the fundamental question and concern he dealt with and in order to do so he studied the works by Moser, Pütter and Majer.

Clearly, the Holy Roman Empire was conceptualized in different terms. Not signing up for a decision of where sovereignty was located was thus not necessarily a sign of the deficiency of the imperial constitution for many *Reichspublizisten*. This was true for

Pufendorf, and as Boyd points out, the same was certainly true for Moser. Building on the idea of a composite state and the objective legal connection, sovereignty vested in fundamental laws and an impersonal conception of the state, this was less the case for Pütter, who reached back to the earlier tradition of Limnaeus. Of all these publicists, Majer departed most thoroughly from the tradition – elaborating an axiomatic concept of the state. In this book, we discover just how deeply Hegel was influenced by Majer's theoretical and historical writings. For much of the earlier tradition, as long as the question of sovereignty between the emperor and the imperial estates was still disputed, the mechanisms of the imperial constitution were still functioning. We are shown how this tradition of thought found a distinctive echo in Hegel's approach to the imperial constitution. In view of the revolutionary and Napoleonic wars, Hegel could not afford such a position any longer, and Boyd scrutinizes in detail how Hegel had to shift ground. When he provocatively claimed that 'Germany is no longer a state', Hegel underlined that his starting point for what was to follow had to be seen in the 'older teachers of constitutional law'.[3]

The figures of the earlier tradition of *politica* had never given up on the categorization of the constitution because during the Thirty Years' War so much depended on determining where sovereignty was exercised. After the Peace of Basel, and certainly during Rastatt and after Lunéville that incited another frenzy of writing activity, the question of the *forma imperii* was revived. That the Empire was a theoretical state, but that in reality was non-existent was Hegel's answer. Understanding how Hegel arrived at his positions thus requires understanding how he built his argument on the 'older teachers' and the moderns who had given up trying to fit the constitution to a specific form, above all Moser and his empiricism, to a lesser extent Pütter and Majer who remained within the scope of the *forma imperii* and thus influenced Hegel in a manner consistent with the earlier tradition. Boyd judiciously demonstrates the extent of Hegel's knowledge of the imperial constitutional tradition and early modern German public law, which in turn informed Hegel's conception of a modern constitutional state. This ambitious study proposes a fresh and insightful reading of the historical, constitutional and confessional context of the Holy Roman Empire that shaped these debates in the late eighteenth and early nineteenth centuries. We encounter a Hegel that has so far not been discovered, which makes this study a fascinating read.

Peter Schröder
May 2025
London

Acknowledgements

This has been a work of incredibly long gestation and has been warmly supported along the way. I want to thank Louis Carré, Tim Stanton and Peter Schröder above all. Louis backed me as a postdoc from 2020 to 2021 at the University of Namur, during which time I wrote an initial draft of this book. From 2021 to 2023, Tim took me on as a postdoc as part of his Leverhulme Trust Research Leadership Award RL-2016-044t – Rethinking Civil Society: History, Theory, Critique at the Department of Politics and International Relations, University of York. Much of the advanced research and many of the more developed iterations of this book were undertaken during that time. Tim has also generously read through the entire book and improved it immensely. Peter has consistently supported my work since 2018. He has also read the book and contributed the depth of his expertise and refined it in numerous ways. To say the least, I am honoured that he has written the Foreword.

I am very pleased that Martti Koskenniemi immediately recognized the substance of this study when I sent it to him. I hope it is able to one day join the pantheon of his works and those of the late Michael Stolleis – or, far less ambitious, to at least transform the minutiae of our scholarship on the early Hegel and bring to light what I see as his lasting perception of public law. I want to thank Martti for his keen interest in the book and for encouraging me to submit it to Bloomsbury and overseeing the process.

The two anonymous peer reviewers were incredibly insightful and economical in their comments. I hope to have sufficiently responded to some of their suggestions by more extensively elaborating on Gans and Savigny in the book, especially with regard to the dissolution of Hegelianism and the ascendency of the Historical School of Law. I have also rewritten the Introduction and expanded the Conclusion in view of their perceptive remarks. Obviously, any remaining faults or inconsistencies are my own.

Friends too travel with a book. I wish to thank Haseeb Ahmed, Andrea Bardin, Alexander Bornschein, Kris and Kathy Cuppens, Adrien Lucca, Francesco Ronchi and Samo Tomšič.

If friends do, family even more so. My daughter Isa has accompanied this book in almost every way. It is fitting that it carries her name in dedication. She has become and will remain my principal source of inspiration.

Note on the text and translations

All German and Latin translations in this book are my own but have been vetted. In the first case, my dear friend Donald Goodwin has kindly offered his time and highly gifted competence; in the second, my father (and brilliant Latin teacher!) Alan P. Boyd has been no less generous. For all Hegel references and citations, I have exclusively used the German critical edition (*Gesammelte Werke. In Verbindung mit der Deutschen Forschungsgemeinschaft herausgegeben von der Nordrhein-Westfälischen Akademie der Wissenschaften und der Künste*). I firmly believe this should be the principal source of navigation for contemporary Hegel research in any language.

Abbreviations

Cited works by Hegel

GW (followed by volume number, sub-volume and title abbreviation): *Gesammelte Werke. In Verbindung mit der Deutschen Forschungsgemeinschaft herausgegeben von der Nordrhein-Westfälischen Akademie der Wissenschaften und der Künste*

ABH	*Abhandlung Bibliothek Hegels*
DS	*Differenz des Fichteschen und Schellingschen Systems der Philosophie*
E1817	*Enzyklopädie der philosophischen Wissenschaften im Grundrisse (1817)*
E1827	*Enzyklopädie der philosophischen Wissenschaften im Grundrisse (1827)*
E1830	*Enzyklopädie der philosophischen Wissenschaften im Grundrisse (1830)*
FE	*Frühe Excerpte 1795–1800*
FsG	*Fragment zur Philosophie des subjektiven Geistes*
FSI	*Frühe Schriften I*
FSII	*Frühe Schriften II*
GW	*Glauben und Wissen*
JN	*Jenaer Notizenbuch*
JSI	*Jenaer Systementwürfe I*
JSIII	*Jenaer Systementwürfe III*
NR	*Über die wissenschaftlichen Behandlungsarten des Naturrechts*
PdG	*Phänomenologie des Geistes*
PdR	*Philosophie des Rechts*
RV	*Fragmente einer Kritik der Verfassung Deutschlands*
SdS	*System der Sittlichkeit (Critik des Fichteschen Naturrechts)*
SE	*Beitrag zur Spinoza-Edition*
ÜaI	*Über das absolute Identitäts-System und sein Verhältniß zu dem neuesten (Reinholdischen) Dualismus*
VGP	*Vorlesungen über die Geschichte der Philosophie*
VL	*Verhandlungen in der Versammlung der Landstände*
VNR	*Vorlesungen über Naturrecht*
VPR	*Vorlesungen über die Philosophie des Rechts*
VWG	*Vorlesungen über die Philosophie der Weltgeschichte*
WLI	*Wissenschaft der Logik, Erster Band*

Cited works by Majer

AEP-Fr	*Allgemeine Einleitung in Privat-Fürstenrecht überhaupt*
AF-As	*Autonomie vornehmlich des Fürsten- und übrigen unmittelbaren Adelstandes im Römischen deutschen Reiche*
ATSK	*Allgemeine Theorie der Staatskonstitution*
GUrV	*Germaniens Urverfassung mit einer Vorrede über den akademischen Vortrag der teutschen Reichsgeschichte*
SSrG	*System der Staatsregierung im Grundrisse*
TSK1	*Teutsche Staatskonstitution. Erster Band*
TSK2	*Teutsche Staatskonstitution. Zweyter Band*
TwSR1	*Teutsches weltliches Staatsrecht abgetheilt in Reichs- und Landrecht. Erster Band*
TwSR2	*Teutsches weltliches Staatsrecht abgetheilt in Reichs- und Landrecht. Zweither Band*
TwSR3	*Teutsches weltliches Staatsrecht abgetheilt in Reichs- und Landrecht. Dritter Band*

Cited works by Moser

CJP	*Compendium juris publici moderni regni germanici. Oder Grund-Riß der heutigen Staats-Verfassung des teutschen Reichs*
GhSv	*Grundriss der heutigen Staatsverfassung des teutschen Reiche*
NG	*Neueste Geschichte der teutschen Staats-Rechts Lehre und deren Lehrer*
PJP	*Praecognita Juris Publici Germanici Generalissima. Oder Tractat Von der Lehre der heutigen Staats-Verfassung von Teutschland überhaupt*
TSR2	*Teutsches Staats-Recht. Zweither Theil*

Neues teutsches Staats-Recht

NtSR1	*Von Teutschland und dessen Staats-Verfassung überhaupt*
NtSR3	*Von denen kayserlichen Regierungs-Rechten und Pflichten. Erster Theil*
NtSR8	*Von der teutschen Justiz-Verfassung*
NtSR13	*Von der teutschen Reichs-Stände Landen*
NtSR14	*Von der Landeshoheit derer teutschen Reichsstände überhaupt*

Cited works by Pütter

AN	*Anfangsgründe des Naturrechts*
BtS-FR1	*Beyträge zum teutschen Staats- und Fürsten-Rechte. Erster Theil*
BtS-FR2	*Beyträge zum teutschen Staats- und Fürsten-Rechte. Zweyther Theil*
EB1	*Erörterungen und Beyspielen des teutschen Staats- und Fürstenrechts. Band 1*

EG	*Elementa iuris publici Germanici*
HD	*An Historical Development of the Present Constitution of the Germanic Empire*
IG	*Institutiones juris publici Germanici*
KB	*Kurzer Begriff des teutschen Staatsrechts*
LtSR1	*Litteratur des teutschen Staatsrechts. Erster Theil*
LtSR2	*Litteratur des teutschen Staatsrechts. Zweyter Theil*

Lexicons

GG	*Geschichtliche Grundbegriffe*
GGP	*Grundriss der Geschichte der Philosophie*
GpD	*Geschichte des politischen Denkens*
HRG	*Handwörterbuch zur deutschen Rechtsgeschichte*
HWPh	*Historisches Wörterbuch der Philosophie*

Introduction

Understanding the genesis of modern legal and political thought often requires the structural study of overlooked historical contexts. This book offers an original interpretive framework for Georg Wilhelm Friedrich Hegel's (1770–1831) legal, political and historical philosophy by engaging with imperial public law – a tradition that has up to this point remained at the margins of scholarly discussion. My approach illuminates hitherto unexplored dimensions of German public law itself, as no prior comprehensive study has been devoted to Hegel's profound relationship with this specific legal tradition and the central figures explored here, thereby filling a crucial gap in scholarship. German public law, especially through its imperial tradition, played a crucial and transformative role in shaping foundational philosophical concepts that were instrumental in the formation of European political and legal thought, influencing ideas such as sovereignty, the state and the diverse legal systems that emerged from them.

How did Hegel come to understand the German public law of his time as a form of private law – that is, as primarily based on contractual and proprietary relationships rather than a unified sovereign will – and how did this structure his alternative conception of the state? What did his unique notion of universal public law – a discipline that involved determining the rights of sovereignty, government in its internal and external relations and the obligations and freedoms of subjects – entail and how did it converge or diverge from the tradition? The answers to such questions are built up cumulatively through the four substantial chapters of this book, each of which deals with a major figure of imperial public law: Johann Jacob Moser (1701–1785), Johann Stephan Pütter (1725–1807), Johann Christian von Majer (1741–1821) and Hegel. This forms a convenient chronology of the literature of later imperial public law, proceeding from the old to the new, to Hegel as the philosophical finale.[1] Crucially, each chapter also meticulously examines Hegel's relationship, whether postulated or proven, to the specific lawyers under consideration. By bringing Hegel's conceptualizations into continuity with a tradition and historical context that have so often remained at the fringes of his thought, if not excluded entirely, this book enriches our understanding of his political, legal and historical philosophy and the public law literature.

This book decisively alters our view of Hegel's intellectual development, revealing the critical and constructive influence of imperial public law on his distinct concepts of public law and the state. In the process, other related issues come to the fore such as his interpretation of private law and its distinction from public law. By starting from a historical context that Hegel had actively engaged with, connected issues arise. For example, we gain another perspective from which to view Hegel's denunciation of the contract as an element of political order. This not only stems from his critical reception of natural law. His critique extends to the then-prevailing universal public law and the capitulation theory (which posited the imperial state's foundation as a series of constitutional contracts). Crucially, this connects to the German reception of Roman private law and contract law.

By placing Hegel's critique of Roman law within a historical-contextualist perspective, this study fundamentally revises existing perceptions,[2] incrementally building its analysis across dedicated chapters on key figures: from Moser's vast and empirical compilations on territorial supremacy that were a de facto record of how the Empire actually worked, to Pütter's aristocratic despotism and Majer's theoretical works, which divided the Roman private law concept of property from supreme authority or rule, thus laying the foundations for a truly public legal order of the state. Moser, through his sheer volume of collected cases and legal opinions, painstakingly documented the Empire's unique decentralized structure and, in doing so, unintentionally demonstrated the pervasive 'private law' nature of public relationships. This book unearths a vital underexplored legal history that stretches from Hermann Conring (1606–1681) onwards, which laid the foundations of a unique legal discipline. Through the mediation of Conring's student Ludolph Hugo (1632–1704), Moser and Pütter, in their pragmatic engagement with the Empire's actual functioning, reluctantly accepted Roman private law as a way of formalizing the legal relationship of the imperial estates among themselves and to the Empire. With Hegel's Tübingen professor Majer, this became an entirely established field *adjacent* to public law, the doctrine of private princely law (*Privatfürstenrecht*). This book demonstrates how this intricate legal history profoundly shaped Hegel's critique of the Empire and ultimately led to his alternative idea of public law and the state.

Each chapter reveals crucial, hitherto neglected facets of German public law. The chapter on Hegel's Tübingen professor Majer, however, is particularly pivotal as his work represents a critical turning point in the tradition and offers a uniquely direct insight into Hegel's intellectual development. Majer's thought is remarkably overlooked in the critical literature, especially considering how it anticipates concepts central to the later historical sociology of Max Weber (1864–1920), offering a crucial analytical link for understanding the intellectual lineage of the sociological description of the state. While Majer's influence on the most important German philosopher of the nineteenth century has been a subject of conjecture since Franz Rosenzweig's (1886–1929) classic *Hegel und der Staat* (1920) (Hegel and the State),[3] this book provides the first exhaustive analysis of his writings, substantively considering them alongside Hegel's *Fragmente einer Kritik der Verfassung Deutschlands* (1799–1803) (Fragments of a Critique of the German Constitution) or what is popularly known as the *Verfassungsschrift*.[4] What is modern in Hegel's state was initially derived from Majer's theoretical expositions. This was then retained in Hegel's maturity within the legal order of civil society, where protection of property was identified with freedom and a legal constitution. Majer's thought is an important fringe product of the twilight of imperial public law. My analysis of Majer's decisive role underscores a core premise of this study: the enduring, transformative power of imperial public law in shaping foundational philosophical concepts that only later came to prominence in political and legal theory, even as the Empire itself faced dissolution. Hence Majer's profound, yet underexplored, impact exemplifies the enduring significance of imperial public law for understanding the genesis of modern political thought and the future of German public law.

Building on this insight, a central structuring assumption of this book is that we will find ourselves in a much better interpretive position to assess the development of Hegel's legal and political thought – *and* the contents of his philosophy of law and world history – *if we take imperial public law seriously*. This tradition persisted through change. In the form of the theoretical speculations of universal public law and Pütter's natural law, it was carried forward in the productions of German Idealism or classical German philosophy.[5] The structures of thought, patterns of life and divisions of labour to which imperial public law had given rise did not entirely cease with the collapse of the Empire on 6 August 1806. Rather, its methodology continued unbroken into the Confederation of the Rhine (1806–13). This novel political structure offered publicists – the scholars of public law, political theory or state affairs – the opportunity to transfer the legal tradition of *Reichspublizistik* to the Napoleonic period, to a different legal and political context which might otherwise have lacked the appropriate tools for analysis, adapting existing conceptual foundations rather than starting from scratch.[6]

The initial development of Hegel's legal, political and historical thought cannot be separated from the Empire. German public law constituted the background stock of cultural knowledge with which the young Hegel first became acquainted during his formative years in Stuttgart (1777–88), then as a student in Tübingen (1788–93) and which he applied in Frankfurt (1797–1800) and Jena (1801–7). This book shows how he first attempted to shape public law anew within the imperial context and, after its demise, beyond it.

In other instances, *Reichspublizistik* had profoundly shaped the practical training of the individuals at the helm of the reforms in the Napoleonic and post-Napoleonic periods in Germany and certainly those in Hegel's later circle in Berlin. Among publicists, no one was more instrumental than Pütter in this respect. The book demonstrates how Hegel's conception of limited monarchy and public law shares a significant degree of continuity with Pütter's reform absolutism and universal public law. Undoubtedly, this brought Hegel's political thought into favour with the Prussian reformers who had all been moulded by the *mos Gottingensis*. The Göttingen method of legal teaching emphasized the direct application of natural law alongside systematic and encyclopaedic approaches aimed at practical training. Hegel's mature textbooks corresponded in many respects with the *mos Gottingensis* and thus found common cause with the Prussian reform. He was appointed to a professorship in Berlin in large part due to this coincidence of method and interest. The reformers were on the look out for a scientific counterweight to the Historical School of Law and the spread of irrational romanticism in order to hem in the growing reactionary nationalist forces while transforming the state.

Hegel lived and breathed the dissolution of the Holy Roman Empire of the German Nation. Its collapse and the communication of its public law methodology to the new epoch coincided with the most productive intellectual period of Hegel's biography, the Frankfurt and Jena periods. Rosenzweig even went so far as to identify the crisis of the constitution directly with a personal crisis in Hegel's biography.[7] Later, this was generalized into a transitional psychological stage in the philosophy of subjective spirit.[8] But, as Rosenzweig emphasized, 'very personal experiences are mirrored in these very factual sentences'.[9] Hans Maier did something similar, directly linking the reality of the imperial constitutional crisis with a crisis in Hegel's thinking.[10] These judgements in their different ways capture an important truth: the collapse of the constitution marked Hegel's lifeworld not only at the turn of the century *but also* thereafter.

The generation of publicists that came before Hegel – and we might add before the far more radical Johann Gottlieb Fichte (1762–1814) and his *Reden an die deutsche Nation* (1808) (Addresses to the German Nation) (given that Hegel was always a patriot but never became, like Fichte, a revolutionary nationalist) – held fast to the belief that living together in the Empire as a whole was the only way to guarantee peace, justice and freedom, that this was the source of strength and vigour and could have a beneficial influence on Europe as a whole. The Reign of Terror (1792–4), the First Coalition War (1792–7) and the Second Coalition War (1798–1802) altered the historical and political situation irrevocably.[11] Nevertheless, the universal (European) tradition of the Empire continued, particularly in the Mainz reform circles to which Hegel might have belonged. Drawing on a mythology of the Carolingian renaissance that saw the Franks and the French as a Germanic people, Karl Theodor von Dalberg (1744–1817), for example, considered Napoleon Bonaparte (1769–1821) as a possible saviour of the Empire.[12]

Like Friedrich Schiller (1759–1805) in the fragmentary poem *Deutsche Größe* (1797) (German Greatness) discovered after his death,[13] Hegel had separated the political fate of the Empire from the intellectualization of its concept. In order to emphasize the importance of the legal tradition of *Reichspublizistik*, it sometimes seems necessary to restate simple facts, for example, that Hegel termed the final fourth empire or realm of the philosophy of world history variously: *Germanisches Weltreich*, *Das germanische Reich*, *Das Germanische Princip und Reich* and *Das germanische Reich*.[14] What would an audience that had in recent history lived through the political collapse of the Empire have heard in these titles that has been lost on us? Hegel's Germanic Empire, principle or Germanic World Empire, just as the tradition of imperial publicism from Samuel von Pufendorf (1632–94) to Pütter,[15] began with the Franks and Charlemagne.[16]

Hegel's world-historical conception – already present in outline in the fragments of the *Verfassungsschrift*[17] – is a perfect example of Hegelian sublation (*Aufhebung*): the Holy Roman Empire of the German Nation had been in reality abolished but at the same time raised to a different (spiritual) and higher plane.[18] Hegel stands out from the tradition of imperial public law since Conring as he reaches even further back to the medieval universal conception of Empire that had appropriated the four Empires or monarchies doctrine from the book of Daniel.[19] This had first been denounced by Jean Bodin (1530–1596).[20] But it had been at the centre of Protestant reform circles, notably Philipp Melanchthon (1497–1560), along with the similar translation theory of Empire from Ancient Rome to Germany. Melanchthon had developed the doctrine in his revised and expanded edition of universal world history in the *Chronicon Carionis* (1559); it forms an overarching historical-theological framework in which the Holy Roman Empire is viewed providentially.[21] The *Chronicon* became the principal textbook for the teaching of history in Protestant universities of the early modern period. Hegel maintains the doctrine in his universal world history, which is also a philosophical eschatology and theodicy. On the other hand, the translation theory structures his understanding of the reception of Roman private law.

Even if imperial public law did not survive the dissolution of the imperial constitution in its entirety as a legal discipline, its ideas could be transformed and have an overwhelming impact far beyond it. Still, the novel constitutional considerations arising from the French Revolution (1789–99) began to have an effect on legal and political thought. If there is one publicist that can be singled out in this respect, it has to be Hegel's Tübingen professor Majer – he stood at the centre of such innovation.[22] His ideas – his pathbreaking analysis of the concept of the state, the axiomatic division between private and public law, the distinction between government and constitution – are strikingly modern.

In Hegel's aptly titled chapter 'Begriff des Staats' (Concept of the State) in the *Reinschrift* (1802–3), he directly followed Majer's terse theoretical analysis from the opening pages of *Allgemeine Theorie der Staatskonstitution* (1799) (General Theory of the State Constitution) or the first volume of *Teutsche Staatskonstitution* (1800) (German State Constitution).[23] Furthermore, Majer's distinction between the status quo (*Staatsverfassung*) and the modern concept of 'constitution' (*Konstitution*) significantly influenced Hegel's early speculative system.[24]

The present study analyses *System der Sittlichkeit* (1802) (System of Ethical Life) as a political programme for the reform of the Empire or, similarly, as a revised corporate doctrine for a territorial state like Hegel's native Württemberg – an 'institutionalism' that actively contended with the French Revolution's individualism and its reception in Fichte's political thought. This offers an entirely novel method for studying the development of Hegel's legal and political thinking, providing unique insights into the materials that led him to the idea of 'an authentic conceptual form', his structured monism of the state and the steps he already took in that direction in Frankfurt that led to an internally unified real system of speculative philosophy that sought 'to grasp the entire world of actuality'.[25] On the one hand, it shows how imperial and territorial structures shaped absolute idealism; on the other, it shows how Hegel utilized the pre-critical substance metaphysics of Gottfried Wilhelm Leibniz (1646–1716) and Baruch Spinoza (1632–1677) to overcome the formal natural law of Immanuel Kant (1724–1804) and Fichte all the while furthering the insights of reform absolutism.

The Holy Roman Empire of the German Nation and its supra-territorial public law, governing the imperial estates, may provide, in the great treaties, the first example of a truly public international law.[26] The various autonomies of the Empire, balanced between the diverse systems of imperial and territorial governance, are an important part of the history of early modern European parliamentarianism, federalism and subsidiarity – not to mention their world-historical singularity.[27] How do such structures impact the development of Hegel's organic notion of the state? In contrast to the Roman principle of unity, the Latin World and the ministerial centralization that had been introduced with the French Revolution and Napoleon, Hegel's Empire of ethical life preserved the principle of subsidiarity: 'for freedom is in the form, and in the fact that the individual part, acting for itself and its own determinateness, is a subordinate system of the whole organism'.[28]

As the book argues through its various chapters, we cannot sufficiently explain why Hegel understood German public law as largely a system of private law if we do not keep this unique legal history in view. When he denounced the aristocratic form of constitution or sovereignty (concepts traditionally designated as *forma Reipublicae* or *forma imperii*)[29] and the despotism that the territorial princes sought to establish against the territorial estates, it was no accident that he connected this to Rome. Second, Hegel attacked the French Revolution in comparable terms and his critique here is deeply intertwined with his understanding of the German reception of Roman private law. The point being that private legal existence had in the same way been raised to the political, causing chaos and confusion in the public order of the state. This perspective also stems from his rejection of the formal equality of the French Revolution and Fichte's political thought. Importantly, what each of these cases re-explain is Hegel's understanding of individualism as an element of private law in the emergence of modern civil society and the significance of a constitution as an eminently public legal order.

This book focuses principally on Hegel's early period, but it does so with an eye to wider gains – in particular, a more thorough interpretation of his mature political, legal and historical thought that belongs to the afterlives of imperial public law and reform absolutism. I reach this dimension of interpretation particularly in the final chapter when I turn to the doctrine of law and consciousness in the state, to a modern ethical life that grew out of an attempt to answer the unique problem of religion and politics in the Empire, to Hegel's notion that there could be no radical change in legislation and political constitution without at first a reformation.[30] This connects Hegel to the earlier Protestant tradition of universal world history and provides the materials through which *ethos* and *nomos* coincide in the Germanic World or Empire. The book argues that Hegel's philosophical eschatology was a last gasp of imperial public law, which is why the break with his philosophy became world historical. In the *Vormärz* (1815–48), a radical right in the form of consciousness developed in conflict with law that was transmitted to the revolutionary epoch.

It must be acknowledged at the outset that it simply would not have been possible to undertake this study without several relatively recent advances in the scholarship on German public law and in the critical Hegel literature.

The monumental scholarship of Michael Stolleis (1941–2021) in the four volumes of *Geschichte des öffentlichen Rechts in Deutschland* (History of Public Law in Germany) – and especially the first untranslated volume – has transformed our perception of the legal and political tradition in Germany and the Holy Roman Empire. Prior to Stolleis, Hanns Gross (1928–2006) had paved the way for the study of this neglected literary genre in *Empire and Sovereignty: A History of the Public Law Literature in the Holy Roman Empire, 1599–1804*.[31] The latter work has remained the principal resource in English on early modern public law – at least until very recently.

Gross has now been supplemented by the depth and range of the latest book of Martti Koskenniemi, *To the Uttermost Parts of the Earth. Legal Imagination and International Power (1300–1870)*, which comprehensively studies the German legal context and evolution.[32] Even so, Gross's work remains a vital resource in English on this early modern legal-philosophical tradition in Germany – albeit with the stipulation that some of its interpretations are by this hour quite dated.[33] The first point is amply confirmed by Koskenniemi's use of Gross in the final part of his study, which concerns the German public law tradition. Both authors conclude their studies with Hegel, although in very different ways.[34]

As far as the Hegel scholarship is concerned, I am reliant on the critical edition of his works. All students of Hegel's thought are indebted to the editorial labours that made possible the complete reorganization of Hegel's fragments on the imperial constitution on the basis of a revised chronology,[35] replacing the artificially reconstructed text that had for such a long time held the field.[36] Likewise, to the immensely valuable commentary of Kurt Rainer Meist (1944–2013).[37] The two together represent landmarks in the possible interpretation of Hegel's relation to the public law tradition and to the last days of the Holy Roman Empire.

With these debts acknowledged we can now proceed to our principal analytical tasks. These will take us down untrodden paths in the history of legal and political thought, exploring the doctrines of Moser, Pütter and Majer, revealing their distinct contributions to imperial public law and their collective influence on Hegel's intellectual development and his philosophy of law more generally. In the process, the deep structures of Hegel's comprehension of public law will be brought to light, illuminating his corresponding monistic order of sovereignty and the state and, in doing so, offering a fundamentally distinct understanding of his political thought's genesis in the crucible of early-nineteenth-century Germany.

1

Imperial public law in *statu cadentis imperii*: Johann Jacob Moser

1.0 Prologue

1.0.1 Moser and Hegel

The famous Württemberg publicist Johann Jacob Moser's death was marked by the young Hegel during his days as a student at the Eberhard-Ludwigs-Gymnasium, before he left for Tübingen and the seminary, with the following Latin epigram: 'qui tot, quot perlegere humana non sufficit aetas perscripsit libros'.[1] Roughly translated, Moser wrote more books than a human life has sufficient time to read.

The allusion was without doubt to *Neues teutsches Staats-Recht* (1766–75) (New German State Law), an encyclopaedic collection of some twenty-three volumes, sub-volumes aside, which assembled every dimension of imperial public law and detailed the territorial right of governance in all of its forms. Moser's work was unique in its almost total rejection of the philosophical. Unlike most contemporary approaches, which followed doctrines such as waning Protestant Aristotelianism, *ratio status*, or ascendant natural jurisprudence and imperial history, Moser's methodology stood apart. He became famous in part for his rigid empiricism and the positivism that was a consequence of this methodology.[2]

In the later imperial public law literature, the state constitution (*Staatsverfassung*) was treated ubiquitously. While this did involve defining the imperial constitution, it had less and less to do with the Aristotelian typology or the specific form of sovereignty categorizing the Empire and – certainly with Moser – more with the positive collection of imperial foundational laws: the Golden Bull (1356), the Peace of Augsburg (1555), the Peace of Westphalia (1648), the capitulations, the statutes, the titles and territorial claims that had been passed down from time immemorial. The empirical-positivist feature of Moser's public law doctrine set a pattern for the subsequent considerations of the imperial state and descriptions of its constitution.[3] Not only had he abandoned the Aristotelian categories and largely shunned natural jurisprudence, but he had also rejected the speculative approaches of universal public law.[4] As Moser saw it, imposing an Aristotelian mould onto the state constitution was perpetually contentious precisely because such an artificial fit inevitably created a partisan advantage for either the emperor or the imperial estates, clearly demonstrating the hidden political agendas.[5]

Hegel would have been acquainted with Moser's work not only from direct study, as the publication of the critical edition *Fragmente einer Kritik der Verfassung Deutschlands* establishes beyond doubt in the commentary by Kurt Rainer Meist,[6] but also because of Moser's famed position as a representative of the resistance of the Württemberg estates against the Duke of Württemberg Karl Eugen (1728–93).[7] This had cost Moser more than five years of his life, imprisoned in Hohentwiel.[8] Hegel's father, Georg Ludwig Hegel (1733–99), was a bureaucrat, secretary to the revenue office at the court of Karl Eugen.

Furthermore, Moser became the fountainhead of the last phase of German imperial public law. For any study that wishes to illuminate the fragments of Hegel's *Verfassungsschrift* and its relation to the literary genre of public law, Moser's encyclopaedic knowledge must be considered the most natural place to start. For example, Johann Stephan Pütter – whose theorizations were taken up almost ubiquitously in the Empire – set out from Moser's method, even though he sought to systematize public law, a purpose alien to Moser. Moser had recognized the younger lawyer's genius when shown his intentions for writing and teaching in public law by Gerlach Adolf von Münchhausen (1688–1770).[9] Even if Pütter's systematization were foreign to Moser, it would not have been possible without the Württemberger's exhaustive and voluminous compilations of material that it sought to reduce to lexical order.

1.0.2 The dismissal of the *forma Reipublicae*

Whereas Moser's compilative method had risen in renown to become an almost universally accepted approach in later imperial public law, the same cannot really be said about his repudiation of the search for the form of the state. In this respect, the historical literature ought to have balanced Moser's dismissal of the *forma Reipublicae* with the following corrective: 'But it still remains always necessary for every theory of constitutional law not to leave the question unanswered from the outset: What kind of government a state has?'[10] This authoritative quote from Pütter directly challenged the dilemma Moser had introduced through his disavowal of the *Staatsverfassung* and its *forma Reipublicae*, a question Moser considered merely a consequence of description.

Practically speaking, Hegel saw that Moser's explication was contradictory. On the one hand, Moser's imperial patriotism, which viewed the Empire's strength in its legal circumvention of despotism, affirmed the constitution's unitary and juridically monarchical character. On the other hand, by simultaneously sanctioning *Landeshoheit* (territorial supremacy) as an ancient right of the imperial estates, he inadvertently liberated these estates from oversight, thereby legitimizing the very power that could be wielded despotically against the territorial estates themselves. Nonetheless, *Landeshoheit* was variegated for Moser, encompassing far more than merely the power vested in the territorial lord.

Even if he considered the categorization of the constitution as of no practical use or advantage, Moser had clearly not escaped the problems that had haunted the earlier *politica* and the pointed question of where *maiestas* resided.[11] Just as determining the constitution was pertinent to defining the locus of sovereignty during the Thirty Years'

War (1618–48), so too was its salience evident when the coordination of the body politic fell apart during the Seven Years' War (1756–63), which Hegel had isolated as a constitutional or internal conflict of the German estates with each other.[12]

This historical crux brought with it the confirmation of another imperial system, which was increasingly giving way to an alternative structure of independent states or different forms of federation. The extent of imperial jurisdiction was severely restricted by the rise of Austro-Prussian dualism. Prussia, as an imperial estate, usurped imperial privileges, evading its obligations in times of war and peace. The imperial ban went unrecognized, as did declarations of war, even extending into the subsequent peace:

> This war had in common with older wars the character that it was an internal war between the German estates. After the decrees of the Imperial Diet, some estates sent their troops to the Imperial Army of Execution; others, by contrast, completely withdrew from this relationship with the German Empire and, as sovereign estates, allied themselves with Prussia.[13]

Evidently, Hegel's interpretation was strongly marked by the historical context in which he was writing. The extremes reached during the First Coalition War and its conclusion in the Congress at Rastatt (1797–9), to which the theoretical endeavours of the first fragments of the *Verfassungsschrift* belong, revealed a body politic in fragmentation and the increasing independence of the imperial estates. Presumably, Hegel took his initial use of the empirical body politic comprising a head and members from Moser; it had replaced the contested issue of the *forma Reipublicae*.[14]

The young Hegel traced in detail how the imperial fundamental laws were shaped by the private interest and property of the competing larger imperial estates. These are what determined the imperial state constitution, not the activity of a sovereign state itself. By locating the standard evolution of the Empire in its fundamental laws, laws that were defined by an ever-increasing complex relation between the emperor and imperial estates, Moser had excluded the constitution as a guideline.[15] In this way, Hegel – arguably following Moser – saw how the electoral capitulations, house contracts, peace treaties and imperial court mandates had all become an integral part of public law even if they often represented highly particular interests, displacing the universal.[16]

It was in similar terms that – as Hegel later observed – the imperial court, the highest legal authority in the Empire, had transformed into a court of arbitration. It was little more than a site of legal conflict that came between the contesting powers of the various imperial estates.[17] Public authority was reduced to the application of law but had little power to make it.[18] The Empire had become a diverse sum of private legal claims; it neither had a constitution in the Aristotelian sense nor did it possess a public (in the sense of *political*) law. Hegel's use of Moser's method served a different turn. It showed that the massive collection of rights contradicted the very idea of a constitution: 'The principles of German public law therefore cannot be derived from the concept of a state, or the concept of a particular constitution, a monarchy, etc. German constitutional law is not a science that follows principles, but an *urbarium* of the most diverse of constitutional rights acquired in the form of private law.'[19]

1.0.3 Historical context: The body politic and the results of an empirical methodology

For Hegel, what the First Coalition War had shown and what the Second Coalition War (1798–1802) had further brought home was the loss of harmony between the parts and the whole – a lack of *coordination* between the head and limbs of the imperial body politic.[20] Moser's favoured metaphor for emperor and Empire had lost all meaning. Once again, Moser had relied on empirical description that circumvented the issue of the *forma Reipublicae*. As historical events unfolded, for Hegel this revealed that the Holy Roman Empire had been reduced to a mere shadow of what it was; it had become an empty name. Put simply, the body politic had transformed from 'the absolute ethical order' and 'eternity of the people' – as the absolute idealism of *System der Sittlichkeit* had it – to an artificial totality opposed to a nature, which had been degraded to conflict.[21] Nature itself, however, could be used descriptively to approximate understanding: 'From this point of view the German Empire, like the realm of nature, is inexhaustible in large things, and unfathomable in small things, and it is this aspect which fills those initiated into the knowledge of the infinite details of rights with that admiration, that amazement at the venerability of the German body politic.'[22]

Armed neutrality was the reality revealed during the Seven Years' War. Balance had emerged as *the* principle. Yet this equilibrium was destroyed during the First and Second Coalition Wars. In this respect, the issue of the *forma Reipublicae* expressed in theory what empirical observation confirmed in practice that the Holy Roman Empire did not have or 'want to give itself a constitution … to protect its members against foreign enemies.'[23] From this point of view, Hegel's was the latest criticism that stretched back to the Thirty Years' War: the tissue of the imperial structure was dissolving and fraying at the seams, Moser's metaphor of the *harmonized* whole in tatters.

Already with the Peace of Basel (5 April 1795), which saw the reality of Prussian state interest secure a separate peace with republican France, the highly contingent character of any imperial union was demonstrated for all to see. Insightful commentators have observed how the final crisis and collapse of the constitution was historically inevitable once Prussia left the First Coalition War in order to secure its own aggrandisement.[24] Predation took place within the confines of the imperial political space. For Hegel, this also corresponded to imperial political history and the evolution of the history of public law. Moser's approach to the historical sources embodied a contradiction: it simultaneously justified both imperial public law and, at the same time, the legal principles governing territorial rule. Hence, his doctrine of public law really was an eclectic compilation of different parts of private law.

The intricacy of the constitutional situation in the Holy Roman Empire directly influenced the formation of political and legal thought. Not only involving the electors and their territories, but also other imperial estates, as well as cities, bishoprics, imperial knights and princes, the German constitution was a compound structure: 'The German state constitution is thus based in general on a universal imperial government and a particular government of states.'[25] Even if territorial supremacy entailed a particular right of governance separate from imperial jurisdiction, as can be observed in this passage, it still drew its significance from the context of universal imperial government. What Moser's observation demonstrated theoretically – although he did not deduce it himself, as that would have been anathema to him – was a working idea of a system of 'double rule' (*duplex regimen*). The territorial lords stood alongside the emperor and together represented the Empire.

What Moser's empirical methodology traced was the reality of a constitution that had been legally built upon layer by layer, by continuous accretion throughout its history. The result was a juridical structure composed of multiple strata of interpretation that pressed together into a legalistic idea of the state that was constitutional (*rechtsstaatlich*) in orientation or governed in a unique way by the rule of law. To think of it as a constitution in the modern sense is incorrect.[26] The dismissal of any attempt to conceptualize what he had discovered in imperial legal history in terms of the *forma Reipublicae* simply left Moser with empirical sources as the principal element. Thus, he had turned titles, statutes, custom and tradition into a melange of rights that he called the state constitution, the Empire.

Hegel's perspective on Moser's work seems to have remained unaltered from the *Verfassungsschrift* until he began to work again on the question of the role of the Württemberg estates in his second *Ständeschrift* (1817) (Proceedings of the Estates Assembly) and the lectures delivered on the philosophy of law in Heidelberg (1817–18).[27] The emphasis continued to be on how the German Empire had been transformed into an object of private property: its supreme authority, sold or handed off (literally 'capitulated') by the head to the members who pursued their *iura singulorum* (individual or subjective private law) in an entirely 'unlawful' (*widerrechtlich*) fashion:

> Where these laws came from could not be seen, nor that they were constitutional laws which the individual cannot possess. *Moser* now presented all these laws in one work, both the constitutional laws [*Staatsrechte*] of the individuals and their private rights [*Privatrechte*]. The revolutions of more recent times belong here. There were estates and individuals who were entitled to the rights of the state [*Rechte des Staats*], especially in relation to duties, such as freedom from taxation and jurisdiction, as private rights. And in our times a step has been taken towards the rational existence of the state that has not happened for a thousand years; the law of reason has been asserted against the form of private justice [*Privatrecht*].[28]

This powerful critique, drawing on Moser's extensive documentation in *Neues teutsches Staats-Recht* concerning territorial supremacy, highlights Hegel's profound reinterpretation of imperial legal practice.

1.0.4 Outline

What was largely left to guesswork for the earlier critical scholarship has been confirmed by the discovery of an important fragment 'Der Nahme für die Staatsverfassung' (The Name for the State Constitution) in which Moser directly appears.[29] In this respect, it becomes far more plausible to suggest that the towering figure of Moser stands behind the young idealist's discussion of the modern teachers of German state law. This insight, first owed to Franz Rosenzweig, will be justified in what follows.[30]

This chapter breaks new ground, reassessing Hegel's relationship to Moser and studying Moser's work with a view to Hegel's. This sheds fresh light on Hegel's understanding of and relation to the last phase of German imperial public law, and equally on his connection to the earlier tradition that followed the Aristotelian arrangement of constitutional forms. My analysis confirms that Moser's rejection of the categorization of the Empire must stand behind Hegel's polemic at the outset of the *Reinschrift*, directed at the modern state law teachers or public lawyers. This position, however, goes back to the earliest Frankfurt fragment, 'Sollte das politische Resultat' (Should the Political Result) which demonstrates a significant degree of continuity in Hegel's plan for the introduction to the *Verfassungsschrift*.[31]

The chapter is structured into four sections. First, I discuss Moser's methodological approach in more detail and how it diverged from the philosophical tradition (Section 1.1). This in turn isolates his singular manner of proceeding and clarifies the ambiguity of Hegel's relation to his methodology. On the one hand, I show how elements of Hegel's approach rely on Moser, on the other how they equally subject him to criticism.

Second, I consider how Moser took no decision on where sovereignty resided in the Empire (Section 1.2). Leaving this question aside, however, he was unable to avoid examining the issue of *Landeshoheit* (territorial supremacy) and the extensive rights this entailed, which he enumerated in volumes fourteen to sixteen of *Neues teutsches Staats-Recht*. This firmly established the freedom and territorial autonomy of the imperial estates, starkly contrasting with the absence of a determined *forma Reipublicae*.

Third, I analyse the notion of the head and members that Moser raised to the status of a definitive description of the Empire (Section 1.3) and how he followed certain figures in the history of German political thought in doing so, going beyond his formally purely descriptive methodology. Within this context, we also examine Hegel's connection to this tradition.

Finally, I take up the issue of Hegel's Aristotelianism as a particular theoretical approach to German public law and his relation to the contention over the *forma Reipublicae* (Section 1.4), which he developed into an historical framework, into a world-historical periodization of the Aristotelian types of constitution that can already be discovered in embryonic form in the fragments of the *Verfassungsschrift*.[32] This involved a unique periodization of world history that drew extensively from the imperial patriotic tradition, as well as the idealism of Schiller and Gotthold Ephraim Lessing (1729–81).

Schiller's influence can be observed in the poem *Resignation* (1786). It stands at the entry point to Hegel's philosophy of world history in the lectures delivered on the philosophy of law in Heidelberg and was integrated into *Grundlinien der Philosophie des Rechts. Naturrecht und Staatswissenschaft im Grundrisse* (1821) (Elements of the Philosophy of Law. Natural Law and Political Science in Outline).[33] Hegel had been citing from the poem since at least 1794.[34] Lessing's notion of the education of the human race, taken up by Schiller in his notion of aesthetic education, was adapted by Hegel to the various *forma Reipublicae* which were stages on the path towards the complete realization of freedom, with modern constitutional monarchy, a state power divided between a monarch and estates-representation – which he considered idiosyncratically Germanic – that must be grounded in positive public laws.[35] In another way, Hegel's spiritualization of the idea of the Holy Roman Empire of the German Nation shared with Schiller the notion that the ethical Empire could be separated from its political fate.[36]

1.1 Moser's methodological empiricism

1.1.1 Statelessness and statistics

The famous words, repeated as a leitmotif throughout the *Verfassungsschrift*, are that 'Germany is no longer a state'.[37] One central issue, apparent from the earliest drafts and becoming increasingly acute as Hegel progressed in his analysis, was that the constitution could not be grasped conceptually. Public law consistently evaded the Aristotelian concepts of the *forma Reipublicae* that would have given meaning, *reality* to the constitution.[38] This line becomes even more emphatic at the outset of the *Reinschrift*.[39]

For the historian Mack Walker (1929–2021), Hegel's position, his use of the verb *begreifen* in this context, spoke not only to the efforts to systematically and rationally comprehend the constitution but also carried a strong political overtone, in the sense of seizing or laying hold.[40] By contrast, for Moser, the fact that the imperial constitution could never be fully grasped was one of its principal merits. He thus drew the following conclusion: 'Germany is governed in German, and in such a way that no scholastic term [*Schulwort*] … or the way of government of other states are suitable to make our way of government comprehensible.'[41] Further, the very attempt to grasp it by means of a particular concept had *always* been overtly political. Not only did Moser put little stock in such theories; he looked with a great degree of suspicion and apprehension upon any political use of jurisprudence. Hegel was led to the following conclusion: 'In order for the problem of how Germany is a state and at the same time not a state to be solved, it must, in so far as it is a state, exist merely as a theoretical state [*Gedankenstaat*], whereas the non-existence of the state must be the reality.'[42]

It is worth citing these lines here as they immediately foreshadow how aspects of Moser's own methodology were remoulded in Hegel's hands. The famous Württemberg publicist was the first to emphasize that any analysis of the *Reich* had to assume that there was a difference between the state as a thing of thought (*Gedankending*) and the state as it existed as a reality.[43] According to Moser, this doctrine of the imperial state constitution concerned the systematic organization of its existing elements, piece by empirical piece, to facilitate efficient and clear future decision-making on relevant matters. It was thus a practical construction, not a formal structure or principle-driven idea in the philosophical sense, focused on assembling various components to enable effective governance.[44] Admittedly, Hegel bent this to wholly other ends. Nonetheless, the fact remains that he borrowed this approach directly from Moser.

Another methodology that must be mentioned in this connection is the statistical method. Whereas the Württemberg publicist rejected the conceptual categorization of the Empire along Aristotelian lines,[45] he did use the *notitia rerumpublicarum* or statistics as a method in order to arrive at a more precise knowledge of the imperial constitution.[46] Aristotelianism as well as the study of legal philosophy or the philosophy of universal public law for Moser was 'unnecessary ballast'.[47] Walker even went so far as to identify Moser as an *anti-philosophe*.[48] Yet the empirical side of statistics could and should be retained. Probably the reason why Moser rejected the philosophy of universal public law was because he was able to intuit that, as it had unfolded since the seventeenth century, it was little more than the theoretical part of the earlier Aristotelian practical philosophy. In this respect, it was simply a product 'of the process of specialization [that] led to the distinction between a theoretical and a practical part of science, which was originally understood uniformly as practical philosophy'.[49]

The *notitia* in Moser's hands became wholly empirical, solely practical; it thus had nothing to do with the Aristotelian concepts of the *forma Reipublicae*. Rather, it dealt with the reality of the state constitution through assessing the strengths or weaknesses of a given country, the maxims of government and matters of income and finance for example, all of which went beyond an interest in strictly legal issues. In this way, a constitution was a composition of the observed knowledge acquired about its real condition.[50]

Much of this empirical approach was taken up in the *Verfassungsschrift* when Hegel considered population, economics and military organization, applying them broadly to analyse the Empire (*notitia status imperii*), notably in comparison to other states. Hegel also drew up detailed tables – manuscripts that have not survived but are recorded by Karl Rosenkranz (1805–79) – which had three columns comparing Bern, Italy and the German Empire. Furthermore, it is almost certain that he laid out the history of the Empire in tabular form while working on the imperial constitution.[51] While the comparative approach was common to the statistics practised in Germany, so too was the drawing up of tables to do so.

Gottfried Achenwall (1719–72), professor of law and politics in Göttingen, who put the term *Statistik* into general currency after 1750, derived the name from the Italian *statista*, statesman, and the *ragione di stato*, reason of state, referring to the knowledge a statesman was required to possess. In Germany the resulting discipline was closely interwoven with recent history and politics and comparative in character, because in contrast to the *studia antiquitatum*, which documented similar material for ancient and biblical times, *Statistik* involved existing European states whose interests were mutually affected by the mechanism of the balance of power.[52] It took all sorts of considerations into account in its reflection on the condition of the Empire but – and unlike the earlier Aristotelian tradition – without attributing to it a specific form of government. Rather, it aimed at observing all of the elements that made up a state constitution. For Moser, this signified the mass of facts that could be assembled about the Empire – for Hegel, its non-existence as a state:

> The legal question of the state constitution in spiritual and secular matters could not supersede the examination of the more comprehensive reality of the state and its applicable constitution. The more *the real state constitution of empires and states is taken into consideration*, the greater the *benefit* of *science*, which also appears as *political prudence* [*Staatsklugheit*]. Accordingly, the question *about the formam Reipublicae* lost more and more importance as a *useless dispute* in the general descriptions of the constitution of the state.[53]

1.1.2 The futility of *politica*

This idea that quarrels over the *forma Reipublicae* had become futile, though expressed here in the words of the theologian and popular philosopher Johann August Eberhard (1739–1809), was first and foremost to be attributed to Moser. Historically reflecting on this contention in the first volume of his *Neues teutsches Staats-Recht*: *Von Teutschland und dessen Staats-Verfassung überhaupt* (1766), he considered every earlier attempt to categorize the constitution as not only unproductive and pointless but even detrimental. The endeavour to fit the state constitution into this or that type of Aristotelian mould was always unfavourable to one or other of the parties, the emperor or imperial estates, thus attesting to underlying political interests. Hence, there was another reason why the earlier discipline was called *politica* – beyond its mere reliance on Aristotle's *Politics*. The Thirty Years' War had revealed the full vehemence of the problem.[54] More sardonically, Moser simply ridiculed this theoretical approach: 'As far as I am concerned, this whole question, although others make a fuss about it, write whole books about it, and treat each other harshly enough about it, is not only quite useless, but also not even worthy of taking the trouble and the time.'[55]

There is a compelling unity to be discovered in Moser's thought. Irrespective of the subject to which it was applied his methodology remained identical. Just as with statistics and its issues of population and governmental edicts which, compiled together, were integral, if not identical, to the essential reality of the state constitution, so too with legal matters. The same overarching logic can be observed. Only after the actually existing rights and duties of its members had been enumerated could the type of constitution, in any sense, be considered. Without exception, Moser continually worked his way up piecemeal to the consideration of the state. It was not the end product of some theoretical process or deduction – no teleological objective – but rather the collection of everything considered along the way. Following this reasoning, a given form of constitution was a consequence and nothing more – something arrived at after the fact and in that respect largely insignificant to the preceding discoveries. The state constitution was synonymous with the facts and only arrived at through the compilative method. The latter was its reality.[56] Hegel turned this logic on its head. Moser's exhaustive compilation of the particular legal privileges and rights of the imperial estates contradicted the reality that something called the imperial state constitution even existed:

> Moser's treatment of German constitutional law has swollen into a library not through repetition, but through the real and eternal diversity of things themselves. The endless mass of far-reaching rights contradicts the view according to which Germany is a state body, an Empire – i.e. an empty name for a state, no longer a state, and therefore no longer has a state constitution and in fact no constitutional law. If we wanted to accept that enormous mass of rights as constitutional law, we would actually have to say that they are not the law of the state, but a system of law *against* the state, and that the German constitution *actually* consists in the general guarantee of the abolition [*Aufhebung*] of the state.[57]

This quotation attests directly to the rather complicated relationship Hegel had to Moser's thought, of which he was not entirely dismissive. Moser's approach spoke directly to an imperial political reality in which the Aristotelian concepts of the *forma Reipublicae* no longer applied. For Hegel, this was demonstrated in the loss of the First Coalition War against republican France and the ensuing Congress of Rastatt to which the genesis of the *Verfassungsschrift* was owed.[58] Not only was Moser's compilative method the most appropriate for understanding the irreality of the state constitution, but it was also a symptom that confirmed Hegel's own diagnosis. In this respect, in the words of the *Reinschrift*, Moser thus produced a form of 'constitutional law no longer as a science, but as a description of what empirically exists without conforming to a rational idea'.[59] *Politica*, the Aristotelian scientific approach, that dealt in rational ideas or concepts – what Franz Rosenzweig called 'the old doctor's question concerning the constitutional nature of the Empire'[60] – had definitively given way to a methodology of pure description. Just as Moser's compilative method answered the academic question by foreclosing it, so too did the First Coalition War: 'Deutschland ist kein Staat mehr'. In this way, Moser's empiricism 'obviously only has its place in *statu cadentis imperii*, it is precisely through its flight into a description without concept that it reveals all the more clearly the decay, the "irrationality" of public conditions'.[61]

This position can already be discovered in the earliest fragments of the *Verfassungsschrift*, making the case that Moser was the model for Hegel's description of modern German public law and the modern state law teachers. The Empire wholly defied categorization: 'a multitude of rights which, without unity, without principle, could form more of a collection than a system'.[62] These words from 'Sollte das politische Resultat' reflect the same insights Hegel drew on Moser's almost endless enumeration of far-reaching rights that contradicted the idea that Germany was a state body, an Empire or could accord with any one of the Aristotelian concepts of the *forma Reipublicae* from 'Der Nahme für die Staatsverfassung'. In this respect, Moser's vast compendiums were representative of the last phase of imperial public law for Hegel. They served his turn impeccably. Yet this cannot alter the reality. Moser's firm dismissal, his utter rejection in categorizing the constitution in favour of a compilative methodology was an exception rather than a rule in the public law literature. Pütter's systematic approach that set out to organize Moser's discoveries had asserted as much.[63] But this is something to explore in more detail in the following chapter. What is clear is that the singularity of Moser's approach makes it all the more plausible that *he is* the figure behind Hegel's denunciation of modern public law.

1.2 The question of sovereignty: Territorial supremacy

1.2.1 The *ratio status* and sovereignty

Under the legal question of the state constitution, Moser had examined the spiritual and worldly condition – what the older literature would have called the *status*, politics or reason of state (*ratio status*) – of the Empire.[64] If the type of constitution was not determined, however, this tradition was arguably emptied of its original meaning.

Historically, the *ratio status* set out to preserve or restore a given constitution. This was writ large in the most infamous example, the *Hippolythus* (1640).[65] If the *forma Reipublicae* was undetermined or underdetermined, it would seem impossible to answer the fundamental question of what was to be preserved or restored. In this way, the *ratio status* remained part and parcel of political Aristotelianism.

Leaving such things aside, Moser touched on the central issue of the division between emperor and imperial estates. It was in this context that traditionally the problem of sovereignty would be discussed. Yet Moser left the fundamental crux unresolved of who possessed or exercised such rights. With the locus of sovereignty undecided, as the historical literature has argued, the question only increased in severity.[66] In this way, Moser was unable to see the full ramifications of his own analysis. But Hegel did. Put another way, however, Moser might have been suggesting that sovereignty was simply a distraction, as the Empire seemed to be functioning fine without it.

Moser rarely used the term 'sovereignty'. It did not correspond to his understanding of the German constitution.[67] It was tarred with the same feathers as the Aristotelian typology – a doctrine in the abstract or the general, an object for a philosopher or Platonic jurist but not for the practising lawyer. Moser's condemnation of sovereignty was thus strikingly similar to his dismissal of the question of the *forma Reipublicae*: 'Who has majesty in the German Empire? is one of the most miserable academic questions [*Schul-Frage*]. People play with the word, ... argue with each other about it.'[68]

By now we should be well acquainted with Moser's alternative. To the abstract and the general, he counterposed the observable, the factual and the particular – to the ideal type, the real type. But in relying on description rather than categorization, he still could not escape the question. Rather, he froze it in a kind of *stasis*, implying here both suspension of motion and internal strife. In an attempt to avoid every type of political determination, Moser had inadvertently raised the stakes and increased the contention. This was further aggravated by another central concept in the history of German political thought that found itself in competition with the characteristics of imperial sovereignty.[69]

1.2.2 *Landeshoheit*

If we confine ourselves to the question of authority, what Moser observed was that German public law had undergone a process of devolution – from the imperial to the territorial. Even if there was no answer to the question in the abstract of where sovereignty ultimately resided, there was nonetheless an observable shift: 'As the sphere of public activity had grown, the centres of judicial gravity had migrated from imperial to territorial location, so that the focuses of constitutional issues and activity were no longer immediate to the empire.'[70]

For this reason, Moser considered territorial supremacy in all of its detail. Although not the same as complete sovereignty, or to be placed on the same footing as the rights of sovereignty, *Landeshoheit* represented the traditional rights of the imperial estates to hold the reins of not only local internal government but also external government in the form of war, peace, trade and diplomacy with other states.[71] This had been inherited from a tradition that continued to evolve. And a predominant shift could be identified.

The individual particularities of government law in the territories were being 'eclipsed by the expansion of the Landeshoheit toward a pretense of general sovereignty, toward an unrestrained and arbitrary authority'.[72]

Given the latter, Moser's attempt to avoid conceptual trappings, his rejection of the theoretical side of the doctrine of *Landeshoheit*, was far less successful than in the related case of sovereignty and the Aristotelian typology. He was even given to concede that in some respects territorial supremacy approached sovereignty.[73] Still, he sought out the reality of *Landeshoheit* as a living practice, demonstrating the diversity of different territorial constitutions – beyond the inexorable tendency towards expansion and general sovereignty. Hegel's observation about the French law of the *ancien régime* holds in this context: 'whoever travels through France by stagecoach, changes laws more often than horses'.[74] Thus, the real existing exercise of a multiplicity of rights in governance and jurisdiction that made up *Landeshoheit* differed from estate to estate and subject to subject: 'There are therefore different kinds of *Landeshoheit* which, however, because they are different in each territory (at least in some respects) from those in the others, cannot all be categorized under certain precise classes.'[75]

A further point must be noted. *Landeshoheit* was more than simply law. A quick survey of the titles of the sub-volumes of the sixteenth volume of *Neues teutsches Staats-Recht* reveals this most clearly. Territorial supremacy included almost every possible dimension of governance: from the imperial estates in general, to affairs of justice, taxation, military issues, the police, cameralism, the relations between subjects and their property, to mercy or pardon and ecclesiastical matters.[76] This extended down to the individual of a territory, an extension of scope which saw Moser introduce private law into German public law. Further still, and however reluctantly, he accepted the *Corpus iuris civilis* as a source for the relations between the imperial estates, even if the law of Justinian (482–565) made no sense when applied to the heterogeneity of the Germanic Empire.[77]

The process of the transfer or delegation of power identified above was unstoppable. Historically, it went hand in hand with the constitutionalization that was occurring at the territorial level between princes and their subjects or territorial estates.[78] Recording such conditions for Moser was a world away from providing an abstract answer to the question of where ultimate authority was held. There remained an acceptance, however, that, whatever its form, *Landeshoheit* could only be understood within an imperial constitutional context:[79] 'Thus no one can say with reason that a single imperial estate constitutes such an independent and sovereign state.'[80] Rather, what ought to be followed was the principle of balance that had been enshrined in the great treaties before it was tested during the Seven Years' War: 'In Germany, the emperor can and should hold the balance for the estates, and the estates for the emperor: this yields an equilibrium of government, and it is in this that the common good of the whole state consists.'[81]

But this did not alter the fact that, so long as *Landeshoheit* was not abused, it was freed from imperial jurisdiction.[82] This caveat standing, Moser was as realistic about the nature of power here as elsewhere. He expressed little faith in the ability of imperial authority to contain the imperial estates.[83] Despite his intentions, his work, by illustrating the independent operation of *Landeshoheit*, effectively recast the territories as autonomous states. This de facto independence, however, never gained legal recognition; the imperial constitution always served as the defining context for their status.[84]

1.2.3 Constitutionalization: Origin and custom

Moser's efforts attested to an historical fact: the concept of the constitution first emerged in the context of the preservation of the position of the territorial estates and their privileges over and against their princes or territorial lords, developing from the dynastic house rule that had elementally expressed itself in written form.[85] Thus, a highly organized legal relationship had come into being at the territorial level. This attested to the parity of lord and house, prince and estates, in which the exercise of rights and obligations was guaranteed. It too was the result of an increasing need for more complex administration, the rise of civil servants, administrators and the new tasks demanded for the estates. At the imperial level written contracts had, likewise, become the norm, one that legally secured the rights and duties of the emperor at the behest of the electors and imperial estates. These contracts belonged to the foundational laws and were the principal sources of public law.[86] The concept of the constitution made its appearance in this historical context with the perpetual electoral capitulation (1711).[87] This attempted to establish a permanent, universally binding set of rules for all future emperors, to which every new candidate would have to swear allegiance before their election. Its primary aim was to limit imperial power and prevent the Empire from becoming a hereditary monarchy in the hands of the Habsburgs. It sought to solidify the rights and privileges of the prince-electors and other imperial estates, effectively articulating aspirations for a more proto-constitutional framework for the Empire. Thus, the positive written sources that had appeared in the territories antedated this development by almost a century: 'The statehood shaped in the interplay between rulers and estates on the territorial level thus also differed in its "constituted" dynamic regulations from the conservative overall structure of the Empire.'[88]

It is safe to assume that the growing import of such legal sources as existed in the territories had in part transformed the theoretical object of the discipline of imperial public law. Perhaps this is one of the principal reasons why *Landeshoheit* and territorial governance became central topics in the last phase of German imperial public law.[89] Hegel analysed the evolution thus:

> Territorial supremacy, the pride of the German estates, the pride of their subjects in belonging to a particular state, is, with respect to the whole, the principle by which it is torn asunder; one is incompatible with the other; but it has so many alluring charms, it was so much supported by the character of the people, that every estate overlooked the fact that this segregation is the pit which it digs for itself, that the more it advances in its endeavour to isolate itself, the more it loses strength, that every gain is an increase of danger.[90]

Through the process of constitutionalization as it occurred in the territories, the German Empire had become a juridical rather than a political structure. For Hegel, it was concerned with cementing acquired rights at the cost of the public authority of the state. Private property, following the dictates of *Landeshoheit*, thus carved up the body politic and determined the irreality of the imperial constitution.

The rationale underlying this development was the confusion between private and public law or those elements of private law that had seeped into the imperial constitution to become an inseparable part of its being. As Moser's exhaustive description made clear, so Hegel recognized that territorial supremacy involved far more than simply law. It was to be located first and foremost in an obscure Germanic antiquity. Only at a much later stage was an original appropriation legally established, justifying the rights to regional governance:

> The spheres of power which each created for himself according to character and chance, the possession which he obtained for himself, these changeable things gradually became fixed by the passing of time, and inasmuch as exclusive property completely segregated individual needs from each other, the concepts became the same as what they had connected themselves with, and makeshift laws began to rule.[91]

In this way, Hegel had perceived how *Landeshoheit* with its rights to governance was a form of originary or primitive possession that had been attained through the power of acquisition: 'for possession was earlier than the law, and it did not spring from laws, but what was itself gained was made a legal right'.[92] This agreed with Moser's starting point too, which took tradition and custom as a basis in order to assess how such rights of governance had been accrued.[93]

1.2.4 A centrifugal structure without concept

Whereas Moser had attempted to limit the sphere of action of the imperial estates against emperor and Empire, the supreme head had little more power than to reprimand those who did not obey. Imperial jurisdiction more or less stopped at the given borders of a particular territorial state. The transfer or delegation of power thus entailed a decisive movement away from the centre.

The ideal of balance that Moser had invoked in which emperor and estates were complementary and in parity with each other was adopted by Hegel too. Yet the young philosopher spoke of how private property and the function it had attained in the state had eroded the universal system of governance that originally saw the emperor assembled with the estates: 'This power of the universal, the monarch (Emperor) and the assembly of the estates (*Reichstag*) has thus been left with the necessary character [of] sovereignty in a very weak measure.'[94]

From here, Hegel could and would elaborate further. The central point on which a state hinged was public authority and it had its core in supreme, plenary power – sovereignty. This universal governance directly implied other powers: the right to wage war, foreign relations and diplomacy and the part finances must play in such activities. But in the Empire, things were determined otherwise.[95] Indeed, as we have seen, Moser listed the right to wage war, foreign relations and diplomacy correctly under territorial governance, as an integral part of *Landeshoheit*, with the caveat of course that war be neither directed against emperor nor Empire (*I.P.O.* Article VIII §2).[96] This was an apt description of constitutional reality, as it existed in the eighteenth century and even earlier after the great treaties of the second half of the seventeenth century.

Already at its inception, the fragments of the *Verfassungsschrift* demonstrate Hegel's knowledge of Moser's compendiums on *Landeshoheit* – or so at least it seems to this interpreter. The two early fragments I have been discussing – 'Sollte das politische Resultat' and 'über ihre Entstehung' (on their emergence) – show this convincingly. The orientation of Hegel's discussion in 'Sollte das politische Resultat' brought Moser's descriptions of *Landeshoheit* to their logical conclusion. The interminable listing of the particular rights and privileges of governance contradicted the idea of a universal imperial public authority. The advancement in the territories, the entrenchment of *Landeshoheit*, came at the cost of the constitution or state:

> Thus, a state structure has come into being whose individual parts, every princely house, every estate, every town, every guild, everything that possesses rights with regard to the state, has acquired them for itself; the state has always only had to confirm that which was taken from its power. The share in the power of the state which the individual has acquired for himself is thus withdrawn from the power of the universal. This endeavour to make the power of the state a private property means nothing other than dissolving the state, destroying the state as a power.[97]

It was in this context that Hegel also discussed the Aristotelian typology, agreeing in part with Moser's rejection of this form of classification – though for very different reasons. The compilative method, which enumerated the rights of every member, from the electors and the imperial estates down to the isolated individual, contradicted the very idea of the state and its categorization according to any one of the Aristotelian models of the *forma Reipublicae*. This too spoke directly to the very character of German public law. The individual member of the body politic owed its rights and duties not to the universal, but rather to its particular allegiance to family, guild or estate: 'The principles of the system of German public law [*des deutschen öffentlichen Rechts*] are therefore not derived from the unity of a concept of state law, such as the concept of a monarchy, aristocracy, democracy, and so on.'[98]

The local structures, so thoroughly rooted in tradition and custom, were thus entirely determinative. They codified rights in the imperial constitution through any number of arrangements, from the most insignificant trifles to titles and the order of seats in the *Reichstag*. Remarkable care had to be taken to ensure the preservation of every privilege.[99] Historically, as we have seen, this conformed to the datum that regional constitutional evolution preceded developments at the imperial level. Thus, the endless concern to preserve private property stood in stark contrast to the desultory effort invested in universal governance, public authority and the imperial constitution. All of these rights were codified and determined through the capitulations, the contracts or treaties of imperial public law: from the electoral and imperial legal mandates to the peace treaties of Westphalia which were also constitutional laws,[100] to the most insignificant house contract that had fixed status relations.[101]

1.2.5 The emergence of territorial sovereignty

All of these developments cemented the private interests of each and every estate. It could not be denied. A form of sovereignty had thus in effect become a direct possession of the imperial estates. With the overwhelmingly prevalent use of sovereignty and its cognates,[102] the fragments of *Verfassungsschrift* demonstrate how Hegel had intuited the historical shift that was emerging. This came to a head in the War of the Second Coalition and the later treaties with Napoleon and in the *Rheinbund*. The doctrine of territorial supremacy only figured in the early fragment 'über ihre Entstehung'. It was replaced throughout by the increasingly more palatable notion of sovereignty as a territorial right that destroyed the Empire. In this subtle alteration of concepts, Hegel had thus already grasped how reality would later appear in Article 9 and Article 10 of the Ludwigsburg Treaty (5 October 1805).

Personally dictated by Napoleon, the Ludwigsburg Treaty between Württemberg and revolutionary France was a final attempt by the French to make sovereignty into a reality against emperor and Empire. Aimed principally at destroying the imperial constitution, as it had existed since Westphalia, it was successful in this political objective.[103]

A vestige of the imperial feudal system, *Landeshoheit* no longer applied. Napoleon had thus finally realized a principle of French foreign policy dating back to the seventeenth-century *ancien régime*. During the Westphalian peace negotiations, the rights of sovereignty (*souveranitas iura*) were, in a political sleight of hand, ascribed to the imperial estates in the French draft of the treaties – only to be struck out by the hawk-eyed emperor.[104] In his struggle against emperor and Empire in 1805, the consequences of territorial sovereignty were fully grasped by Napoleon. This change in concepts was through and through *political*. With the dissolution of the Empire and its legal system of courts, *Landeshoheit*, by necessity, must also disappear. Sovereignty was the only category necessary for grasping the thoroughly modern concept of the highest power.[105]

In a different way, what this discussion shows is that as long as the decision over where sovereignty resided was contested, the Empire continued to exist. Indeed, the tension between territory and Empire, the real conflict and opposition between emperor and imperial estates, demonstrated how the legal framework of the imperial constitution, the complex interplay between the various interests, thrived.[106] This was key to its system of compromise and balance for Moser. The Empire was not deficient in leaving the locus of sovereignty in question – in fact that was its strength, integral to its system. The real issue is whether this was still possible in view of the revolutionary wars, the incursion of the French forces under Napoleon. In this context, we do well to note just how much Hegel's early system was marked by the corporate forms of the old Empire. His ideal of sovereignty was that of a monarch alongside the estates. This was the representative system of original Germanic freedom. If only it could be restored, in place of the striving after sovereignty of the imperial estates, it would surpass the French revolutionary model in every way in which abstract equality and centralization, for Hegel, had produced the Reign of Terror.

For Moser, arguments over sovereignty, just like the Aristotelian concepts of the *forma Reipublicae*, were responsible for shattering the collective whole into fragments.

Even so, as we have seen, *Landeshoheit* amounted to a loose kind of imperial sovereignty. Moser thus faced a dilemma. When accepting the juridical formula that *Landeshoheit* was 'envious sovereignty' (*maiestas aemula*) of 'the supreme power of the Empire' (*summae Imperii*),[107] he thus practically recognized its full extent – even if the diverse rights of governance were secured constitutionally in the doctrine of imperial public law. What I am suggesting is that Hegel drew out the consequences of Moser's exhaustive analysis. The diverse multiplicity that had secured their private interests contradicted the nature of public authority, transforming it in turn. Although Moser left sovereignty undefined, his description of *Landeshoheit* was sufficient enough to supplant it almost entirely. In the final analysis, Moser had thus answered the problem of the *iura maiestatis* despite himself. The endless enumeration of private territorial rights had shaped the very contours of public law so completely that it became for practical purposes indistinguishable from them.

1.3 A definitive description of the Empire: The head and members

1.3.1 A metaphor from imperial public law

The compilative methodology defied every attempt to classify. Yet this did not mean that classification was impossible. Moser was a monarchist. Imperial patriotism demanded nothing less. For him, the ideal of emperor and Empire was the only brake stopping the potential despotism of both sides of this equation – something he had experienced at close quarters.[108] He thus held fast to the sanctity of imperial institutions, even if their authority began to wane in the eighteenth century.

In looking around for an appropriate description – *not*, we must stress, a concept – Moser hit upon the representation of the constitution as it had been provided in the Last Recess of the Empire (1654), with its apt political and physiological illustration of a head and members or limbs: 'Our German Empire consists of a single head and several members, some of which are immediate and some mediate [to the Empire].'[109] He referred explicitly, as was his penchant, to imperial public law to support the metaphor: 'What … has been referred in the Peace of Westphalia to a general Imperial Assembly for further deliberation and settlement between the head and the members. And in the electoral capitulation … the Peace of Westphalia is called a perpetual bond between head and members.'[110] The bond was not a 'contract' that could be broken, however, but a continuous, legally defined, almost unbreakable link that preserved the Empire's existence despite its decentralized nature and the frequent conflicts between its members. It emphasized continuity and legal obligation. Moser's idea of a 'perpetual bond' became Pütter's objective legal connection, as we will see in the next chapter. The *negotia remissa* that Moser hinted at in this context left a series of constitutional issues unresolved in 1648, prolonging them into the peace. This meant that the other signatories, Sweden and France, had no influence on these matters, as they would have had they been raised during the negotiations.

A body politic composed of a head and members had numerous advantages. Firstly, it was a living part of imperial public law, a way of accounting for the functioning of imperial institutions. Secondly, it was a powerful metaphor to describe a complex reality: 'The idea of head and limbs, of the parts that are combined and ordered into a multi-membered unit, ... made it particularly suitable for intuiting the political reality of the old Empire and its complex constitution.'[111]

But Moser also went further, first relying on Johannes Limnaeus (1592–1665), the avant-garde of German imperial public law, who had conceived of the Empire as a subject of sovereignty through the rule of foundational laws.[112] Limnaeus had successfully expounded a rather complex theory of the *status mixtus*, which became an authoritative doctrine for the generation that came before Pufendorf.[113]

According to this doctrine the *leges fundamentales* did not come into conflict with sovereignty but gave voice to it and stabilized rule. Whereas real sovereignty (*maiestas realis*) was firmly anchored in the Empire and its foundational laws, represented by the collectivity of estates, the emperor possessed personal sovereignty (*maiestas personalis*).[114] This was an attempt to overcome the doctrine of the sovereignty of the ruler established by the French jurist Jean Bodin and to replace it with a doctrine of the state.[115] The latter was nothing more 'than an organization of the national community, which is itself the subject of sovereign power, of real majesty, both externally and internally within the organization'.[116]

Obviously, Moser would have cared little about these theoretical details. Through the *maiestas personalis*, the emperor's power became bounded by law, something Moser seemed to refute, although his use of purely descriptive language is not explicit enough to be entirely sure.[117] The important matter that Moser extracted from Limnaeus was the notion that only the emperor held the position of the head of the Empire. The fact that this had only become possible through Limnaeus's theoretical innovation, that divided sovereignty into real and personal, was not Moser's concern.[118]

Limnaeus was not alone in the rank of publicists Moser cited favourably in this context to support his description of a head and members. What he found important to stress was that this description in no way implied that there was 'a distinct concept of the German type of government'.[119] The physiological description was particularly apt because it was clear that limbs could do nothing without a head – and that the opposite was also true. If the head for Moser was to a greater degree independent when compared to the members, as it did not require consent to give direction whereas the members consented in following it, it remained laughable to imagine the head acting autonomously from its body – only Cartesians took such foolishness seriously.[120]

Undoubtedly, this all spoke positively to Moser's illustration of balance in the Empire. Referring to another exhaustive compiler of imperial public laws Johann Friedrich Pfeffinger (1667–1730) and an adept student of Christian Thomasius (1655–1728) Gottlieb Samuel Treuer (1683–1773),[121] Moser went further insisting that the emperor was the *only* head of the Empire: 'Pfeffinger and others, and Treuer in particular, made an observation of this title. Sometimes the Emperor is called *head* [*Haupt*] sometimes *superior head* [*Oberhaupt*]: sometimes this word is used alone, sometimes it is added: highest or: supreme, or: vigilant, and so on.'[122]

The importance of such descriptions of the imperial body politic is that they spoke to the ancient imperial harmony between emperor and Empire, preserving the status of the emperor. Yet, in Moser's hands, it was transformed from a metaphor into an empirical account of the unity that could be achieved when the parts were grouped together and suitably arranged into a whole.[123] Moser thus drew from the earlier imperial tradition, but even more directly from the use of the head in imperial public law descriptions which reached back to 1544. References could also be gleaned from the later context of the great treaties: the capitulations and the observed imperial structure in which harmony, balance and equilibrium had become principal ideals emphasized everywhere – almost unanimously. The unity of emperor and Empire, uncontested.[124]

Moser then discussed how the description of the emperor as administrator of the Empire had entered circulation via the electoral capitulations and within the context of writings in the run-up to the treaties of Westphalia that had conceived of the emperor as a legitimate administrator (*tanquam legitimi Administratoris*). Moser went out of his way once again to stress how this in no way involved the irrelevant question of the *forma Reipublicae*. Administration was completely indifferent to the Aristotelian categories.[125] Moreover – and pinpointing how the issue belied all contention – the description of administrator took nothing from but also gave nothing to the imperial dignity. Accordingly, there was nothing in its use among the imperial estates that could be construed to support one party over another.

1.3.2 The conceptual language of Jean Bodin

It is ironic, given Moser's barely concealed loathing for theory, to note that his whole discussion is saturated in the conceptual language of Jean Bodin, which had left deep traces on the German political and juridical literature, of *De Republica libri sex* (1591).[126] In an effort to maintain the monistic character of sovereignty and to attack those who continued to uphold the doctrine of the *status mixtus*, the Angevin cunningly introduced an abstract division between the constitution and condition of the state or republic (*Reipublicae statum*) and the underlying purpose or logic of command (*imperandi ratione*), its governance, government, rule or administration (*gubernatio*).[127] Bodin thus definitively separated sovereignty and its exercise from the office-holder who administered any given governmental function of the state. 'This legal construction', as Helmut Quaritsch so astutely pointed out, 'presupposes the separation of office and office holder'.[128] This had insidiously worked its way into the conventions of German public law to become an object of frequent misinterpretation. But in the legal history that it would establish, it spoke to the division between constitutional and governmental or administrative law. This stretched down into the conceptions of German Idealism, to Kant and Hegel.

For Moser, to follow the idea that conceived of the supreme head as an administrator, it was enough to look to the language of the imperial laws, statutes and treaties – one need go no further. The question of sovereignty in this context, as elsewhere, was completely circumvented. The matter was not even raised. And the like issue of the *forma Reipublicae*, as Moser continually insisted, had nothing to do with administration.

Treuer was almost as punctilious as Moser. As a result, Moser was inclined to accept his learning more or less in its entirety – especially when Treuer insisted on rejecting the idea, which had become rife in imperial patriotic positions that favoured the emperor, that he was (in a political sense) greater than the Empire (*Caesarem (in sensu politico) maiorem esse Imperio*). There was nothing to support this assertion. Finally, there was also no evidence to uphold the theorizations of the opposite camp, which were no less political and, in some cases, even more pointedly radical.[129]

The *Hippolythus*,[130] referred to by Moser in this context, had drawn a good deal of attention by virtue of its obtrusive animus, but it won few friends and, according to historical revisionism, had no formative impact.[131] Notwithstanding its polemical appeal, there was no proof to uphold the idea that the emperor was called director in the imperial laws and acts of the Empire: 'although, if one thinks of it in terms of the imperial constitution, this word, just as little as the title of an *Administratoris*, would not offend either the Emperor or the imperial estates'.[132]

What Moser's passing discussion proved was that even the most violent diatribe against the Habsburgs and the position of the emperor could not escape examining the true intricacy of the imperial political order. Part of the significance of the *Hippolythus* was that, from within the context of the patriotic reform tradition which sought a greater freedom for the imperial estates during the Thirty Years' War, the purity of Bodin's aristocratic *forma Reipublicae* was impossible to uphold.[133]

Leaving this thorny issue aside, although holding fast to the categorization of the *forma Reipublicae*, it might even seem that the *Hippolythus*, in its preference for empiricism and complexity, intuited Moser's later views: 'If the boundlessness of Bodin's extremely harsh opinion [continues concerning the mixture of the diverse forms of republic], I fear you are proved wrong by experience itself, the best teacher of reality'.[134] To account for complexity, one had to consider a position for the emperor. This was nowhere more apparent than in the word 'director' introduced by the *Hippolythus*, which Moser isolated in his analysis but ultimately rejected as a piece of pure theory with no corresponding documentation in the collections of imperial public law. Nonetheless, he tersely recognized the full complexity of its typological discussion:

> H. à LAPIDE considers the state constitution or form of government of the Empire to be aristocratic strictly speaking, but in such a way that the closer administration of certain individual governmental affairs and special matters is in a certain way carried out on a monarchical basis. However, he also establishes a fourfold mixture of an aristocracy a) of the electors, b) of the princes, c) of the prelates and counts, and d) of the imperial cities.[135]

Thus, the *Hippolythus* could in no way simply represent 'the reemergence of a Bodinian view'.[136]

1.3.3 The supreme head and sovereignty

For Moser, the compilative methodology must be carried through consistently to the end. Yet if, at the end, the emperor really *was* the supreme head of the Empire, nothing could stand as a judge over him.[137] Although avoiding the question theoretically, with this Moser came so dangerously close to what he had hoped to avoid at all costs. The classical concept of sovereignty and with it the contested issue of who or what stood above all positive law had raised its ugly head.

Moser thought he had an answer in the purity of his methodology. But this too could be deceptive. What seemed to be so self-evident – a purely empirical and value-neutral enterprise – had reintroduced an oddly familiar set of problems. These problems were so deeply ensconced in the conceptual baggage of early modern sovereignty that they were essentially indistinguishable from it. If the supreme head could not be judged, what happened in the case of a despot like Ferdinand II (1578–1637) with his Edict of Restitution (1629)?[138]

Given that the emperor was the supreme head of the Empire, this meant that he stood directly over the members, the imperial estates. Taken together, the imperial estates approached him in dignity – he was not more sovereign than the Empire – but individually this was not the case. A member did not form an external body but only could be considered as part of a larger whole. The contrast for Moser was clear and it was an expression of his monarchism. Every imperial estate must yield to the emperor who was *in corpore* part of all of its institutions and courts – as supreme head.[139]

A proviso, however, came hazily into view. The collectivity of imperial estates was not obliged to tolerate an emperor who misused his power to repress the members. In other words, they could oppose and offer resistance but could not stand in judgement.[140] Not only did this demonstrate how impossible it was to evade the classical problems of sovereignty, it pointed, too, to the ambiguity of the supreme head and the unresolved contradiction of its potency or impotency. Hegel had a word or two to say about all of this:

> By the very general concept of the supreme head of the Empire, the emperor is thrown into a category with the former Doge of Venice and the Turkish Sultan, both of whom are also supreme heads of state, but the former the most restricted head of an aristocracy, the latter the most unrestricted of a despotism; and because the concept of a supreme head fits the most varied scope of supreme state power, it is entirely indefinite, and for that very reason has no value at all; it pretends to have expressed something and actually has not expressed anything.[141]

With this quote Hegel demonstrated the extent of his knowledge of the imperial constitutional tradition and early modern German public law as it had been communicated down to his own time. This connection has gone entirely unnoticed in the most recent critical literature and commentary.[142] In 1530, an anonymous report was circulated within the reform movement of the imperial estates that considered the emperor akin to the Doge of Venice.[143] The archbishop of Mainz, the traditional representative of reform initiatives, had taken over this idea in turn. By 1539, the Protestant reformer Martin Luther (1483–1546) was using it.[144] But it only became widely known and criticized in German public law circles with its notorious popularization in Bodin's discussion of the imperial *forma Reipublicae*. On the other hand, what Hegel's quote makes perfectly clear is the extent of his condemnation of Moser's discussion of the imperial head or supreme head.

For Bodin, the emperor, as was the Doge of Venice, was even less than a supreme titular head of an aristocracy.[145] At best, he was a *princeps* in the Roman republican understanding of the term – the first among equals.[146] With the Golden Bull, the Holy Roman Empire had transformed from a monarchy into an aristocracy. This first fundamental law gave it its electoral character, fixing the status of the electors as well as their number and exact identity and allowing the Count Palatine to sit as judge over the emperor. The latter in no way possessed *maiestas* but was more akin to a vassal of the collective assembly of imperial estates in which at most three to four hundred members had something to say.[147]

Moser would not have entertained such ideas. Not only did Bodin's radicalism patently contradict the idea of monarchy, but also, through the Count Palatine, it exercised judgement over the emperor – and, in so doing, put this power squarely in the hands of the imperial estates. Ultimately, the formula was a political expression of the efforts of the emergent French nation state which was in the process of attempting to free itself from a feudal order of allegiance.[148] Yet, it also reflected an historical context in which the right of resistance of some of the Protestant estates had emerged during the Thirty Years' War ignited around the Palatinate. But it really had nothing to do with German public law.

Moser too had referred to the equation between the emperor and the Doge, rejecting it as unsuitable, absurd and tasteless.[149] This might have been the source for Hegel's discussion. Quite clearly, even if it was not heretical the idea contradicted reality. The emperor *could* decide against the imperial estates and, if he did so, what had been proposed did not pass into law. Hence, Moser's refutation fell in line with the perspectives of the majority of the imperial patriotic tradition that had been scandalized by the formula. This has been recounted by the historical scholarship in some detail.[150]

1.3.4 Moser and the *Hippolythus*

Moser drove his point home by restating that it was axiomatically false to propose that the emperor could neither depart from the conclusions of the imperial estates nor reach his own decision independently. Germany was thus *some type of monarchy*. In the same context, however, he did find some of the ideas of the *Hippolythus* acceptable – it had intuited the imperial body politic of head and members: 'LAPIDE ascribes the essential majesty, that is, the actual administration of the state, the essence of rule, the true sovereignty and the concept of supreme state prerogatives [*StaatsGerechtsamen*], to the whole Empire, including the emperor, insofar as they constitute a single corpus at general imperial assemblies.'[151]

What is striking is just how close Moser's position came to the ideas of the *Hippolythus* and how closely it conformed to what Moser had discovered in the documents of imperial public law. This was not mere chance. The *Hippolythus* was recognized for its vast erudition as much as its vituperation. Still, there remained more than enough points to criticize. The *Hippolythus* presented a paradox: its extensive scholarship, though undeniable, was fundamentally shaped by its partisan aims, rendering its conclusions highly tendentious and its method questionable. Its conceptual acuity was sullied by the fact that it was directed to purely political ends. Such aspects marked an epoch in which scholarly debate in the literature of public law had been soldered to an actual conflict, the internecine Thirty Years' War.[152] This was brought back to life in Moser's epoch with the Seven Years' War when the German translation appeared as a Prussian propaganda piece, toning down the original invective directed against the electors. The Austrian house was once again depicted despotically, to ignite another union of Protestant estates.[153]

Moser was disinclined to credit many of the claims of the *Hippolythus*, certainly with respect to the supposed cunning of the emperor.[154] He chose to cite a brief between electoral Saxony and the Palatinate (1608). This asserted that, importantly, the designation emperor was not simply an honourable title, something bestowed by the electors and imperial estates. The idea of the supreme head of the Empire embodied much more than this. It conveyed notions of command and ultimate decision and thus reflected, in turn, the pinnacle of a feudal hierarchy.[155] Hence, the emperor was *legibus solutus* according to the classical theoretical terminology which Moser scorned. Yet the purity of description could not avoid the problem entirely, as we have now seen. Moser directed this document against the unknown author of the remarks to the German *Hippolythus*.[156] Given that the document was an exchange involving the Palatinate, Moser might have hoped it would carry even more weight.

Part of the conceptual acuity of the *Hippolythus* was its naturalization of the techniques of the *ratio status* in Germany, which it directed to the Empire. Thus, as Pütter discerned, its title 'was designed to express what the French called *Raison d'État*'.[157] This tradition in Germany closely followed the Aristotelian approach to the *forma Reipublicae*, mentioned above. After identifying the original aristocratic type of government in the Empire, its *ratio status* could then be pursued – bound by no law.[158] The *Hippolythus* thus identified any means necessary for restoring the original *Reichskörper* and the ancient liberty of the estates that had degenerated through the force of monarchical tyranny or despotism: 'as in sick bodies Doctors leave nothing behind that will be injured: as a consequence we may cut back anything that stands in the way of our Government (whose foundation is Liberty, not the decisive mastery of one person)'.[159]

The *Hippolythus* advocated the total destruction of the Habsburgs who were to be driven out of Germany. In this context, the judgement of Niccolò Machiavelli (1469–1527) in the *Florentine Histories* (1532) was cited[160] – that in every state there are families deadly to the body politic: 'This is certainly the fate of our German family, which having sprung from small beginnings, has advanced to such a degree of power that it may be formidable to the whole empire, and indeed disastrous.'[161] From 'Sollte das politische Resultat' onwards, Hegel identified the counter position of the *Hippolythus* with 'the saga of German freedom'.[162]

Even if the supreme head was the imperial judge that stood above every other member or limb and thus enjoyed immunity, as Moser had highlighted, he could still be resisted in cases of tyranny and despotism.[163] Obviously, Moser did not employ the latter terms. To do so would have gone against the grain of his descriptive approach, reintroducing the theories he so abhorred. Such concepts after all belonged to the *forma Reipublicae* and the doctrine of sovereignty.[164] Thus, Moser spoke simply of the abuse of imperial power weighing on the imperial estates. The mere avoidance of terminology, however, cannot alter reality. Despite every effort to evade the contentious debate over the *forma Reipublicae* and the related loci of sovereignty, these concepts proved irresistible, inevitably drawing thinkers to them like a moth to a flame.

1.3.5 Hegel and the *Hippolythus*

For Hegel, the problem was all too obvious. The categorization of the German constitution as an Empire or a body politic united under a supreme head simply gave further expression to it. Thus, Moser's approach was more of a symptom than a method. It represented the failure to ascribe an appropriate *forma Reipublicae* to the imperial constitution. This had originally taken its inspiration from an Aristotelian scientific approach to political and legal concepts. Writ large in the tradition, Moser sought to replace it with whatever the documents of imperial public law might have to say on the matter. This is what led him to the imperial body politic of a head and members in the first place, as we have seen:[165]

> The teacher of constitutional law, who can no longer call Germany a state, because he would otherwise have to admit some consequences that follow from the concept of a state, and which he cannot admit, assigns the title Empire as a concept. Or, since Germany is not a democracy, nor an aristocracy, but should be a monarchy by its very nature, and at the same time the Emperor should not be regarded as a monarch, recourse is taken to the title of supreme head of the Empire, which holds even in a system in which not titles, but certain concepts should prevail.[166]

There is no riddle to be solved in this context. What Hegel had in mind with these concepts, which should also form the foundation of any system of public law, are identified with the Aristotelian forms of monarchy, aristocracy and democracy.[167] Further, in speaking of mere titles and contrasting them to a science of concepts, Hegel followed in the footsteps of the *Hippolythus* and the Machiavellian or Tacitean-inflected genre of the *ratio status* and *arcana imperii* that it had popularized.[168] For this tradition, the mere appearances of rule (*simulacra imperii*) or the appearances of sovereignty (*simulacra maiestatis*) were set in explicit opposition to the secrets of rule (the *arcana imperii*) or the real rights of domination (*iura dominationis*).[169] This followed the political technics of dissimulation and theories for securing power that had been discussed in the *Annals* and the *Histories* – the *arcana imperii*, *arcana domus*, *arcana dominationis* and *arcanum imperii*.[170]

As the historical literature has shown, these were connected to a discussion identifying good and bad *ratio status* which corresponded to the good and bad types of constitution in Aristotle, particularly in the fifth book of the *Politics*. The latter was a study in political pathology that in many ways anticipated Machiavelli's later discussion.[171] In the third part of the *Hippolythus* these technical means for restoring the original constitution were extensively discussed alongside the concepts, drawn from Limnaeus, of real and personal sovereignty – the latter being little more than a titular function.[172]

Just as the *Hippolythus*, so too for Hegel: the Empire had (at one point in time) accorded with a distinct constitutional concept; it belonged 'under the principle of limited monarchy, that is, one based on laws'.[173] As to the question of whether it could be restored to such a condition, Hegel was far less certain. Medicine and politics may have been equivalent sciences in the early modern period, but the mere identification of a poison was never enough for the statesman or political scientist to bring about a cure. In its attempt to prove the de facto 'legal reality of the *Reichskörper* behind the silhouettes of honorary titles and deceptive phrases',[174] the *Hippolythus* had appropriately been led to Machiavelli, as we have observed.[175] The same held true for Hegel. The imperial body politic lent itself to the use of medical metaphors, not to mention the apothecary of distasteful methods that could be gleaned from this infamous political Hippocrates. Drawing a direct historical equation between Machiavelli's Italy and a Germany similarly besieged by French invading forces, Hegel did not mince words: 'Here, however, there can be no question of any choice of means; gangrenous limbs cannot be healed with lavender water; a state in which poison and assassination have become common weapons cannot tolerate any gentle attempts to counteract it; life close to decay can only be reorganized by the most violent means.'[176]

The principle of a limited monarchy based on laws that Hegel had pinpointed was a notion central to Protestant reform circles and Aristotelianism. Philipp Melanchthon, in his famed commentary on Aristotle's *Politics*, had developed a particular typology of kingship: a kingship bound by laws that was to be distinguished from tyranny and domestic rule or despotism.[177] Luther took up the same ideas as his colleague and friend: 'Caesar occupies a civil office [magistracy], not a despotic one, as Aristotle specifies.'[178] After listing the various monarchies in Europe, Luther then referred to the government of Germany as an aristocracy.[179] It was at the same time that he referred to the anonymous legal opinion that had surfaced among the reformers that referred to the emperor as the Doge of Venice.

The conception of the Empire as a limited monarchy based on laws inherently recognized that the imperial estates could oppose a legal breach by the supreme head, a principle consistent with Moser's (and Luther's) own guarded terminology that explicitly avoided any reference to the emperor as a despot in this regard.[180] Still, when considering the imperial *forma Reipublicae*, for the reformers Aristotelianism provided the dominant semantic field in which they developed and honed distinctive concepts that were then passed on to the German tradition of imperial public law.

We can now turn to study Hegel's Aristotelianism in more detail and, more precisely, to the way in which he developed it in opposition to Moser's modern public law doctrine.

1.4 Hegel's Aristotelianism and the Germanic World

1.4.1 The impossibility of form: Transition to legal culture

When Hegel came to define the imperial constitution conceptually, as the earlier political Aristotelians and professors of public law had done, he immediately concluded that it could no longer be considered a constitution, a state. From 'Sollte das politische Resultat' onwards, he summarized – and, indeed, in painstaking detail – how the Aristotelian inflected tradition had run aground in its efforts to determine the imperial *forma Reipublicae*.[181] In a later template for the *Reinschrift*, 'Diese Form des deutschen Staatsrechts' (This Form of German Constitutional Law), Hegel was even more explicit in identifying the failure, which he linked directly to a German character trait, respect for law.[182] However admirable and praiseworthy as a general rule, when applied to *every* law, in a situation in which, as Moser's work testified, the sheer number of laws to which the same individual might be subject could boggle the mind, it was unreasonable and presented a formidable obstacle to the formation of the state without which public law was impossible. Pushing the analysis further, Hegel arrived at the conclusion that the 'political condition [of Germany] would have to be regarded as a legal anarchy, its constitutional law as a legal system against the state'.[183]

The transition from the law of the land, the right to private warfare (*Faustrecht*) – little more than brute acquisition and force – to politics, according to Hegel, did not necessarily signify a shift 'from anarchy to a constitution, [for] the true principle has not changed, only its exterior'.[184] Germanic prehistory confirmed this suspicion: what had been acquired by violent appropriation – implying a ripping away from the common stock – following the reception of Roman law, was simply made legal. This spoke directly to Moser's vast compendiums – a sum of rights that, for Hegel, contradicted the idea of the state, public authority and public law. What the volumes of *Neues teutsches Staats-Recht* demonstrated was how a true system of German public law was impossible. Moser's collection, in essence, reflected an historical logic traced by the Halle philosopher Johann Christoph Krause (1749–1799): 'The territorial and imperial estate privileges had to be solemnly recognized not as innovations, but as *ancient* law.'[185]

Neues teutsches Staats-Recht had set out to compile, to archive every discoverable law, but it also simultaneously conveyed the living character of the imperial constitution with its complex division into territorial and imperial jurisdictions. It revealed how the formalization of public law had been equally shaped by private interest. For Hegel, it demonstrated how the rights of the territories essentially outweighed the rights of the emperor. What had been previously attained by force had then become custom and practice only to be ultimately codified as law by an increasingly refined legal culture.

For Hegel, the underlying objective everywhere remained the same: the securing of private political gain that sapped the essentials of public authority. At the same time, this continuity of purpose was accompanied by a shift in means: politics and law had replaced private warfare and the blood feud as the prevailing methods, even if they originated in the latter.[186] Whereas in Germanic prehistory individuals would respond to any slight with violence and seek to secure even the smallest possession through force, modern subjects employed varied means. Hence, it became necessary to delineate the subtle contours of a gradual historical process: 'This transition from the condition of manifest power to the condition of calculated power did not, of course, take place all at once; on the contrary, it was brought about by a legal constitution.'[187]

This constitution was what Hegel recognized as the constitution of fiefs (*Lehensverfassung*) that had arisen during the Middle Ages and that brought an end to the law of the land with the institution of public peace (*Landfriede*).[188] Further, it produced the peculiarity of the original imperial *forma Reipublicae* as a limited monarchy or kingship bound by laws. It had culminated in the diverse systems of representation of Hegel's day, the *Reichstag* and the *Landtag*, the Imperial Diet, the Territorial Diet.

1.4.2 From the constitution of fiefs to the *simulacra imperii*

Even if the constitution of fiefs represented the necessary historical abolition of open violence and its replacement by law and culture, this did not quiet the powers that had been originally integrated into it. Whereas the *Lehensverfassung* produced a modicum of stability insofar as 'the power of the state was divided into many parts, [and] because of the number of parts, some were not powerful enough to oppose the whole',[189] there were, nonetheless, individual independent elements that continued to consolidate their power.

What this constitution essentially lacked was a necessary and unitary legal bond that tied the people collectively to 'the power of the state'.[190] Thus, as Max Weber characterized it, it represented 'the most extreme type of systematically decentralized rule'.[191] Hence, the principal historical result of this form of constitutional development in Germany was the 'gradual transformation from an originally fairly unitary state into a federalistic organization of *de facto* sovereign states'.[192] This was precisely the history that Hegel detailed in 'Sollte das politische Resultat' and elsewhere. This is to say nothing of the fact that fiefdoms in the German Empire came under the control of foreign powers through inheritance, marriage and alliance which produced what Hegel called the 'northern barbarism of the Roman Empire':[193] 'Just as the old Roman Empire was destroyed by Nordic barbarians, the principle of the destruction of the Roman-German Empire also came from the north. Denmark, Sweden, England, and especially Prussia are the foreign powers whose imperial status gives them both a separate interest from the German Empire and a constitutional influence in its affairs.'[194]

An essential problem with the *Lehensverfassung* that had produced the imperial *forma Reipublicae* as a limited monarchy or kingship bound by laws was its continuation into a period when it was apparent that a system involving largely independent states was emerging, through the gradual concentration of power in the territories. The confessional issue that had united the Protestant estates against Ferdinand II furthered this process, which evolved into an ideological struggle against what became the bogey of universal monarchy.[195] The *Hippolythus* had been representative of this trend, its *ratio status* a solution to the crisis of the *Reich* in the period of the Thirty Years' War.

This was so completely different from the historical context of the Seven Years' War in which Prussia was the obvious aggressor. What was farcical in the mid-eighteenth century had become downright absurd by the Peace of Basel. This is not to mention the fact that by concluding a separate treaty with France, Prussia had egregiously violated the imperial constitution and forsaken the loyalty it owed to the emperor.[196] Hence, as Hegel expressed it in language that has determined the reception of the fragments of the *Verfassungsschrift* ever since: 'So foolish are men, due to ideal visions of the disinterested salvation of freedom of conscience and political liberty, and in the inner heat of enthusiasm, to overlook the truth that lies in power'.[197] If the genius of Augustus

(63 BCE–9 CE) and Tiberius (42 BCE–37 CE) had been to preserve the external forms, the *simulacra* of the Republic under the Principate, 'for the opposite purpose, in Germany all signs of the German state association have been conscientiously preserved for centuries, when the thing itself, the state, has disappeared and it has not dissolved into open anarchy but into many separate states'.[198]

Hegel went on to speak of the coronation of the emperor – the titles, signs and insignia of the supreme head of the imperial body politic during investiture. Beyond wearing the crown and bearing the sceptre and orb of Charlemagne (747–814), the very same coat, jewels and even the same shoes were worn. This was emblematic of how original signs and appearances, the *simulacra*, were upheld under very different political conditions, in a period in which limited monarchy had all but disappeared. Hegel drew attention to the fact that the relation to the Margrave of Brandenburg remained the same as it had always been during the ritual symbolism of the coronation. The Brandenburg envoy presented the emperor with oats, despite the fact that instead of some 2000 regulars, its standing army now maintained some 200,000.[199]

The moral of the story was that the interpretations of the *Hippolythus*, certainly by the time of the Seven Years' War and even more emphatically with the Peace of Basel and the First Coalition War, were correct: the emperor had the mere appearance of sovereignty (*simulacra maiestatis*); the imperial estates – albeit in many cases now individually and *not* collectively – wielded real sovereignty (*maiestas realis*).

1.4.3 Historical continuity

There is a rather uncanny continuity to be observed in this context: Hegel maintained the idea of the transfer of Empire (*translatio imperii*) from Ancient Rome to Germany which had been an object of scorn for the majority of publicists since the mid-seventeenth century. This connection, however, spoke not of imperial public law and the imperial public office but everywhere of private legislation. In this way, the form in which Ancient Rome had come to Germany was demonstrated by Hegel in the notion of aristocracy, whereby internal and external sovereignty had collapsed in on themselves, producing an anarchic reign of private law oligarchy. This dissolved the original German unitary state with its limited monarchy.

Hegel had adopted this position from his study of Edward Gibbon (1737–1794) who had isolated the secret poison that sapped the vitals of the Roman state in private life.[200] Hegel extended Gibbon's thesis to the German reception of Roman law and the German cultural esteem for everything legal. Germanic freedom in this context meant nothing more than the legalization – through the formalism of the ancient Roman law of the *Corpus iuris civilis* – of the private land acquisitions of an unbending *manorial aristocracy*. Since 1648, this aristocracy of increasingly independent rulers, the imperial estates, had solidified their rights over their territories, advancing private interests in public constitutional law.

To reiterate, for Hegel this is what Moser's compendiums of *Landeshoheit* had shown in such exhausting detail. Admittedly Moser would have seen things very differently. After all, it was only with great reluctance that he made the *Corpus iuris civilis* a source of private law for the imperial estates. By stark contrast, the German reception of

Roman law for Hegel demonstrated how German public law was equivalent to a form of private jurisprudence. The legal anarchy that Hegel identified directly with the Roman Republic and the Principate that followed in its wake was what allowed the imperial estates to legalize their claims against the emperor and thus carve up the constitution. Without the written legal culture of Roman law, which was above all private law,[201] the rational process of writing down, collecting and analysing all sources and varieties of law never would have been set in motion.[202]

1.4.4 The philosophy of world history and the *forma Reipublicae*

Initially following Voltaire (1694–1778) and others, Hegel spoke of the German constitution as an anarchy, a structure without rule: 'Voltaire has directly called its constitution an anarchy; this is the best name if Germany is regarded as a state; but now even this name is no longer valid, because Germany can not at all be regarded as a state.'[203] Hegel linked this interpretation of the Holy Roman Empire of the German Nation with the decadence of Ancient Rome. This viewed public law strictly as a form of private jurisprudence, directed against any consolidation of the Empire as a state.[204] Further, Hegel singled out aristocracy as the worst type of constitution in *System der Sittlichkeit*[205] – the same perspective taken up in the mature *Rechtsphilosophie*: 'The fact that moderation is the principle in aristocracy entails the incipient divergence of public power and private interest, which at the same time touch each other so directly that this constitution in itself is on the verge of becoming the harshest condition of tyranny or anarchy (as witness Roman history) and so destroying itself'.[206]

Aside from despotic states, for Hegel, which essentially lacked a constitution, no other country had a more miserable composition than the German Empire which had inherited the deplorable anarchy of Ancient Rome.[207] Even the degenerate *forma Reipublicae* of tyranny was to be prized higher, for even in that instance the relation to the state remained explicit. Crudeness or barbarism was identified with a condition that could only see 'the relationship of lawless rule of state power, blind power, and servile subjugation; the way out under communal fixed laws was unknown'.[208]

In his Heidelberg lectures on the philosophy of law (1817–18), after enumerating the Aristotelian doctrine of constitutional forms and their changes as the preliminary stages of a teleological philosophy of history,[209] Hegel decisively separated the concept of Empire from monarchy: 'Empire is distinguished from monarchy, so Germany was called the German Reich, here it can mean anarchy, for the obligations of the princes to obey depended on their power.'[210] Hence, the German Empire, like the ancient Roman body politic with its disavowal of public interest, the uncontrolled growth of the polyp of legal formalism, was like a corpse, dead but containing the life of worms:[211] 'the individuals reduced to private persons and thus all to equals and only an abstract capriciousness, driving itself into monstrous forms, held them together'.[212] The levelling of aristocracy confirmed everywhere the nature of pure private interest, the corrupt *forma Reipublicae* of oligarchy. The ancient Roman and the Roman German Empire were differentiated only by the nature of the individuals that composed them; in the latter these were none other than the imperial estates.

Hegel's attempt to uphold the *translatio imperii* in the fragments of the *Verfassungsschrift*, even if purely in the destructive sense of the anarchy of a legal formalism, reflected his exasperation with the imperial *forma Reipublicae*. It also followed in outline the contemporaneous perceptions of his former professor in Tübingen, Johann Christian von Majer, in *Allgemeine Theorie der Staatskonstitution* (1799): 'No state in the world is so badly off with its constitution, for which one thinks this, another that, and the third again something else, than the *German Reich*.'[213] Yet, whatever its demerits, the *Lehensverfassung* with its principle of representation, a monarch assembled with estates – a kingship bound by laws – formed an epoch in world history: 'The context of the formation of the world has led the human race, after oriental despotism and the rule of a republic over the world, from the degeneration of the latter to this centre between the two, and the Germans are the people from which this third universal form of the world spirit was born.'[214]

What we see here, admittedly in embryonic form, is Hegel's later world historical conception – a three- but not fourfold scheme.[215] Just like Polybius (200–118 BCE), Machiavelli and Jean-Jacques Rousseau (1712–78) before him,[216] Hegel grasped the alterations of the *forma Reipublicae* temporally as part of a teleological philosophy of history or – as understood in the terms of German public law and its imperial patriotic tradition – an eschatology.[217]

States, like individuals, were exposed to finitude in their mutual relations. For Hegel, this was the tragedy of ethical life. But it also produced in turn the higher dialectic of the world spirit, which he conceived as universal and free of all limitations. Here belonged too the speculations of absolute spirit – of art, religion and philosophy. It was only in this higher realm that the problem of judgement was ultimately resolved: 'Schiller's dictum that world history is a world judgement are the most profound thing that can be said.'[218] Later, Hegel spoke of a 'turning point' – what may well be a *crisis* or more emphatically a decision – whereby judgement had ultimately come to an end: 'the reconciliation as the objective truth and freedom appearing within self-consciousness and subjectivity'.[219]

This work had been carried to completion in the public law of the constitutional and representative monarchies of the modern Germanic Empire, the historic successors to the Holy Roman Empire which began with the Frankish kingdom of Charlemagne, the last of the four empires or kingdoms (prophesied in the book of Daniel: 2:31–5 or 7:2–7) into which Hegel had divided history. The *Lehensverfassung* was thus identified in the *Verfassungsschrift* with a distinct system of representation that became a distinctive feature of every modern European state.[220]

Moser rejected the eschatological scheme drawn from the book of Daniel and prominent in early modern imperial public law, a scheme central to Melanchthon's revised and expanded *Chronicon Carionis*.[221] He contended that the affirmation of the idea of fourth universal monarchy 'only happened in earlier times, and probably only by private scribes. But it has never been used as a chancellery title; much less in the present day'.[222] Perhaps, unlike Hegel, he was too closely tied to the *Reichspublizistik* that developed after the foundational critiques of the *Hippolythus*, Conring and the *Monzambano*. From this perspective, all continuity had been broken; it was simply impossible to retrieve the *translatio imperii*. On the other hand, he may have intuited, rightly, that the *forma Reipublicae* was lurking there somewhere in the background.

Since the Protestant Aristotelian tradition had begun in Germany, the *forma Reipublicae* had been mixed with the eschatology of the four kingdoms, Empires or monarchies.[223] Hegel even referred explicitly to the earlier doctrine in Heidelberg when elaborating his own four world historical realms (*Reiche* – here best understood as 'empires' given their historical and theoretical connection to the *translatio imperii*, the Holy Roman Empire and the four monarchies). What Hegel affirmed in this division was that the history of all other nations was tied to the history of those that were world historical: 'In the past, world history was treated according to the four monarchies, and this was based on relating the history of all other peoples to the world-historical peoples. In these four worldviews, it is through these stages that the spirit has come to know itself.'[224] When he consequently proceeded to elaborate the four world historical realms – the Oriental, Greek, Roman and Germanic – he tied each of them to a distinct Aristotelian constitution.[225] In the fragments of the *Verfassungsschrift*, this was related to the formation of the world. More explicitly, in the mature *Rechtsphilosophie*, to the 'question of the perfectibility and education of the human race'.[226]

It is true that Hegel discussed the frustrations of the earlier attempts of *politica* to categorize the constitution in the fragments of the *Verfassungsschrift* and also stated the impossibility of applying the models of antiquity directly to modern conditions.[227] Nonetheless, he remained steadfast in his commitment to a conceptual approach. On the other hand, Hegel fully recognized the reality disclosed by Moser's empiricism. This reflected both the actual conditions of the imperial constitution in *statu cadentis imperii* and the very character of its public *qua* private law. Divested of the concepts of Aristotelian *politica*, public law was no longer a science, but pure description.

It was necessary for Hegel to devise an alternative method of conceptualizing the Empire. Neither the *forma Reipublicae*, the Aristotelian typology of monarchy, aristocracy and *politeia*,[228] nor the corrupted forms of tyranny, oligarchy, despotism and democracy, by themselves, adequately served his turn. As we have just seen, Hegel found his alternative in a teleological philosophy of world history. It is thus hard to square this direct historicization of the Aristotelian typology with the claim that he pushed the question of the *forma Reipublicae* aside as one of purely academic interest.[229]

The seeds of Hegel's wider philosophy of world history are contained in the fragments of the *Verfassungsschrift*. Further, the temporal inclusion, yet decisive historical sublation, of the *forma Reipublicae* in modern European constitutional monarchy, its '*inner differentiation*' into different 'moments' – each of which was characterized by a distinct Aristotelian constitution – belies any interpretation that would attempt to divorce his ideas from *politica*.[230] In another way, the *forma Reipublicae* speaks to the history of early modern European parliamentarianism which saw state power divided between a monarch and estates: 'This system of representation is the system of all modern European states; it was not in Germania's forests, but it emerged from them; it is epoch making in world history.'[231]

Like Schiller, Hegel's modern Germanic Empire, as a world historical entity, was the result of a process of 'spiritualization', an internalization of the Holy Roman Empire of the German Nation, which had become a speculative object for the absolute spirit in art, religion and philosophy. This Germanic Empire which Hegel projected into world history as the final historical form that contained the diversity of *forma Reipublicae* as moments was explicitly contrasted with the actual fate of the political concept of the imperial state constitution: 'It is a higher law that the people from which a new universal impulse is given to the world will itself ultimately perish before all others.'[232] Or, as Schiller put it: 'While the political empire crumbles, the spiritual empire has formed ever more firmly and perfectly. ... This empire is flourishing in Germany; it is in full growth and amidst the Gothic ruins of an old barbarian constitution.'[233]

1.5 Epilogue

1.5.1 Eclecticism

While the *Verfassungsschrift* prioritized the Aristotelian conceptual perspective in contrast to Moser's methodology, we must not lose sight of the fact that his decidedly empirical approach to public law left a significant mark on Hegel's working methods. Even a superficial glance at Hegel's manuscript fragments reveals Moser's undeniable influence: it structures Hegel's approach to imperial public law and his assessment of the Empire's collapse, evident in his use of recent history, statistics and various compiled documents. How else would a competent interpreter explain all of the historical details Hegel was discussing, let alone all of the documents compiled, the excerpts and notes recorded from a variety of reports, decrees and commissions?[234]

Indeed, Hegel was intensively involved in compiling documentary sources of his own. This was equally part and parcel of arriving at a better understanding of public law and a more complete knowledge of the condition of the Empire and its constitution. He took this methodology from Moser and the modern historical school of public law that the Württemberg publicist essentially founded. Yet, as we saw, the empirical body politic of a head and members, as described by Moser, was found wanting. To compass his ends, Hegel had leveraged the terms of the *Hippolythus*, contrasting the mere appearances of rule or sovereignty (*simulacra imperii et maiestatis*) to the real rights of rule, Moser's empiricism to a science of Aristotelian concepts and more broadly to the conceptual notions introduced into German public law through Bodin. Machiavelli, the political Hippocrates, also made an appearance, as did the history of the reception of Roman law. We see why Hegel's perspective and way of working has thus been described as eclectic in the scholarship:

> Hegel's position on the famous controversial question of which form of government the Empire belongs to is complicated. On the one hand, Hegel brushes the problem aside as academic and in this respect seems to approach the point of view of the younger (historical) school of constitutional law (J. J. Moser), which was no longer concerned with the conceptual construction of the imperial constitution, but with collecting the documents of imperial law and the genetic recording of the prevailing state practice. On the other hand, however, he criticized the empiricism of this school, which purported to be science, for example when he rejected the term 'imperial head' for the Emperor as an insufficiently distinguishing term that

could be applied to all possible forms of state and called for 'certain concepts', rather than 'titles'.[235]

1.5.2 The unity of Moser's public law with the imperial constitution

For Hegel, Moser's work was a construction intertwined with the imperial constitution itself and the diversity of its laws. Moser's extensive efforts to describe territorial supremacy, however, ultimately contradicted the very idea of sovereignty and the state. This contradiction, Hegel argued, mirrored the grim reality of the Empire, especially amidst the wars with revolutionary France. Whereas *Landeshoheit* was one of Moser's accepted concepts in *Neues teutsches Staats-Recht*, *maiestas*, much like the *forma Reipublicae*, remained a watery abstraction. Given that their territorial rights were obscured in the mists of antiquity, the imperial estates were free to assert them against the emperor without fear of contradiction. For Hegel, the consequences of Moser's approach were thus clear: 'the edifice of the German state signifies nothing other than the sum total of rights that are withdrawn from the state, rights that are protected with the greatest conscientiousness. And this justice is the principle, the soul of the constitution.'[236]

Moser's *Neues teutsches Staats-Recht* had effectively codified this reality. Its positive collection of imperial foundational laws, capitulations, statutes, territorial claims and privileges constituted the sole true sources of public law and were synonymous with the discipline itself.

Dissatisfied with a methodology that essentially denied the public authority of the state in a period wracked by war, Hegel found common ground with the older teachers of state law who had explicitly drawn on an Aristotelian tradition of *politica*. But their approach was unequal to the needs and nature of the present and could no longer be revived. History, as with much else, had sealed its fate: 'There is no longer any dispute about which concept the German constitution falls under, what can no longer be grasped is no longer.'[237]

Yet at the same time, history too might provide a solution – but only if the subject of history was recast, as Hegel cast it, as the advance of states towards constitutional monarchy, which united the disparate parts, or members of the political body, under a true sovereign. This was the education of the human race.[238] At the same time, it made it possible to bring the state under the control of 'certain concepts' and to explain how and why the external manifestations of political order, which were extremely variable in character, did not yet conform to a proper understanding of the truth. It raised the hope, third, that reality and idea could and would one day be reconciled – a conclusion which offered a measure of consolation to those who lamented the miserable condition to which the German Empire had actually been reduced and the interminable decline it seemed to portend. How large a measure of consolation it amounted to is a different matter and one that Hegel would grapple with throughout his philosophical development, particularly as he sought to reconcile the ideal realm of absolute spirit with the often harsh realities of the forever-finite state.

2

The Empire as the impersonal legal connection of the composite state: Johann Stephan Pütter

2.0 Prologue

2.0.1 An epoch of imperial public law

Johann Stephan Pütter stands as a metonym for a distinct period in imperial public law, his name indelibly connected to the faculty of law at the University of Göttingen which has been considered 'as the most successful, most typical, most modern, to a certain extent *the* epoch-making university'.[1] Pütter was as famous as his faculty. His lectures were attended sometimes by more than two-hundred listeners, coming from all over Europe, surpassing a quarter of the student population.[2] His public law doctrine was almost universally accepted in the Empire, his natural law textbook *Elementa iuris naturae* (1750) (Elements of Natural Law) co-authored with Gottfried Achenwall formed the basis for the teaching in the discipline of natural law down into the critical era of philosophy of Immanuel Kant, his followers and beyond.[3] Without *Elementa iuris naturae*, it is difficult to imagine how Kant's metaphysical doctrine of law could have come into being. The Königsberg philosopher lectured twelve times on it.[4]

2.0.2 Hegel and Pütter

During his Jena period (1801–7), Hegel lectured on *ius naturae civitatis et gentium ex dictatis* (1802) (the law of nature of the state and nations from dictated exercises), *ius naturae ex dictatis* (1803) (the law of nature from dictated exercises), *ius naturae* (1803–4) (the law of nature) and, on this last theme, for the final time in 1805.[5] One wonders if *Elementa iuris naturae* might not have been studied or used as a basis for the lessons in this context. Even if the speculative dimension of natural law was given pride of place, notably following Fichte and Friedrich Wilhelm Joseph Schelling (1775–1854) alongside the approach to law as custom or spirit after Montesquieu (1689–1755) and the ancient Aristotelian approach, the rational natural law of *Elementa iuris naturae* could certainly have been a source of inspiration. It would have been known and recognized as the principal textbook on these subjects.

The obvious place to begin any account of the relation between Pütter and Hegel is, however, with the evidence. The nature of Hegel's connection to some other public lawyers is a matter of conjecture; but here there is an abundance of material in the fragments of the *Verfassungsschrift* that establishes a connection and supplies us with the means for interpretation. The evidence does not stop there. The extent of Hegel's knowledge of Pütter goes beyond the summarizing efforts of many of the fragments, which are in some cases little more than annotations from any one of the three volumes of *Historische Entwickelung der heutigen Staatsverfassung des Teutschen Reichs* (1786/7, 1798/9) (Historical Development of the Present Political Constitution of the Germanic Empire), which he read and interpreted in an altered historical context, updating as he went along.[6] This has been argued by Kurt Rainer Meist.[7] Meist has also pointed to the fact that Hegel may have encountered Pütter's work during the time he spent at the University of Tübingen (1788–93). Hegel, one might add, had defended a doctorate in constitutional law and ecclesiastical law.[8] This suggests that he probably had much more than a superficial knowledge of the Göttingen public lawyer, having even made an intensive study of his public law. As Meist observed, 'during his student days at the Tübinger Stift Hegel was able to regularly attend lectures within the law faculty by one of the professors active at the time, which were based exclusively on the publications of perhaps the most respected constitutional lawyer of the time'.[9]

Franz Rosenzweig argued long ago that Hegel adopted the differentiation between constitutional law and government law from Pütter, or from the lectures he had heard in Tübingen that explicated this reigning public lawyer's doctrine.[10] Meist's claims reinforce this in a way that explains everything in general and nothing in particular: he declines to identify precisely which professor or professors impressed themselves upon Hegel.[11] For Rosenzweig, there was an obvious candidate Johann Christian von Majer.[12] Yet if one surveys the course catalogue during Hegel's Tübingen period, there is clearly more than one plausible candidate.[13] Lectures seem to have also been delivered on other materials than *Historische Entwickelung.* Rather, the methods of Pütter's *Elementa iuris publici Germanici* (1754) (Elements of German Public Law), *Entwurf einer juristischen Encyclopädie* (1757) (Outline of a Legal Encyclopaedia) and *Neuer Versuch einer juristischen Encyclopädie und Methodologie* (1767) (New Attempt at a Legal Encyclopaedia and Methodology) were taught. This does not alter the fact that the first book was Pütter's most successful. In any case, the course catalogue suggests that Pütter's methodological approach was widely applied: 'Almost all German universities teach constitutional law in the same way.'[14]

2.0.3 Doctrine and impact

Pütter's intellectual reach extended deep into the nineteenth century, to the most brilliant minds in politics and diplomacy of the later generation. Through his students Gustav Hugo (1764–1844) and Karl Friedrich Eichhorn (1781–1854), he had a direct influence on the formation of later nineteenth-century legal scholarship.[15] It was through Pütter's work that the later systematization of law, the overcoming of Roman legal order and the discipline of constitutional historiography first became possible.[16] With its focus on the historical development of the imperial constitution, Pütter's principal work *Historische Entwickelung* paved the way for the Germanic branch of the Historical School of Law.

At the University of Göttingen, Pütter's lectures covered a wide range of subjects from imperial history, constitutional law and imperial process to princely law, private law and natural law to name but a few. He followed Moser in part, accepting the positive foundations of imperial public law. Still, the influences of rational law methodology cannot be overlooked. His connection to natural jurisprudence and, by consequence, the speculations of universal public law was far more than simply a product of the *Zeitgeist*.[17] The notion that he was just another legal positivist would be contradicted by even a cursory analysis of his works. Particularly representative in this respect are the chapters he contributed to *Elementa iuris naturae*.

On the other hand, as Pütter himself admitted, in reference to Christian Wolff (1679–1754) and the philosophical method that many had tried to introduce into legal scholarship, himself included: 'it would be ungrateful to Wolff's true merits if one were to fail to recognize the influence that his teachings and writings have had, even indirectly and often unnoticed, on the teaching of the majority and most deserving modern legal scholars'.[18] In this way, Pütter decisively balanced the positive legal sources of Moser's imperial public law with a rationalist methodology which set about organizing them into a structured framework that followed the principles of natural jurisprudence.

Natural law introduced another dimension into debates about the diversity of the forms of government. For example, the state of absolute monarchy ought to be a constitutional state.[19] This led to the notion of reform absolutism that had a profound effect on Hegel's legal and political thought which brought it into consonance with the Prussian reform in Berlin.[20] Whereas natural jurisprudence was an interpretive means, its use of reason was a compass to find one's way through a dense forest of laws which could not be navigated otherwise, to set limitations on rulers. Hence, natural law for Pütter was a form of positive law.[21] With the establishment of the state on the basis of natural legal principles, however, an essential contradiction arose. The contract of submission that stood at its genesis introduced a structural inequality: families subjected their will to the will of a ruler which then became *the* guiding principle.[22] Just as the tradition had done, it was necessary to distinguish political rule from *despotism*: 'The contract of submission demands "absolute" political (and therefore ruler) power, but sovereignty has its counterweight in fundamental legal principles.'[23] Had Hegel said anything different when he stated that the monarch exercised supreme power in the state but that this was counterbalanced through the universal power of the laws?[24] For Pütter, absolutism was also limited in practice by a universal teleological objective, the common good or welfare.[25]

Once absolutism as an historical concept arose in the 1830s, replacing the notions of autocracy and despotism, it obscured the fact that a type of absolute power had once existed that followed the dictates of rational and legal reform. Hegel's protégé Gans was instrumental in this respect. The Hegelian doctrine of the philosophy of law only really gained popularity through him along with the concept of absolutism which took the place of the previous despotism.[26] This has arguably obscured the rather close proximity of Hegel's understanding of monarchy as decidedly constitutional and Pütter's restricted typology. Dividing monarchy into a dualistic typology deduced from the state of nature, Pütter endeavoured to make this fundamental distinction as transparent as possible: 'Rule either exists over all actions of subjects or it does not. The former is called *despotic*, the latter *restricted*. Therefore, the unequal society is either *despotic* or *restricted*.'[27] Despotic states were everywhere uniform; the restricted, by contrast, knew countless forms. This typology stood at the centre of Kant's political thought which divided states into republican and despotic forms.[28] It also returned in Hegel with his critique of Virtue and Terror as well as ministerial centralization in revolutionary France and the similarly enlightened rational principles that predominated politics in Prussia at the time. Following Pütter, he termed this political phenomenon of monocratic centralization aristocratic despotism. In the Empire, this saw the imperial estates attempting to destroy the territorial estates and the system of representation.[29] Both France and Prussia followed the dictates of the power state that the young Hegel denounced as a form of centralized mechanism.

The first point to take away from this discussion is that through natural law and the *ius publicum universale* Pütter had introduced independent legal sources to supplement the deficiencies of purely positive law where a rule to orient its activity had been lacking.[30] This allowed him to set about organizing Moser's unstructured mass of sources, which could now be systematized. But perhaps most importantly, existing constitutional law could be aligned with a rational form of state organization that furthered the essential interests of reform. In this way, the principles of rational jurisprudence were made actual in concrete administrative and constitutional law. Pütter provided the intellectual tools to transform absolutism into a constitutional state. A roster of the names of those who attended his lectures included the most prominent politicians and reformers of the subsequent generation: Karl Theodor von Dalberg, Karl August von Hardenberg (1750–1822), Friedrich Karl Baron vom und zum Stein (1757–1831) and Karl Sigmund Franz Freiherr vom Stein zum Altenstein (1770–1840). Excepting Baron vom Stein, each of these figures had a distinctive role to play in Hegel's biography.[31]

Pütter's work had thoroughly integrated philosophical reason into the law faculty. In Berlin Hegel had taken over the torch from Pütter, similarly aiming at rational reform and constitutional monarchy. There was thus much common cause between the reformers who had been shaped by Pütter and Hegel's absolute idealism, far more so than the Historical School of Law. With Hegel, we see the philosophical theorization of law coming directly from the other faculty in the struggle against romanticism and reaction. The concord of philosophy with the reforming state was the reason why Hegel had been brought to the University of Berlin under Altenstein, the Prussian minister of education, in the first place. Gans's legal thought carried this further, deploying Hegelian philosophy methodologically against the Historical School. For Gans, Hegel's philosophy was identified with German classicism which, like Roman law, challenged the romanticism and mysticism of the Historical School that were the true threats to law's autonomy.[32] This reveals a contest of the faculties and how philosophy since Wolff had sought to assume the leading position in training the civil service and enlightened state bureaucracy. With Pütter's student Gustav Hugo natural law was collapsed entirely into positive law. Consequently, the *philosophy* of law became unrecognizable in the way Hegel and Gans still understood it. Altenstein, Hegel, Gans and the Hegelian School lost the battle.[33]

2.0.4 Outline

This chapter is divided into three principal sections.

In Section 2.1, I analyse Pütter's place in the debates over the imperial *forma Reipublicae* and his relation to the literature of German imperial public law, to the reigning conceptions of the *Monzambano* and the systems-theoretical perspective. To grasp Pütter's conception of the composite state, I examine its distinction from other forms of association he discussed and the idea of the real connection between the composite body politic of the head and members. The latter touches on his monistic, objective and impersonal conception.

In Section 2.2, I pursue these ideas in more depth considering Pütter's categorization of the imperial state, sovereignty, territorial supremacy and the restrictive typology which was emblematically expressed through the electoral capitulations and in the existence of the diets at both imperial and territorial levels. Pütter construed the Imperial Diet as akin to a modern parliament. The electoral capitulations were typical of a contractually based idea of the state that fell under the censures of Hegel's critique of the imperial constitution and natural law. These perspectives are contrasted to Hegel's alternative conception. Through assessing the philosopher's critique of the Empire, another source of his rejection of the contractually based organization of the state comes into view. This section concludes with a disquisition on imperial public law and government law and the true citizens of the Empire, the imperial estates.

The final part of this chapter (Section 2.3) covers Hegel's reliance on Pütter's concept of aristocratic despotism and how the imperial estates set out to undermine the territorial estates. I demonstrate how this shapes Hegel's interpretation of Roman law, slavery and despotism, the relationship of this jurisprudence to the imperial constitution and to Hegel's interpretation of the decadence of imperial Rome that had coincided for the young philosopher with an equalization between the estates. I analyse how Hegel's interpretation of Roman law and the imperial constitution had deep roots in the history of German public law and the famed formalization of the imperial estates as *cives imperii*.

This idea stemmed from Hermann Conring,[34] but it was popularized most notably by the Hanoverian Vice Chancellor Ludolph Hugo, the most adept of Conring's students and a contemporary of Pufendorf and Leibniz who had most adequately theorized the idea of a quasi-federal state. I then demonstrate how once the imperial estates were treated as private persons under the dictates of Roman private law and its concept of property (*dominium*), the door was opened to aristocratic despotism. As I argue, this fundamentally shaped Hegel's analysis of Roman law and the imperial constitution. This can provide us with a much more comprehensive historical-contextual basis to assess his relation to Roman law and the territorial state which grows out of an interpretation of Pütter's ideas and German public law more generally as we have already seen with Moser and as we will see with Majer in much greater detail in the third chapter.

2.1 *Diversae reipublicae formae* and the Empire as a composite state

2.1.1 From the simple to the complex

In *Beyträge zum teutschen Staats- und Fürsten-Rechte* (1777–9) (Contributions to German Constitutional and Princely Law), at first glance it seems that Pütter initially adopted a perspective on the Empire that had been popularized by Pufendorf's *Monzambano*, only to be carried further by Thomasius.[35] This perspective, reflecting Pufendorf's evolving views, increasingly tended towards the system of states (*systematibus civitatum*) or the systematic alliance or federation (*foedus systematicum*) – a robust theoretical legitimation of irregular state systems. This offered a systems-theoretical perspective on the state constitution which went decisively against the Aristotelian approach.[36]

There was a significant shift in perception between the first edition of the *Monzambano* (1667) and the revised edition that appeared one year after his death (1706). The Latin edition in Hegel's library was a reprint of the first edition published by Thomasius with commentary (1703).[37] Even if the idea of the Empire as 'irregulare aliquod corpus et monstro simile' (some irregular body similar to a monster) was excised from the second edition, Pufendorf's original intentions are made clearer if we look at 'De republica irregulari' (1669). There we find an endorsement of the concept and a demand for 'a precise analysis of such constitutions – just like that of the monstrous animals and plants in natural philosophy'.[38]

Like Pufendorf and Thomasius, Pütter had recognized the fallacy of trying to match the imperial *forma Reipublicae* to any one of the simple Aristotelian forms. From 'Sollte das politische Resultat' onwards, Hegel's approach to the imperial constitution was similarly sceptical.[39] Indeed, there was a great degree of unanimity in the public law tradition after the *Monzambano* – a common cause that could even be discovered in Moser, although the Württemberg publicist had no interest in categorizing the constitution more generally. It is important to highlight, however, that Pütter had emphasized the inadequacy only of the *simple* Aristotelian forms. In other words, he was not necessarily dismissive of a more complex arrangement. This is what he elaborated in *Beyträge zum teutschen Staats- und Fürsten-Rechte* and elsewhere. When setting out to categorize the imperial constitution, he summarized the principal failing of previous efforts:

> In all the writings which I have yet come across on this subject, the fundamental error has been committed, if I am not mistaken, of adopting an incomplete standard, by adhering merely to the Aristotelian division of states into monarchies, aristocracies, and democracies; – a division which is quite correct as far as it extends, and as far as one knows how to divide restricted or unrestricted, hereditary or elective monarchies and aristocracies properly from one another.[40]

What this quote makes immediately clear is the rather equivocal nature of Pütter's dismissal. On the one hand, the *simple* taxonomy must be rejected; on the other, if nuanced in the various ways mentioned, a more adequate standard could be attained and the classification could prove more correct. To this we can even add Pütter's affirmation of the Polybian or mixed form in *Elementa iuris naturae*.[41] This mixed form had been thoroughly denounced by Bodin, for whom the logic of sovereignty ought to remain indivisible or monistic, but it was revived by the German theoreticians in their attempt to categorize the imperial constitution.[42] The *Monzambano* dismissed the *status mixtus* in favour of monstrosity – the use of mixture itself little more than a placeholder for irregularity.[43] Sovereignty, this time more explicitly following Thomas Hobbes (1588–1679), must be indivisible.[44] Still, Pufendorf's system of states involved something more: 'Mixture is loose, implying neither fixed proportions nor the bonding of elements; composition, however, involves fixed proportions in specific arrangements, and results in a new compound property.'[45]

Pütter adopted a similar line of reasoning. Yet he did so in his differentiation between composite states and 'states united without a new common authority [which], however much they may pursue a common purpose, do not form a new state, but only a *confederation of united states*, or *associated states*.'[46] This was the case with the Netherlands and Switzerland which 'were merely a set of several connected independent states'.[47] Obviously, Pütter's approach was above all eclectic, referring to the systems-theoretical perspective and composite bodies politic alongside a more nuanced understanding of the Aristotelian *forma Reipublicae* and the Polybian *status mixtus*. Thus, to state that he was entirely dismissive or that he abandoned all Aristotelian divisions is to contort his meaning.[48] On the contrary, he aimed at a more complex and so a more complete classification.

2.1.2 Hegel's eclecticism

Hegel too was partial to eclecticism. Whereas at first glance it seems that he polemically dismissed the failure to reach a consensus on the imperial constitution, we find on closer inspection that he also pursued an explicit Aristotelian doctrine of politics in this period.[49] Moreover, the conundrum Hegel isolated in 'Sollte das politische Resultat' was very similar to Pütter's. However, Hegel pointed in particular to the character of the legal claims that the imperial estates were able to make on the Empire which undermined any crude taxonomic approach and which made it impossible, in practical terms, to fit the imperial constitution to any one of the simple Aristotelian *forma Reipublicae*: 'the lectern statisticians who had the official duty to classify the constitutions of the state, and to assign them to the classes of monarchy, aristocracy and so on specified by Aristotle, never knew how to do justice to German rights'.[50]

The issue of classification returns in the *Reinschrift* with its characteristic emphasis on the more theoretically inclined conceptual and scientific approach of Aristotelianism against the moderns who 'believe they can give the German state nothing more than the name of an *Empire* or a *body politic*'.[51] Hegel referred to the body politic at numerous places in the *Verfassungsschrift* and *System der Sittlichkeit*. He did so in a fashion strikingly similar to Pufendorf's endorsement of monstrosity and irregularity – but also critically alongside an emphatic affirmation of the *status mixtus*:

> Like the empire of nature in its productions, the German Empire is in its law unfathomable in the great, and inexhaustible in the small, and it is this side

> which fills the initiates into the infinite details of rights with that wonder at the venerability of the German body politic, and with that admiration for the system of the most elaborated justice. This justice of preserving every part in its separation from the state and the necessary claims of the state upon the individual members of it are in the most perfect contradiction.[52]

In this context, it becomes clear how the issue of private law – the codification of originary rights, titles and claims – made it impossible to apply the simple Aristotelian taxonomy, let alone refer to public authority and the state in the modern sense. All else failing, Empire and body politic were thus placeholders, a way of solving the irresolvable. Hegel weighed the body politic composed of members alongside the *status mixtus*, which was a real organizational form: 'The state requires a general centre (a monarch and the estates) in which the various authorities, relations to foreign powers, military power, finances relating to it, etc. are united.'[53] This makes clear that the idea of pure monarchy was not his ideal, but rather the royal principle maintained alongside representative government and the estates: 'The advantage of the mixed constitution over the simple one is based solely on the good organization of the basic constitution of the state, through which the predominant parts of the supreme power are placed in a just relationship and balance with each other.'[54] Such ideas followed the principles laid down by Montesquieu, in both his eulogy to the freedom of the Germanic tribes and in his opposition to despotism, centralization and absolutism.

2.1.3 The taxonomy of the *civitas composita*

Moser had leveraged the body politic composed of a head and members as an empirical *description*. Pütter, by contrast, deployed it far more actively as a *concept*. This was part of his systematic approach to the constitution, which he developed into a distinct type of state. In his hands, it was thus less the picture that emerged from the panoply of documents of imperial public law than something theoretically explicative of the intricacies of the Empire. It was taxonomic. The composite state (*civitas composita*) was an *impersonal* legal connection ruled by foundational laws.[55] Hence, it was a form of categorization and belonged to that issue that Pütter stressed everywhere was necessary (implicitly in contrast to Moser) – the determination of the *forma Reipublicae* or the imperial form of sovereignty (*forma imperii Germanici*) and its type of constitution.[56]

A composite body politic emerged when states with independent internal governments united for their external affairs, subordinating to a higher authority.[57] In this respect, the Empire was still a state (*una respublica*), but a complex one. Pütter admired legal intricacy, the variety of jurisdictions, the imperial estates as immediate subjects under the emperor which, as territories, presented their own separate systems of governance. Their respective subjects were only at a distance from or mediated through the imperial estates and their representative governments to the emperor and Empire. Hence, the *forma imperii Germanici* 'remains monarchical as a whole, whose individual members, however, are again composed of several members, so that the latter, as members of a member, or parts of a part, are only indirectly, whereas those who are only parts of the whole, and not of another part, are directly under the universal head.'[58]

With the emperor, as Pütter saw it, a *real* connection had been provided to unite the various states. The main difference between the Holy Roman Empire as a composite body politic and the Swiss and Dutch models of confederacy, for example, was that these were based on a mere personal union.[59] They lacked the overarching character of imperial sovereignty or majesty, which Pütter viewed *monistically*, forming a *Realverbindung*:[60] 'the real connection, on which the unity of every other state is based, also keeps all particular German states in the ties of a single Empire, … an Empire which consists of several particular states that are still subordinate to a common higher authority'.[61] This distinguished the Empire wholly from 'a mere system of united states (*systema foederatarum civitatum*)' or the association of states discussed above, which were more explicitly the object of Pufendorf's analysis.[62]

Part of Pütter's innovation was to recognize that the imperial body politic of head and members was a distinct, objective form of state. Moreover, through the functional division of government that was structured according to rights of sovereignty, the end of the traditional conception that had emphasized the property basis of power was at hand.[63] The exercise of government had become autonomous. Office, no longer viewed as a private heritable possession, thus reemphasized the differentiation between despotic and political rule. This applied to both the imperial estates *and* the emperor. In this way, the emperor was invested with an *administrative* office, while the imperial and territorial rights of government were no longer viewed as antagonistic personal possessions but as administrative tasks to be exercised in parallel.[64] Majer would carry this forward by separating private princely law from public law as such.

Pütter theoretically grounded the composite body politic in the objective legal connection between head and members. This was where a transformed conception of sovereignty, focused on the imperial state as a *civitas composita*, emerged. It stressed the political interrelation between the diverse parts and accepted the fact that various forms of government could be found in the Empire – electoral principalities, bishoprics, monarchies, aristocracies and democracies.[65] In every example, Pütter stressed how the part was of lesser standing in relation to the whole and to the imperial head that united all of the different members. The same held for territorial law which was subordinate to imperial public law. In sum, the Empire as a complex state of states or structure composed of different wholes was still united for all that into a larger composite arrangement: '*The GERMAN EMPIRE is a kingdom divided into several obviously different states, which nevertheless have been till now in the manner of a republic arranged systematically under a shared sovereign power – monarchical, kept within limits, more chosen* [*electicio*]'.[66] Here we have everything essential: a divided kingdom of systematically ordered states under a legally restricted and common sovereign monarchical elective power.

This conception even found its way directly into Rosenzweig's reflections.[67] Pütter's perspective was the predominant one in the last phase of imperial public law and his definition, so Rosenzweig reckoned, was all the more remarkable, 'as the general doctrine of the state was otherwise in no way compatible with the concept of *civitas composita*'.[68] On the contrary, Pufendorf's concept of the *systema civitatem* was more comprehensible in the world of strictly sovereign states under international law which was without a head.[69] The *civitas composita* that existed in a *unum imperium* (single empire) had even deeper roots and was explicitly at odds with the *Monzambano*.[70]

What Pütter had done was to make the body politic of head and members into a distinct form of state. Hence, above the simple Aristotelian division, 'we must conceive of a higher one, which, in the same way as there are simple or composite societies, there can also be simple or composite bodies politic'.[71] The *real* connection of the emperor that drew on a monistic conception of sovereignty distinguished this form of government as an actual political authority. As we shall see, what was central to Pütter's analysis, however, was not so much the monarchical *forma Reipublicae* but rather its limitation.

2.1.4 Critique

Pütter's idea of the imperial head and its capacity to bind the members into a common unity – the monistic *Realverbindung* of the *civitas composita* – came under increasing scrutiny. In the changed circumstances after the Peace of Basel – and certainly after Rastatt and Lunéville (9 February 1801) – it was no longer self-evident that the Empire had 'a centre [which] would also have the necessary power to assert itself and its decisions and to maintain the individual parts in their dependence on itself'.[72] Indeed, the *civitas composita* united under a common authority was fundamentally being called into question by unfolding historical events.

The Peace of Basel had ensured the neutrality of Northern Germany and historically resulted in the flowering of Weimar classicism and the Jena idealism of Schiller, Fichte, Schelling and Hegel,[73] but it was also a serious violation of the imperial constitution and the loyalty owed by Prussia to the emperor.[74]

Moreover, there was plenty of evidence for the disintegration of the *civitas composita* into a system of states with the rise of Austro-Prussian dualism in the late eighteenth century. In truth, this had already sounded its death knell. If Pütter could not see this clearly, blinkered by his imperial patriotism, it was obvious enough to the authors of the *Fürstenbundpublizistik* for whom the principles of armed neutrality and balance were essential to their interpretations of the imperial constitution. This fell in line with the idea that Hegel put forward, reflecting on the wars of Friedrich II (1712–1786) that 'the wars of this period can be called constitutional. … Even the Seven Years' War can be called constitutional.'[75] In other words, these were conflicts waged by German estates as quasi-sovereign entities within a system of states or association of states.[76] Hegel further isolated the wars of the revolutionary period in Germany. These were all wars that attempted to alter the status quo, to attain more legal privileges and political advantage for the members of a constitutional order in which a higher personal authority was no longer a given.

2.2 Defining elements of sovereignty: Electoral monarchy and the *status mixtus*

2.2.1 Decomposition: The *civitas composita* and *forma Reipublicae*

If Pütter set out to meticulously define how a composite state came into being, Hegel arguably pursued the opposite trajectory in the fragments of the *Verfassungsschrift*.

Whereas the Göttingen publicist focused on the Empire as a *real* and *impersonal* legal connection, which resulted in an objective understanding of the Empire as a state of states, the young philosopher, by contrast, concentrated on the process of *decomposition*. Yet, Hegel's proposals for *recomposition* – of how Germany could become a state or what was necessary to that end – will not be lost on any perceptive reader of the fragments. Indeed, what the First Coalition War and the subsequent Congress at Rastatt so aptly made visible was the breaking apart of any previously unified consensus. 'In the last war, four political systems appeared in Germany, one the Austrian, the other imperial, [the third] the neutral, the fourth the Prussian.'[77] In view of these entirely altered historical circumstances, it was clear that the same association, the esteemed *civitas composita*, was dissolving openly into a competing world of independent states or political systems. In this respect, Hegel's analysis with its emphasis on state sovereignty seems to conform rather neatly to what Pufendorf had developed under the concept of the *systema civitatem*. Even so, there is more than a single system in evidence here – thus contradicting any idea of a unified association of states.

To delineate the essence of a *civitas composita*, it was necessary to show how 'from several states united under a common rule, which have the same fundamental law, a state arises again'.[78] This resulted in the characteristic division Pütter identified between particular government law and constitutional law. Within the imperial order, constitutional law or public law trumped territorial government law. Identifying the genetic process by which a *civitas composita* came into being, the legal superiority of imperial public law over government law became obvious: 'Either the former rule of the individual states that have joined together then ceases, or it remains in the individual communities but is subordinate to the one supreme rule.'[79] What this implied was nothing less than an emergent legal theory of the Empire as a quasi-federal state. Pütter's theorization demonstrated the gulf that divided it from the four political systems Hegel identified in which the one supreme rule was absent – although the imperial order was indeed present, it was nevertheless a separate system. For Pütter, as he reiterated everywhere in his discussion on the *forma imperii Germanici*, the Empire 'as a whole is still monarchical'

> but restricted, not absolutely monarchical; and so no one will find any more offence or misgivings in revering the Emperor as a monarch, even if this means that the imperial power is anything but completely unrestricted, or that it can be exercised in any other way than with the reservation of the territorial supremacy of each imperial estate in its territory.[80]

If the Empire fell within the confines of a limited monarchy, once more this fundamentally contradicted the reigning propositions of the *Monzambano*: 'But they [are not so easily baffled, who allow the Emperor to be a Sovereign, but Limited King, and ascribe unto the States great Liberties, but tempered too by Laws], and so place Germany in the List of Limited Monarchies.'[81] For Pütter, as he detailed historically, the German Empire had always been monarchical. Yet it had come to be progressively limited by the imperial estates assembled in the *Reichstag*. Indeed, this conception applied throughout the Empire. So, for instance, the *Länder* 'have a type of monarchical government' restricted by their territorial estates in the *Landtag*.[82] The *iura reservata Imperatori* (imperial reserve rights) were prerogatives of sovereignty, proving the monarchical *forma Reipublicae*. These, along with the *regalia*, demonstrated how 'the person of the Emperor, irrespective of his hereditary lands, is entitled to sovereignty and what is attached to it both in community with other European crowned heads and as a special property of the imperial dignity'.[83] Given that the imperial estates took part in governance and were attributed with the *regalia* as well, Pütter had to account for complexity: 'In addition to the person of the Emperor, not only do the imperial estates have an important share in the government of the Empire as a whole; but each imperial estate also has territorial supremacy in its own particular state, on which the status of the imperial estate is duly based.'[84]

It was precisely in this context that Pütter went out of his way to analyse the differential character of associated states that either possessed or did not possess a common authority.[85] Whereas the German Empire could be compared to other states or empires like France or Spain insofar as it likewise had a universal public law that applied to the entirety of its territory – having nothing above this except for international law – it was also clearly in a class of its own, given the distinction between the universal and the particular legal dimensions. This is to say nothing of the fact that the imperial estates since 1648 were permitted to conclude treaties with foreign states and wage independent wars. Within the Empire, particular state laws could be distinguished that were binding within a larger legal hierarchy or system of imperial superordination in which the universal held sway: 'Every particular German constitutional law is subject to the common German constitutional law, just as every particular state is itself subordinate to the German Empire and must therefore still recognize positive laws or other regulations of a higher power, which does not take place in the case of independent states.'[86]

In *Beyträge zum teutschen Staats- und Fürsten-Rechte*, Pütter gave this classification an increasingly empirical foundation in his attempt to determine the imperial *forma Reipublicae*. Monarchies that were absolute in form, like those of France, Denmark and Spain, little resembled the Empire. By contrast, the monarchies of Sweden and Great Britain, which were bound respectively by their diet or parliament, were strikingly similar – even if hereditary and non-electoral.[87] Hence, he attempted to view the Imperial Diet along the lines of a modern parliament – however implausibly.[88] The Empire was not a pure monarchy as the power of the emperor was restricted and circumscribed by the authority of the imperial estates (*potestas Imperatoris auctoritate statuum imperii circumscripta*). Thus, the Imperial Diet put limits on the extent of state sovereignty. At another level, this was no less true in the territories where a structural analogy was drawn. The territorial princes were monocratic (yet for the most part hereditary, excepting the ecclesiastical estates of Mainz, Cologne and Trier) and likewise constrained by the authority of the territorial assembly of estates (*auctoritate ordinum provincialium*), the provincial diets or *Landtag*.[89]

2.2.2 Centrifugal political evolution and the Imperial Diet

What for Pütter was a positive process resulting in the composite state, for Hegel proved by and large negative in a transformed political context. Nevertheless, freedom for Hegel subsisted only in a form that took on the character of subordinate systems existing within the larger state organism.[90] This gives an inkling of the degree to which the Empire as a *civitas composita* impacted Hegel's early absolute idealism in *System der Sittlichkeit*.[91] This is studied in greater depth in the final chapter of this book. For now, it must be emphasized that, to Hegel's mind, what remained insurmountable was the fact that Germany had suffered a prolonged centrifugal political evolution in which the diverse parts had torn themselves away from an original whole:

> The principle of the original German state, which has been spread from Germany to all Europe, was the principle of monarchy, a state authority under a head for the administration of general affairs and with the participation of the people, through its deputies, the form of which has remained in what is called the *Reichstag*, but the thing has disappeared.[92]

Clearly, Hegel held fewer illusions than Pütter about drawing any direct equation between the Imperial Diet and a modern parliament. Yet he too consistently upheld the imperial legal order – or at least for as long as conceivably possible. In this, he too belonged to a publicist reform current and Europe-wide debate that looked to a universal order still based on the Holy Roman Empire, which irrefutably ensured the balance of European powers.[93] Arguably, this brought his thought into contact with the *Fürstenbundpublizistik* and the Dalberg circle.[94] It should come as little surprise then that Hegel was even considering the relationship between the emperor and Germany on the whole in an imperial patriotic way into the early Jena period. Eulogizing the emperor in the interests of the freedom of the Third Germany of the smaller imperial estates,[95] he even claimed that 'the great interest of the people has returned to its source; as a need which, however, has not yet found its satisfaction through a state organization appropriate to it'.[96] As far as Pütter's valorization of the *Reichstag* was concerned, Hegel's view, however, was damning. This was most pointedly expressed in a later gloss in his *Jenaer Notizenbuch* (1803–6) (Jena Notebook). There he reflected on the words of Hugo Grotius (1583–1645) reproduced by Heinrich Luden (1778–1847) in his biography of the Dutch natural lawyer:

> At that time rumours were spread that the king (Gustav Adolph after the Battle of Lützen) was still alive; he had faked his death for good reasons. 'Sharp-witted people mock us', Grotius says, 'as if we were dullards who believe a dead man to be dead. This is the shrewdness of the Germans.' Similarly, when a philosopher judges a state or the like, that it is dead – then it is said, 'But it still lives, the *Reichstag* etc.' This is the shrewdness of the Germans![97]

Hegel's later observations here thoroughly detailed how Pütter's earlier claims for the Imperial Diet in no way lived up to reality. However much imperial patriotism was justified towards the emperor and Empire during the wars, a suitable political structure was still absent. Yet, it can be argued that *System der Sittlichkeit* had the objective of constructing this appropriate state organization or, similarly, a revised corporate doctrine for a territorial state like Hegel's native Württemberg. Moreover, it detailed in a very precise fashion the division between state constitution, constitution in the modern sense and government – thus, aspects germane to late imperial public law. Hence, even its incredibly speculative character cannot detract from the fact that it could also be interpreted from a publicist reform angle. All of this lends credence to Rosenzweig's intuition that 'Hegel's engagement with the German constitution might perhaps have influenced the system.'[98] It is not by chance that the final writing up of the *Reinschrift* coincided with *System der Sittlichkeit*.[99]

With its similar discussion of the 'estate of the free' – the only citizens capable of governing – that stands in opposition to the 'system of needs and labour' (the 'estate of the unfree') and the 'system of justice, of property and ownership' (the 'formal universal estate'), Hegel's contemporaneous *Naturrechtsaufsatz* pursued the same purpose.[100] This strikingly reflected a political situation in which the imperial estates were considered the only true citizens of the Empire. The 'estate of the unfree' comprises those engaged in the 'system of needs and labour', whose efforts are directed towards individual gain and private property. As Hegel further elaborated, this category includes both the 'second estate' (the bourgeoisie or class of understanding, engaged in differentiated economic activity) and the 'third estate' (the peasantry or elemental class, whose direct labour with the earth fulfils basic needs without complex intermediaries). While the labour of these unfree estates does not inherently involve the 'danger of death', the elemental nature of the third estate means it provides the fundamental mass for the first estate, which embodies absolute ethical life through its willingness to face death.[101] Whereas with the *cives imperii* 'the duties of the state have become private rights', nonetheless, as Hegel glossed, 'in this separation from the state lies the possibility of forming a state'.[102] Thus, the 'estate of the free', whose capacity to govern stemmed from their independence from the 'system of needs' and their indifference to the property and wealth of the 'formal universal estate', also held the potential for the most direct political relation to the state.[103]

The imperial estates could become the 'individuals of absolute ethical life' – an 'estate of the free' that served as a conduit to the state. The imperial estates were obviously more than simply individuals; they were, instead, complex corporate bodies: territorial states composed of provincial estates. These estates were then active in the *Landtag* and represented their constituent 'single individuals' (the subjects of the territories): Pütter's indirect 'members of a member or parts of a part'.[104] According to Hegel's analysis, there were thus two distinct levels of mediation from the subjects upwards in this hierarchy. Firstly, the provincial estates mediated the 'single individuals' into their own corporate structures: from the practical (elemental) to the legal (bourgeois) and the ethical (nobility).[105] Secondly, the 'estate of the free' at the higher level of the Empire were its true citizens: the imperial estates. Whether considered territorially or imperially, the nobility acted as a crucial layer, mediating the relationship to absolute ethical life. But how could the potential despotism of the imperial estates be averted; and how could the tendency towards oligarchy be contained? Hegel drew directly on

Plato (427–348 BCE) who had emphasized the royal art – that of monarchy that held the nobility in check – and had denigrated property, 'the entire endless expansion of legislation':[106] 'The royal art ... conquers and casts out that which, through its evil, violent nature, pushes towards godlessness, arrogance, and injustice, by means of death, exile, and ultimate disgrace.'[107]

In each case, the 'individuals of absolute ethical life' – whose ultimate composition and function Hegel set out to describe – were immediate. They stood in a direct relation to the ethical totality of the state and served to raise the 'single individuals' to this higher corporate plane. The 'single individuals', the subjects of the unfree estates, then became the 'organs' of the 'individuals of absolute ethical life' through their elemental and formal labour, materially constituting parts of an ethical whole 'which, viewed from the side of its indifference, is the absolute living spirit, from the side of its objectivity the living movement and the divine self-enjoyment of this whole in the totality of the individuals as its organs and members'.[108] This stressed another point in Hegel's consideration of the possibility of the Empire existing as a state – as a structured or differentiated whole. In contrast to the simple *forma Reipublicae*, as Pütter had recognized, the imperial constitution was precisely this complex of immediate and mediate subjects. Hegel concurred: 'That a state counts among its subjects serfs, citizens, free nobles, and princes who themselves have subjects.'[109]

2.2.3 Contract law, the capitulations and the imperial state

Yet for a state to be considered a concept at all, sovereign rule was required. Pütter recognized this fully. The absolute superiority of the ruler 'is therefore not bound by any positive law, is not subject to any courts or penalties and lives in natural freedom'.[110] Hegel followed a similar logic: this centre 'is certain due to the reverence of the peoples and sanctified in its immutability in the person of the monarch determined by a natural law [*Naturgesetz*] and by birth'.[111] If sovereignty, according to Hegel, was the final will of the state, it was also true that the will was something personal and, as such, had therefore to be exercised through a natural person. This explains why Hegel's monarchical principle was inherently hereditary. From a functional perspective, it was necessary to ensure that sovereignty should be passed on from one king to his successor without interruption so that the form of state was preserved unchanged. This spoke merely to the state's organization; the essential matter was the existence of public authority, with all else being pure *adiaphora*.[112] By contrast, Pütter's understanding of imperial sovereignty cannot conceal the reality that the requisite fundamental law – the capitulation that established the state and the rights and duties of the emperor upon election – was *not* positive.[113] Hegel was markedly at odds with the contractual character of this political order, which in principle if not always in practice passed the sovereignty of the state into the hands of the people with disconcerting frequency: 'The first of the principal sources of public law were the fundamental laws of the Empire. They were first and foremost contracts, which the emperor recognized in the electoral capitulations.'[114]

In the more complex *forma Reipublicae* of electoral monarchy, the monarch was an *organ* elected to an official role by the *members*: 'If the elected person rejects, another must be elected. If he accepts, he is ruler without further ado, but bound to the capitulation as fundamental law.'[115] Prior to election, furthermore, the person of the ruler had no rights.[116] Thus, the electoral capitulation perfectly demonstrated the contractual foundation of the imperial state, a structure that had been particularly pronounced since the peace negotiations in Münster and Osnabrück in which contract law had emerged as an essential methodological doctrine:[117] 'At the imperial level, written contracts existed between the emperor and the imperial estates in the form of electoral capitulations. They belonged to the circle of fundamental imperial laws and laid down anew the rights and duties negotiated for each Emperor.'[118]

In Hegel's political thought, we do not have to look far to find the rejection of this contractually based idea of the state. It was perhaps most famously discussed in the mature *Rechtsphilosophie*.[119] In every case, the central issue for Hegel was the transference of a private law doctrine (contract law) to the higher ethical spheres of family and state.[120] Nonetheless, as he still put it in the fragments of the *Verfassungsschrift*, 'whether the possessor of power be one or several, whether this one or the several, be born or elected to this majesty, is indifferent to the only thing necessary, namely that a multitude constitute a state'.[121] The problem with a public authority structured on the basis of a capitulation was that the capitulation itself, a contract, effectively carried the true marks of sovereignty by positioning itself above positive law. Hence, Hegel's comprehensive grasp of the imperial political tradition was another core experience which made it impossible for him to accept the full scope of natural jurisprudence. In other words, he could view this through the nullity of the imperial order in his own time, which had been so thoroughly hollowed out by contract law and the capitulations:[122]

> That is to say, the nature of the relation in an elective realm in which the *particular* will is made the final deciding factor means that the constitution becomes an *electoral capitulation*, i.e., a surrender of the state power to the disposition of the particular will, from which results the transformation of the particular powers of the state into private property, the weakening and loss of the sovereignty of the state, and thus its internal dissolution and external disintegration.[123]

As the fragments of the *Verfassungsschrift* acridly detailed, imperial sovereignty was so thoroughly constrained by the electoral capitulations that it had essentially been reduced to contingency. Reliant on the imperial estates to secure election, the emperor increasingly granted extensive rights and privileges that, in turn, were transformed into fundamental laws – he even waived his imperial right of jurisdiction (*privilegia de non appellando*), which granted a kind of quasi-sovereignty to the estates.[124]

A parallel can thereby be drawn between the doctrine of the social contract and the prevailing conditions in early modern imperial Germany in which the law of contract, through the capitulations, was used to theorize the doctrine of the imperial state. Perhaps the resemblance was most transparent in the case of the vacancy of the imperial throne. Without the head of their union, the members of the imperial body politic fell back into a state of nature.[125] In this way, sovereign jurisdiction itself had been parcelled out to the private interests of the imperial estates that, in their natural condition, existed as equals just like the individual in social contract theory. The contract law establishing the capitulations had unequivocally demonstrated how the private interests of the imperial estates contradicted a universal order such as the state. Yet, as we saw above, the private interests of the imperial estates for Hegel still contained the possibility of forming a state. This is because, at the most fundamental level, it is only through public law that the order of private law can be secured.[126] Thus, the public authority of the state was necessary for every citizen that stood in an immediate relation to the emperor and Empire.

2.2.4 The objective legal connection of the state

The electoral character of the Empire is readily apparent: 'The legal relationship between the person who is elected and the people, who elect either themselves or through the nobles, is determined by the nature of the contract by which the electing people transfer rule to the elected person.'[127] At bottom, there is thus very little distinction between natural law and public law in *Elementa iuris naturae*. In fact, if we follow the dictates of Pütter's jurisprudence to the end, the necessary foundational law that established sovereignty was always a contract.[128] Each state form or form of sovereignty was constituted on a contractual basis which subsequently gave structure to the form of government or administration.

In this way, popular sovereignty, which for Pütter took on the form of a pre-political society of families and corporations, was the exclusive foundation of the state. This manifested itself particularly in situations of interregnum or election where the rights of sovereignty reverted either to the entire people or certain nobles, resulting in transitional or representative rule and thereby maintaining continuity in the state and the functioning of government.[129] This stressed the idea that 'a contract, which is entered into between the people and the ruler over the supreme authority, is called, with regard to the state it concerns, *the fundamental law of rule* [*lex imperii fundamentalis*]'.[130] This gave further credence to the idea of the imperial constitution as an impersonal legal connection ruled by foundational laws: 'All these very laws can be considered as fundamental GENERAL laws of the whole of Germany, in so far as they hold together whatever concerns the *bond* [*nexum*] either between the Emperor and the Empire or between states and citizens of the Empire in the fashion of mediators.'[131]

There remain several important points worth highlighting in this approach. For example, what this quote perfectly displays is how the imperial body politic functioned as an objective medium governed by foundational laws. These connected emperor and Empire. The imperial estates, as the *cives imperii*, were the direct members or citizens implied in the latter concept. By contrast, the subjects of the *Länder* themselves (Hegel's 'single individuals' or 'organs') were only parts of a part (as indirect members of the Empire through a given imperial estate). They thus stood in a mediatized relation to the universal head – a mediation that occurred through multiple layers.[132]

For Pütter, true sovereignty, as Bodin had defined it, entailed nothing less than the exercise of the rights of sovereignty.[133] Whereas the Angevin had attributed those to the pure aristocratic collective of imperial estates, where some three or four hundred members had something to say,[134] this had long been relegated by the imperial patriotic tradition, to the complex of emperor and Empire.[135] When Pütter brought his discussion of the *forma Reipublicae* or *forma imperii* to a conclusion in *Beyträge zum teutschen Staats- und Fürsten-Rechte*, he consequently emphasized its monarchical, legal, limited and non-despotic character.[136] The same held true for the territories or imperial estates with their exercise of territorial supremacy, which Pütter identified as an ancient right and thus far removed from any type of despotic power.[137] This perfectly conforms to the revisionist historiography: 'the "modern state" was not absolute monarchy – absolutism was a contemporary synonym for despotism – but "constitutional" monarchy. Not only was Bodin's principle of sovereignty regarded as decisive, but also the internal limitation of the sovereign in such a way that he must respect fundamental laws, rights and political freedom. Only the combination of these made up the modern state.'[138]

The ideas of the capitulation and the contract as *the fundamental law of sovereignty* were obviously in contradiction with the very fundaments of Hegel's legal and political thought. The politically dissolutive existing rights and freedoms of the imperial estates contradicted the concept of the imperial constitution or state. It was thus precisely on the basis of the lessons that could be learnt from German constitutional history that individual fundamental rights were excluded from his otherwise constitutionally oriented modern political conception that followed in outline the dictates of reform absolutism as pioneered by Pütter in his natural law and universal public law.[139]

2.2.5 The *societas herilis*: Despotism and a kingship bound by laws

With the theoretical context of modern constitutionality in view, Pütter nevertheless clearly demonstrated his connection to the tradition, to the notion of a kingship bound by laws. From Herodotus (484–425 BCE) to Plato, from Xenophon (430–355 BCE) to Aristotle, the king had been contrasted with the tyrant, and despotic rule to political rule. Monarchy arose as an agreement between the will of the people, the ruler and the laws of the state, whereas tyranny directly opposed this form by explicitly following the arbitrary desire of the ruler against the laws.[140] Despotism simply represented this arbitrariness in a legal form – rule based on the private law relations of the head of the household, a *societas herilis*.[141]

Thus, as Pütter elaborated through his method of demarcation, the distinct limits that were established for *political* authority stressed that, in direct contrast to the despotic, its condition was bound by laws regardless of form. In this way, common welfare formed the basis of the contract of submission. This was, moreover, *the* fundamental law by which the state was established which could not be altered.[142]

This natural-legal deduction demonstrated Pütter's lucid theorization – the pure construction of submission to contracts in which the purpose of the state was identified in the realization of the common good, welfare and security, both internally and externally.[143] Thus, as he noted: 'Despotic rule is not really political [*bürgerliche*] rule, and a people subjected to despotic rule does not really constitute a state'[144] – 'a *rule* that is not even bound by natural limits is called *despotic*, one that is circumscribed only by natural but not arbitrary limits is called *absolute*, one that has arbitrary as well as natural limits is called *restricted* or *limited in particular*'.[145]

For Pütter, every type of truly *political* organization involved not only the exercise of sovereignty but also its *restriction* – it was through limitation that a novel typology of countless forms was produced: 'Many individual rights of sovereignty can be conceived, and just as many limits can be set [to them], and, as is self-evident, different ones in each state, so that in this sphere alone there are innumerable different kinds of states which have a limited rule.'[146] This enumeration corresponded very precisely to his demand for a greater complexity to the Aristotelian approach to the *forma Reipublicae*.[147] It also agreed with the Bodinian taxonomy which prioritized a restricted or royal monarchical form in contrast to the tyrannical. If the state was confused with private property, it simply did not exist.[148]

2.2.6 The *status mixtus* and the composite state

The *plenitudo potestatis* did not extend beyond the aims of the common good or welfare which remained everywhere the objective purpose of the state.[149] This led to the taxonomy encountered above, the absolute, limited by natural law – government still based on the consent of the governed and the common welfare through the fundamental law or contract – to the *restricted* or *limited in particular*. Each type here followed the dictates of reform absolutism or early enlightened liberal constitutional theory. This even led to the mixed constitution:

> Since the government of a commonwealth may be divided in various ways, there is nothing to prevent a *mixed* form being composed of several forms of state [*reipublicae formis*, *Staatsformen*], such as, for example, that the monarch is given supreme power, but a certain part of the state government [*administrationis reipublicae*, *Staatsregierung*] is entrusted to the nobles or to the people as a whole.[150]

Most likely, Pütter rehabilitated the *status mixtus* from the earlier imperial public law tradition of Limnaeus.[151] Historically, this doctrine had offered a pragmatic way out of the difficulties of categorizing the imperial constitution.[152] Even so, it went directly against the prevailing theorizations of the *Monzambano* where the mixed form was simply a fool's attempt to tame monstrosity – behind the mask of order lurked the irregular state: 'all kinds of mixture can produce nothing at last but [a monstrous deformed Government]'.[153] Additionally, with his notion of the objective legal connection Pütter followed the doctrine raised to prominence by Limnaeus – the *maiestas realis* of the state. Authority was seen rather to derive from a constitution, contract or fundamental law and *not* from the personality of the ruler. Rather it was a *Realverbindung*: 'With the "functional" representation of state activities, organized according to individual sovereign rights, again divided into Empire and territories, the end of the traditional personal conception, which could only imagine sovereign rights "in the hands" of a bearer, is at least hinted at in favour of a transpersonal conception of the state.'[154] Thus, while the Roman legal formula of Ulpian (*c.* 170 BCE–228 CE (possibly already assassinated in 223 CE)) *princeps legibus solutas* was central for any understanding of sovereignty, in Pütter's view it was increasingly supplanted by the fundamental laws (*leges imperii*) that in this case directed governance and ensured continuity in the state.[155]

If we sum up what we have learnt thus far about Pütter's categorization of the imperial constitution, we would be forced most likely to resort to a *status mixtus*. Without doubt, this model goes furthest in explaining the complexity of the foundational legal connection of a body politic of head and members with superordinate universal public law and subordinate territorial government law that for Pütter was also monarchical but limited in form. Each of these components taken together definitively made up the composite state, which was a state of states, as did the electoral character of the emperor by the Empire, a monarch which was thus doubly limited, first through election by the imperial estates and then by the fundamental laws that established his reign.

Further, Pütter very precisely differentiated between the authority of rule and the civil service and public office that were necessary in managing the affairs of a modern state.[156] The latter might well have been administrative functions, but they still remained assigned by the sovereign power. Thus, he did not argue that mixture could take place, as Bodin had done, merely in how government was organized. On the contrary, the issue when considering the imperial *forma Reipublicae* – forever and always – remained the division of sovereignty, an impossibility for the Angevin.[157]

While the emperor was alone in exercising the imperial dignity of the *iura reservata Imperatori*, the *regalia* by contrast were parcelled out among the imperial estates which were, as Ludolph Hugo put it, possessors of superiority which represented the rival or envy of the highest sovereignty or imperial majesty (*summae aemula Maiestatis*).[158] *Landeshoheit*, undefined by law, unknown in written law, had its origin solely in ancient custom:[159] 'Territorial Superiority therefore received the name from its similarity to Imperial Superiority. We also bestow kingly attributes [*Regalia*] on the Princes.'[160] For Pütter: 'Each imperial estate had to exercise not just one or two individual *regalia* in its territory, but the entire territorial authority as an entirety of all rights of government [*Regierungsrechte*], with the exception of the imperial reserve rights.'[161]

Consequently, imperial sovereignty with its *iura reservata Imperatori* could remain untouched without this affecting the reality of an essentially divided rule in the composite state – that the imperial estates possessed complete territorial authority. Government and government law, which later in the nineteenth century became more commonly recognizable as the administrative law of a federal state, understood in this sense, might have indeed been subordinate to imperial public law and its sovereignty, but the role the imperial estates played, with their wielding of the *regalia*, far outstripped the bare functionality of a civil service. In this way, the *status mixtus* was real.

For one insightful commentator, *System der Sittlichkeit* had elaborated a model not unlike Pütter's categorization of the imperial constitution as a *status mixtus*: 'The final brief notes on the forms of constitution are interesting because they tell us that Hegel was consciously operating in the tradition of the "mixed" constitution.'[162] That this was related to the fragments of the *Verfassungsschrift* was likewise intuited.[163]

2.3 Aristocratic despotism

2.3.1 Slavery, corporate inequality and the *cives imperii*

In *System der Sittlichkeit*, Hegel went out of his way to distinguish the corporative absolute structured through the estates from 'the estate of slavery [that] is not an estate, for it is only a formal universal; the slave is related as a single individual to his master'.[164] Hegel grasped this formal relation in the idea of empirical universality, the notion of an abstract equality.[165] Through an expansive system of legislation, the relation between the absolute, the estate of the free and the property-owning estate (the bourgeoisie) had been levelled. Arguably, the key concept to this interpretation was *dominium*, the Roman idea of property. The concept of the political, based on the nobility, as Hegel understood it, had disappeared. He weighed this against the equality of belonging to an absolute, to an estate, which was 'not an equality of citizenship'.[166] Corporate egalitarianism was corporate affiliation. It was neither the abstract equality of the French Revolution nor the related formal idea of an organic central authority, which had initially aligned itself with it. Both had followed a purely negative concept of freedom, establishing individualism as the fundamental principle at the basis of the state:[167] 'I set myself as an individual in opposition to another particular individual while *I* ascribe to *myself* a sphere for my freedom from which I exclude the other, and to *the other* a sphere from which I exclude myself.'[168]

The identical issue of formal equality and of slavery that appeared in *System der Sittlichkeit* was similarly traced in the *Naturrechtsaufsatz* with a view to the decadence of imperial Rome. Through an equalization of the estates, the corporative system of ethical life with its hierarchy of rule, of those destined to govern, to live as a free citizen (*politeúein*), which Hegel drew from Plato and Aristotle,[169] had dissolved and 'with the cessation of freedom slavery has necessarily come to an end'.[170] Through its system of contract and property, Roman law had prioritized a formal legal individuality above all else – or at least this is how Hegel construed it. Having destroyed the system of estates, it supplanted the relation of universal to universal, replacing it with that of particular to particular, of the single individual: 'The principle of universality and equality first had to take possession of the whole in such a way that it substituted a mixture of the two estates for a separation; in this mixture, under the law of formal unity, the first estate is in truth completely abolished [*aufgehoben*], and the second is made the sole people.'[171] Through the application of *dominium* to the imperial estates, Roman private law had dissolved the constitution.

Obviously, Hegel's critique is not really directed at Roman antiquity. On the one hand, it is connected to Fichte and the French Revolution.[172] The other perhaps far less obvious reference is to the aristocratic despotism treated by Pütter. Hegel appropriated this in the fragments of the *Verfassungsschrift*. It is connected to the reception of Roman law in Germany – the imperial and territorial context with the direct members or citizens, the *cives imperii*. As we will see, this demonstrates a far more comprehensive historical-contextual basis from which to assess Hegel's relation to Roman law and the German territorial state that grew out of his engagement with Pütter's ideas but also imperial public law more generally.

The private law relation, which is what Hegel essentially understood by Roman law, was what the imperial estates had won against the emperor once they were treated as *cives imperii*: 'that the constitutional relationship and its obligations are not determined according to universal, genuine laws, but rather in the manner of civil laws'.[173] Such criticism displays a reach of consciousness into the German public law tradition that everywhere marks the profound genius of the fragments of the *Verfassungsschrift*. From

Ludolph Hugo to Moser and Pütter, the private law of the *Corpus iuris civilis* had been used to formalize the relations between the imperial estates, alongside other sources such as custom and usage – the precise origins of territorial supremacy being in any case obscure.[174] This eventually evolved into a distinct subject which Majer decisively separated from public law: *Privatfürstenrecht*. Pütter had treated *Fürstenrecht* at such length that 'until 1918, his writings on this subject, due to their precise systematization, were the authoritative legal source for the inheritance and family law of the ruling houses in Germany'.[175]

Reaching back to Ludolph Hugo's first formulations, the evolution of princely law also tells us something distinctive about how government law was theorized in the composite state and why *Fürstenrecht*, more generally, was made up of equal parts of private law and public law:[176]

> When different States unite under one common Empire, they are reduced in a certain way to the condition in which individual private housefathers [*Patresfamilias*] are in ordinary States. For the government of a great State has its place, to which the smaller States are subject, to which private families are subject to their own individual States. Hence, we call the Imperial States themselves Citizens of the Empire; a name which in other States belongs to the private housefathers.[177]

For Hegel, this use of Roman private law had indelibly altered the political character of the imperial constitution, transforming it into a system of jurisprudence directed against any political formation beyond strict private interest. This inexorably modified the very nature of public law, not to mention the political status of the nobility: 'the relationship of each estate to the whole is something particular in the form of property'.[178] Public law had become a contradiction, for those treated under private law were for all practical purposes almost equal to sovereign authority. This cemented the idea that aristocracy was the worst *forma Reipublicae*, strictly equivalent to oligarchy as it was solely grounded in ownership by which the universal, the state, became an object of *dominium*. It was this relationship that needed to be transformed. The fact that Ludolph Hugo had to speak tautologically about *private* housefathers signalled a confusion between legal registers: the territorial lord considered the housefather of the state, a species of public law.

What we can observe in Hugo's quote is how private law could indeed *become* public law in a quasi-federal state, a means by which to explain an intrinsically political relationship that connected the imperial estates to a superordinate legal entity. This had been arranged through hereditary rights, laws determining the possession of office, electoral rights, lands and political capital more generally – in every conceivable way. Roman law had codified the customary – what had been won by the territories and their princes from time immemorial.[179] Hence, it is thoroughly 'misleading to think of a sharp division between Roman law, on the one hand, and the Germanic customary laws on the other'.[180] Rather, as Montesquieu perceived, Roman law under the Germans had become a universal personal law, a territorial law.[181]

On the other hand, the reduction of everything to private law relations confirmed Hegel's diagnosis. Those who were destined to govern, the Germanic estate of the free, the nobility of the *Naturrechtsaufsatz*, had become indistinguishable from the bourgeoisie insofar as private property and ownership became the sole issues of concern when considering the nature of the imperial state. The Roman World, as Hegel conceived it, could only take on the aristocratic form – monarchy alien to it. Thus, the reception of Roman law sapped the vitals of the original German monarchy. The one thing that singled out the aristocratic *forma Reipublicae* was the fact that only by means of the greatest hardship could it be united.[182] This was no less true in the Holy Roman Empire. The Roman jurisprudence leveraged by the imperial estates sundered them completely from the whole, just as the territorial estates, in pursuing their own privileges, proved in fact no less separate.[183]

2.3.2 The Roman legal concept of ownership: *Dominium*

Tellingly, Ludolph Hugo found the connecting link between territorial government law and private law in the Roman legal concept of ownership: *dominium*.[184] This central notion detailed the property relation to the household (*domus*) and the lord of the house (*dominus*).[185] In the early Roman period, it was directly connected to the *Patresfamilias* with their corresponding paternal power; it was thus part of a comprehensive doctrine of domestic rule.[186] This understanding highlighted how, in the imperial courts, the estates, despite their political standing, often appeared as private persons engaged in litigation.[187]

The attribution of *dominium* to the imperial estates opened the door to despotic power and the *societas herilis*. This equation was taken up in *Elementa iuris naturae* which spoke of the *ius herile et dominicum*, precisely detailing how, stemming from the concept of slavery, this society of ownership could become despotic – the slave having no natural freedom against the owner.[188] Pütter, as we have seen, contrasted truly despotic societies (which he argued were not genuine states) with those that merely placed limitations on sovereignty. This distinction found a corresponding historical analogy when he observed how the German aristocracy or princes verged on despotism when they attempted to levy taxes on their subjects without consent, denying the significance of the territorial estates.[189]

Directly following Pütter, Hegel traced the same development in the fragments of the *Verfassungsschrift*.[190] In the name of the German freedom of the imperial estates, the territorial princes set out to destroy the participatory rights of the territorial estates through the development of artificial systems of taxation, legislation and standing armies. In this context, Roman law provided a body of formal and rational (in the Weberian, though not Hegelian, sense) legal techniques. These techniques facilitated centralization and the establishment of an administered bureaucratic state.[191]

Since Emperor Maximilian I (1459–1519) had issued an edict in 1495, Roman law had been the imperial *ius commune* with the constitution of the Imperial Cameral Court.[192] Quickly, however, this jurisprudence fell into the hands of the princes who saw in it a way to 'counter the independence of over-mighty feudal lords'.[193] Essentially, it went hand in hand with that historical 'reconfiguration of lordship and its practice of protection in which the prince claimed to be the sole lord'.[194] Ultimately, this development consolidated the territorial state.[195] Moreover, the struggles of the princes against the territorial estates, as Pütter put it, 'were gradually productive of the most important change in the constitution of Germany, as many of the most powerful States began now to maintain a permanent military establishment or standing army'.[196] Through this historical development, many imperial cities and territorial estates lost much of their freedom:[197] 'the development of a standing army created and maintained, outfitted and trained according to the system of bureaucratic administration at state expense, spelled the death of the feudal and social order of estates'.[198]

Just as for Pütter, so too for Hegel – only by means of the refusal of Emperor Leopold (1658–1705) to ratify what had been proposed by the college of princes was the degeneration into aristocratic despotism thwarted. For some scholars, this aspect of Hegel's position was part of the patriotic reawakening of the smaller imperial estates of the Third Germany to which he and his close friend at the time Friedrich Hölderlin (1770–1843), as children of Württemberg, belonged.[199] Writing in this spirit, Hegel perceived that the real interests of the people – German freedom – had returned to its source. Hence, 'the Emperor's relationship to Germany appears in a different light; and his relationship is very different from that of Prussia'.[200] This can be observed even more clearly in Hegel's favouring of the principle of the nobility maintained in Austria which had preserved its connection to the system of representation against the bourgeois principle in Prussia and France. Or, to put the matter more directly, Austria had upheld the significance of its territorial estates.

The territorial estates were common heritage among the majority of German states. If the monarch of the Germanic World must be the centre from which all power derived, in charge of national affairs and in particular the external relations with other states, law and legal power resting in his hands, this was counterbalanced by the fact that 'the estates have a share in the legislation, and they provide the means by which power is maintained'.[201] This underlined the advantage of the mixed constitution: 'Without such a representing body, freedom is no longer conceivable.'[202] Through the power of law, it also evaded the problem of a monocratic despotism and the related fear that the individual estate would be suppressed.[203] By the eighteenth century, despotism had become a synonym for slavery. Despotism implied excluding subjects from government and legislation, consolidating all power in a single will unbound by written law – divesting the ruler of responsibility towards the people or representative bodies. The despot governed solely through arbitrary whim and personal discretion.[204]

Hegel's perspective aligns with the ideas shared among authors on the territorial estates constitution and reform absolutism such as Pütter's: that 'the original spirit of the German peoples' was in 'striking contrast with the mode of thinking and customs of military despotism'.[205] This had of course been writ large in the German reception of Montesquieu, especially in the interpretation of Roman law in the context of a struggle against the absolutism of Louis XIV (1638–1715).[206] It was further elaborated in Kantian legal philosophy with its state typology, which, while preserving autocracy (monarchy), aristocracy and democracy in both the form of rule (*forma imperii*) and mode of administration (*forma regiminis*), was essentially divided between republican and despotic forms.[207]

In all likelihood, Kant was directly following the theorizations of *Elementa iuris naturae* and the imperial conditions so thoroughly described by Pütter. After all, it was the Göttingen publicist who had first formalized this dichotomous *forma Reipublicae.* Kant had also taken the *societas herilis* directly from *Elementa iuris naturae* to conceive the difference between the temporary (contractual) service of lordship and bondage against the permanency of slavery and the slave as the absolute subject of the absolute master or lord of property.[208] In *System der Sittlichkeit*, the same issue resurfaced. Hegel went out of his way to distinguish the relationship of lordship and bondage with its corresponding system of estates from slavery. Even if vestiges of the personal relation remained in this context, linking the bondsman to the lord, the contract had largely been given priority, which bestowed a legal character on the relationship, one of (temporary) service: 'What connects with the head through necessity, connects … only as an absolute person through contract, and for a specific time. Because everyone is an absolute person, they should be able to achieve their living totality, to become a housefather.'[209] For Hegel, the personal relationship of lordship and bondage in this respect had been replaced by relations of service and labour. Thus, the head of the household is related to lordship only superficially.

A larger contrast demands articulation here, between the use of the *Corpus iuris civilis* to codify the relations between the imperial estates as *Patresfamilias* and the applicability of this jurisprudence to German public law more generally. Imperial union proved impossible given the utter diversity of the imperial estates, in their holding fast to their private interests as *cives imperii*. But this was also no less true, as Hegel noted, when considering the particularism of the territorial estates. The codification of their customs and freedoms also separated them thoroughly from any idea of political universality. In other words, the universal, in the form of public law, did not govern, but only civil rights. This was a contradiction. Without public law to ensure a subordinate legal order, there can be no such thing as private law. Thus, the same structural tension between private interests and the political was evident at the territorial level between the territorial estates, their princes and the Empire.

2.3.3 The *Hippolythus* and the rejection of Roman law

Of the early modern epoch and the political struggles of the *Hippolythus*, Hegel wrote: 'German freedom meant nothing other than the independence of the estates from the Emperor, either slavery and despotism – or the abolition of state union – no third option was known in earlier times.'[210] With its vociferous rage against *everything* Roman, *everything* imperial, the *Hippolythus* had so thoroughly destroyed the older ideas of imperial public law that those ideas collapsed under the weight of its propaganda. In the name of *teutsche Libertät*, the *Hippolythus* sought to rally the imperial estates against the Habsburgs and to tear off the imperial mask of sovereignty. It was not the emperor who possessed *maiestas*, but the Empire, the aristocracy of the imperial estates.[211] As Pütter famously claimed, the *Hippolythus* 'perhaps had caused greater damage to the imperial court than a few lost battles':[212] 'The designs of the Emperor … were totally frustrated by the effect of a single book; a book which deserves on that account a place in the Historical Development of the Constitution of the Germanic Empire, as much as the history of many of the wars or treaties of peace.'[213]

Historically speaking, Conring completed the process the *Hippolythus* had begun when he translated its animus into an innovative new discipline: legal history. This purported to demonstrate the complete inapplicability of Roman law and Roman legal concepts to the study of German imperial public law.[214] What the reception had actually accomplished was simply the codification of whatever had been left unwritten in Germanic customary law,[215] a role Montesquieu later also perceived.[216] This process has been significantly detailed, noting that where written law already existed, the influence of Roman law held less sway.[217]

For Hegel, the deep recesses of Germanic prehistory revealed how power preceded law. In *System der Sittlichkeit*, this was further identified as the sphere of practical feeling where 'there can be no question of a legal foundation or [a] side of possession here at all'.[218] Spheres of power and chance took hold of changeable things which were only then gradually fixed through the passage of time; what had been appropriated was made legal after the fact and thereby transformed from an originary appropriation into a possession and thence into property.[219] This indicated the direction in which the imperial constitution had evolved on the basis of Germanic custom as well as the nature of its public law. Hence, as Hegel put it in the *Verfassungsschrift*, 'this diverse property does not form a system of laws, but a collection without principle'.[220] This unprincipled collection was akin to barbarism, to the very Germanic tribes that had caused the collapse of the Roman Empire and, if I am permitted the historical inaccuracy, had seemingly absorbed both its aristocratic principle and its jurisprudence in the process.

For Aristotle, barbarism had been identified with a particular type of rule: despotism. Distinct from the political rule over the free citizens of the *polis* that was regulated by law, it was an extension of household rule - private *not* political.[221] Without law, there could be no talk of a constitution in the proper sense.[222] The continuity between this tradition and that of *Elementa iuris naturae*, in Kant as well as Hegel, is palpable. A barbarian was akin to a slave, and slavery best described its government. For Hegel, however, this condition was not wholly without law; rather, its laws were strictly private, fundamentally undermining both state and constitution.[223] This opened the door to the rule of the despot. The *cives imperii* were *Patresfamilias* that possessed paternal power over their subjects, which fell under the Roman concept of *dominium*. In the quasi-federal state, as Ludolph Hugo articulated it, they were to be treated as public *Patresfamilias* - a contradiction in terms if there ever was one. This produced a condition of barbarism in which private law subverted the state, confusing the very character of what ought to be public law.

2.3.4 Hermann Conring and Germanic legal history

The foundation of a particularly *Germanic* legal history has long been attributed to Hermann Conring.[224] Based on the innovative use of historical sources, he exploded the idea of the transfer of empire (*translatio imperii*) from Ancient Rome to Germany that justified Roman law as a native (imperial) law. He dismissed as groundless the supposed introduction of the *Codex* and the *Digest* by Emperor Lothar II (III) (1075–1137) in the Middle Ages.[225] Methodologically, Conring showed how the German reception took place through legal scholars returning from study in Italy. This had much more to do with knowledge transfer, through scholarly exchange from crossing and recrossing the Alps, than it did with an ideologically laden mythology such as the legend that Emperor Lothar II had adopted Roman law as the *ius commune* in the twelfth century – thus transforming, through the *translatio imperii*, the Empire into the Holy *Roman* Empire of the German Nation.[226] Hence, Conring carved out a distinctively Germanic conception of the Empire and attempted to divest it of what had now become *the* foreign law. Hence, 'this Empire in which he lives is not that of the Romans, but that of the Germans'.[227] In this way, he refuted the similar idea of the continuity between Ancient Rome and Germany contained in the doctrine of the four monarchies.[228]

With the emergence of what Krause called the historical school, identified in its first phase with the *Hippolythus* and Conring, custom and usage became stronger indicators of how territorial supremacy and the system of imperial sovereignty had come into being.[229] Consequently, the traditional legal analysis, which had previously interrogated concepts like 'iurisdictio' in the *Digest* and the *Codex*, the 'regalia' in the *Libri Feudorum*, or their connection with canon and ecclesiastical constitutional law, now shifted its focus. The *Corpus iuris civilis* began to lose much of its standing and legitimacy when applied to the position of the emperor and the interpretation of the Empire.

For Krause, the emergence of the early modern historical school coincided historically with the period of the Thirty Years' War and its concluding peace treaties.[230] Roman legal elements were jettisoned and increasingly appeared alien. Historically, this contrasted starkly with the first phase of German legal scholarship. The legists and decretists, as he put it, 'were ignorant of German laws and rights'.[231]

Yet the separation of Roman law from imperial public law decisively served the state formation of the imperial estates. If the German emperors could no longer lay claim to the Roman Empire and its laws, their universality was broken – their eternity, on the basis of the biblical exegesis of the four empires, disproved. This was consequent to a secularization of the idea of Empire, a more strictly empirically oriented, yet politically normative procedure, which could simultaneously legitimize the Empire and territories.[232] On the other hand, through electoral rights, the imperial estates directly shared in power.[233]

A good part of the evolution of German public law evidently involved breaking away from the juridical notions of Roman law that were indiscriminately applied to explain the constitutional authority of the emperor and the imperial estates.[234] The authors of the Middle Ages had attempted to view the emperor, princes, Imperial Diet and the free cities through the lens of Roman legal ideas of *summa potestas*, *praesides provinciarum*, *senatus* and *municipia* respectively.[235] But, as Pütter would decisively state, this was a way 'to understand everything only from the Roman state constitution according to the Justinian code of law, but nothing of German things'.[236] Pütter might have simply been incapable of seeing just how powerful a source Roman law had been in the Middle Ages. After Conring, it was very difficult to view that part of German legal history in the same way. Yet with the Reformation, the universality of the Empire – following the doctrine of the *translatio imperii* – was threatened but not yet lost.

The German emperors, according to Conring's interpretation, were no longer the legitimate heirs of Justinian and Augustus, but 'merely the rulers of Germany and the Imperial dignity was an incidental supplement to the original title of *Rex Germanorum*'.[237] The idea that Roman law could be legitimized on the basis that it was an indigenous law, as it had been for Peter von Andlau (1420–1480), 'the first and only writer on constitutional law of his time', had become completely impossible.[238] Nevertheless, the process was protracted. Throughout the Reformation and down into the Thirty Years' War, a bitter struggle raged. To give up universality meant many things, not only the sanctioning of confessional pluralism but also the decline of universal Catholic rule through both Church and Empire. Canon law also lost its universal significance. With the *translatio imperii* broken, the Holy Roman Empire simply could not lay claim to what then became foreign law.[239] Since the Germanic Empire was *wholly* Germanic, its purported Roman vestiges all but disappeared. Or so it would appear.

2.3.5 The return of Roman law

Appearance can be deceiving. It is important to note that Conring, just like his successors and unlike the *Hippolythus*, was not opposed to Roman law per se. Paradoxically, his disquisition on an exclusively *Germanic* Empire bereft of all Roman vestiges allowed Roman private law to ascend via the concept of the *cives imperii*. Despite its initial rejection, Roman law found its way back into the legal framework. Shown the door, it had crept back in through the window. Hegel perceptively noted the profound historical consequences of this development for the unfolding history of German public law and its effect on the Empire: 'Conring and Hippolithus à Lapide, however, made this distinction between Roman law and constitutional law more, it seems, to dissolve the state than to unite it; they constituted the estates as states, in which case, of course, private law is not applicable to them.'[240] Hence, not only was Hegel aware that the *Hippolythus* and Conring had rejected entirely the status of Roman law as a form of constitutional law applied to the emperor – a status based on the *translatio imperii* and thus deemed his special province – but he had also intuited the foundation of the *cives imperii* in these authors.

This quote underscores the extent of Hegel's grasp of the tradition of German public law and the contradiction at the heart of Ludolph Hugo's application of *dominium* and Roman paternal power to the imperial estates, which treated them under the terms of private law in a quasi-federal state. No doubt, Hugo followed in the footsteps of his teacher when he rejected Roman public law and the *lex regia*. However, he paradoxically reintroduced its private jurisprudence to explain the association among the imperial estates themselves and within the Empire at large, as *cives imperii*. In this respect, he considered Roman private law as a way of grasping the further differentiation between government law and constitutional law. The imperial estates as citizens of the Empire, however, were princes who could govern almost as kings or even autocrats – or, perhaps more appropriately for our discussion, with the despotic power of the *paterfamilias* over wives, children and, most importantly, slaves.[241]

This was a contradiction almost impossible to disguise. On these terms, private law significantly influenced German public law, or more precisely, the structure of rule operative in the imperial composite state. Furthermore, *dominium* could be instrumentalized politically and directly equated with the consolidation of the territorial states. Thus, Roman law, for the young Hegel, closely corresponded to the paternalistic ethos of the German territorial state.[242]

2.3.6 Hegel and Roman law

Something essential occurred in this context that runs through the imperial public law literature directly to the last phase of its theorizations and Hegel's denunciation of German public law as a form of private law. The result was the vacuity of German public law as such – a constitution disembowelled by Roman private jurisprudence. In other words, by an historical sleight of hand, Conring's purely Germanic Empire – through the innovation of the *cives imperii* and Hugo's attribution of Roman private property law to explain the relationship between the estates – had become, in effect, a *Privatum Imperium Romano-Germanicum*.

For Hegel, the imperial state thus lacked the dimension of sovereignty that served as *the* marker of the early modern state because its *citizens* possessed powers directly equivalent to it in their own right. Considered under the Roman legal concept of *dominium*, the power exercised by the imperial estates carried with it corresponding notions of despotism and slavery. This degeneration, however, was initially visible in the emperor himself, particularly in 'the political and religious despotism of Ferdinand'.[243] This very despotism had, in turn, prompted the creative destruction of the *Hippolythus* in the first place with its rejection of all things Roman and its struggle for the German freedom of the imperial estates. In the later epoch that Pütter and Hegel had discussed, this despotism had definitively fallen into the hands of an aristocracy of imperial estates.

For the French legal philosopher and historian Michel Villey (1914–1988), Hegel's grasp of Roman law left out what was most admirable in the original framework of the Roman *civitas* which had preserved its republican elements even under the *Principate*.[244] Hegel's interpretation, according to Villey, was heavily influenced by the questionable readings of Montesquieu and Gibbon.[245] Villey found Hegel's notion of the slave as a wretched object of domination particularly historically questionable. He argued that Roman law lacked a specific study of the relationship of rule or power, contending that things and persons were not strictly divided in this context. Instead, it was the German Idealism of Kant, Fichte and Hegel that had introduced this as a *radical* opposition.[246] Thus, *dominium*, the principle of property related to the household (*domus*) and the lord of the house (*dominus*), was never to be confused with absolute despotic power in Roman law.[247]

Had Villey been more of an adept contextualist, however, he might have seen things otherwise. As Pütter pointed out, Karl V (1500–1558), perhaps seeking to solidify his imperial power despite uncertain German ancestry, had explicitly used the institution of *patria potestas*.[248] This precedent, arguably, blazed the trail for the imperial estates to become *cives imperii* and individual *Patresfamilias*, thus thoroughly confusing the doctrines of private and public law. Regardless, what the example in any case demonstrates is how whatever came within the circumference of the legal purlieu of the emperor, irrespective of the precise character or origin of any particular law, could and did become imperial public law. Moreover, the fact that *dominium* went hand in hand with the practice of territorial state consolidation could easily make the equation with absolute despotic power tangible.

In the absence of a truly sovereign state, public law, in both the Roman imperial and modern senses, could scarcely be conceptually grasped.[249] Following such logic, there was nothing that stood in the way of translating the *dominium* that described the household rule of antiquity into political law. On the one hand, this was the very nature of despotism as Aristotle had described it: the conversion of the private realm of the *oikos*, of the differentiated rule over women, children and slaves, into politics and the constitution (*politeia*), which was meant to concern rule over the free.[250] Crucially – and in responding to Villey's criticism – if such application of *dominium* was indeed foreign to antiquity, this merely reinforces the fact that Hegel's critique is likely derived from his intensive study of German legal history and Pütter. In the contemporary context in which Hegel was writing, practically every political relation of public law had been carefully codified under the dictates of Roman private law. This had then been fully integrated into the relations between imperial public law and *Fürstenrecht*, as a form of government law.

Fürstenrecht significantly impacted the public law of the German imperial state. The *cives imperii* were princes that, as Ludolph Hugo pointed out, were akin to the private individual *Patresfamilias* in regular states. The contradiction was thus tangible. Hugo had noted the actual success of private law in explaining the complexities of public law in a quasi-federal state. Nonetheless, as he also detailed, these private individual *Patresfamilias* wielded autocratic power in their territories which was in competition with the very idea of imperial sovereignty.[251] For Pütter, only the emperor could prevent the effects of such despotic power.[252] Hegel followed him in due course. In the literature of reform absolutism, the question would thus naturally arise as to whether such citizens were rightfully endowed with a similar power over the subjects of their domains as the housefather over his household.

Undoubtedly, this particular application of Roman law corresponded to what has become known as the patrimonial state. In this precise way, Hegel's analysis has been vindicated by historical sociology. Although it may not, as Villey rightly noted, have much to do with the Roman law of the *Corpus iuris civilis* as practised by the jurists of antiquity, the Hegelian perception can still tell us much about the peculiarity of the historical phenomenon of the reception of Roman law in Germany.

2.4 Epilogue

2.4.1 Pütter's imperial *forma Reipublicae*

This chapter has studied Pütter's place in the debates and his definition of the imperial *forma Reipublicae*. We have seen how his ideas were drawn to a more complex characterization of the simple Aristotelian enumeration. This resembled, in some ways, the reigning conceptions of the *Monzambano* and the systems-theoretical perspective, yet the *civitas composita* was, in fact, a unique legal construct.

Importantly, Pütter articulated the legal connection between the head and members of this composite body politic that provided the aspects necessary to develop an objective doctrine of the state, both monistic and impersonal. The gist of this approach is perhaps most fittingly summed up by the limitations Pütter argued could be placed on the Roman legal formula, taken from Ulpian and made famous by Bodin: *princeps legibus solutas*. In the process, Pütter emphasized the rule of the foundational laws. He set out to rehabilitate the 'patriarch' of German imperial public law or the 'oraculum in iure publico' – Limnaeus.[253] This led to a distinctively patriotic theory of the imperial state that grappled with the idea of a *status mixtus*. For the *Monzambano*, there was nothing to suggest that Limnaeus had more than 'a mediocre understanding of sound politics'.[254] The *status mixtus* rejected entire. Pütter profited from the luxury of historical distance, which lent enchantment to the view. The terms of the debate had shifted to such an extent that Limnaeus could appear in a more positive light. In this way, an objective doctrine of sovereignty and the state had emerged through the objective legal connection of foundational laws.

There is a striking similarity between Pütter's object legal connection, intrinsically part of German public law, and Hegel's conception of *Staatsgesetze*. For Hegel, it must be the power of these public laws that ensured the legal exercise of sovereignty – that set limits on monarchical rule. Everything hinged on this in the constitutional organization of the state. Before these *Staatsgesetze* could be considered, however, the power of the state had to exist.[255] Hegel spoke simultaneously of the *personality* of the monarch, Pütter's *Realverbindung* and the objective power of the state. For Hegel, the monarch's wielding of sovereignty was synonymous with the very existence of the state. In contradistinction to this form of limited monarchy, the imperial head for the young philosopher was a mere title and legal fiction of the theoretical state. With true political power practically non-existent, the Empire had left the issue of sovereignty and supreme power unresolved. Without the reality of these concepts, there could truly be no public law. Indeed, the body politic of a head and members followed a tradition that heavily relied on a patriotism that favoured the imperial estates, where 'the Emperor does not have the sovereign power in his own right like an owner, but he exercises it merely as an official, as the first official of the state'.[256] Yet this cannot alter the fact that the *regulae administrandi* were part of a wider set of legal relations that had made possible the very transformation of sovereignty, from strictly a personal possession into an objective legal order in the first place.[257]

2.4.2 The restrictive typology: Electoral monarchy

Pütter went to great lengths in detailing more precisely the nature of the imperial state, sovereignty, territorial supremacy and the restrictive typology. The nature of his public law was integrated with his approach to natural jurisprudence which was treated as a form of positive law. This expressed itself emblematically in an analysis of the state's contractual foundations, particularly the Empire's electoral character and its peculiarly restricted monarchy, established through the capitulations. The nature of this monarchy restricted by the contract in the form of the capitulations gave Hegel's critique of the Empire its point of entry. Likewise, it provided a cue for his rejection of modern natural law and the idea that individual rights ought to be codified as the foundation of the modern constitutional state. Still, we do well to note that the form in which sovereignty was organized – whether monarchy was electoral or hereditary – was an indifferent matter; there was only one essential thing: the existence and power of the state.[258]

2.4.3 The critique of Roman law

The rejection of Roman law as imperial law by the publicists of the seventeenth century served as a preface to its immediate return as a source for explaining the relationship of the imperial estates among themselves and within the Empire at large. For Hegel, this private law source undermined everywhere the public legal nature of the Empire. In this way, Hegel's grasp of Roman law, slavery and despotism must be framed by the overarching imperial legal context. This marked his relationship to this jurisprudence, which fundamentally shaped the contours of the early modern territorial state in Germany.

Hegel's interpretation of Roman law and the imperial constitution had deep roots in the history of German public law and the famed formalization of the imperial estates as *cives imperii*. This private law was the Serpent in the Garden identified by Hegel in his analysis of the decline of the Holy Roman Empire. Whereas it provided a legal basis for the idea of a quasi-federal state, the fact that it had applied private law to members who were obviously more than simple citizens eroded imperial political power and undermined the very character of public law. Once treated as private persons under the dictates of Roman private law and its concept of property (*dominium*) the door was opened to an aristocratic despotism by the imperial estates. Reflection on the historical context of the imperial constitution thus conducts us to a new way of interpreting the early Hegel's relation to Roman law.

3

The twilight of German imperial public law: Johann Christian von Majer

3.0 Prologue

3.0.1 Majer's modernity and Hegel

Speculation about the influence of the Tübingen professor of constitutional and feudal law Johann Christian von Majer on the young Hegel's political and legal thought has abounded ever since Franz Rosenzweig's *Hegel und der Staat*.[1] Majer's second stint as rector of the University of Tübingen (1790–1) overlapped the period in which Hegel studied theology at the Tübinger Stift (1788–93). Rosenzweig suggested that Hegel attended Majer's lectures. Hegel was possibly influenced by the historical approach to the imperial constitution that Majer developed in his lectures on Publius Cornelius Tacitus (56 BCE–120 CE), eventually published as *Germaniens Urverfassung* (1798) (Germania's Ancient Constitution).[2] Hegel's study of Tacitus went back to his early student days in Stuttgart when he attended the Eberhard-Ludwigs-Gymnasium.[3] Majer had been translating and publishing on Tacitus since 1774, notably in Christoph Martin Wieland's (1733–1813) *Der Teutsche Merkur*, the most influential literary review in Germany.[4]

Majer made his name, in part, by furthering the separation between constitutional and government law (*Verfassungs- und Regierungsrecht*), which his far more famous contemporary, Pütter, had raised to prominence.[5] In dividing the status quo of the state, the political condition, from the constitution in a strict sense as government, Majer coupled his ideas to revolutionary modernity. Government law consisted in the exercise and scope of state sovereignty over citizens, encompassing their mutual relations and private property. This was the objective side of internal state law (*inneres Staatsrecht*). The subjective side concerned how sovereignty was organized, in terms of the specific form of constitution. Rather an indifferent matter when compared to the former, this denoted how sovereignty existed for the ruler who gave the state life and activity.[6]

Rosenzweig registered the significance of these formulations for Hegel when pinpointing the ways in which *System der Sittlichkeit* mobilized government and constitutional law as an active system against the inactive existence of the people in the state, the political condition (*Staatsverfassung*).[7] In recent historical scholarship, Majer's further innovations of Pütter's division have been recognized as a decisive conceptual advancement: 'Majer in 1799 went so far as to assert that "the epitome of all circumstances apparent in the same [the state]", that is the Verfassung in the older sense, can no longer be termed a "constitution", but rather as the "status quo", while the term "constitution" is reserved for the legal norms governing state power.'[8]

That Hegel clothed Majer's innovations in speculative language does not detract from his direct appropriation of Majer's terminology. This can be observed in Hegel's discussion of what Majer termed the status quo, which Hegel similarly conceived as the political condition (*Staatsverfassung*) or 'the system of ethical life at rest'.[9] On the other hand, 'the absolute subsumed under the absolute concept, the *absolute movement*, or the process of ethical life' conformed in outline to Majer's discussion on government and constitutional law. Not only did this fall under Hegel's disquisition on government (*Regierung*) in *System der Sittlichkeit*, but also his analysis of 'the true constitution' (*die wahre Constitution*) which he identified it with.[10] In this way, he was in complete conformity with Majer's scheme, viewing the *Staatsverfassung* as the state's condition or status quo. This aligns with Majer's distinction: the constitution (in the active sense of government) represented the modern element, while the political condition (*Staatsverfassung*) signified a pre-existent, essentially indifferent entity, reflecting the older understanding of the term. Thus, the two different words distinguished two distinct concepts. Through this differentiation of concepts, Hegel decisively appropriated the modernity of Majer's political thought, identifying the thoroughly modern sense of constitution with the active force of government.[11]

We can then add a critical note on Rosenzweig's otherwise illuminating perceptions in *Hegel und der Staat*. Unable to fully grasp the extent of Majer's political modernity, Rosenzweig equated it directly with the *mos Gottingensis* and attributed the innovating move solely to Hegel:

> Hegel recognized that that which was newly called '*Konstitution*' and which began to play such an enormous role in political thinking, was not to be grouped in the sense of Pütter and Majer's division with 'constitution' [*Verfassung*], but rather with 'government' [*Regierung*], and that it was not related to the resting existence of the people in the state, but rather was the law according to which the state acted against that being at rest.[12]

At another level, *Allgemeine Theorie der Staatskonstitution* and the first volume of *Teutsche Staatskonstitution* (1800) began by constructing a concept of the state that has striking formal similarities to the identically titled section of the *Reinschrift*.[13] The introductory part of the *Reinschrift* took up some of the materials that had already formed the basis of the original opening gloss 'Sollte das politische Resultat' and the core issue of the categorization of the imperial constitution, which the modern public lawyers could only deem an Empire or body politic – so thoroughly defying the Aristotelian concepts of the *forma Reipublicae* – before detailing the concept of the state. When treating simple forms of state, Majer referred to the Aristotelian schema and used it as a basis, although it remained insufficient.[14] It formed part of his taxonomy of the state constitution, from the regular types of monarchy, including its limited form, aristocracy, to which he added the body politic of a head and members, democracy and the mixed constitution. Hence, *Allgemeine Theorie der Staatskonstitution*, following the noble lead of the *Hippolythus* to which Majer stood in awe, expressed similar exasperation before elaborating its concept of the state.[15] This structural correspondence between Majer and Hegel continues to be a subject of considerable scholarly interest.[16]

3.0.2 The shift towards law in Tübingen and the religious question

Astute biographical accounts emphasize a significant shift in Hegel's focus from theology towards law during his time in Tübingen.[17] We have already noted that during that time Hegel defended a dissertation that dealt with ecclesiastical and state law.[18] This would have brought him directly within the ambit of Majer's work which specialized in hierarchical homologies and theocracy,[19] as well as the lectures Majer delivered during the same period on ecclesiastical, canon and public law.[20] Indeed, a large part of the Tübingen publicist's later theoretical reflections on the imperial constitution and the singularity of its public law were considered under what he had termed the religious principle.[21]

For Hegel, admittedly, the implications were viewed differently. Nonetheless, he considered civic freedom as something 'holy' under the section of the *Reinschrift* that had followed Majer's concept of the state in outline.[22] Importantly, this civic freedom was unique to the Germanic peoples and had developed in a highly distinctive fashion through the history of internecine religious conflict.

From the early outline 'über ihre Entstehung', Hegel had seen this perceptively. Territorial supremacy was tied to religious and political freedom, the original right to reformation (*ius reformandi*).[23] This earlier right, granted to the territorial lord in 1555 by the formula 'cuius regio, eius religio' (whose realm, his religion), which permitted rulers to determine confession, faced an important restriction in Article V of the *Instrumentum Pacis Osnabrugensis* (*I.P.O.*).[24] This article referred back to the 1624 *Normaljahr* settlement, which ultimately resolved the denominational question.

With the Peace of Westphalia, the territorial prince was no longer in a position to alter confession. The preference of denomination rested in the hands of the individual. Thus, Hegel recognized that 'in tearing the state completely apart, religion has at the same time, in a wonderful way, nevertheless given an intimation of some principles on which a state can be based'.[25] Imperial public law had sanctified freedom of conscience with the extension of the right of religion to the individual. This resulted in an expansive doctrine of toleration in the Holy Roman Empire.[26] Whereas it indeed produced division following 'the stubborn character of the German nature for independence', which 'cannot be understood otherwise than as resistance to the reality of union',[27] without this radical diremption the need of philosophy, so articulately outlined in the *Differenzschrift* (1801) (The Difference between Fichte's and Schelling's System of Philosophy), would never have appeared in the first place:[28] 'on the one hand, the territorial supremacy of the prince or the imperial city flowed together with freedom, especially religious freedom; on the other hand, the union of the Empire'.[29]

This spoke perfectly to the condition of the state constitution in which 'necessary division is a factor of life which eternally forms itself through opposition'.[30] The state, the truly modern state, however, must be a profound reconciliation: 'Totality, in its highest vitality, is only possible through restoration from the deepest separation.'[31] True unity in legal and political life is thus not found by avoiding dissension and conflict but by engaging with and ultimately transcending the most serious divisions through a dialectical process of dynamic restoration.

3.0.3 State of the art and *forma Reipublicae*

The recent publication of the critical edition *Fragmente einer Kritik der Verfassung Deutschlands* has decisively widened the scope of inquiry into the connection between Majer and Hegel through innumerable references to the last phase of imperial public law.[32] Even if the allusions to Majer are infrequent compared to Pütter, Kurt Rainer Meist's masterful commentary insightfully demonstrates that the references to the Tübingen lawyer extend beyond what Rosenzweig had already indicated.[33] This places a different emphasis on the material.

The focus of the rather sparse yet promising contemporary research on the relationship between Majer and Hegel has arguably taken up and furthered Rosenzweig's original intuitions on the concept of the state.[34] In this connection, Majer's notion of the sovereignty of the Empire has been particularly emphasized.[35] Majer had originally viewed the condition of the constitution in his own time through the lens of the *Hippolythus* in *Allgemeine Theorie der Staatskonstitution*. He drew direct parallels between the historical context of the Thirty Years' War and his own lived experience of futile attempts to categorize the state constitution. This was a lament that he repeated, although no longer citing the *Hippolythus*, at the outset of the first volume of *Teutsche Staatskonstitution*. The wretched situation of living with the effects of war and occupation in the imperial territory of Württemberg that had been ravaged by French forces, already for five years, shaped the urgency of the theory of the state constitution.[36] The importance of the *Hippolythus* was that it had acutely grasped the political conditions and needs of its epoch. Bogislaw Philipp von Chemnitz (1605–1678) 'deeply affected by the miserable condition of the fatherland during the Thirty Years' War, had no other intention in his learned and powerful book',

> than to portray in the most vivid colours to the princes of the German Empire what was averse to the constitution [*konstitutionswidrige*] in the German history of his time. He hoped thereby to incite them all the more to unite most fervently in favour of the maintenance or restoration of the German imperial constitution [*Reichskonstitution*]; but for all his thorough scholarship of the state, he did not know how to find a clear and definite formula for this.[37]

Majer then proceeded to run through many of the currently prevailing definitions – recognizing the insufficiency of the *Hippolythus*.[38] These included descriptions ranging from a grotesque body composed of large and small sovereigns, to half-monarchical and half-aristocratic forms and even the *Monzambano*, mentioned in passing. Through these examples, Majer emphasized how a confusion reigned between the condition (the status quo of the state) and the constitution itself, as the legal norms of political power.[39]

When Majer mentioned the *Monzambano*, it was in the course of reflection upon lectures delivered on Pufendorf by the Strasbourg professor of history and rhetoric Johann Daniel Schöpflin (1694–1771), who had spoken of the Empire as a 'formless and confused chaos' (*informe et confusum chaos*).[40] Majer lifted this concept and coined the neologism *Unformlichkeit* to describe the evolution from the simple to the complex to the dissolutive. This *Unformlichkeit* expressed the impossibility of categorizing the constitution, characterizing its form as essentially formless. This was contained in the politics of *Landeshoheit* that stemmed from the ancient Germanic system of manorial property 'which had remained intact during the overthrow of ancient Germanic freedom and the people's constitution'.[41] The Empire was a singular entity among the European nations as this ancient past could more be readily observed in its present political structure: 'Most of the European nations had much of the same constitutional laws in common with Germany at that time. But in few other states would the influence be as visible up to the present day.'[42]

Hegel would later acidly note this phenomenon. The ancient system of manorial property that eventually led to the constitution of fiefs and the system of representation in all modern European states had been preserved in Germany into a later epoch: 'The German state succumbed to the convulsions of this transition, the members tore themselves away to become completely independent, the state dissolved itself.'[43] In slight contrast to Majer, Hegel spoke of the 'obstinant adherence to formality' that 'cannot be understood otherwise than as resistance to the reality of union, which is averted by the assertion of that formal essence, and this immutability of the form is passed off for immutability of the thing'.[44]

The recent critical literature has recognized the need to comprehend the process of modernization in Germany in terms that stress continuity as much as discontinuity with the tradition.[45] This is no less true for the history of concepts. Hence, an original division designed to describe imperial and territorial political conditions in a composite state could later be leveraged to explicate the modernity of government and constitution more generally – taking leave of the imperial context. Furthermore, these terms would historically evolve to become applicable in the organization of federal systems. Both Majer and Hegel belonged to this fluid conceptuality. The same tendency can be observed in the framework of reforms. The overwhelming predominance of a legal culture that had existed for many centuries did not cease with the collapse of the Empire on 6 August 1806. Rather, imperial public law could be viewed as continuing unbroken into the Confederation of the Rhine that publicists saw 'as the appropriate means to communicate the tradition of *Reichspublizistik* to a new age'.[46]

Hegel's spiritualization of the imperial constitution into the Germanic World or Germanic Empire belonged to this trend – the fragments of the *Verfassungsschrift* that contained it *in nuce* a last imperial patriotic expression of an epoch in decline.[47] That he developed a universal theory, however, out of the welter of these conditions and not one simply applicable to the Empire or any particular German state can be demonstrated in several ways.

Firstly, it is plain that Hegel never departed from the *forma Reipublicae* as it was conceived in this context: the *personality* of the monarch as the power of the state but also as a regent bound by the universal, by laws. In a word, *constitutional* monarchy resolved the potential contradiction between supreme sovereign power and the individual.[48] To this extent, Hegel had recognized the insufficiency of the Aristotelian paradigm in its particular attempt to classify the imperial constitution. But he also historicized the typology, identifying it with different epochs of world history. Finally, he sublated it into constitutional monarchy, the ultimate expression which contained all of the previous forms.[49] This was most recognizable in his maturity but already in the last pages of the *Reinschrift* this culminating *forma Reipublicae* was defined. Further, it was explicitly contrasted to the Empire where 'legality [is] such that the exercise of the laws of the state does not come about'.[50] Secondly, and intimately related, was his concept of freedom, of the organized legal connection structured through a corporative system of the estates.

The first lectures on the mature *Rechtsphilosophie* in Heidelberg show how Hegel applied the state concept and *forma Reipublicae* developed in the *Verfassungsschrift* to the southwest German states of the *Rheinbund*. A similar spirit oriented his Berlin period – the universal theory now applied to the Prussia of the Stein-Hardenberg reforms.[51] What this shows is how concepts unique to imperial publicism or shaped in that particular context could pertain to entirely different political conditions, conforming to Stolleis's insights about the legacy of the tradition of *Reichspublizistik* and its application to the revolutionary age, how authors used the political situation to 'break the internal resistance to long overdue reforms', 'pleaded for sovereignty, integration of the new parcels of land, and energetic legislation'.[52]

Just as for the Empire, so too for the modern Germanic World, each is a universal – *not* a particular nation state called Germany. With the abdication of Emperor Francis II (1768–1835), the categorization of the imperial *forma Reipublicae* lost all significance. Already in 1800, Majer was teaching something similar: 'The *German* state constitution [*Staatskonstitution*] must therefore be divided into the constitution of the German *Empire* and the constitutions of the sovereign *individual* German territories.'[53] Hence, the development of political theory at the territorial level continued and 'tended predominantly towards constitutional relativism and at every stage of development showed apologists for absolute monarchy as well as for monarchy limited by the estates'.[54] With his theory of *constitutional* monarchy balanced by the estates which belonged to the peculiarity of the Germanic World, Hegel rather aimed at a universal.[55] By contrast, Majer's 'development is an example of how even what is deemed to be relatively recent natural law, insofar as it conceptually systematized and rationalized above all historical circumstances, tended fundamentally to constitutional relativism'.[56]

Meist has made similar claims to the ones I am making here, but with respect to the far more explicit influence of Pütter rather than Majer. If we leave the precise details aside, what emerges in any case is once again the importance of the literary genre of public law on the formation of Hegel's political thought that is traceable to a very early period. Hence, when he was composing the fragments of the *Verfassungsschrift*, so frequently interrupted by the historical events of the period, he most likely would have been revisiting materials that he had already thoroughly studied in Tübingen or heard from the lectern.[57]

To this we can add the not unimportant point that Majer's later theoretical and historical works were being published at the same time that Hegel was reflecting on the status of the imperial constitution, from *Germaniens Urverfassung* to *Allgemeine Theorie der Staatskonstitution* and what can be considered its companion volume *System der Staatsregierung im Grundrisse* (1803) (System of State Government in Outline), to the two volumes of *Teutsche Staatskonstitution*. If *Allgemeine Theorie der Staatskonstitution* covered the *forma imperii* or *forma Reipublicae* and the constitution in the modern sense, *System der Staatsregierung im Grundrisse* detailed the *forma regiminis* (form of government or administration). Evidently, this followed the Pütterian scheme of the subjective and objective organization of sovereignty: 'According to the system of recent theoreticians of constitutional law, the *regent* (le gouvernement) should be distinguished from the *sovereign*.'[58] Finally, as I have noted above, a structural correspondence between these publications and the *Reinschrift* ought to be considered. Hence, Majer is just as natural a source as Pütter and Moser.

3.0.4 Hegel's first *Ständeschrift*, Majer and Württemberg *Landtagspublizistik*

Before moving to our principal investigative tasks, a final point of interest concerns Hegel's first *Ständeschrift* (1798) (That the Magistrates Must be Elected by the Citizens). We can consider what insights might be garnered from a closer look at this manuscript in connection to Majer.[59] This political tract on the Württemberg parliamentary reform discussion continued the initial publicist frenzy surrounding the division of war reparations which had been imposed by the victorious French forces of Jean Victor Marie Moreau (1763–1813) after the defeat of Württemberg in the First Coalition War.[60] In autumn 1796, the estates were assembled for the first time in twenty-six years to discuss the raising of taxes to procure the compensation demanded by the French. This quickly degenerated into a bitter power struggle between the Duke Friedrich Eugen (1732–1797) and the state parliament. Majer had entered the fray of reactionary publicists. His interventions were sharply criticized for putting an even greater burden on subjects and sparing the princely chamber estates.[61] For each of the friends from Tübingen that were engaged with the Württemberg *Landtagspublizistik*, from Hölderlin and Hegel to Isaac von Sinclair (1775–1815) – the only one of their number to have actually studied law in Tübingen between 1792 and 1793 – each would have known Majer (if not his publications) on the issue.[62]

Hegel's first *Ständeschrift* suffered the same fate as the *Verfassungsschrift* – it never went to press. This was in accordance with the advice of an anonymous friend.[63] That it belonged to the same complex of problems as Majer's occasional pieces cannot alter the radical incommensurability of the positions taken. Yet this might be precisely why a comparison between Majer and Hegel in the Württemberg *Landtagspublizistik* is potentially instructive.

Majer's arguments belonged to the uncompromising opponents of reform. He provided the theoretically most cohesive, apologetic-restorative answer to the various parliamentary reform movements. This resulted in a unique historical constitutional typology that categorically rejected universal citizenship and national representation as incompatible with the peculiarity of the diverse German territorial state constitutions.[64] The contrast could not be more decisive. Hegel turned to the people and raised the spectre of revolution should privilege not cede to the greater good and undertake reforms that were clearly in the offing.[65] Still, this was tempered by the fact that the political system he sought to construct was to be grounded in German freedom.[66] Thus, while the stances were diametrically opposed, both remained wedded to an estates system. Hegel belonged to the left wing of the publicists but still wanted to avoid revolutionary activity and sought reforms through the estates parliament.[67]

The first *Ständeschrift* is important for yet another reason. It demonstrates a shift in Hegel's perception that shaped the imperial patriotism of the fragments of the *Verfassungsschrift*: 'he regarded the French demand that the Rhine should be the border, which only came to light in the Rastatt Congress after March 1798, as a "crime" committed by "the custodians of the great nation", thus as a betrayal of the ideas of 1789'.[68] This change demonstrates just how different Hegel actually was to the Jacobin radicals in Mainz. Georg Forster (1754–1794) had basically followed the dictates of imperial French policy in Germany when he 'declared Mainz to be part of the French Republic and the left bank of the Rhine to be its natural and proper boundary'.[69] In the final chapter we will see the extent to which Hegel's organic state was structured as a response to the French Revolution and the enlightened machinery of a centralized state. The development of Majer's idiosyncratic constitutional theory also went directly against the French political system or what he termed the 'autocratic free people's state' (*autokratischen freyen Volksstaate*).[70] The contributions in *System der Staatsregierung im Grundrisse* were similarly critical. From this angle, Majer discussed how the anarchy of the French Revolution was forced to return to the question of state government from 9 November 1799 onwards in order to preserve peace and order and the common security for freedom and property that was characteristic of his proto-sociological concept of the state.[71]

Majer's constitutional relativism was shaped by a different, although related, polemic. National representation, akin to the revolutionary model, was excluded and opposed to the legal principle that held sway among the German territorial states.[72] Perhaps the gulf between Hegel's position and Majer's can be minimized by focusing on how each maintained a corporative ideal and looked to German constitutional history. Given what little survives in the manuscript tradition, Hegel's stance in the first *Ständeschrift* still remains rather unclear.[73] Such a comparison, by weighing Majer's view against Hegel's, might help fill this gap, particularly by exploring whether Majer's writings on the Württemberg parliamentary reform debates were once present in the volumes devoted to *Landtagspublizistik* in Hegel's library.[74]

This subject, despite its clear merit, will not be pursued in this chapter. I am far more interested in investigating Majer's theoretical and historical publications and their possible impact on Hegel's early legal and political thought in the fragments of the *Verfassungsschrift*. This seems to me to be the more rewarding approach to the riddle of Majer's possible influence for the present book.

3.0.5 Outline

This chapter sets itself apart from existing Hegel scholarship on the relationship with Majer by taking the Tübingen publicist as a subject worthy of study in his own right. It begins by analysing his legal and political thought and its assessment in the literature of German public law (Section 3.1). What specific relationship to the last phase of imperial public law did Majer have? What was his connection to the developments of this discipline since Moser and Pütter and how radically did he diverge from them?

Central here is Majer's use of Ludolph Hugo and the doctrine of parallel, which he employed to explicate the imperial and territorial systems. This came down to an appropriation of a famous axiom from the tradition of public law in the sixteenth century, as I detail. In this section, I also examine Majer's discussion of the impossibility of categorizing the imperial *forma Reipublicae*, his introduction of *Unformlichkeit* or the formless form. Through the use of recent imperial history, every attempt had proved in vain. This brought his analysis into connection with Hegel's examination and, ultimately, to the aristocratic body politic of head and members that will be studied in the final section of this chapter (Section 3.4).

I then turn to reconstruct Majer's Tacitus reception in relation to the historical ideas of Justus Möser (1720–94) (Section 3.2), which Majer shaped into a particular historical construction of the ancient imperial constitution and a new method for treating imperial public law. This resulted in an idiosyncratic constitutional theory of the German territorial state, which he opposed to the French revolutionary state.[75] The question of the relationship between this interpretation and Hegel's in the *Verfassungsschrift* is answered through a study of *Germaniens Urverfassung* and the private land appropriation that structures the foundation of the German territorial constitutions for Möser, Majer and Hegel.

I then take this examination a step further (Section 3.3), examining Majer's relationship to natural law and the development of an historical sociology. This section will explore his positive description of German freedom and Germanic law in contrast to both the negative deductions of natural jurisprudence and the Roman law of persons.

The chapter draws to a close (Section 3.4) by studying the most obtrusive connection between Majer and Hegel: the concept of the state. It provides a wealth of evidence to solidify the hypothesis of a connection between the Tübingen publicist and the young philosopher. It turns as well to analyse the history of the *Hippolythus* and its reception in Majer and Hegel, which illuminates the aristocratic *forma Reipublicae*, the formation of private princely law and its connection to the disintegration of the state.

3.1 Assessments and doctrine

3.1.1 Critique

Majer's work, like many key texts from the final phase of imperial public law, has received scant attention in historical scholarship.[76] He does not appear, for example, in the comprehensive overviews of the history of German public law, either in Hanns Gross or Michael Stolleis. Majer is also notably absent from Martti Koskenniemi's latest and otherwise incredibly comprehensive work.[77] For an initial assessment, we have to turn to his more esteemed opponent, Pütter,[78] and then, after the demise of the Holy Roman Empire, to the later transformation of public law literature into the histories of the political and legal sciences, of Robert von Mohl (1799–1875)[79] and Ernst Landsberg (1860–1927)[80] respectively.

With the exception of Majer's fellow Württemberg patriot Mohl, the voices are unanimously critical. For Pütter, Majer's proposal for a new doctrinal system for the teaching of constitutional law, while at first sight appearing to be based on his own popularization of the division between constitutional and government law,[81] 'will [Pütter observed sardonically] hardly be applauded'.[82] For Landsberg, Majer, prone to 'discursive and flat reasoning', represented little more than 'the rule of a colourless natural law' that supplanted the enlightened tenor of Carl Friedrich Häberlin (1756–1808) and the Göttingen School.[83] Häberlin had based his textbooks on Pütter's methodology.[84]

In stark contrast, Mohl juxtaposed Majer, as the principal exponent of a more scientific tendency in public law, to the new historical school of Moser and Pütter and the former's compilative method.[85] Mohl saw clearly the core difference between these publicists. Moser, and especially Pütter, resorted to territorial law when the provisions of imperial public law were lacking – which they often were. This was an appropriate way of arriving at common law. Majer's method of *legal analogy* ran precisely in the opposite direction: the territorial princes possessed their rights in relation to their states because they had the similar position as the emperor in relation to the Empire.[86] This relied on the notorious formula of David Mevius (1609–1670) which had been ridiculed by Moser. There was nothing to be gained for the territories in drawing this out analogically; it signalled a diminution, rather than an extension or more comprehensive exercise, of political power: 'even those imperial estates which do not demand to assert completely unrestricted government and territorial supremacy, at least take it upon themselves that they are less restricted in their territorial government than the emperor in the government of the whole Empire'.[87]

3.1.2 Parallel, analogy and the nameless form

Mevius was a principal practitioner of the *usus modernus* in the seventeenth century.[88] He rejected the notion that the Roman legal tradition should be merely parroted verbatim. Krause listed him as a prominent figure of the early modern historical school, alongside Conring and the *Hippolythus*.[89] The essence of his formula was 'that any Prince you please can have as much power in his territory as the Emperor in the whole Empire'.[90] This is what Majer analysed as 'the well known saying "every lord is Emperor in his own territory"'.[91]

The recent historical scholarship, perhaps unwittingly echoing the trend established by Moser and the Göttingen School, or else correctly recognizing its veracity, has reversed the political emphasis. It has thus essentially acknowledged that even the power of the emperor 'came from his own position as a territorial prince'.[92] Majer's viewpoint, when taken axiomatically, was anachronistic, if not contradictory.

For Johann Nicholas Hert (1651–1710), the editor and popularizer of both Hugo's and Pufendorf's writings, *De statu regionum Germaniae liber unus* (1689) (One Book on the Condition of the Districts of Germany) – in pointed contrast to the *Hippolythus* and its seemingly aristocratic determination of the Empire as well as the debates over the Aristotelian typology – had introduced a new type of state that was as yet unknown to the ancients, as yet lacking any proper name; this nameless type approximated a federal *forma Reipublicae*.[93] Majer had spoken of this nameless form when he stated that he had an intense interest in what Hert had said in his 1689 preface to Hugo's treatise.[94] Moreover, when speaking of 'the multiplication of the organization of sovereignty', Majer implicitly took up Hert's characterization of Hugo's discussion by referring to the nameless form in *Allgemeine Theorie der Staatskonstitution*.[95] Majer even differentiated the nameless form explicitly from the composite state insofar as the latter, in his view, was made up of independent states.[96] The importance of the nameless form, the quasi-federal state at the core of Hugo's theorizations, was that it had a role to play in restraining the politics of *Landeshoheit*. Through an extensive quotation from *De statu regionum Germaniae*, Majer highlighted the importance of legal analogy for Hugo – emphasizing the division between government and constitution: 'Because that is to say, as we have shown that Princes exercise the power which Emperors had had before them, and began to administer Districts in much the same form by which Emperors were governing an entire empire: what else could then be said than that Princes in a certain way portray themselves as an Emperor in their domains?'[97]

In the run up to this interpretation, Hugo tellingly referred to the principle of legal analogy and to Mevius's formula.[98] These were clearly deployed to draw a direct correspondence or *parallel* between imperial and territorial governance. Only through a novel determination of the *forma imperii* or *forma Reipublicae* – and in turn, of the *status Imperii*, the condition of the Empire – was another form of government possible. When publicists cursorily assessed Hugo's work they did so with a particular intention in mind: 'These writers were looking only for what the title promised: the *regionum status*. They did not realize that the *status regionum* was determined by a new insight into the *status Imperii*.'[99] This permitted Landsberg to characterize the impact of *De statu regionum Germaniae* in the following manner: 'The book offers not only an historically well-founded and documented description of the constitutional situation in the territories, but also a *parallelization* of the same with imperial law under the guiding idea of explaining the relationship of the Empire to the territories on a *federal* level.'[100]

Hugo advanced the hypothesis of different and distinct public laws, imperial and territorial, and consequently, distinct modes of political or constitutional law and government or administrative law. He thus stands at the origin of these terms, before Pütter had popularized them: 'Moreover, it seems that also this power was divided between the Imperial State and the management [*administrationem*] of the Territories. For one power is limited by general laws throughout the whole Empire, a different power is limited by particular local statutes.'[101]

Mevius's formula was historically binding as it spoke directly to how imperial conditions shaped the contours of territorial state practice. Hugo was thus able to foresee the direction later imperial public law was to take. Only through the system of imperial sovereignty did the equation of supremacy become possible in the territories or gain any degree of significance. Without the quasi-federal imperial *forma Reipublicae*, there simply was no *Landeshoheit*. The French of the *ancien régime* and Napoleon saw this contingency clearly, thereby forcing the question of complete territorial sovereignty.[102]

3.1.3 Classification and the turn to contemporary history

We are by now familiar with the division between an imperial public law and territorial administrative or government law. Each testified to a complex system of rule that incorporated the estates into a quasi-federative union, as integrative parts of a larger whole. This complex system was evident in both Pütter's *civitas composita* and Hegel's system of the estates, which he viewed as the organization of the true constitution through the ideal of government, contrasted with the *Staatsverfassung* – Hegel having directly appropriated Majer's terminology. By these means, the individual territorial state, according to the classics of public law, fell under an overarching system of constitutional law, yet this did not affect individual styles of governance or, specifically, government or administrative law. In comparison to the actual construction of public authority in the state, even the particular type of constitution was an indifferent matter in the same way as 'the form of administration in general can be equally independent of the state and can be just as irregular'.[103]

> Gradually the dispute over the problematic German state constitution [*Staatskonstitution*] became wearisome, and the constitutional scholars finally calmed themselves with the fact that in practice this point could be left undecided especially since it could be regarded as a merely academic question. On the other hand, the German study of history rose increasingly. Only with regard to the science of constitutional law was there a great lack of proper orientation.[104]

This was precisely how Hegel had begun 'Der Nahme für die Staatsverfassung' and the opening section of the *Reinschrift* when he discussed how the modern public lawyers gave up the task of defining the appropriate constitutional concept of the Empire.[105] This exasperation, however, originated with the earliest gloss 'Sollte das politische Resultat', which discussed the task of the lectern statisticians who sought to classify the type of constitution but could reach no consensus, particularly regarding the traditional Aristotelian forms.[106] Not only did Majer set aside the type of constitution in this context, directly focusing on its connection with contemporary historical development that led his discussion to imperial formlessness; in *Teutsche Staatskonstitution* and *Allgemeine Theorie der Staatskonstitution*, he also developed an aristocratic idea of the head and members that became central to Hegel's analysis. The fact that the imperial *forma Reipublicae* remained undetermined did not help the Empire in the imperial wars against France or the ensuing peace negotiations: 'The most recent history of the German Empire provides the most striking evidence that this lack of form has also given the German Empire a very specific and serious defect.'[107]

The turn to contemporary history proved the deficiency of the Aristotelian typology and the impossibility of assessing the imperial constitution according to the simple types. Majer was forced to speak about the Empire's formlessness as its specific characteristic – the formless form, obviously a contradiction in terms.

This followed the particular evolution from the simple to the complex through the politics of *Landeshoheit* that destroyed the original hierarchy of the imperial state with its monarchy. As with Hegel,[108] this was connected to the principle of religion that introduced a fundamental division into the state with Protestantism.[109] For both authors, territorial supremacy in the epoch of Seven Years' War and the later Peace of Basel was in the process of becoming full-blown sovereignty. It was to this extent that Majer characterized the body politic as aristocratic. A similar trajectory is apparent in the fragments of the *Verfassungsschrift*; it symbolized the final deathblow to the last vestiges of monarchy – though not necessarily to the state as such.[110]

After the Peace of Basel that Prussia had signed independently, the system of territorial supremacy had so utterly undermined the original worldly hierarchy that the integral parts of the composite state were disintegrating into wholly independent states. For Majer, this produced *Unformlichkeit*, for Hegel, the four separate political systems, as we have seen.[111] The rights of the imperial estates, which had been prevented by Emperor Leopold from degenerating into an aristocratic despotism, were now free to determine everything of consequence. In large part, they had become monocratic. Further, the consent of the imperial estates had become a binding constitutional norm in public law: 'Under no circumstances can the Emperor command them to do this; nor can he do the opposite of what they say about the matter.'[112]

This marked the fundamental shift towards the aristocratic body politic that had been idealized by the *Hippolythus* in a markedly different age. Hegel recognized the same transformation in the titles Empire and emperor that contradicted the Aristotelian typological concepts as well as the concept of the state, which, as we will see (Section 3.4), he took directly from Majer. For Hegel, the title of supreme head had replaced the monarch of the originary unitary state and essentially indicated the emergence of the aristocratic body politic – the Doge as the most limited head of an aristocracy.[113]

3.1.4 The exception to the rule: Monarchy and the aristocratic body politic

We have already observed how for both Hegel and Majer the Empire must be viewed as an exception to the rule.[114] While the hierarchical form elsewhere in Europe led to hereditary monarchy with the participation of the estates in legislation, the freedom of the constitution of fiefs in Germany ultimately fragmented, the unregulated growth of *Landeshoheit* and its competition with *Reichshoheit* spawning the chaos of formlessness.[115] The imperial estates not only held a legislative function but also directly exercised executive power – as the true rulers over their districts.[116] In the 1770s, Majer still held fast to the idea that 'the Roman-German Empire is a most restricted monarchy, whose majesty, after the entire territory of the Empire had been fragmented into so many subordinate states, now immediately contains only that which does not fall within the scope of German territorial supremacy'.[117]

Admittedly, this was already a very minimal conception of what imperial public law might look like. Nonetheless, these early works, with their notion of a monarch, however limited, reveal Majer's attempt to accommodate territorial governance within a superordinate imperial system. The same argument cannot be made so decisively for the later works. Instead, they demonstrate the overwhelming effect that the wars with revolutionary France had on the Empire as well as the Peace of Basel in which the example of unrestrained aristocracy made its appearance for the first time in the history of the Empire, making a contemporary case for the importance of the *Hippolythus*:[118]

> In the political condition [*Staatsverfassung*] of Europe the *monarchical* form could become so general and, so to speak, the rule; only this has not remained without exception. The most remarkable example of this, which history presents, is precisely our *German Empire*, which differs and distinguishes itself from all the other states of Europe in such a striking way, by its present form, or, as some think, by its very peculiar *formlessness*.[119]

This concept of formlessness was linked to the political condition, the status quo that had a direct impact on the constitution understood in the modern sense. The members of the imperial body politic assembled in the Imperial Diet behaved towards the head as if he were a restricted monarch, but this came into conflict with reality.[120] Majer concluded *Allgemeine Theorie der Staatskonstitution* with an extensive citation from an anonymous imperial report, excerpted by the *Fürstenbund* publicist Johannes von Müller (1752–1809). This dealt with remarks on the royal Prussian declaration at the Peace of Basel.[121] It traced a history we are familiar with from the previous chapter: the introduction of a form of aristocratic despotism in Germany.[122] This arguably laid the foundation for the first real historical example of Majer's idiosyncratic form of the body politic of head and members, which was peculiarly aristocratic.[123] The imperial struggle against the introduction of despotism was placed in the contemporary historical context by the anonymous author in order to grasp the evolution of what now threatened to become an '*unrestricted and unbridled aristocracy*. There is no telling where such things could lead. The *overextension* of the aristocracy might prepare the opposite',[124] in other words, the monocratic territorial state.

Hegel pursued the same type of logic in the fragments. What had emerged from the forests of Germania and blossomed into a hereditary (restricted) constitutional monarchy with the participation of the estates elsewhere in Europe – 'a centre in which all power is concentrated in a manner freely determined according to law'[125] – fell on fallow ground in Germany. The imperial estates, in the name of German freedom, sought to carve out space for and preserve every aspect of their particular privileges, creating a contradictory system of constitutional law based strictly on the legal positivization of private interests, principally landholdings and estates. This paved the way for the aristocratic body politic of a head and members. Both Majer and Hegel contrasted the head of this body politic to the monarch of limited monarchy.[126] These discussions are distinguished in an important way from Pütter who, when treating the imperial *forma Reipublicae*, still considered it a form of (limited) monarchy, as Majer had done in the 1770s. Conspicuously, the Müller fragment spoke in similar terms as Hegel had done: 'There will no longer be *balance*, a *centre* in the *constitution*; it will succumb to the *overwhelming power of the great*.'[127]

By bringing the imperial constitution directly into connection with the historical devolution of limited monarchy with its right of veto, aristocratic despotism and anarchy had emerged.[128] For Majer, the imperial head could not stand over and against the members. The governing person was the single, indivisible body politic as such. Although the body politic of a head and members did not belong to the simple Aristotelian forms,[129] it was aristocratic since there could be no talk of the independence of the supreme head – no type of *co-imperium* involved. The indivisible could not be divided.[130] Like the collegial system, the Doge of Venice, or even the *princeps* in the Roman republican understanding of the term, the head was the first among equals and no more. In other words, even if it consisted of component parts, sovereignty was vested in a single corporate entity.[131]

Importantly, Hegel saw how the principle of the original German state resided in the idea of monarchy in exactly the same way as Majer did with reference to hereditariness and the hierarchical form.[132] Even so, this was a restricted or constitutional type for Hegel – it was limited by foundational laws and involved the direct participation of the people, through their representatives. In looking to the original Germanic constitution, Majer would have agreed. This type of monarchy could still be observed in the functioning of the Imperial Diet in Hegel's own day, although its substance had disappeared.[133] In the concluding chapter of *Allgemeine Theorie der Staatskonstitution*, Majer traced the history of how the hierarchical dignity of kingship had been deformed in the Empire. Every imperial attempt to maintain the characteristics of hierarchy was thwarted by the princes through the doctrine of ancient Germanic freedom, which in turn destroyed those same attributes in the integral parts of the state all the more easily.[134]

Whereas the European state constitutions were monarchical in general, the Empire had followed a different path of political development: 'the transformation of the hierarchical dignity of kingship' in which the original constitution had been destroyed through the territorial princes and the practice of *Landeshoheit*.[135] Hegel had pinpointed the same development, reflecting as well on the fact that 'Germany, together with almost all the states of Europe, started from a single state' but in contrast to many others has 'disintegrated into a number of independent states'.[136] The issue of religion was discussed in the immediately preceding context, which harked back to how *Landeshoheit* was treated in the early fragment 'über ihre Entstehung', discussed above. Further, the *Hippolythus* had played a central role in diagnosing the true status of the constitution for Hegel: 'In the Peace of Westphalia, this statelessness of Germany was organized; writers such as **Hippolythus a Lapide** have clearly expressed the inner character and tendency of the nation; in the Peace of Westphalia, Germany gave up trying to fortify itself as a secure state power and surrendered itself to the good will of its members.'[137]

Just like for Majer, so too for Hegel: the sovereignty and the public authority of the original German state had been destroyed or had developed in a centrifugal fashion through the extension of *Landeshoheit*. There was no longer a supreme point of union to connect the different members. This is why the title of head or supreme head, while descriptive, remained ultimately empty – a mere simulacrum of sovereignty.[138] Furthermore, as we have seen, it was to be thoroughly distinguished from the idea of the monarch and monarchy – even of the variety that had involved a constitutional provision or 'a constitutional *measure* of *reserved* civil *freedom of the people* in the obedience of the state'.[139] This was what Majer had detailed as explaining 'the spirit of the form' of limited monarchy in contradistinction to the aristocratic body politic of a head and members. Nowhere was the monarchical conception further out of reach than in the historical context in which Majer and Hegel were writing. Both authors had fully recognized this in recent imperial history. The emperor had lost all suzerainty over his supposed vassals, the imperial estates. The pyramid of the feudal hierarchy had been inverted.

Hegel discussed the formlessness that Majer had deduced through tracing the history of the expansion of *Landeshoheit* in comparable terms with respect to the failure to classify the type of constitution. Thus, Hegel brought Majer's reflections on formlessness, on the distinction between the condition, the status quo and constitution of the state in the modern sense, to a methodical closure: 'should Germany be a state, one could only call this condition of dissolution anarchy'.[140] German freedom likewise meant no more than the princely striving after sovereignty.

Hegel would have agreed with, if he was not directly influenced by, Majer's view of the increasingly aristocratic character of the Empire. Importantly, he too considered the body politic among the aristocratic forms, certainly when he compared the imperial supreme head or head to the Doge of Venice as the most restricted cipher of an aristocracy.[141] In limited monarchy the people ultimately remained in a state of subjection. This form was thus characterized by a reservation that ensured the constitutional freedom of the people, but little else.[142] In striking contrast, there was no right of veto for the head of the aristocratic body politic: 'Never will it be possible to reconcile with the spirit of this form of state constitution [*Staatskonstitution*] a real right of *veto* on the part of the *head over* and *against* the *united collective will of the members*.'[143] The historical foundations for this system were rooted in the idea of ancient Germanic freedom: 'the abhorrence of all association in political association and of even the most well-organized political command and rule'.[144] With the survival of the ancient Germanic system of landownership into the early modern period, the fate of the imperial state and the worldly hierarchical form was sealed.[145] Somehow the free association of lords, a mere assembly of private housefathers, had been transferred to modernity:[146] 'This state of affairs, in which not laws but customs united a multitude into a people, in which common interests, not a general command, represented the people as a state, was called German freedom.'[147]

For Majer, manorial aristocracy survived the destruction of both the ancient constitution and Germanic freedom. It was based on blood inheritance and really did not deserve the honorary title of aristocracy which, as he noted, dealt rather with the organization of the state among the best and the wisest – according to the ancients and Aristotle.[148] Historically, the rights of non-ratification and veto had been uninterruptedly held in the possession of the emperor. In this way, the conception of limited monarchy had initially held ground. What was now being claimed by the anonymous author of the imperial report was that the emperor could never again determine the part the imperial estates played in the government of Germany – imperial power was reduced to mere learned opinion.

The consequences were extreme. What Emperor Leopold had managed to prevent by using his veto against the Imperial Diet on 3 February 1671 to block the introduction of aristocratic despotism against the territorial estates could no longer be held in check.

There was no longer a centre of the constitution that could do anything collectively for the German nation. With no balance left, only the power politics of the German freedom that Majer directly identified with the imperial princes remained.[149] Hegel spoke in similar terms. In his affirmation of the Third Germany *and* given the historical context framed by the Peace of Basel, what was formerly called German freedom ought to take safeguards against both Austria and Prussia as the most powerful imperial estates.[150] Majer then began to trace the genealogy of the aristocratic body politic of head and members to the deepest roots of Germanic antiquity.[151]

With this fundamental shift, the typological ideal of the *Hippolythus* was becoming a reality – the German Empire truly emerging as an aristocracy.[152] This was the historical lesson to be learnt from recent imperial history. What it meant was the ultimate victory of the imperial estates over the emperor. This was the final step in 'the transformation of the former imperial princely districts into *independent* principalities and *states*'.[153] This was a history that could be linked for Hegel no less directly to the first publication of the *Hippolythus* in the seventeenth century: 'The Peace of Westphalia consolidated the principle of what was then called German freedom, namely the dissolution of the Empire into independent states, reduced the number of such independent states, the only remaining possibility of the whole gaining superiority over the parts, and strengthened the separation by merging them into larger states.'[154]

In this context, we can observe how history was interpreted retroactively by Majer and Hegel. The period under discussion overlooks the fact that the Empire continued to function quite successfully and reform itself for another 150 years. But it must have been practically impossible to look back on things without bias. The consequences of the Peace of Basel were everywhere visible, only to be compounded by the losses of the First Coalition War and the Second Coalition War.

At this point it is necessary to return to Mevius's formula, mentioned previously, and to examine its significance for the growth of territorial power. In the process, I will assess its reception in Majer and Pütter and how the latter's interpretation of it attests to the significance of territorial supremacy in his thought.

3.1.5 The interpretation of Mevius's formula: A final assessment of Majer

From the perspective of the theoretical works of early German publicism in the seventeenth century, Mevius's formula was part of a prolonged political struggle that sought to free the territories from the overarching authority of the emperor. More recent historiography of German public law claims that this predominantly involved the reception of the concept of *maiestas* in the territories, where it began to be equated with the much older custom and practice of territorial supremacy.[155] Although in actual usage *Landeshoheit* was never exercised unrestrictedly, the temptation to draw analogies with sovereignty, both territorially and imperially, was obvious – the concepts at times overlapping.

Perhaps the principal appeal of Mevius's formula was that it ran in two directions, simultaneously. On the one hand, it attributed an excessive degree of power to the emperor; on the other, this could then be wielded, and to the same extent, territorially. For Hugo, as we have seen, the *parallelization* between the emperor and the great territorial lords was historical fact. It may have no longer applied to the position of the emperor, but it still structured the system of imperial public law and the territorial government law that existed alongside it.

Pütter had also contemplated Mevius's formula historically.[156] The path to territorial supremacy was first paved when the imperial estates began to exercise the *regalia* and rights that they had been granted by the emperor in their own name. Both Hugo and Majer had asserted something similar, highlighting the extension of such imperial dignities to the territories.[157] The widening of these rights involved both legal jurisdiction and executive governance. Thus, what had initially only remained in the hands of the emperor, who maintained a right to intervene and supplant local courts with imperial ones, was in the process of undergoing a decisive transformation.

Given the precise phrasing, Pütter was undoubtedly following Hugo when he stated that 'the imperial power seemed to be in general competition with that of the imperial estates'.[158] This was nothing other than Hugo's famed *summae aemula Maiestatis*.[159] Or so it seemed. It is noteworthy, however, that Pütter had inverted the terms of the rivalry. This speaks directly to the character of his system of public law. For Majer, something similar coloured the Göttingen publicist's interpretation of Mevius's formula.[160] All of this allowed Pütter to draw the opposite conclusion: 'that according to the German imperial constitution, the imperial power in all of Germany can do exactly what the authority of the territorial lord is able to do in every territory'.[161] This corresponds fittingly to Pütter's ironic legacy in imperial public law that gave primacy to the private law of the princes in his theorization of territorial supremacy. He was responsible, more than anyone, for legalizing the very historical developments that were to be the undoing of the imperial constitution.[162]

For Hugo, if the correspondence between the imperial and territorial rights of rule proved true, this was a consequence of usage observed in history, which had much more to do with custom than with written law. This was the significance behind Mevius's maxim: 'By these means the newly formed system of territorial supremacy, for which there were few positive legal sources, was supposed to be endowed with the analogy of positive imperial state law.'[163] This chimed with Hugo's observation that 'it is difficult … to write anything about territorial supremacy, since it is not limited by laws and to such an extent is untested by written law'.[164]

It seems a rather open question as to whether Majer's effort to solve the contention between territorial supremacy and imperial sovereignty, which relied on Hugo and the principle of legal analogy, fared any better than Pütter's historicization of the unfolding of territorial supremacy. Indeed, the positions are not as opposed as Majer depicts them in *Teutsche Staatskonstitution*. Still, at the turn of the century, we can see how the functional division between constitutional and government law allowed for a different type of politics: 'This legal analogy was only meant to be limited to *government* law, but not at the same time to be interpreted as referring to *constitutional* law.'[165] In this way, Majer considered the rights of sovereignty of emperor and Empire heterogeneous.

The cleft between the state constitution and government was not supposed to touch the concentration of power in a single centre or imperial sovereignty. Its devolution, as we saw above, however, was unstoppable. Historically, *Landeshoheit* belonged to the broader concept of lordship – the feudal hierarchy forming a vast imaginary that functioned analogically and reached into the deep recesses of Germanic prehistory. Yet Majer emphasized the grievous error in reversing the direction of Mevius's formula. This falsified the nature of imperial authority, reducing it to contingency. Yet it was overwhelmingly symptomatic of existing conditions that saw a far more nuanced discussion of territorial supremacy in contrast to imperial sovereignty.[166] As Majer stated, against Pütter: 'In order to get further and more quickly behind the historically correct meaning of this proverb, I also note that it does not by any means say: "*Imperatorem tantum posse in imperio, quantum quilibet status in suo territorio*", and it is not at all a matter of indifference to invert the order of the persons in the saying.'[167]

With this, Majer set out to critique the principal public lawyer of the last phase of imperial public law. His use of Mevius's formula followed Hugo – providing a positive legal basis for territorial supremacy anchored in the imperial public law of the nameless form of the quasi-federal state. What may have worked analogically in terms of governmental law simply did not run in the opposite direction. Although the imperial and territorial legal systems were not utterly incommensurable, the doctrine of sovereignty, its legal basis in emperor and Empire that rested on the religious principle of the *sacrum imperium*, was far too heterogeneous to allow for a direct equation to be drawn with that of territorial supremacy.[168] *Summa potestas* meant very different things at the levels of constitution and government:

> In *constitutional* law the disparity between the two (imperial and territorial) systems of sovereignty is so great that I consider it almost impossible to compile them without confusion.[169] I have always been of the opinion, and still am, that this [Pütter's] compilation is not readily justifiable according to the rules of good method, at least as far as *constitutional law* is concerned, or the *German state constitution* [Staatskonstitution], which amounts to the same thing; this is due to the great disparity between the constitution [Konstitution] of the Empire and that of all individual imperial territories.[170]

For Majer, the fact that 'the sovereignty of the individual German lands is an entirely new creation, and quite different from that of the Empire'[171] had wide ramifications for the applicability of territorial materials at the level of imperial public law. Quite simply, from his perspective, it was incorrect to use common territorial law as a means of completing the forever-unfinished project of imperial public law.[172] The use of territorial provisions could not be adopted as common law in the absence of imperial law.[173] Thus, Majer had 'recognized that a mass of facts does not yield a common rule of law; rather that these must be derived from a common basis'.[174]

In conclusion, Majer – and indeed in his penchant for hierarchy – only accepted that the provisions of imperial laws and treaties, the statutes and customs intended for imperial government, were justified materials for common territorial law: 'But this is because the imperial princes stand in the same relationship to their states as the Emperor does to the Empire.'[175] This was the significance of his use of Mevius's formula and legal analogy, as we have now seen; it was also integral to his doctrine as well as his thorough rejection of both Moser's and Pütter's supplementation of imperial public law, which drew on common territorial law, and their methods of legal analogy. Whereas 'the *government law* of the whole Empire and the sovereignty of the individual German territories may somehow be put together', constitutional law was another matter entirely.[176]

The diversity of the types of territorial legal order listed here shows definitively how the German states were too distinct to provide a norm, territorial supremacy functioned differently in discrete governmental or administrative systems.[177] Thus, the *summae aemula Maiestatis* was an antagonism – it meant that no strict equality existed. To this end, Hugo had cited the Lutheran imperial patriot Dietrich Reinkingk (1590–1664): '*Princes are empowered in their own domain, though an Emperor is empowered in the whole Empire by comparison to the law – not by equality and fullness of power*.'[178] Majer reproduced the quote.[179] It attested to the relatively subordinate conceptual status of *Landeshoheit* in comparison to the full extent of imperial sovereignty – at least prior to the emergence of *Unformlichkeit* after the Peace of Basel and during the epoch of the Second Coalition War.

We now have an idea of Majer's method. We have also seen how the use of recent imperial history permitted him to draw out the consequences that were undermining the imperial state. This was comparable to the approach adopted by Hegel in the fragments of the *Verfassungsschrift* which also started from the impossible categorization of the imperial *forma Reipublicae* and ended in a denunciation of the aristocratic body politic of head and members. Initially noting that barely a single historical example of this type existed, by *Teutsche Staatskonstitution* it had become a norm. Following Justus Möser, Majer discovered a primitive origin to explain the system of territorial supremacy and the respective state constitutions of Empire and imperial estate. To this I now turn.

3.2 Justus Möser and Tacitus: Agriculturalism and the ancient constitution

3.2.1 Obscure antiquities

For Johann Jacob Moser, the approach Majer followed to comprehend the German constitution had without doubt fallen prey to the 'most abstruse German antiquities, which are of no use to anyone, but merely serve as curiosities'.[180] Such things for Moser were completely unsuitable for shedding light on the imperial constitution.

In the twilight of imperial public law, this critique went unheeded. The use of such antiquities had become a trend that could not be reversed. Thus, Majer traced the freedom of the ancient constitution in his interpretation of Tacitus in *Germaniens Urverfassung* drawing direct analogies with the imperial and territorial constitutions as they existed in his own time.[181] For Hegel, the antiquity of German custom was viewed in similar terms. It had become an interpretive method by which to explain how the formation of a state in Germany had run aground. The primitive constitution did not raise universal public law to a principle of the state. It was unwilling to sacrifice the individual interests of its members and remained in that condition into much later historical periods. This led to a fundamental contradiction. The imperial state structure was founded on the ancient custom that had united individuals against the state: 'The rights of separation from the whole, which the individual estates have won for themselves, are sacred and inalienable rights, on the preservation of which the entirety of what we call the state structure rests.'[182]

The granting of historical authority to the early Germanic period over later constitutional conditions had never been accepted by the earlier generation. What we can observe with Majer and Hegel, however, is how this had now become a standard for the interpretation of the origin of the imperial and territorial constitutions and a way of justifying or criticizing how contemporary political conditions had developed.[183]

The drawing of such direct analogies in *Germaniens Urverfassung* was already apparent in the second volume of *Teutsches weltliches Staatsrecht abgetheilt in Reichs- und Landrecht* (1775) in which the imperial system was conceived of as having developed from a mass of small free tribes, that very peculiarity that would ultimately prove so fatal to the Empire.[184] In this work Majer spoke of German freedom and *not* ancient Germanic freedom, as he later did.[185] This in part attests to the conceptual equivalence of the terms, which we also find in Hegel. Majer's discussion was critical and laudatory at the same time, just like Hegel's, and thus not the one-sided glorification of Montesquieu and the earlier seventeenth- and eighteenth-century German Tacitus enthusiasts.[186] There is a comparable notion in Majer as to how German freedom involved a negative fate; it left the smaller estates prey to the larger and destroyed the possibility of political association. There is also a developed analysis of how German freedom, when subjected to the imperial courts, demanded an ever-greater share in the constitution of the same.[187] Hence, just like Hegel's depiction, what ought to be central to state authority and state power had, in coming under the influence of ancient German freedom, remained private property.[188] This Majer considered under the manorial system of landownership that followed the insights of Justus Möser, providing a novel way of interpreting the system of territorial supremacy, as we will see.

Hegel spoke in very similar terms as Majer. And he did so historically, viewing the Empire as an exception to the rule, in which the gradual disappearance of the monarchical determination of the sovereignty of public authority and the legal and political division introduced into the state by the imperial estates eventually dissolved the Empire into an aristocratic complex of head and members.[189] With constitutional monarchy, however, Hegel also viewed this form as characteristic of the Germanic contribution to world history. But, as we saw in the first chapter, the historical principle that the Germans had given to the world outlived them.[190] Speaking of the development of modern European constitutional representative monarchies, Hegel connected every one of these states to the Germanic World: 'Most of these states were founded by Germanic peoples, and their constitutions developed from the spirit of these peoples. In the Germanic peoples every free man originally had a share in the deeds of the nation, just as his weapon was counted on, so also his will.'[191]

At every level, Majer could be viewed as an important source for Hegel's break with the glorification of ancient German freedom: 'The original, unrestrained character of the German nation [which] determined the iron necessity of its fate.'[192] Meist intuited as much, observing that Hegel might have followed the same tendency if not *Teutsches weltliches Staatsrecht* first hand: 'Majer's explanations give no less the impression that they could have formed a direct model for Hegel's deliberations.'[193] Either the Tübingen publicist's admiration of Tacitus was at the basis of Hegel's perception of the ancient constitution or the work of the Roman author himself – or both. In any event, as Rosenzweig stated, we must recognize that 'the views on the ancient Germanic sense of freedom were common property of the age'.[194]

3.2.2 The genealogy of the composite state

In both *Allgemeine Theorie der Staatskonstitution* and in the first volume of *Teutsche Staatskonstitution*, Majer followed the typology that had been introduced into imperial public law by Hugo, Pufendorf and Pütter: simple and complex forms of state. This enumeration was the only way to account for the Holy Roman Empire of the German Nation where, 'through the emergence of *territorial supremacy*', it became 'a *composite* state or a *system of states*'.[195] For Pütter, the complexity of rule in the Empire necessitated the separation between imperial public law and the law of the territories with which we are so familiar. He treated the rights of the German princes as a separate subject, drawing from the sources of both private and public law. The fact that Germany was divided into so many different states, each with its own government, but was still considered a composite state that further united these different polities into a common system, resulted in the peculiarity of the imperial constitution and the unique character of its public law.[196] With this, Majer wholly agreed. It was the quest for the origin of this system that set him on the path that would lead him to Tacitus and Möser.

For Pütter, the genealogy of the composite state reached back into the murky history of the Middle Ages. If only one could acquire a more exact knowledge of earlier epochs, perhaps a more precise image of the imperial constitution might come into view.[197] The emergence of territorial supremacy – and thus consequently the seeds of the composite state system – was a gradual process that could in no way be reduced to a single piece of legislation. Even so, Pütter could not resist the temptation of emphasizing the years 1220 and 1222. That was when Emperor Friedrich II (1194–1250) first granted to the ecclesiastical estates and then to the secular estates 'general assurances of their sovereign rights'.[198] For Pütter, this amounted to the formal recognition that it was impossible to hinder the growing power of the imperial estates.

Majer referred explicitly to Pütter's discussion on the visibility of the ancient constitution in the present day.[199] He saw his own achievements as meeting the task of reconstructing the ancient constitution, even if inadequately so.[200] He praised Pütter's call to research the historical lacunae of the Middle Ages as an essential prehistory of the imperial state constitution. This was central to his own efforts that sought to grasp the Empire as it had developed since the Middle Ages and, in *Germaniens Urverfassung*, in the thickets of historical antiquity with Tacitus.[201] Yet he took issue with Pütter's more general methodological approach, which considered sovereignty partly subjective and partly objective, thus dividing the entire corpus of German public law into constitutional and governmental law.[202] But as we already know, it is deceptive to see this as the real issue because Majer himself took up these terms.[203]

3.2.3 Novel principles for territorial law: Primitive private land acquisition

For the Tübingen publicist, history had become an unwaveringly positive source that spoke to the legitimization of constitutional form. This methodology had initially emerged in Göttingen with the discipline of *Reichshistorie*.[204] That said, *Reichshistorie* was not political in the sense used here. It in no way set out to justify existing conditions. For Majer, however, it did and it went along with natural law that, used selectively, could warrant the manorial property that pre-existed the state.[205] This gave further historical significance to the division that had been introduced into the imperial constitution.

Majer had come into direct contact with Möser's historical-sociological innovations. These had rejected natural law in favour of an ideal-typical representation of primordial landownership to explain the very formation of political association. This established completely new (contradictory) principles for public law – private land acquisitions and agriculturalism were given primacy, shedding light on the character of the imperial constitution that had been undermined in the process. Without doubt, this provided Majer with additional materials to explain the private legal character of princely law.

The consequences were fully apparent to Hegel. They explained the nature of German public law as such, which he considered indistinguishable from private law. The originary private land appropriations, described so extensively by Möser and Majer, were based on power and acquisition. The saga of German freedom detailed a history in which force preceded law. This definitively shaped the later character of the imperial constitution for Hegel, affecting the very possibility of the Empire as a state:

> From this idiosyncratic behaviour, which alone was called freedom, circles of power over others were formed, according to chance and character, without regard to a universal, and with little limitation from what is called state power; for this, in contrast to the individual, was almost non-existent. These circles of authority became fixed as time went on; the parts of the universal power of the state became a multiplicity of exclusive property, independent of the state itself, and distributed according to no rule or principle.[206]

Such ideas could be intricately related to Majer's prehistory of manorial property and agriculturalism in *Germaniens Urverfassung*, 'the raw concept of freedom … the possession of private property against the estate of the unfree and the poor',[207] just as much to Möser's political and legal thought which Majer directly followed with the ideal of a golden age of German history.[208] Möser had looked to the past for his political ideal and found it in the freedom and equality of property-owning landlords and farmers of the earliest epoch of German history.

The freedom of corporate equality and cooperative autonomy among original property owners in *Osnabrückische Geschichte* (1768) (The History of Osnabrück) was projected by Majer in *Germaniens Urverfassung* into the ancient Germanic prehistory described by Tacitus which, alongside *Teutsches weltliches Staatsrecht*, most likely informed Hegel's perceptions of German freedom.[209] The descriptions of this earliest epoch are the common fount of each of these authors, however far their political interpretations stand from each other. What is emphasized in each case is the private character of the original association. Thus Friedrich Meinecke (1862–1954) was able, from another perspective, to discuss the influence of Möser on Ludwig von Haller's (1768–1854) foundation of politics as based on a series of private law relationships.[210] Hans Maier has noted the unexpected similarity between Hegel's description of German public law as a private legal system or mere collection of private rights and the Bern patrician's inegalitarian patrimonial order, although the accents are obviously different.[211] With the loss of the Empire, the object of Möser's imperial patriotism disappeared. But in other respects, his doctrine found credence. This is the case with his determination of law as historical evolution that found an echo in the Historical School of Law against the dictates of rational jurisprudence. The same can be said of his notion of cooperative autonomy. This was carried forward into the communal reform of Baron vom Stein, even if regional rather than corporative, more emphatically into Otto von Gierke's (1841–1921) association doctrine of the state.[212]

Möser's sway over Majer has been mentioned in the historical scholarship since Landsberg.[213] Still, an exploration of the relationship has never been undertaken. Majer's interpretation of Tacitus and the earliest epoch of Germanic prehistory focus on landlordship and the originary appropriation of land for private usage. This was a central facet of Möser's thought, which resulted in a historical-sociological redescription of the origin of political association in agricultural prehistory.[214] For Majer, this resulted in the predial conception of the state that consisted of an association of landlords – comparable to the hierarchical inegalitarian state doctrine of Möser.[215] Ultimately, this provided a new foundation for *Landeshoheit* and a way of explaining the dissolution of the imperial state and the weakness of its public law. It was a model that Hegel followed.

3.2.4 Tacitus and the ancient constitution

Alongside Möser, *Germaniens Urverfassung* followed in the footsteps of the earlier humanistic movement of Tacitism. This was part of a fundamental shift that had already occurred in the early modern period away from certain classical authors of republican Rome, such as the historian Livy (59 BCE–17CE) and the statesman Marcus Tullius Cicero (106–43 BCE), towards Tacitus and Seneca (5 BCE–65CE), the authors of the Principate.[216] In part, this spoke to a change in literary tastes, away from the Renaissance and towards Mannerism.[217] Yet, at a more profound level, it attested to the transmogrification of the political. Seneca taught how to live under Nero (37–68 CE). Tacitus's language dictated how to speak around tyrants, in the military camp and on the battlefield. He was brief and cryptic, indicating the connection between things while also encoding them.[218] In this way, these authors more readily responded to the historical context and the political pressures of living under the early modern princely territorial state.[219]

Admittedly, this was the Tacitus of the *Annals* and the *Histories*. It was not the Tacitus of the earlier *opera minora* to which the 'remarkable effort in ethnography' of the *Germania* belongs.[220] This was the manuscript that stood at the centre of *Germaniens Urverfassung* and laid the foundation for the myth of Germanic or German freedom. Tacitus had used the history of the Germanic tribes and the description of their systems of election and assembly to critique life under the Roman Empire. By Majer's time, scholarship brought the Roman historian's brief information about the original constitution of the Germanic tribes into genetic continuity with the constitutional reality of the imperial and territorial estates. In this way, Tacitus's portrayal of the ancient Germans could serve as a norm to measure entirely different political realities and answer the needs of particular political intentions.[221]

The discovery of the *Germania* in the fifteenth century represents a far more important watershed in reception history than it does in terms of the historical study of the ancient Germanic lands and their peoples.[222] Also ruled by ethnographic preconceptions, it is of little historical use.[223] The *Germania* is structured into a first ethnographic part and a second part, a catalogue of the constituent elements of the various tribes.[224] In *Germaniens Urverfassung*, Majer provided an overview of the editions and commentaries of his own period.[225] This showed how Tacitus had been transformed into an author of the highest standing among publicists, supposedly depicting the ethnographic commonplaces of the original Germanic peoples.[226] Since the latter had no writing system, there was a complete lack of indigenous primary sources for a historical reconstruction of the ancient constitution.[227] It was thus necessary to rely on classical Greek and Roman writers.[228] Majer listed Strabo (63 BCE–23 CE), Caesar (100–44 BCE) and Pliny (23–79 CE): 'But in Tacitus *Libellus de situ moribus et populis Germaniae* we have a source that is all the more valuable because it was the intention of this already excellent historian to describe the condition of this crude Germanic people to his nation, which was in the highest degree of culture.'[229]

Due to Tacitean style and presentation, however, Majer admitted a certain obscurity had arisen.[230] He added there were other issues to consider, such as the fragmentary nature of the Germania, possible falsifications copyists may have introduced into it,[231] whether Tacitus himself had first-hand knowledge of what he was describing,[232] and, finally, the Latin translation of ancient Germanic terms and (legal) institutions, which could cause confusion.[233] On this latter point, Majer turned to a citation from the preface of the first edition of Möser's *Osnabrückische Geschichte*: 'What I felt most was this, that our language had become a betrayer of noble liberty and had lost the expression which fitted my notions. The oldest historians of Germany did not write in our language and gave the strong German body a completely foreign colour.'[234]

Further, as Möser insightfully added later: 'Therefore we can only make general assumptions about the origin of our ancestors, their first settlements and wars.'[235] In the same context, he repeated a statement made by Tacitus from the *Germania* on the lyrical character of Germanic histories:[236] 'Perhaps they have had their heroes and poets just as well as other peoples and both deeds and songs have been forgotten.'[237] The young Hegel spoke in comparable, if not even more critical, terms about the loss of ancient Germanic history and its culture and customs: 'Christianity has depopulated Valhalla, cut down the sacred groves and eradicated this popular fantasy as a shameful superstition, as a diabolical poison, and in its place has given us the fantasy of a people whose climate, whose law-making, whose culture, whose interests are alien to us, whose history has absolutely no connection with us.'[238]

For Majer, language was a natural distinguishing mark of tribes and attested to the fact that the Germanic peoples belonged to the few indigenous nations of Europe.[239] Yet, decisively, the countless names Tacitus listed for the different tribes revealed a striking overall lack of political unity. The second half of the *Germania* contradicted the very idea that such an entity existed.[240] Quite simply, there was no common name because there was no common connection between the various peoples. They were merely a mass of small associations that could barely be described as having a culture and certainly not a unified one.[241]

Hegel interpreted all this in a very similar fashion. First, there was the power that preceded law: the private property the individual had acquired and consequently transformed into a right separate from the whole. Second, there were the customs that had united the Germanic peoples without a principle of common command.[242] Majer concurred, pointing to 'the disgust against all state-societal connections and even the well-ordered command and sovereignty of the state' which he traced to the ancient Germanic free assembly.[243] This corresponded to how 'the individual stood for himself, unbowed by a universal, without subservience to a state, and how his honour and his fate were his own concern'.[244] Hence, the customs Tacitus had described were based on separation rather than the universality of law, which could be identified directly with the authority of the state. The inner logic of German freedom had led to a particular form of constitutional development: 'The individual member of the body politic owes his authority in the state, as well as his rights and duties personally to his family, his rank, or his guild; and the rank, guild, etc., has them from the chance of former times.'[245]

This latter point referenced what was common to Möser, Majer and Hegel: the originary private land appropriation that formed the earliest epoch of Germanic prehistory that continued to have a hold on later constitutional conditions. This period of primitive accumulation appeared for Hegel with those spheres of power, character and chance. It became the essential basis of territorial supremacy in all of its guises. Hegel could have gleaned this simply by looking at the relevant titles of those volumes dedicated to the subject in Johann Jacob Moser's *Neues teutsches Staats-Recht* in which he could observe how 'legislative, judicial, ecclesiastical and military authority are mixed, divided and combined in the most irregular manner and in the most disparate portions, just as diversely as the property of private people'.[246] In striking contrast to Moser, however, what was common to Möser, Majer and Hegel was the perceived origin of *Landeshoheit* in the mists of the antiquity described by Tacitus. This contradicts other assertions made simultaneously by Majer as we have seen.

To prove the theory, Majer emphasized how the various Germanic tribes were not nomadic. They lived neither from robbery, nor hunting and fishing. Rather – and instinctively following Möser – *they were agriculturalists and cattle raisers*.[247] In this way, the ancient accounts of Caesar, Pomponius Mela (d. 45 CE) and Strabo, which argued for the collective or communal nature of property among the ancient Germanic tribes, were utter falsifications.[248] Caesar's statement about 'the most warlike nation among the Germans' from *The Gallic War* (58–49 BCE), the Suebi tribe, categorically contradicted the model of private landownership and thus must be in error.[249] Referring to another passage about the Germanic peoples more generally, Caesar stated: 'For agriculture they have no zeal. No man has a definite quantity of land or estate of his own.'[250] Tacitus must have carried more weight than Caesar. The Tacitean description of the ancient Germanic constitution directly agreed with Möser's conceptions, as 'he tells us about so many special circumstances from the Germanic constitution, which alone, but even more so when taken together, make Caesar's reports unbelievable and leave almost no doubt about a common *private* property'.[251]

Evidently, in this context, Majer sought confirmation for his own hypotheses and those of Möser in Tacitus's account of the ancient constitution. What Tacitus had described could be used to interpret present historical development.[252] The refutation of Caesar's assertions was of the highest necessity, as they wholly contradicted the agricultural hypothesis and common private landownership. To prove Caesar wrong, Majer used a source equally, if not more, suspect in its claims to be doing history – but this cannot concern us here.[253] The essential task, as he saw it, was to trace in detail the ancient legal relationships outlined in the *Germania*. From here, the archetype of the original private *cum* political association would come fully into view.[254] In this way, continuity could be established from the ancient Germanic period down to the patrimonial and freeholder states. What was collective or communal was simply primitive private appropriation as such.

For Majer, this entailed a fourfold division: between those who have and those who have not, which resulted in a system of manorial rule (*Grundherrlichkeit*); the landed property of the free and the unfree that are bound to them in every way; the family system; the national association; and the institution of warlike retinues (*Institut der kriegerischen Gefolgschaften*).[255] All land in ancient Germania was composed of districts, either great or small, in the hands of *private* families or persons. This is what laid the foundation, as Hegel saw it, for the personal rights and duties that then belonged to family, rank and guild: 'The enduring status which those possessions gradually acquired produced a multitude of rights which, without unity and without principle, could form more a collection than a system.'[256]

The concept of common private landownership as a form of primitive accumulation was equivalent to independence, to the freedoms of the ancient Germanic constitution. This was viewed as an historical antecedent of the estates for both Majer and Hegel. Majer had raised the status of the private legal relationship into a fundamental organizing principle: 'the entire ancient Germanic private and national constitution was based solely on *common private land ownership*'.[257] Clearly, this shows how his conceptual framework was influenced by later legal scholarship, the *Aufklärung*, Roman law principles of absolute property and the German common law (*Gemeines Recht*) tradition.

3.2.5 Private law as public law

At an historical level, all of the preceding demonstrated how the system of estates had come into being through the jurisdiction of district courts that were hereditary as well as territorial assemblies and parliaments.[258] Obviously, confusion would abound in this particular case between the distinct status of private and public law. In essence, these spheres were indistinguishable. So-called public office was a private inheritance. The earliest period of Germanic prehistory, characterized by private land appropriation, was thus epoch forming. Known for its oral legal tradition that far preceded the reception of Roman law, once the latter was received, this came at the behest of the powerful private landlords determining the very character of the national association as well as the German zeal for law.[259] This highlights once again what we saw in the second chapter, that it is deceptive to think of a hard separation between Roman law and Germanic customary law as the former simply codified the ancient property rights of the latter.[260] As Montesquieu put it, Roman law was a universal personal law, a territorial law.[261] For Hegel, this historically shaped every aspect of the imperial constitution in his own time, undermining the universal idea of public law:

> The German state structure is nothing other than the sum of the rights which the individual parts have withdrawn from the whole and *this* justice, which carefully guards that no power remains to the state, is the essence of the constitution. ... According to its original legal basis, therefore, German constitutional law is actually a private law and political rights are a legal possession, a property.[262]

Osnabrückische Geschichte had proposed an entirely new method of historiography, looking at private landownership as *the* distinctively constitutive part of the nation, which consequently gave public law another face. This provided unity to history, as Möser saw it, as well as another way of looking at the later formation of territorial supremacy or the aristocratic despotism that took its place.[263] Möser referred to the initial period of landownership in which private rights were identical with political rights.[264] Not only did this form the basis of *Germaniens Urverfassung* and its interpretation of Tacitus, but it also found a distinctive echo in the fragments of the *Verfassungsschrift*. It was writ large in Hegel's judgement that 'German public law is therefore a collection of private laws'.[265]

The imperial estates were involved in litigation at the imperial level, having appointed the judges trained in Roman law. Ludolph Hugo had already isolated this paradox when he stated that 'Let the judicial decisions concerning the right of Territory be established between the regular successions of Empire as an example of private judicial decisions.'[266] To put it in Möser's language: 'The real associates established their rights themselves, every associate, without difference in estate, follows the Mark court, which he appointed, the judge whom he elected.'[267] Hegel discerned the same tendency and observed critically how it influenced the very functioning of the judiciary, defining the character of public law: 'The administration of civil law and that of state law are mixed in the authority of the imperial judges; state law and private law are subject to the same courts; the imperial courts are the supreme courts of appeal for civil law cases and for state law.'[268] Such contradictions were omnipresent. For example, Ludolph Hugo had seen just how useful private law was when dealing with territorial law: the imperial estates, involved in litigation in the imperial courts, appeared as private persons.[269]

All of this was part and parcel of 'the obstinacy of the German character' for Hegel, 'their drive for freedom' that 'prevented the Germans from becoming a people subject to common state authority'.[270] Their exaggerated respect for (private) law was their undoing.[271] From this angle, he was able to perceive how primitive accumulation, the spheres of power and chance, determined every facet of the later imperial constitution. This emboldened the principle of separation that dictated the nature of any form of union. For Hegel, the character of the universal was the same as that contradiction-in-terms Majer had identified as *common* private landownership. In this way, 'the imperial association through the imperial courts is not an association, Archduke Karl spoke of it in appeals for defence, but imperial courts a) are not powerful, have no authority, b) the state power is not the subject of a court, namely with regard to the distribution of state power'.[272] By contrast, the courts merely upheld the principle of complete separation through raising the status of private law as pre-eminent over the political. This came into direct conflict with the concept of the state: 'political powers and rights are not state offices calculated according to an organization of the whole, the deeds and duties of the individual are not determined according to the needs of the whole'.[273] On the contrary, they were calculated on the basis of private property which determined the personal rights and duties of family, rank and guild.

Möser's description of primitive agricultural life and Majer's analysis of the ancient history recounted by Tacitus led to organic or corporate concepts and essentially to the patrimonial and freeholder ideas of the state. Each was encapsulated in Möser's stock theory, where governance consisted of political shares based on private landownership, which from a novel historical-sociological perspective seemed to be proven by the continued existence of large landowners (the nobility) and rural agricultural systems (farms) in European history:[274] 'The Europeans, as agriculturists, laid … the ownership of a farm designated for each estate, called a manse, as the basis of their union. Only the true owner of such a manse was a member of the nation'.[275] Private property was thus the essence of all political capital.

From here, it is easy to grasp how Möser's political and economic theory was founded concretely on a viewpoint that saw historical society as consisting of nothing more than a collective association of freeholders. It was a revolutionary theory. It coincided very precisely with what Majer had traced in *Germaniens Urverfassung* – the rural, agricultural, archaic and primal ideal of common private landownership that he saw in Tacitus. Only with the gradual decline of the Carolingian constitution did this golden age begin to decay. It was telling that this was also the epoch in which feudalism first began to make its appearance. For Möser, this had exchanged genuine possession of property for mere services.[276]

Concrete rural agricultural existence was a way of life originally free of feudal ties and manorial duties.[277] Möser waxed lyrical about hereditary allodial lands and the political intimacy of the freeholder on his tract of earth and his participation in the popular assembly, just as Majer had done as well as Montesquieu before him. Through the inheritance of fiefs passing 'to more distant relatives' these 'justices that were patrimonial' resulted in the development of mediatory institutions between the crown and the lord that resulted in the corruption that characterized the later feudal epoch.[278] Irrespective of historical change, the free association of private landowners and their legal communities ought to remain the guideline for interpreting constitutional evolution as well as contemporary constitutional reality. By the turn of the century, for Majer the idea of a political share in governance stopped at the landowning nobility, the only true constitutional people of what he termed the freeholder state, which served the interests of the Germanic estate of the free:

> The age-old Germanic difference between the estate of free and unfree – which was originally just *private* law, has now also become *constitutional* and now gives constitutional preference in the territorial constitutional systems against the territorial subjects and the dependents of the landlords. The landowners and landlords appear at the provincial assemblies, deliberate and decide, entirely for themselves and in their own name: and *in no way* as *deputies*, *representatives* or *mandataries* of their dependent citizenry and peasantry.[279]

In this way, Majer precluded the possibility of any other occupants possessing a political share: the Territorial Diet was based strictly on the ownership of land, the predial principle, and was thus alien to the idea of national representation – even representation as such.[280] Here was the true genesis of the patrimonial and freeholder states in which private law had become constitutional. These state forms in Majer's later political thought were utterly opposed to that history of representation that Hegel had constructed as the unique character of the Germanic World or Germanic Empire. For the young philosopher, this had been the logical historical outcome of an increasingly complex political life in the modern state, retaining the connection to constitutional monarchy, legislative power shared in part with the estates.[281]

Majer was able to re-envision the doctrine of imperial public law by giving primacy to *common* private landownership. Obviously, this idea came into contradiction with the notion of a public law as such. Indeed, Majer's emphasis was on a *private* primitive accumulation, the *Urverfassung*, that shaped the bases of territorial governance. He set out to prove the political logic at work in the territorial states, connecting it to Tacitus's account of the Germanic tribes. In the process, Majer had sought to prove Möser's thesis on originary agricultural existence. Hegel too took these issues into account in his excursus on the obscurity of the spheres of power and chance that he saw as fundamentally shaping the character of the imperial constitution, making public law a private thing. The private legal nature of landownership that determined the constitution moved to the centre of his analysis and, for Hegel at least, essentially contradicted the concept of the state.

3.3 The predial principle: Historical sociology, patrimonial and freeholder states

3.3.1 New political foundations

In his later works, Majer still employed natural jurisprudence – not least with his concept of the state, to be analysed in Section 3.4. But he did so in a much more restrictive fashion. Möser, whom he followed closely, even utilized the contract theory – *the* shibboleth of eighteenth-century natural law and public law – in order to arrive at his stock theory.[282] Whereas universal natural law was based on negative liberties, the patrimonial and freeholder states made the existing private rights of lords positive or constitutional. The contract which established the political order did not take place at a single (unspecified) moment in time between every free individual but rather over time between large landowners and agriculturalists. With this move, a foundation for the state quite different from the redescription of natural right in the state of nature as a real sphere of contractual relations had been provided. The anthropological basis that saw the mutual co-determination of individualist and social traits disappeared and was replaced by the positive historical fact of manorial existence that demonstrated how the state was based on *real* landownership. Given the veridicality of this history, readily demonstrated by the primitive existence of landownership and the forms of governance that these had acquired, this represented a historical-sociological transformation of contract theory.

Unlike natural law, the formation of patrimonial and freeholder states did not imply depoliticization. They were to be clearly distinguished from those based on universal rational principles. Majer still discussed the philosophical foundations of natural jurisprudence and its deduction of the state. But, in the main, it now also represented a specific historical form. It had appeared with the autocratic free peoples' state, the type of state in revolutionary France, with its constitution based on the national legal principle. Founded on resolution, agreement and the contract of a free people with themselves, sovereignty was conceived as a shared property: 'Thus the people's free right of disposition over the same is the legal principle on which the legality of the constitution and every form given to it by the people is based.'[283] This description was important, as it provided the counter model to the patrimonial and freeholder states.

Majer contrasted the egalitarian and inegalitarian models at some length. Each followed a separate derivation, which, in the main, emphasized either philosophical or historical origins. The speculations of philosophy and the facts of history radically diverged. If the first elaborated a doctrine of rational freedom and national sovereignty, based on individualism, the second showed the utter subordination of human beings to their bodily nature which tied them to the ground and soil, for nourishment and necessity. For Majer, this had a factual basis reaching back into human prehistory which confirmed the antiquity of the manorial system of rule.[284] Through this, he was able to legitimize a certain type of political order indicating not only its validity but also its real-historical foundations which could be readily rediscovered in the structure of the existing constitutions in the German territorial states against the rational-based deductions of natural jurisprudence.[285]

What was implied in this context was a growing gulf between the doctrine of rational natural law and what can be termed a nascent form of historical sociology that, nonetheless, emerged out of it.[286] The rational philosophy of natural law was thus only one way of theoretically deriving the state – and a much later one at that. This could also be done with reference to historical reality: 'In this way, the system of fundamental manorial lordship that is to be presupposed for the constitutional people always grants it the same independence and freedom as that in which philosophy allows mankind to be born, to unite into peoples and to give the states founded by them their constitution according to the principle of national law.'[287]

All of this formed part of Majer's constitutional relativism. This meant that there were those states, like revolutionary France, based on the people, organized on rationalist egalitarian and national foundations as well as those based on the predial principle – the freeholder and patrimonial – which were equally as lawful and legitimate and also could be considered as based on a peculiar national (territorial) principle.

Majer's productions at the turn of the century set out to justify the *forma Reipublicae* of the German territorial states in this fashion. The constitutional people were the ancient Germanic estate of the free. Structurally inegalitarian, these were the private landowners and agriculturalists possessing tracts of land and everything held on them, including any subject population, the estate of the unfree.[288] Constitutional relativism allowed for the legitimacy of any given type. This simply had to be measured in terms of how well the point of departure was taken up and preserved, how the common good, the objective character of sovereignty, was maintained. This still led to rather paradoxical looking formulations that appeared to present a mixture of private and public objectives: 'The authority and command of the landlord has his private benefit as its purpose. The latter, together with the multitude of his subjects and serfs, is nothing less than in an actual society, by which a *common good*, a common welfare, should be promoted.'[289] Insofar as the common welfare remained an objective, the patrimonial and freeholder states were distinctive legal orders which could also be affixed with the national principle.

3.3.2 Ulpian's dichotomy

If natural law and its contract doctrine shaped the egalitarian foundations of the revolutionary state, the freeholder and patrimonial models developed out of an interest in preserving the private property of large agricultural holdings, manors that historically became estates. In the first instance, this occurred among multiple landowners; in the second, with a single lord. Perhaps the stunning paradox of Majer's private law association, constructed on the foundation of common private land appropriation, is that it had been theorized in the epoch when the cleft between public and private law, so sharply distinguished by the Romans, was first appearing as an integral part of the political consciousness of publicists. This was nowhere more apparent than in his own works.[290]

In *Allgemeine Einleitung in Privat-Fürstenrecht überhaupt* (1783) (General Introduction to Private Princely Law in General), Majer still discussed this issue in terms of representation, a compound of private and public law. The prince was the private owner of *representation* but as the *representative* of the state, he acted in a public capacity. The private and the public were thus deftly separated and united. Later, Majer's follower and Hegel's Heidelberg colleague Karl Salomo Zachariae (1769–1843) would claim that the *ius publicum Europaeum* was little more than a legal relationship between governing *houses*: 'that, in a word, it was regarded more as a private law of these houses than from the point of view of a public law'.[291] Yet this is hard to square with Majer's view. In quoting from the Halle public lawyer Justus Henning Böhmer (1674–1749),[292] Majer emphasized how the domestic order of the house was alien to the public authority of the state: 'Those actions are private that have no relation towards the condition of the state [*statum*]. … The private affairs of individuals chiefly pay attention to *domestic* advantage, but *public* affairs pay attention to the safety and preservation of the entire state.'[293]

In this way, territorial authority could not be directly identified with the *dominium* that, as we have seen, was current in the tradition since Ludolph Hugo furthered the legal status of the *cives imperii*. It was simply impossible to equate domestic and political rule. If public law relates to the organizational structures that govern social and political life, private law ought to be restricted to the interactions between individual members as exclusive legal units (persons).[294] Or in other words, since political authority fell under the *potestas publica*, resorting to Roman private law to understand it was a contradiction: 'The evil in the state by which the public is treated in an unnatural way as something private could be called privatism; it is called *despotism*.'[295] For Majer, this meant the subjection of public law to the private benefit and private purposes of the prince.

What all of this meant was that even the patrimonial state – insofar as it was a *state*, that is a *public* legal order – could in no way have a merely private legal character. The emphasis on household rule and its communication to the political was pathological, despotism being standing in contrapuntal opposition to politics and modern constitutionality. This sets a different tone to the whole debate. The predial principle under which the association of lords or the single lord organized the constitution of the freeholder and patrimonial models did not have private interest as an end. This was simply due to the fact that they had established a state, the theoretical object of public law. Private law, in becoming constitutional, had lost its purely private legal character. The words of Krause are instructive in this respect: 'the German public constitution emerged from armed associations of free housefathers into a public state [*civitas*]'.[296] With its aim to ensure public security and the mutual enjoyment of private property and freedom, state sovereignty was clearly an issue for public *not* private law: 'The manorial relationship rests solely on a mutual private advantage; the civil state relationship is aimed at the common good.'[297]

For Majer, neither public law nor private law could be treated objectively – only *subjectively*, that is, according to their respective legal persons. There was thus the (moral) legal person of the state to consider and the private legal persons that stood arrayed in opposition to it.[298] The Holy Roman Empire of the German Nation, as we have seen on numerous occasions, had introduced a complication with the *cives imperii*. To this extent, Majer spoke of *private* princely law. This entailed the private law of succession and the law of the princely families, each of which had direct implications for public law. Still, almost everywhere, as we have seen, Majer's work conformed to the insight that 'the dichotomy of Roman imperial law into public and private law was understood around 1800 in a new constitutional and philosophical climate'.[299] Perhaps this was nowhere more the case than in his careful demarcation between the immediate property law of *dominium* in Roman law and its counter concept *imperium*.

3.3.3 The distinction between *dominium* and *imperium*

The patrimonial state may have been constructed on the basis of the private property of a single landlord as an *absolute* legal foundation, but '*to govern* remains once and for all, even in *patrimonial* states, something different from *to dominate* [*dominari*]'.[300] Thus, it was necessary to make a crucial distinction between *dominium* and *imperium*.[301]

For Majer, the confusion between these two Roman legal concepts remained a sore point for recent constitutional law, as he put it in *Allgemeine Theorie der Staatskonstitution*.[302] This repeated an earlier observation: 'Such exercise and administration of the power of society itself cannot at all, due to the nature of things, consist in the use of one's property (*usus rei suae et dominium*) but in rule (*imperium*).'[303] As he definitively expressed it: 'for the sake of the great difference between the persons, the things of the state must be distinguished and separated from the private things of the prince among the actions, transactions and things belonging to him.'[304] Here is the distinction between public law and private princely law. If direct continuity were established between the private and public persons, despotic governance emerged. The private law concept of *dominium*, the legal order of the house, was in no way applicable to political rule: '*To govern* [*regere*] is always something actually different from *to dominate* [*dominari*]; and *dominium* may and should never be mixed up or interwoven with *imperium*.'[305] Further, if the state was identical with everything that belonged to it, it would be bereft of its legal personhood and cease to exist.[306] Thus, similarly, the private legal order was preserved. Majer's theoretical contribution to patrimonialism is idiosyncratic. His patrimonial state is a distinctive concept of *public* law and not a taxonomy of overlapping private legal orders of subordination and superordination as we find with the Bern patrician Haller.[307]

For Majer, there were distinctive reasons why *dominium* was not an acceptable way of interpreting rule for a public legal order like the state. The most obvious was that *dominium* was directly related to the house (*domus*) and to the household rule of the head of the family (*erilis*) – just like its cognate to dominate, which he rejected, as we saw above. *Herilis* or *erilis* in the medieval period took on a range of meanings related to the system of fiefs. Etymologically connected to the Frankish *hero*, it meant lord, maitre and seigneur. Thus, as a substantive *erilis* signified seigneur, lord; adjectivally, seigneurial – of a lord.[308]

Majer referred critically to such notions by citing a lawyer of the *Reichskammergericht* Georg Melchior Ludolf (1667–1740) who had stated that the German territorial states could be governed *modo magis herili*.[309] What was at issue here was the transference of the despotic rule of the head of the household over his slaves and its passage to the political that, for Aristotle, marked the boundary between legitimate and illegitimate forms of public rule.[310] This was nothing other than the aristocratic despotism we have explored in detail in the previous chapter. It was the symbolic of Roman law that for Hegel corresponded to the paternalistic ethos of the German territorial state.[311] In this respect, Majer had broken with Ludolph Hugo and the tradition of the *cives imperii*.

With Haller, the more famous theorist of patrimonialism, the emphasis was decidedly different. The despot and despotism were legitimate concepts which could be used politically. This reached back to the original meaning of the term as the head of a household or head of a family. It implied a reduction of content, while simultaneously denying real constitutional implications.[312] It justified the authority of the ruling patricians over the inhabitants of the countryside as a great and necessary law of nature.[313] There was no constitution or state in the proper sense of public law, but rather an infinite number of private legal relations. Haller had constructed a feudal imaginary in which every law which threatened the private right of the lord was anathema. Prioritizing the immediacy of rule, the property owners and landlords decided for themselves and in their own name: 'territorial estates do not represent their subjects, but only themselves'.[314] What was originally characteristic of private law, family and estate had thus become immediately *constitutional*.[315]

Yet Haller's 'will to particularization'[316] was against every form of public law or the administration of justice which must 'be regarded as much a duty as a right of the public power [*Macht*], which rests just as little on the discretion of individuals to entrust it to an authority [*Macht*] or not'.[317] In other words, the state must be a wholly independent public legal order which pre-existed the private individuals that fell under its power. It was in no way based on the private legal order. Majer's approach remained far too close to natural jurisprudence and universal public law to fall in line with Haller's conceptions. Quite simply, the patrimonial idea of the political in which a single landlord expanded his *dominium* or estate into a form of territorial supremacy transformed the nature of the private property involved into a public power: 'the owner can no more be ascribed ownership of the members of the state and all that belongs to them, or of the state itself and all that belongs to it, than he can be ascribed ownership of the administrative right to the corporate authority or suzerainty in the true sense of the word'.[318] The historical growth from the manor or private estate to state had truly altered the nature of the legal and political relationships. Only the moral person of the state was invested with sovereignty, even if the law of succession was strictly bound to the house or dynastic politics outlined in *Privatfürstenrecht*.

To establish the exact contours of public law, Majer identified three exemplary types of individual overlordship and separated them from social overlordship. In the first case, there existed the rule of parents over children, the household power of the *pater familias* over his servants and *despotism* – a type of supremacy that sought to make political society submissive to a single individual's interests.[319] Majer counterbalanced these private law notions to the political ideal type: 'Social supremacy is the supremacy of a society, which, for the sake of its commonwealth and its promotion, is vested in it over its individual members, considered apart from their social relations and as individual persons.'[320] Obviously, this followed Ulpian's dichotomy.[321] Majer sought to account for an *independent* element directing the activity of the patrimonial prince which forbade treating the subjects of the state as objects of private property. The degeneration of a patrimonial state occurred when the princely estate was no longer organized for the benefit of humankind but solely for the household.[322] If a strict correspondence was established between the individual prince and the state, the latter would lose its moral personhood and cease to exist; by definition there is no public thing – no *res publica* – if that thing is treated as a private possession.[323]

What remains constant in all of these discussions, from Majer's early to later works, is what passes under the name of the civic freedom of the people or the common good – like Pütter, the true theoretical object of universal public law.[324] Majer had thus averted the despotism that had been popularized in the theoretical literature of his time.[325] The administration and the exercise of power by a patrimonial prince still had the common good of the state as an end purpose.[326] It is thus difficult to see how Majer's nuanced position on *dominium*, despotism and their differentiation from *imperium* which recognized the categorical division between private and public law could be viewed as a passage or preparation for Haller's patrimonial state theory.[327] Rather, with his refined notion of a public legal order and corresponding concept of the state, Majer laid the foundations for Hegel's comprehensive grasp of public law and its distinction from private law, property and private rights.[328]

3.3.4 Private princely law

Majer's treatment in *Allgemeine Einleitung in Privat-Fürstenrecht überhaupt* was not primarily concerned with the moral person of the state, as we can observe from the title. The moral person of the state implied sovereignty, explicitly related to public not private law. Private princely law, however, formed a separate and indeed liminal case – also with respect to the private law applicable to subjects and citizens.[329] The legal personhood of the prince was itself demarcated: 'rights and obligations must be divided into constitutional and private laws and rights'.[330] In other words, there was private law related to the dynasty or house and the public law of the state.[331] The two disciplines were separate or, as Majer also put it, autonomous.[332] He further reflected on constitutional law in two respects: internally, which corresponded to the common good (*ius publicum internum*, *inneres Staatsrecht*), and externally, in the foreign relations to other states (*ius publicum externum*, *auswärtiges Staatsrecht*).[333] For those Hegelians among us, these are familiar conceptions that divide the textbooks Hegel lectured on in his maturity.[334]

What Majer's comprehension of the Roman dichotomy cannot alter is the fact that for the earlier political tradition continuity had existed between the house order of rule and the political. Indeed, they were often synonymous. For example, the Pandectist formulations of Johann Gottlieb Heineccius (1681–1741) and the rationalism of Wolff continued to view the creation of the *civitas* along the lines of its central foundation in the domestic life of the household economy.[335] The household was envisioned as an ordering principle that, as with much else, followed a Roman legal concept: *familia*. This represented the seat of private property which was strictly codified and regulated under Roman private law.[336] Shaping the legal contours of the space in which personhood and the citizen-subject unfolded as a private sphere, as a *res privata*, this was intrinsic to the early modern state – akin to a form of domestic government.[337] These ideas coincided with the traditional conception of civil society *in the political sense* that was composed of ruling estates (*Herrschaftsstände*), families or houses which consisted of the corporate associations of lords.[338]

Majer knew these concepts very well; he deployed them in his analysis of representation in the early 1780s. In a monocratic state, which corresponded to the majority of the German territorial states, the prince possessed the right of representation – *personally*. This was in harmony with the existing basic public laws of the state.[339] For Majer, such property could take on many different modifications partly through the prince limiting its exercise to this or that extent, due to the consensus needed to be maintained between himself and the corporate body of territorial estates. In this context, *dominium* actually did play a distinctive role. Majer could not alter the nature of feudal law that had codified these relationships: 'The right of ownership to which such representation is entitled is either divided between two persons, for instance according to *dominium directum* and *utile*, or it is sometimes undivided, sometimes halved to be shared among several, or it belongs perhaps to a whole family.'[340]

What cannot be lost on us in this discussion is that the private part of princely law concerned the mere ownership of the right of representation, the law of succession. This may have indeed emerged as a dynastic right, but it still remained something completely different from the public capacity of the representative as an actor in the state, which involved *imperium* not *dominium*. As we have already observed, the difference between the two concepts was at once significant and highly consequential.

While the Roman legal concept of *dominium* was indivisible, monistic as it were, nonetheless, there remained two different types of property in the *Libri Feudorum*, which was included with the three original law books of the *Corpus iuris civilis* (*Digest*, *Institutes* and *Codex*).[341] Originally having emerged in Lombardy, the Northern Italian part of the Holy Roman Empire, the *Libri Feudorum* dealt with the rules governing the relations between lord and vassal. In it, *dominium* was leveraged to explain how the feudal order functioned more generally – direct property was the possession of the lord; the use of property was in the hands of the vassal.[342] In the interpretation of the constitutional relationship between the majesty of the emperor and the territorial supremacy of the imperial estates, *dominium directum* and *dominium utile* were used.[343] Majer employed the concept to explain how the private right to representation in the state, essential to private princely law, was divided: into the hands of the territorial prince and into a heritable property.

For the historical literature, the reason why this private law theory took on such a prominent role in the German principalities was because the public law of the *sacrum imperium*, of emperor and Empire, did not apply analogically to the territories.[344] Majer had turned private land appropriation into a fundamental constituent of public law, establishing the greater importance of the patrimonial and freeholder states. Hence, the hereditary property of Germanic freedom, following the law of succession, was the essential element. Even once the state had been formed, this private dimension remained as it codified the possession of political office and the right to exercise it that followed the logic of dynastic inheritance. It was in this way that private law had become constitutional: 'The nature of this legality consists in the fact that the relationship under constitutional law and its obligations are not determined by general, actual laws, but in the manner of civil rights; the relationship of each estate to the whole is something particular in the form of property.'[345]

3.3.5 Positive freedoms: Germanic law versus Roman law and natural jurisprudence

In contrast to Roman law and natural jurisprudence, the Germanic legal order of custom, tradition and oath contained purely positive freedoms, for example, 'in Germanic law, the status relationship was that of a free man, whose status, through voluntary subordination to a military chief, who looked out for his livelihood, was not lowered but raised, particularly when the chief was a prince or a king'.[346] Such positive liberties were worlds apart from Roman law in which freedom consisted only of *not* being a slave, *not* being a servant or *not* being in service.[347] Among the Germanic tribes, as Tacitus put it, the 'inferior status of freedmen is a demonstration of freedom'.[348]

Majer had analysed this passage from the *Germania* in order to distinguish the precise character of Germanic freedom and to differentiate the system of bondage from slavery.[349] Hegel did the same, distinguishing the very idea of an estate, which grew from the system of fiefs, from slavery.[350] Tacitus refined this point further in another of the *opera minora*, the *Agricola*, when he ridiculed the Roman imperial system: 'Nero's freedman Polyclitus, so far from being able to negotiate with rebellious Britons, is mocked by them because "the power of freedmen was as yet unknown, since freedom still flourished among them"'.[351] In Germanic law, freedom was not a quality attached to the person. By contrast, in Roman law it fell under the discussion of status: 'He is a free born who, as soon as he is born, is free [*ingenuus est qui statim ut natus est, liber est*]'.[352]

Justus Möser highlighted just how strange it was that Roman law had to express itself in this fashion. It betrayed the attempt to distinguish the noble from the freed: 'liberti in solo respectu ad manumissionem' (the status of freedmen is defined or understood exclusively in relation to the act of manumission).[353] On the other hand, for natural jurisprudence all were free in the state of nature just as all were unfree by comparison in the state. Hence, the two legal doctrines could only speak of freedom in negative qualities or terms. This is how we should understand Hegel's attack on Roman law as an equalization of estates. Thus, Manfred Riedel (1936–2009) got it wrong when he stated that it is a 'historical falsity' to say that 'Roman law in its cultivation of the concept of the person in no way annuls the distinction between classes [sic!] named by Hegel but rather establishes this very distinction in the title *status libertatis*'.[354] Hegel's point is the same as Möser's and Majer's in their criticisms of the Roman law of persons: 'equality existed in the Roman world – because it is linked to the despotic principle. – Under a despotic government, all subjects are slaves'.[355] Further, in Roman law one is always either born free or freed, in each case distinctions made on the basis of slavery.

Heineccius had arrived at a similar insight, as Hegel noted in the mature *Rechtsphilosophie*: 'as far as what in Roman law is called the law of persons is concerned, a person is only considered to be a person when he has a certain status (**Heineccii Elem. Jur. Civ. §. LXXV.**); in Roman law even personality itself is, as compared to slavery, only a *status*, a *condition*'.[356] In the oral additions and handwritten notes, Hegel expanded on the idea further by quoting directly from *Elementa juris civilis* (1728) at much greater length in order to arrive at a comprehensive understanding of the Roman law of persons and its relation to slavery:

> §75. A human being is one to whom belongs a mind endowed with reason in a human body. A person is a human being decreed with a certain status. §76. Status is a condition whose legal warrant people employ by differing law. §77. And so, the slave is a human being, is in addition a person, insofar as he is inspected with the state of nature, but with reason his *civil status* is 'faceless'. §89. He is a free born who, as soon as he is born, is free – and yet he could be sold by his father – earlier killed.[357]

In this way, the Roman expressions *ingenuus* and *ingenuitas* – the Latin terms for the nobility, those born of a free father, the freeborn – simply could not do justice to ancient Germanic freedom, which contained something more.[358] Majer used the same argument in his analysis of modern revolutionary philosophy, 'the natural freedom of man'.[359] Natural jurisprudence was 'connected with a purely negative characteristic'.[360] The natural equality and independence it hymned were vacuous. By contrast, the corporate character of the Germanic estate of the free possessed something wholly concrete in landed property, inheritance by birth and the allodial system, a type of ownership that was absolute and irrevocable: 'The estate of the *free* in ancient Germania was therefore a *real* estate by *birth*.'[361] Even the relationship of the vassal to the lord was based on freedom: 'Everywhere the vassal (in the specific meaning of the word) had to be a freeman, not subordinate to the patrimonial power of the lord.'[362]

The inegalitarian system of estates in general was viewed as a bulwark against despotism, the extension of the house over the public order. By comparison, as we have seen on numerous occasions with Hegel, despotism was identified with systems of abstract equality, with Roman law no less than the French Revolution that had abolished the system of estates and its relation to the system of fiefs and representation. For Majer, 'landlordship and manorial rule was thus the entire epitome of all the *power* and *authority* over the *land* and the *people* measured on it arising from unrestricted *property rights*'.[363] This was the nature and spirit of the freeholder and patrimonial models: '*He who sits on another's ground is also his, belongs to him and is lorded over [verherrt], is a pure subject*.'[364] The combined resources of Tacitism, imperial history and Möser's historical sociology provided the Tübingen publicist with the tools needed to construct a novel doctrine of the freeholder and patrimonial states.

It was a strange, perhaps somewhat uncanny construction. The historical continuity between the ancient constitution and the much later genesis of territorial supremacy becomes almost tangible. In the same respect, the division between the citizens – the imperial estates of the Holy Roman Empire – and their mere subject populations was proven in a vast historical antecedent. In this way, Pütter's remark from the second volume of *Litteratur des teutschen Staatsrechts* (Literature of German State Law), about how German public law had retained a continuity with its past, readily observable in the political present, took on almost fantastical proportions.[365] The legal principle of the earliest epoch of Germanic prehistory had become a living and present connection.

All of these Germanic elements were contrasted, in like manner, to separate constitutional systems. In this case, it was not Roman law that was at issue but rather the French revolutionary constitutions based on the national principle or the contract of all with all.[366] The territorial constitutions of Germany were grounded on the predial principle – *private* rights that had become *constitutional* insofar as the state was initially brought into being for the preservation of the private property of the house or the single lord. Once the state had emerged, however, as we have observed, the public legal order could not be avoided *imperium* supplanted *dominium*, which was, appropriately, relegated to private law where it belonged.

With respect to the national legal principle, revolutionary natural law and its premise of rational individualism, Majer enjoyed pointing out the difficulties involved in maintaining the form of mass democracy. If the people were to enjoy the advantages of a state, they would have to concede in some form or fashion the fictional character of their claim to be ruled by their own will. Popular sovereignty must inexorably give way to government. The immediacy of the general will could only be practically conceivable for the smallest type of state. The ideal of popular sovereignty inevitably augmented bureaucratic rule in the autocratic free peoples' state where, 'in the hundreds and thousands of *integrated parts of the state*, sovereignty with the government of the people must be left solely to *state officials*'.[367] In a similar way, the true exercise of sovereignty fell to the people's representatives in the French National Assembly: 'This *national assembly* with *autonomy* is the *spirit* of the form of such an autocratic free peoples state.'[368] It was quite impossible to maintain this state without representation, a binding necessity: 'The *more numerous* the people are in a state formed in such a way, and the more its direct government requires *uninterrupted activity*: the less it can then assemble itself otherwise than through deputies and *representatives*, who are set up by the people according to certain divisions, which then remain *assembled* together.'[369]

The contours of this argument were reproduced in the *Verfassungsschrift*.[370] Hegel too emphasized that representation was a necessary phenomenon due to the size of modern states which also required the concentration of political authority in a single centre for administration.

3.3.6 Lordship and bondage

The predial principle that Majer put forward as characteristic of Germanic freedom, along with its rather exacting description of the estate of the unfree, the bondage and dependency of the resident farmer, serf or peasant, introduced a new problem: servitude. How could one square the complete subordination of the serf with the account of Germanic freedom? Majer did not mince words: 'Mankind lay so deeply oppressed in *free* Germania, chained by its unfree state of birth to the yoke of servitude and the harshest rule of manorial aristocracy.'[371] There simply could be no talk of liberty when it came to those bound to the land, the estate of the unfree. Tacitus's eulogy to the freedom of the Germanic tribes fell on deaf ears, even when compared to the decadence of imperial Rome. Still, Tacitus admitted that the kind of slavery existent in Germania was based on household rule and that each controlled their own holding and home.[372] Hegel followed a similar logic and conceived it as a basis for the family principle at the foundation of his early speculative system of the state.[373]

This provides evidence of the Germanic character of Hegel's developing idea of the state. It follows a conception in which the expansion of individual rights and property is of a contractual nature which would eventually become part of abstract right and modern civil society. The ideas for this can be discovered in the relationship of authority that had 'turned feudalism into an approximation of the *Rechtsstaat*, at least in comparison to pure patrimonialism with its juxtaposition of traditional prescription and appropriated rights, on the one hand, and arbitrariness and discretion on the other'.[374]

For Majer, the problem of bondage was difficult – even impossible – to solve. The very legal principle he identified as characteristic of the ancient Germanic constitution and had later conveyed as the essence of the German territorial state more or less forbade it. To do otherwise would be equivalent to falsifying history. Yet there was a further division at the level of the estate of the unfree. Majer read this into Tacitus in an attempt to distinguish ownership over the body (*Leibeigenthum*) or serfdom (*Leibeigenschaft*) from mere bondage (*Hörigkeit*). On the other hand, he wanted to make explicit a distinction between these Germanic concepts and the Roman notion of the slave – *servus*.[375] For him, Tacitus suggested as much 'by distinguishing the *Libertos* and *Libertinos* from the described Germanic unfree persons (*Servis*)'.[376] In this, he followed Möser who also cited Tacitus's account of the notion of the freed, which he rightly recognized applied to those who had been set free or emancipated through manumission. This did not apply to the Germanic concept.

Möser repeated Tacitus's insight about the low opinion of freedmen among the Germanic tribes, even in comparison to the serf: 'Therefore the freemen [sic!] among us are worse off than serfs who depended on heirs, half heirs and cotters; and such a serf would not easily give his daughter to such a freedman.'[377] Moreover, Möser asserted that a freedman was hardly to be recognized as a category (*genus hominem*) among the Germanic tribes – just like Tacitus. Freed was that which was excluded from common defence.[378] It was thus, by far, better to belong to the land – to be unfree and a serf and to come under the jurisdiction of a lord and be protected.[379] For Tacitus, what was once the epitome of Roman republican virtues had disappeared and was only to be found among her most bitter foes: '*Libertas*, once the Roman ideal, becomes the greatest threat when possessed by others, and that is why the Germans matter.'[380] Hence, Tacitus played off the status hierarchy of Roman law against the Germanic estate of the free, which was in no way related to the law of persons. In Ancient Rome, slaves were part of the household and had to be maintained as such.[381] By contrast, the serf had to support himself and his family even if he finds himself as part of the family inheritance on the lord's land.[382] The serf was certainly no freeholder, but he had a holding even if in loan. This betrays, in part, the distinctiveness of the Germanic concept and its imbrication in the constitution of fiefs.[383]

What remained true everywhere was that those who were unfree were poor. This poverty was what led to bondage. In order to cultivate a plot of land, the peasant required not only the land from the lord but the means with which to work it. In this way, he obliged himself and his family to bondage. Yet he was also able to pass the land on to his descendants and in so doing the following generations would, as part of the land and property, no longer have to enter into bondage.[384] Through an increase in population, through the development of the towns and cities, we can have a glimpse here of the origin of the later subjects of the princely territorial state and the territorial estates. Majer arrived at the following conclusion: 'That German serfdom meant something similar to the abominable Roman concept of *servus*; that a *specific* burden of servitude was connected with it, and that it made the serf or peasant absolutely incapable of having anything of his own against his master – does not seem to be historically correct.'[385] Hence, Majer sought to emphasize the heterogeneity of the Germanic estate of the unfree – the German slaves or serfs described by Tacitus – from the Roman legal concept of slavery and the discussion of freedmen (*Libertos*) and the sons of freedmen (*Libertinos*).

From here Majer turned his attention once again to Tacitus, remarking that the descriptions of the *Germania* were mainly concerned with the estate of the free. Yet, as the Roman historian noted, it is 'difficult to distinguish between master and slave by the delicacy of their upbringing; they live together among the same flocks and the same earth floor until maturity sets the free apart and valour claims them'.[386] This was Hegel's original dialectic of lordship and bondage. The willingness to risk death in the struggle for recognition set the free apart from the unfree, distinguishing the absolute labour of death from mere labour to meet needs: 'in reality, on the other hand, the inequality of life is posited, and with it the relation of lordship and bondage; for in reality there is form and individuality and appearance, that is, difference of potencies or of power'.[387]

This division was central to *System der Sittlichkeit*. Hegel remarked that the people organized for war in absolute ethical life were equivalent to the criminal in private law insofar as both infringed the sanctity of private possession.[388] Thus, the collective defence of property was identical to the raw concept of the state – its conflagration in the ethical order had another significance entirely. War belonged to the first estate, the Germanic estate of the free. The estate of the unfree, however, was connected to war through its relation to manorial property – its service in the system of needs to the first estate. The estate of the free for Hegel, just like Majer before him and Weber after him,[389] was the estate with the true capacity for politics; it had separated itself from necessity through the inheritance of property and wealth. This provided for the independent livelihood and the potential indifference to private property that was proper to the political: 'To this estate Aristotle assigns as its business that for which the Greeks had the name *politeúein*, which expresses living in and with and for one's people, leading a universal life belonging entirely to the public.'[390] Organized for the absolute labour of death, it was indifferent to self-preservation 'but is the being and preservation of the whole of the ethical organization'.[391] The subordination of the serf to the lord bearing arms was based on this dialectic. With the universal estate as developed in his mature philosophy of law, Hegel opened this dimension to talent – dissolving the absolute distinction of living 'from' and 'for' politics through the patriotic disposition towards the ethical organization of the state.[392]

As relayed by Tacitus, everything was carried out under arms in the ancient parliaments – weaponry the emblem of the Germanic estate of the free, like the toga among the Romans.[393] Thus, the estate of the free, provided with the liberty of arms, joined the warlike retinue and so rose in rank.[394] 'There are grades of rank, indeed, within the retinue, determined by the chief whom they follow. There is great competition between the followers to gain the highest place in the chief's estimation, and among the chiefs as to which one has the largest and bravest retinue. This is their form of prestige, this means power for them.'[395] What the continuation of Tacitus's quote demonstrates is that this also worked the other way around, 'that the chiefs gain glory and renown if they excel others in the number and valour of their followers'.[396]

By contrast, the peasantry, lacking political existence, was forced to follow the laws laid down by the lords and was separated and isolated on the various manors or estates. This corresponded to the constitution of the Germanic people of the earliest epoch which consisted of a moderate number of families: of freemen, landlords and free lords.[397] The national association was little more than the meeting of freemen under arms; it was a gathering of householders and the sons of families who had grown up and belonged to the estate of the free.[398]

What becomes visible with *Germaniens Urverfassung* are the first fruits of Möser's self-proclaimed and lauded novel method, which permitted, in his eyes, the complete toppling of all previous systems of public law and imperial and territorial state history. This allowed for the circumscription of imperial and sovereign rights on the basis of entirely new principles.[399] What Pütter, with patent irony, had slighted in Majer's innovative proposals for another teaching method for positive German constitutional law was, in most particulars, little more than Möser's fascinating theoretical approach in different clothes.[400] It represented the emergence of an historical sociology that had redescribed the state of nature through human agricultural prehistory and the ancient constitution in order to explain the emergence of the state and the various constitutions relative to it.

3.4 The concept of the state

3.4.1 On the necessity of the state and the *adiaphora*

What remained of natural jurisprudence in Majer's later theoretical endeavours at the turn of the century can largely be perceived in his pared down concept of the state. The opening passages of both *Allgemeine Theorie der Staatskonstitution* and the first volume of *Teutsche Staatskonstitution* set out the theory in summary form. The preservation of individual private freedom and property is the end of political activity; the state is viewed as a security complex driving the logic of sovereignty and its exercise. However parsimoniously, this still represented a philosophical jurisprudential foundation, what Majer called 'the principle of *national* law' that 'proceeds from the innate human right of *freedom*'.[401] Since the 1770s, he had followed natural law in deducing the objective order of the state from subjective rights and liberties.[402] But, as we have seen, this could also be set in opposition to the historical-sociological method that elucidated the religious and predial principles, describing the real existing constitutions of the Empire and the German territories: the fact that 'all residents of Germany were divided into the free imperial and the unfree dependent residents of the landlords'.[403] The avowedly universal rational basis, however, did not necessarily have to come into direct conflict with the estate of the free and the estate of the unfree:

> For the state is, after all, nothing other than a social association, by which the freedom and property of *every individual and private person* is to be secured by means of the sovereignty it establishes. Also, the excellence of such an institution consists solely in the fact that *each individual citizen and private person*, from the first to the last, is to be granted security for his own with the least possible sacrifice of his private liberty and property to the greatest possible extent.[404]

What we can observe here is something we are already familiar with from the foregoing examinations: the supremacy of public law that secures the private realm of freedom through the establishment of the state, of *imperium* over *dominium*. The highest political order, irrespective of what Majer called the spirit of its form, was a universal security complex for private freedom and property. Hence, structural features of the state such as protection, security and freedom are inseparable. In this way we can see how 'the state as a peaceable entity does not arise and live from a discourse free of domination, but rather it is the state that first creates the conditions for a discourse free of domination to become possible'.[405]

The impact of Majer's theoretical endeavours on the *Reinschrift* has long been conjectured in the critical literature – proposed initially by Rosenzweig, extended in depth by Rolf K. Hočevar and commented on by Akira Hayase.[406] For both Majer and Hegel, the state is the absolutely necessary institution. For the Tübingen publicist, 'one of the most indispensable and salutary institutions among the human race is undoubtedly the state. Its first and immediate purpose is to provide general *security* for private freedom and property'.[407] For Hegel, on the other hand, the point was 'to elevate the truth that freedom is only possible in the legal union of a people to a state, to the belief of the peoples or to a principle of a political science'.[408] Yet, as Hegel also recognized critically, in view of the historical actuality of the imperial constitution and the decay of its once unified political form, 'the right of the state, … in order to exist, cannot of necessity, permit private law in all its consequences; even the taxes which it must demand are an abrogation [*Aufheben*] of the right of property'.[409] This put a markedly different emphasis on the theoretical material than the one stressed by Majer, even though he too noted the differentiations: 'The epitome of all rights and obligations, which concern all citizens as one corporation in the state relationship, is *state* law, which is therefore opposed to the *private* law of the citizens. With the state relationship itself, therefore, state law is divided into the *external* and *internal* [*das Staatsrecht in das* äußere *und* innere *ab*]'.[410] In other words, it is separated into the public law proper of the state and the *coordination* order of public international law. Hegel considered this in the same fashion: 'das äußere Staatsrecht' concerned the outward-facing relations of independent states.[411] Just as the private individual cannot be a real legal person without actual relationships to other individuals, so too with the state: it also requires other states for self-actualization and recognition.[412]

The unique character of the state was recognized everywhere by Majer in the public aspect of its legal order. This ensured the common good through security, with little regard to the particular *forma Reipublicae* attached to it or the mere 'subjective' organization of sovereignty. For Hegel, it was also to this extent that forms of constitution as well as administration were nothing more than *adiaphora*. In the first section of the *Reinschrift*, which Hegel entitled 'Begriff des Staats', he must have drawn on Majer's groundbreaking discussions in *Allgemeine Theorie der Staatskonstitution* and the first volume of *Teutsche Staatskonstitution*. In each of these publications Majer had detailed the essential characteristics of the state. *Allgemeine Theorie der Staatskonstitution* then used this as a basis by which to analyse different legal norms governing power in various constitutions; the two volumes of *Teutsche Staatskonstitution* pursued a similar task, firstly with respect to the Empire, secondly with respect to the imperial territories. Hegel did not have this analytical aim. Rather, he was more preoccupied with the minimum of what was required in reality to have a state as such: 'For a multitude to form a state, it is necessary that it should form a common defence and state power; but the manner in which the particular effects and sides of the union flowing from this are present, or the particular constitution, is indifferent to the fact that a multitude forms a power.'[413]

In identifying the particular *forma Reipublicae* as a separate subject that directly concerned the constitution but not, strictly speaking, the existence of the state, Majer was able to discuss how the patrimonial and freeholder models as explicit public legal orders upheld the common good as ably as those organized on a purely national basis. The constitution, no less than the administration, did not affect the necessary and essential aspects of public authority. This was how he managed to resolve the potential tension between natural jurisprudence and states based on the religious and predial principles. This implied a nuanced distinction between private and public law. Even the patrimonial state in no way contradicted the objective order of state sovereignty. Thus, the mere subjective organizing principle of the political was inconsequential. Only the collective defence of property and territory mattered. Everywhere in 'Begriff des Staats', Hegel concurred with the conclusions Majer had reached:

> What belongs to this particular manner can exist in a most diverse way, and in a particular state itself there can be a complete lack of rules and irregularity about it; and we must separate from each other in the consideration, that which is necessary for a multitude to be a state and a common power, and that which is only a particular modification of this power, and belongs not to the sphere of the necessary, but for the concept to the sphere of the more or less better, but for the reality to the sphere of chance and arbitrariness.[414]

Majer had made the case first and foremost for the necessity of the state and considered this the *objective* principle, detailing how sovereignty was exercised. Only after this initial theoretical enquiry had clarified the characteristics of the political did he then move on to the second and far more indifferent matter by comparison – the nature of the particular type of constitution or *forma Reipublicae*. Rather than speaking of this as defining the structure of public authority and law, Majer considered it as the *subjective* principle, one which strictly concerned the typology of the variety of state constitutions that he then proceeded to analyse in a relative manner.

It was evident to Majer that this had little to do with the actual organization of sovereignty. First came the necessity of the state, then the question of how its constitution fitted into a particular taxonomy or how it was categorized. Hence, the variety of state constitutions the Tübingen publicist analysed was a second-order problem. To this extent, 'the *concept* of a patrimonial state does not concern or determine anything in the *inner* content and essence of state sovereignty itself':

> but solely and exclusively only the *circumstances outside of their organization.* It merely refers to the *subjective* determination of the same and leaves state sovereignty, considered *objectively*, *as it is* and *as it should* be according to its nature, namely as law and power, the purpose of the state, common security, as to bring about the common welfare of all fellow citizens.[415]

With this, we can observe how natural jurisprudential deduction in Majer's hands was still able to maintain the universality of individual preservation in the security complex of the state organized around the common good, even in an explicitly inegalitarian *forma Reipublicae*. Indeed, it was precisely through the indifferent character of the state constitution that he was able to balance the objectives of natural law with the novel historical-sociological method that justified the foundations of the manorial system.

In this context, the same nuance that we have now come to expect from Majer's discussions of private and public law is everywhere in evidence. We already saw how he had separated the private and public legal orders in the patrimonial state in the earlier works through the notion of the private right to representation and the public function of the representative, the prince. The same pattern of argument may be detected in his separation of *dominium* and *imperium*. What can be observed in the later theoretical works is how the objective organization of sovereignty is the mainstay of state power which remains in every case unaltered. The central idea of state sovereignty considered *objectively*, as Majer put it, was the principal concern for a public authority such as the state. In 'Begriff des Staats', Hegel followed a similar logic:

> To that part of the reality of a state which belongs to chance must be reckoned the manner in which the whole power of the state exists in a supreme point of union; whether the possessor of power be one or several, whether this one or the several, be born or elected to this majesty, is indifferent to the only thing necessary for a multitude to constitute a state.[416]

Obviously, Hegel was building on Majer's reductive theoretical structure: 'A *state* is formed from every social connection to the common security for freedom and property against the violation of others, which is to be procured and managed by means of a common command.'[417] Or, in Hegel's words: 'A multitude of human beings can only call itself a state when united in the common defence of the entirety of its property.'[418] There is thus little need to dig much deeper into history to find an axiomatic concept of the state that could have influenced Hegel's early political thought – no necessity really of discussing the doctrine of the *ratio status* or of treating Hegel's grasp of public law as wholly idiosyncratic.[419] It suffices to have the opening sections of Majer's theoretical works in hand when analysing the raw concept of the state in the *Reinschrift* – as Hegel himself surely did.

What might Hegel have heard in the Tübingen lecture hall when he and Hölderlin were increasingly drawn to the law faculty where their mutual friend Sinclair was a student? We already know that Majer's security complex of the state had been propounded since the 1770s. It was further developed in the 1780s to become central in the publications at the turn of the century. The fissure between private and public law was nowhere more theoretically pronounced.

It should be added that this same circle of friends was engaged in the peace negotiations at the Congress of Rastatt. Sinclair, representative of Homburg vor der Höhe, brought Hölderlin along with him to the conference where the likes of Napoleon,

Johann Wolfgang von Goethe (1749–1832) and Klemens von Metternich (1773–1859) were present. Hölderlin for his part was instrumental in bringing Hegel to Frankfurt. Both poet and philosopher were engaged in lively discussions about the political events and the imperial constitution at this time.[420] Thus, Hegel was at one stage removed from the political context. Even leaving such speculations aside, there is the simple fact, noted above, that as Hegel worked on the fragments of the *Verfassungsschrift* several of Majer's most important theoretical publications were appearing, publications in which the concept of the state had a central place along with the analytical divisions between the subjective and objective organization of sovereignty, private and public law. 'Begriff des Staats' suggests that their impact on Hegel's thinking was considerable.

3.4.2 The essential criteria and the return of the *Hippolythus*

Majer set the tone for a realistic concept of the state defined very precisely by certain minimal criteria, which then could be employed analytically: 'unity, integrity, simplicity, autonomy, independence or freedom'.[421] He gave primacy as well to political power and its exercise over a territory, the defence against external threats. These criteria defined the very concept. Majer had raised the status of the state to the pre-eminent institution that made political life, private freedom and property possible. Further, he had introduced the concept *qua* concept, making it a predominant idea in public law and political theory: 'Without the enjoyment of general security, which the state is supposed to provide, all development of the powers invested in mankind and all progress in the great goal of man, in the perfection and happiness of which mankind is capable, are – almost impossible.'[422]

It followed that if the criteria Majer had outlined were lacking, then the disintegration of the state was at hand. Hegel concurred: 'a theory of the state is called a state and constitution only in so far as it is real'.[423] The dimensions of territory, sovereignty and command which Majer had considered as central objective organizational elements must not come into contradiction with political reality.

For Hegel, Majer's reductive concept remained *the* theoretical foundation by which to gauge such actuality. Not only was the *forma Reipublicae* an indifferent matter, but Hegel also added that the heterogeneity of civil law was equally as inconsequential – so too the variety of relationships that existed between the various estates. This was obviously tailored to take a complex legal and political order like the Empire into account, to make the case that it too could become a state without sacrificing its polyarchic or quasi-federal character.[424] In this way, the patrimonial and freeholder states, existent within the larger imperial *civitas composita*, could be left alone on similar terms:

> That a state counts among its subjects serfs, citizens, free nobles, and princes who themselves have subjects, and that the relations of these particular estates themselves as particular political members do not exist purely but in infinite modifications, does not prevent a multitude from forming a state power any more than that the particular geographical members constitute provinces of different relations to the internal law of the state.[425]

This fell into line with how Majer elaborated the essential criteria, contrasting complexity with simplicity. This was the very taxonomy that had been popularized in the public law tradition since Pufendorf and the emergence of systems theory. Unity and integrity could still be retained in a *civitas composita* or state system.[426] If the state was composed of families and private corporations, it retained everywhere a simple form, the private separated from the public and the political – the moral person of the state. Yet divisions in a given state could be altered:

> If such divisions of a state form *independent* special states by the emergence of their own sovereignties and if it is the case that, according to *international law* [*Völkerrecht*], they neither isolate *and* separate themselves completely from each other, nor merely *coalesce* with each other or with a third party, but, notwithstanding this preceding revolution in the divisions of their original state, remain in a constitutional relationship with the same, as before.[427]

Imperial history, as it rapidly unfolded in the wars with France, set the pace by which this composite concept was increasingly hollowed out and no longer readily applied. The *civitas composita* with its integrating parts was undergoing a process of dis-integration – fragmentation. For Majer and for Hegel, the logic underlying this development was to be found in the aristocratic body politic of a head and members.

Majer spoke of the imperial state as having an aristocratic *forma Reipublicae*, with a particular modality, as he termed it: the body politic of head and members.[428] Initially, he had proposed that there were no real historical examples of this form.[429] But, in truth, he vacillated.[430] What remained somewhat ambiguous in *Allgemeine Theorie der Staatskonstitution* was, however, clarified in the volumes of *Teutsche Staatskonstitution*.[431]

Although Majer did not mention the *Hippolythus* when referring to the aristocratic *forma Reipublicae*, no other German publication could be referenced – it was alone in its affirmation of aristocracy. That *Allgemeine Theorie der Staatskonstitution* set out from a reference to the *Hippolythus* and the miserable condition of the Thirty Years' War cannot be lost on us. This was something no doubt mirrored in Majer's own time under the French occupation – after the Peace of Basel, after his study of the Müller excerpt.[432] For the *Hippolythus*, the emperor was not *legibus solutus* but constrained by constitutional laws. Under the sway of the collectivity of the imperial estates, the emperor was subordinated to the *Reichstag*, the *maiestas realis*.[433] While the emperor was maintained as an administrator or director, he essentially became a mere cipher: the apex of a pyramid composed of several aristocracies.[434] Similarly, for Majer, the emperor was *Reichsoberhaupt* – imperial supreme head of an aristocratic collective.[435] In its analysis of the imperial *forma Reipublicae*, the *Hippolythus* famously conceived it a mixed aristocracy: 'How truly this imperial Status may be mixed from differing aristocratic forms.'[436]

Whereas Meist singled out Krause's *Abhandlungen aus dem deutschen Staatsrechte* (1797) (Treatises on German State Law) as the most important reference for Hegel's interpretation of the *Hippolythus*, to my mind considerable doubts must be entered on the question of direct influence.[437] Meist may be correct that Krause was the source, but Hegel need not have taken this directly from a reading of the Halle philosopher: an intermediary source is far more likely. Majer treated the *Hippolythus* in the first volume of *Teutsche Staatskonstitution* that set out from an extended examination of Krause's periodization of state law and its division into various schools, combined with Pütter's *Litteratur des teutschen Staatsrechts*.[438] Given that Majer combined the analyses of Krause and Pütter, Meist failed to exploit an important source.[439] Rosenzweig missed making the connection by a hair.[440] He proposed, however, that Hegel took the idea of public law as private law from Majer, although no mention of Krause's interpretation of the legists and decretists is made:

> The *Romanizing* publicists made their mark on the science of German constitutional law in two ways. They often applied principles from Roman *private law* to *state* relations in a quite unseemly manner; in addition, however, their idea of the Emperor and the Roman Empire led them to neglect the system of constitutional law of the individual self-governing German states far too much.[441]

Admittedly, this is to tell only half the story. Hegel had seen through the problems of the political tradition, the history of *cives imperii*, the Roman private law of *dominium* that Ludolph Hugo had raised to interpret the imperial estates in a quasi-federal union. But Majer's private princely law was in fact a very different creature. Far more successfully than Pütter and the earlier tradition that followed Hugo, he divided the private from the public and could thus be seen as an important starting point for Hegel's critique of the application of Roman private law and *dominium* to the estates. When the *Hippolythus* attacked Roman law as constitutional law, no substitute was suggested. Conring separated the Roman from the Germanic elements of the constitution in his interpretation of Tacitus, but in introducing the *cives imperii*, Roman private law returned almost immediately as a way of formalizing the relationship of the imperial estates among themselves and to the Empire.[442] If the estates had become states, which stood at the centre of Hegel's interpretation of the *Hippolythus*, 'then, of course, private law is not applicable to them'.[443] Hegel could have learnt all of the refined distinctions he drew between private and public law from Majer who, as we have seen, made a point of separating these legal orders – dividing what had been confused theoretically in the tradition since Melanchthon, *dominium* and *imperium*.

For Majer, the ancient Germanic property right to land and soil and the jurisdictions that followed by consequence were intrinsic to the subjective legal principle that continued to form the foundation of the German territorial state constitutions. Everything was determined by the private association as described by Tacitus: from the decision on family marriage, to the question of the inheritance of private landed property, which allowed a member to participate in the primitive national assembly. In other words, everywhere the ancient Germanic constitution concerned private *not* public law.[444] The positive nature of Germanic freedom existed in the fact that the private property owner, the lord, was also the active holder of a political right, which was not ceded at the formation of the ancient constitution but actually formed its foundation. Hence, independence was not *personal*, it did not rely on the distribution of titles; it was *real*, born with the hereditary right of landownership. Majer had viewed the nobility of his own time as 'a holy relic of Germanic high antiquity born in the crudest age and brought up in the mental darkness of the Middle Ages'.[445] For Hegel, this produced the later condition of barbarism in the Holy Roman Empire that 'consists in the fact that a multitude is a people without at the same time being a state, that the state and the individuals exist in opposition and separation'.[446]

If this system were to be translated into a form of constitutional law, it would seem almost certain to become contradictory. Hence, while the *Hippolythus* could be held in esteem for correcting the misuse of Roman jurisprudence by the legists and decretists that had, until that point in time, shored up imperial power, it essentially offered no viable alternative for the imperial constitution. In this way, it solidified the territorial principle and territorial constitutional development. The historical import of the *Hippolythus* thus lay in the establishment of the constitutions of the individual German states. It was nothing more than a symptom of its age.[447] The defence of collective property, which involved the external relations of the state, must be categorically distinguished from the defence of private property. Yet, in the absence of the state, any distinction between private and public law was impossible. Hegel isolated this contradiction at the core of the doctrine of the *cives imperii* and the private princely law that had evolved from it that could neither be absorbed into the *ius civile* nor was properly a part of *ius publicum* although it was understood in this way in the seventeenth and eighteenth centuries:[448]

> Political rights [*politische Rechte*], in so far as they are supposed to have the force of private laws, involve a kind of self-contradiction, for they would presuppose that those who had such fixed political rights against each other were in a legal relationship under a powerful and sovereign authority. But in this case the reciprocal rights would no longer be political rights, but private, property rights.[449]

For Majer, the development of the aristocratic *forma Reipublicae* followed the logic of *Landeshoheit* and the Germanic manorial system that survived the collapse of ancient German freedom.[450] This was structured equally, as we have seen, through Möser's novel methodology.[451] Majer even spoke of the natural history of territorial supremacy as Möser had done of bondage.[452] Still, this was initially maintained alongside the system of imperial sovereignty. *Landeshoheit* may have destroyed the secular imperial hierarchy, but it initially left *Reichshoheit* intact.[453]

This resulted in a form of parallelism, two powers: the glory attributed to the ancient Germanic practice of landlordship and the equiprimordial imperial sovereignty, 'the putative daughter of heaven, born in the church and raised and educated by it for the service of the church and the protection of the Empire'.[454] Hence, if the first was based on the predial principle, the second was founded on the religious principle. The fact remains, however, that *Landeshoheit*, through Protestantism, eventually eviscerated the religious principle and thus imperial sovereignty as such. The older universal and essentially medieval character of the Empire had become problematic – a secularization of the concept occurred.[455] For Hegel, *Landeshoheit* pursued a singular logic; it was connected to Protestantism, the aristocratic *forma Reipublicae* and the *Hippolythus*; it had dug its own grave: 'The striving of the imperial estates offers the spectacle of a crowd throwing itself onto a frozen stream, from whose ice each one strives to tear off as much as possible, unaware that the more he enriches himself, the more hastens his own ruin and that of all.'[456]

3.4.3 Disintegration of the state

If one were to measure the Empire according to Majer's defence concept of the state, as Hegel had done in the epoch of the Congress of Rastatt and during the Second Coalition War, it would be found wanting.[457] The Tübingen publicist's theoretical productions at the turn of the century explained how the territories were emerging as the sole political reality. Perhaps it was this that justified the reasoning behind Hegel's use of sovereignty to describe the imperial estates. Germany had begun to provide evidence for another model in which the private interest of its integrating parts was in the process of corroding the imperial state and *Reichshoheit* – the objective sovereignty of the state exercised territorially. Even with the unity that had been attained in the composite state, the seeds of its own destruction had been planted through the principle of territorial supremacy that after 1648 had bestowed on the imperial state constitution a significant part of its form. Nonetheless, the fact remains that 'territorial supremacy cannot be thought of as anything other than *subordinate* to *imperial sovereignty under constitutional law*'.[458]

An integral part of the history of modernity and the development of the Germanic World, for Hegel the *Hippolythus* realized the aristocratic *forma Reipublicae*.[459] This resulted in the constitutional guarantee of supremacy in the treaties of Münster and Osnabrück (*I.P.O.* Article VIII §2). In Heinrich Gustav Hotho's (1802–73) transcript of Hegel's Berlin lectures on the philosophy of world history (1822–3), the conclusion of the Thirty Years' War had a weight that anchored the contradictions at the heart of imperial public law for generations to come: 'With regard to Germany, the war ended through the constitution of law; that is the constitutions of each fixed state.'[460] Thus, as Hegel concisely summarized: 'There is no talk of a common state purpose, rather the idea of German freedom was only that of a complete particularization and establishment of private law.'[461] The other transcript of these lectures by the influential Prussian military strategist Karl Gustav Julius von Griesheim (1798–1854) referred directly to the *Hippolythus*: 'With the constitution, that is the establishing of the private laws of the various princes, peace is made a Lapide. Here one sees most clearly that the idea of German freedom contains only particularization.'[462] This simply repeated a logic, some twenty-odd years later, that had first been made in the *Verfassungsschrift*: 'state law has become private law'.[463]

For Hegel, the estate of the free in the Holy Roman Empire had become oligarchical through its private legal status as *cives imperii* and the use of the Roman private legal concept of *dominium* to codify the relations between the imperial estates among themselves and to the Empire. Rather than aiming at the preservation of property rights, the nobility ought to be indifferent to their destruction through a free ethical relation to the state based on independence and freedom. For Hegel, the failures of the imperial army to adequately hold ground against revolutionary France was the product of a political history that reached back to 1648, defeat written into a constitution.

The *Hippolythus* was a symbol that, like Pütter, must have a prominent place in the interpretation of constitutional development.[464] With the great treaties, the imperial estates gained complete control over military forces, the right to wage war as well as to conclude treaties of alliance and peace with foreigners.[465]

For Majer, this development resulted in the dissolution of the imperial worldly hierarchy and ultimately led to the spirit of the formless form.[466] The criteria of integrity and unity that codified central aspects to the concept of the state could still be maintained in a quasi-federal *civitas composita*, even after the rise of the territories, given that subordination to a higher legal order was implied. A state may lose its simplicity, like the Empire, but this did not necessarily imply the forfeiture of its unity and integrity. Rather, its component parts remained integral having developed into independent states. All of this was evidently being called into question by recent imperial history, not least since the Peace of Basel. This led to the irreality of the imperial constitution, *Reichshoheit* and the inapplicability of Majer's reductive concept of the state to the Empire:

> Germany is united for its common defence according to laws and words; but we cannot here distinguish between laws and words on the one hand, and fact and reality on the other, nor say that Germany does not defend itself collectively in fact and reality but nonetheless according to laws and words; for property and its defence through a state union are things that relate entirely to reality; and whose ideality has anything but a state.[467]

Hegel's words reflect very precisely Majer's conceptually reductive discussion of the state as a defence complex for property and freedom. They echo earlier iterations in the fragments of the *Verfassungsschrift* that had emphasized the *maiestas realis* over and against the *simulacra imperii*, real existing sovereignty and the state against the mere appearances of rule. Hegel had critiqued the principal theoreticians of imperial public law, such as Moser and Pütter, that had never tired of extolling the many symbols, insignia, claims and titles.[468] These were meaningless when weighed against the reality of power and the incapacity of the imperial state to organize a common defence or military constitution.[469] With the decay of the Empire, made manifest in the revolutionary wars, the lack of both will and power to ensure collective security, property and freedom was more than merely avowed. Thus, as Majer put it, the integrating parts, the states of the dissolving composite state, had recourse to the state of nature: 'Thus, in this fatal moment of time, such an individual state, as far as its existence or autonomy is concerned, is entitled to take any means left to it to save itself from ruin.'[470] Hegel spoke in precisely the same way: 'For since Germany does not wish to give itself a constitution which would enable it to protect its members against foreign enemies, the estate which is in danger, placed entirely in a state of nature, is not only entitled, but obliged by the consideration of its self-preservation, to provide for itself as best as it can.'[471]

What had taken place since the French armies swept through Germany demonstrated for both Majer and Hegel an extensive historical rationale, the origins of which could be traced to the emergence of *Landeshoheit* and even further to the ancient freedoms of the Germanic tribes. Majer had depicted the rise of formlessness, the disintegration of the original hierarchical form, when the integrating parts of the imperial state could no longer see how the common interests of territorial supremacy were to be maintained within a larger composite structure: 'the organization of the sovereignty of the *Empire*, but for the whole and for its integrity, to maintain the once established *hierarchical* form'.[472] The central problem that haunted the composite state was that its unity and integrity everywhere remained contingent on the interests of its integrating parts. The same could not really be said of the private persons, families and private corporations that made up the simple state. The ancient system of landlordship and private princely law had every right to administer the districts. This implied that the territories were states with their own state constitutions; control over the land exercised a power that was the essential marker of sovereignty: 'The district of the territory *occupied* by a multitude of people united for such a purpose and organized in this way is called their state *territory*; and all the members of the state who are subject to the common command, or so-called sovereignty, are in the category of *subjects*.'[473] In Majer Hegel had discovered a realist.

Majer had referred to a simple legal principle of the ancient constitution: those who are on my land belong to me and are my subjects. This also carried with it another equally transparent idea, that of the system of inheritance operative among the original family units that, taken together, constituted the free association of lords. From here, he was able to develop the idea that the primitive national assembly, as relayed by Tacitus, was not akin to a meeting of subordinates under a ruler. Rather, it consisted of the sons of all families that had inherited land discussing common affairs carried out under arms. The army, in this strict sense, was *constitutional*.[474] In this fashion, Majer brought the system of landlordship operative in ancient Germania into direct connection with the system of public law and the theory of the imperial state constitution. A striking continuity could thus be established between the Tacitean description of the ancient Germanic parliament of free lords and the imperial army that had been reduced to naught as it relied on the contributions of the imperial estates. This corresponded very precisely to the prevalent conditions in the imperial state, to the reality of the losses of the Empire in which private law had become constitutional.

With the disappearance of the unity of the imperial estates on the battlefield after the Peace of Basel and the pursuit of their own reason of state, little remained of the imperial state association besides the private rights that had stood at its origin: 'The fact that the state is only a thing of thought lies in the fact that as a state it has no power, but that power is in the hands of the individual.'[475] This was nowhere more obvious than with the incapacity of the imperial army to defend united interests, for such interests existed no longer. Hegel had discussed the four systems with their different nuclei and masses that emerged from the decay of the imperial body politic. For Majer, the aristocratic body politic of a head and members utterly defied monarchy.[476] It led to the exception to the rule with the *formlessness* of the German imperial state and its existing constitution: 'even the most perceptive mind would tire and despair of conceiving a form out of such formlessness'.[477]

In the absence of a sovereign public authority, with no concept of the state proper, the confusion between private and public law was insurmountable. The defence of collective property, which involved the external relations of the state, was a clean different thing from the defence of private property. But these had been mixed in the imperial constitution through the arbitrary extension of private law and the effect it had on the public legal order. A ubiquitous trope in Hegel's thinking was how war was destructive of private property as such. Indeed, the very existence of the state may have guaranteed the private legal order, property and freedom, just as Majer had detailed, but it also implied its infringement through taxation, for example. The importance of the noble warring estate, the estate of the free, was that it dissolved the sanctity of private property in absolute ethical life.[478] Private property belonged to private law, which was guaranteed by public law – and criminal law, through theft and punishment:[479]

> In part it is already a contradiction in and of itself that not only property but relationships that relate directly to the state should have the form of private law, but because there is no longer any state power in Germany, the treatment of political rights as private rights, and the security and firmness of those equal to them, also ceases to exist, and [they] enter into the general rank of political rights.[480]

We are now in a position to respond to a query posed by Hans Maier: to what extent the image of the German past sketched by Hegel, of private law as a form of public law, was already present in the earlier imperial public lawyers?[481] Certainly, Majer's productions must be considered, as we have done here. After all, it was through Majer that Hegel arrived at his raw concept of the state: 'that this union does not merely have the intention of defending itself, but that it defends itself through real defence, whatever its power and success may be'.[482] What has been attributed to Hegel was no less true of Majer: 'the sharp juxtapositions of personal and legal freedom, private and public law etc. show a thoroughly modern awareness of the state that was ahead of its time'.[483]

3.5 Epilogue

3.5.1 Singularity

This chapter has illuminated the significance of an obscure theoretician from the twilight of imperial public law. Majer's significance extends even beyond his connection to the greatest German philosopher of the nineteenth century. Indeed, his singular theorizations, shaped by Justus Möser and an interpretation of Tacitus, brought the ancient constitution into genetic continuity with a historical present on the brink of collapse. Hegel did the same. The chapter has demonstrated the uniqueness and range of Majer's conceptual ideas: from the ambiguity of Germanic or German freedom to the negative deductions of natural jurisprudence, the Roman law of persons and the radical cleft between the private and public legal orders – all profoundly shaping Hegel's conceptions.

3.5.2 Majer and Max Weber

The emergence of an historical sociology was central to Majer's thought. This grew out of a highly restrictive use of natural law combined with Möser's pioneering methodology. Majer's work is best assessed in light of the period's ongoing conceptual shift away from natural law. Employing methods of natural history, this shift led to the redescription of the state of nature as a primitive agricultural society.[484]

Majer conceived ideas which only later rose to prominence with Max Weber. This is evident in his constitutional relativism, an early iteration of the study of types of rule and legitimacy – ranging from patrimonialism to the autocratic free peoples' state (the French revolutionary state) – all while maintaining a consistent set of minimal state criteria. Indeed, Weber himself was a typologist not all that far removed from the these classical debates over the *forma imperii*, as evidenced by his systematic development of ideal types of legitimate rule (*Herrschaftstypen*) in *Wirtschaft und Gesellschaft* (1921).[485] His analysis of patrimonialism and his concept of the *Ständestaat* are even more illustrative.[486] The *Ständestaat*, in particular, represents Weber's sociological attempt to define the constitutional form prevalent in many parts of the Holy Roman Empire and other pre-modern European states. Through his analysis of its structure, the role of estates (*Stände*) in limiting princely power and its inherent tensions, he provides a sociological account of the German state constitutions.

Perhaps most central of all such comparisons, however, lies in Majer's refined theoretically deductive concept of the state. This strikingly anticipates the later Weberian classification of political community, with its comparable standards for territory, defence, monopoly on physical force (sovereignty) and the establishment of a legal order to regulate interrelations among inhabitants.[487] Weber famously defined the state as 'a human community that (successfully) claims the monopoly of the legitimate use of physical force within a given territory'.[488] This definition, while succinct, is the culmination of Weber's historical and comparative analysis. It is a sociological, rather than purely legal or philosophical, definition because it focuses on the means (monopoly of legitimate force) and territory as empirical features, regardless of the state's moral purpose or historical origin.

Majer, in essence, was stripping away older, more normative conceptions of the state and moving towards this more functional and empirical understanding of what a state does and is in practice. In essence, Majer can be seen as a proto-sociologist of the state. While he lacked Weber's explicit methodological apparatus (e.g. ideal types), his deep historical engagement, his shift away from abstract natural law towards concrete constitutional forms, his constitutional relativism and his proto-functional definition of the state all point towards a conceptual trajectory that directly anticipates the more systematic sociological analyses of rule and the state. Thus, Majer's formulations are almost as severely rational as any found in Weber; indeed, they adhere to the rule of a colourless natural law.[489] Hence, assessing the work of this neglected thinker offers an even more concrete conceptual link between the development of Hegel's political thought and the unfolding sociological description of the state.[490]

3.5.3 A definitive connection between Majer and Hegel

This chapter has undertaken a pioneering study of Majer's legal and political thought. It has situated its assessment within the literature of German public law and specifically examined its relationship to the twilight of imperial public law. In so doing, I have stressed just how central Möser's innovative methodology had become. As we have seen, this was no less true for Hegel. Through Möser, Haller had translated primitive land appropriation (Hegel's 'spheres of power and chance') directly into a legal theory that esteemed the rule of the private despot – the stronger by nature – above all else.[491] Majer's theoretical productions were far more nuanced. They resulted in a refined doctrine of public law and the state and its strict separation from the private legal order. He had realized the intricacies of the Roman dichotomy in the emergent revolutionary epoch, strikingly even for the patrimonial state.

The doctrine of parallel, explicated by Majer following Ludolph Hugo, provided an alternative approach to studying the imperial and territorial systems. Starting from the aristocratic *forma Reipublicae*, this analysis eventually demonstrated the impossibility of categorizing the imperial constitution as such, leading to the introduction of *Unformlichkeit* – a concept also central to Hegel's speculative endeavours in *System der Sittlichkeit*. Through the leveraging of recent imperial history, Majer had also demonstrated the contradictions at the core of the imperial concept of the state. This brought his analysis into connection with Hegel's examination, demonstrating a reciprocal influence.

Importantly, the chapter has established, beyond any reasonable doubt, the relation between Majer and Hegel regarding the concept of the state. What was previously purely hypothetical, I have now grounded through structural comparative analysis. As Hans Maier correctly recognized, Hegel, in his maturity, no longer considered the collective defence of the property (and thus Majer's minimal concept) part of the political realm; it was merely an aspect in the formation of civil society.[492] This agrees remarkably with sociological description. Further, it determines the scope and limits of state activity which are also an integral part of the concept of freedom and realization.[493] Thus, Hegel did not abandon Majer's concept of the state but integrated it into his developing concept of civil society. It was relegated to the state of the understanding or the state of necessity: 'If the state is confused with civil society and its purpose is placed in the security and protection of property and personal liberty, then the interests of individuals as such are the ultimate purpose for which they are united and it follows from this that it is something arbitrary.'[494]

Yet, for Hegel, these elements – even if relegated to civil society – are indispensable. It would be impossible to imagine the higher levels of ethical life in the state without the fundamental guarantee of the rights and freedoms – the collective security and welfare – of subjects. In this way, 'the concern for external freedom and security, for the life purposes of the nature of need, already transcends the realm of the merely functional and the delimitation of self-interests'.[495] Thus, Majer's concept of the state, what Hegel terms 'the state of necessity' in his mature legal and political thought, is a prerequisite for modern ethical life and a fundamental development of modern history. It does not disappear with the movement into the higher levels of consciousness but is rather sublated, remaining the condition for the complete realization of the individual. Hence, 'the purpose of every legal constitution is *freedom*'.[496] The second moment of civil society is identified with 'the protection of property by the *legal constitution*'.[497] Private law, covering the legal relations among subjects and their private interests – such as marriage, inheritance, contract, tort, etc. – are elements, nevertheless, which can only exist in a condition of equilibrium through the assurances provided by a public legal order. Thus, the following logic emerges: 'The state as such is always something prior to civil society; the latter only develops within the state and it can only emerge within the complete unity that the state is.'[498]

3.5.4 Public law and *Privatfürstenrecht*

The relationship between Majer and Hegel and the public law tradition since the *Hippolythus* has been examined in detail. This modifies a reception history that had previously overlooked the importance of Roman law, the doctrine of the *cives imperii*, their connection to private princely law and their role in the disintegration of the imperial constitution. This analysis further solidifies the arguments I initially presented regarding Moser and subsequently detailed with aristocratic despotism and Pütter. Majer's thought is singular in its profound recognition of the distinction between the moral person of the state and *Privatfürstenrecht*. No other publicist of his generation attained a more precise knowledge of the division between private and public law while simultaneously understanding how this private law had become constitutional in shaping the idiosyncrasies of the German territorial states.

In the transformed historical context after the Peace of Basel, Hegel could no longer see how the imperial system had in fact functioned quite successfully since Westphalia. With the spirit of the formless form, Majer fell into the same trap. For Hegel, the Thirty Years' War and the Seven Years' War were internal or constitutional wars. They demonstrated how the forces that were to be used for collective defence 'destroyed themselves and Germany tore its own entrails to pieces; what is called the German constitution is not only incapable of preventing such wars, but rather, they are lawful and legitimate'.[499] All in all, this has prepared the way for the analysis of Hegel's position that is offered in the next chapter.

4

The empire of ethical life: Georg Wilhelm Friedrich Hegel

4.0 Prologue

4.0.1 Early biography and imperial dissolution

Unlike the other figures in this book, the most famous German philosopher of the nineteenth century requires little introduction. Even so, it is worth exploring the personal dimension of the precise historical moment in which Hegel composed the fragments of the *Verfassungsschrift* up until the ultimate dissolution of the Empire.

In the critical literature, it has long been asserted that Hegel's biography was intertwined with the crisis of the constitution. He even implicitly spoke of this himself later in his correspondence, pinpointing a personal crisis from which his philosophy slowly emerged:

> I know from my own experience this mood of the mind, or rather of reason, when it has once, with interest and its intuitions, become involved in a chaos of phenomena and when [it], *inwardly* certain of the goal, has not yet passed through it, has not yet come to the clarity and detailing of the whole. I suffered from this hypochondria for a few years to the point of exhaustion; every human being has such a *turning point* in life, the nocturnal point of contraction of his being, through the narrowness of which he is forced and secured and reassured to the certainty of himself, to the certainty of ordinary everyday life, and if he has already made himself incapable of being filled by the same, to the certainty of an *inner* noble existence.[1]

In *Hegel und der Staat*, Franz Rosenzweig demonstrated that this personal turning point belonged to the period in which Hegel first began work on the fragments of the *Verfassungsschrift*.[2] Theoretically, Hegel extrapolated from his personal experience, transforming crisis into a general psychological development of subjective spirit. Importantly, he identified it with a specific period: extending from the age of twenty-seven to thirty-six.[3]

A closer look at his biography, following Rosenzweig, reveals this period uniquely coincided with the beginning of the *Verfassungsschrift*, extended throughout his Jena period and culminated in the collapse of the imperial constitution and his most famous work, *Phänomenologie des Geistes* (1807), conceived as the introduction to his system. Hans Maier has similarly confirmed Rosenzweig's insights by recognizing that the catastrophic character of the *Verfassungsschrift* is 'ultimately rooted in the fact that the decline and fall of the Empire coincided with an inner crisis in Hegel's thinking itself'.[4]

4.0.2 Crisis as concept

It is also important to note that Hegel deployed crisis as a distinct analytical concept. He applied it initially to history and politics and then to medicine, with a striking overlap between these registers in most cases. In the Frankfurt period, Hegel referred to the concept for the first time in the context of his writings on the Christian religion and its emergence out of a schism in the Jewish religion: 'Jesus appeared not long before the final crisis, which brought about the turmoil of many elements of the Jewish fate. In this time of inner turmoil, of the development of this diverse material, until it is gathered into a whole, and the pure oppositions, open war arises.'[5]

On the one hand, this discussion reflects the personal crisis Hegel detailed in his correspondence: the immersion in a chaos of phenomena without having arrived at the detailed articulation of a whole. On the other hand, with its pure contradictions, it aligned with both the Greek etymology, which emphasized how the 'concept imposed choices between stark alternatives – right or wrong, salvation or damnation, life or death', and its application to a philosophy of history, to world-historical judgement.[6]

Generally speaking, Hegel's second usage of the term conformed to these ideas of dichotomization too. It was taken over from Jean-Jacques Cart (1747–1813) whose *Vertrauliche Briefe über das vormalige Staatsrechtliche Verhältniß des Waadtlandes* (1798) (Confidential Letters on the Previous Constitutional Relationship of Vaud) Hegel had translated from the original French and published anonymously during his Frankfurt period.[7] Cart's letters have been interpreted alongside the contemporaneous *Ständeschrift*.[8] Both writings leveraged the threat of the revolutionary masses to incite reform and abolish privilege: Cart's letters targeted patrician Bern by fully exposing its oligarchical nature, while the *Ständeschrift* addressed Württemberg. As Cart wrote: 'May the dreadful movement of the great masses near us, which they have unwisely endeavoured to give us, become an occasion for remedying such crying abuses! May this remedy spare us the spasms and the crisis that always results in death if it does not lead back to health.'[9] In this way, crisis revealed itself to be a choice between an *either* of reform *or* revolutionary Terror. The point being, as H. S. Harris (1926–2007) rightly put it: 'to frighten the self-interested into behaving "justly"'.[10]

This imbrication of the political and the physiological was strikingly evident in Hegel's similar reflections on the Württemberg territorial estates constitution (*landständische Verfassung*) in his first *Ständeschrift*. The nature of the crisis was the same as that of Bern: the discrepancy between outmoded institutions of aristocratic privilege, oligarchy and the *either-or* of revolution or reform. Although the term itself did not explicitly appear, it can be gleaned directly from what Hegel discussed: 'a paroxysm of fever, ends only with death, or when the diseased matter is sweated out, it is an effort of the still healthy power to drive out the evil'.[11] Not only did crisis signify a decisive turning point, a difficult or dangerous situation, but in medicine it also meant a rapid drop in fever in infectious disease, marking the climax and turning point of an illness.

This adheres in almost every respect to the ancient Greek medical definition of crisis as a decision, the decisive turn of a disease, its implied climax and its relation to fever. Furthermore, it should be directly coupled to the concept's extensive discussion in the philosophy of nature in *Jenaer Systementwürfe III* (1805–6) (Jena System Outlines III). Both examples demonstrate how illness and physiological metaphors such as fever, death, crisis and disease could be conjoined with discussions on the constitution or body politic.[12] Moreover, in the philosophy of nature, this involved both the subjective dimension of personal experience Hegel referred to in his correspondence with Karl Windischmann (1775–1839) and in *Fragment zur Philosophie des subjektiven Geistes* (1822) (Fragment on the Philosophy of Subjective Spirit), as well as the objective dimension of substance, the state or politics.[13]

4.0.3 Constitution

Before turning to the philosophy of nature, which concludes the usages of the concept of crisis in the Frankfurt and Jena periods, another instance can be discovered in the fragments of the *Verfassungsschrift*. In 1802, Hegel excerpted and reproduced a copy of a diplomatic document or report on the meeting of the estates in Regensburg-Churbrandenburg.[14] The immediate context was the protracted demise of the Holy Roman Empire in light of the failures of the Second Coalition War, a period where the resolute connection between crisis and an acute moment of decision became emphatic. Indeed, the excerpt stressed every element common to the concept: a decisive point, the climax of a dangerous development and a difficult situation. It thus directly extended the medical phraseology of urgency at a critical moment to politics: 'In the unprecedented situation in which the worthy German fatherland reportedly finds itself at the present time, the extraordinary daily increase in the urgency of the circumstances would make the rapid decision of this crisis a pressing necessity, because solely on it do peace, order and public safety depend.'[15]

4.0.4 Crisis in the philosophy of nature

The examples from the philosophy of nature in *Jenaer Systementwürfe III* securely established Hegel's understanding of crisis in direct connection to Hippocratic medicine.[16] This returned the concept firmly to its Greek etymological origins. It is important to note, however, that in classical Greece, 'the term was central to politics. It meant not only "divorce" and "quarrel," but also "decision" in the sense of reaching a crucial point that would tip the scales'.[17] Thus, it could be argued that a wider political context of world-historical judgement was always implicit in Hegel's use of the concept. This was already evident in the first *Ständeschrift*, where the paroxysm of fever directly addressed a dangerous political situation. The philosophy of nature extended crisis beyond its strictly medical application: 'Freedom, independence on both sides – like the individual and the state, and this is the substance of the latter; this IS *certain* substance, insofar as the substance stands beneath it, it is, as in desire, power over its form.'[18] Hence, what was characteristic of crisis was opposition: between the particular and the universal, the individual and the whole. The roles could also be reversed – the substance of the state opposed to subject:

> *Substance as subject*, there as being; here as negative; the subject is a *determinate negativity*; if the determinateness of the substance becomes unequal to the determinateness of the subject, then the latter is greater still for the subject because the latter as negativity is the *universal*, but the universal to which then its being, which is essentially a determinate one, is not adequate and insofar stands below it.[19]

With its structured monism, Hegel's philosophy of union was an attempt to overcome every dichotomy.

Crisis is a dialectical concept. The turning point it implies is as open to death as it is to convalescence. To overcome disorder, for Hegel the organism had to undergo a crisis, marking the climax of an illness. Disease entailed opposition, with the organism undergoing an activity of separation where particularity or individuality was opposed to the whole.[20] This is what he had recounted in his correspondence with Windischmann. It is also apparent in each of the examples we have reviewed. Disease occurred when the individual as a determinate subject was dissociated from its kind, or when there was an opposition between the individual as determinate negativity and the substance of the state.

Philosophically speaking, this situation arises precisely when an immediate, unreflective unity (like the *polis* of ancient Greece, where ethical life was simply lived) breaks down. When contradictions, tensions and 'diseases' of separation emerge, the living unity can no longer hold itself together spontaneously. It requires thought to comprehend, explain and ultimately reconcile these divisions. Thus, what the disease implies is simultaneously a healing. This diremption, while experienced as crisis, is a necessary stage in the unfolding of spirit. It is precisely this experience of 'diseased' separation that gives rise to the need for philosophy, whose ultimate goal is to achieve union – a conceptual reconciliation that integrates all these oppositions into a conscious, richer and more vitally dynamic whole. Philosophy's task is to demonstrate how these apparent ruptures are internal moments within a larger, self-developing unity and how they find their truth and resolution within a comprehensive system.

4.0.5 The turning point of world history

Hegel's reflections on crisis in *Jenaer Systementwürfe III* coincided with the final collapse of the Holy Roman Empire, the formlessness of its state constitution. As we have seen, this history involved private law becoming constitutional, which led to aristocratic despotism and the oligarchic 'particularization' of the imperial estates. In an entirely different way, for Hegel private law had become constitutional in the French constitution of 24 June 1793 – however immediately suspended by the authoritarian rule of Maximilien Robespierre (1758–94).

What Hegel had isolated in the first *Ständeschrift* was a crisis or fever that either resulted in death or led to convalescence and renewal. This presented a choice: *either* the continuation of politics 'in statu cadentis territorii' or the detailed articulation of a structured whole, a system. As he stated: 'The organism sets itself as a whole against the determinacy; – it as a whole becomes an existence, the individual pathological affection is transformed into the whole and this disease of the whole is at the same time healing [*Heilung*], for it is the whole that is set in motion.'[21]

This also said something about world-historical judgement that for Hegel was a *Heilsgeschichte* (history of salvation/healing).[22] The Empire was a conflictual, non-structured whole, a system of private law particularization inimical to the state, a crisis of madness and death: 'When human sociable nature has once been disturbed and forced to throw itself into peculiarities, such a deep perversity comes into it that it now exerts its strength in its divisiveness from others, and in the assertion of its separation sinks into madness, for madness is nothing other than the complete separation of the individual from its kind.'[23]

This distinctively echoes the dichotomy of crisis which the *Verfassungsschrift* conceived as a shared fate among the Germanic and Jewish peoples.[24] Hegel noted that the idiosyncrasy of the Jewish people made it impossible for them to live with others in a common state; a similar obstinacy marked the Germans, who held fast to every particular right.[25] Jesus had responded to this crisis of the Jewish people.[26] Further, he did so through the notion of love that abolished the law. This was identical with the overcoming of fate and implied a reconciliation with the world.[27] Later, in Hegel's thought, this principle of love was first called life and finally spirit and then, in the philosophy of law, ethical life.[28]

A similar turning point appeared in the mature *Rechtsphilosophie*. This world-historical turning point was connected to the same discussion of reconciliation. The point was the decay of ethical life into a formal legal universality. With its oligarchic state form, the Roman Empire destroyed the free personality and individuality of the demos of Greek antiquity. The diversity of nations disappeared and died in a nameless pantheon. Furthermore, in the brutality of the Roman World 'all individuals sink down to private persons and to equals with formal rights, who are held together only by an abstract arbitrariness that drives itself into monstrosity'.[29] This resulted in the inner migration of the Jewish people into conscience, where 'spirit, pushed back into itself, grasps in the extreme of its absolute *negativity*, the *turning point* that is in and of itself, the *infinite positivity* of its inner being'.[30] In turn, this led to 'the principle of the unity of divine and human nature, the reconciliation as the objective truth and freedom appearing within self-consciousness and subjectivity, which is assigned to the Nordic principle of the *Germanic peoples* to fulfil'.[31] Hegel had spoken of this development as reconciliation with fate. The very idea of separation, of subject opposed to substance, of a member excluding itself from the whole, drove a philosophy of unification even if, as a properly monistic theory, it was independent of it.[32]

Striking continuity can be found throughout Hegel's thought. For example, he had long conceived how the despotism of the Roman emperors had driven spirit from the world, resulting in an objective, abstract God. This had its contrary in the universality of slavery, equality.[33] Jesus was the initial reconciliation, but the Christian religion as it developed was world denying and took over the formalism of Jewish law in its relation to works, miracles and superstition. Only with the appearance of the right to make reforms in religion did reconciliation with the world become possible: 'the German character fervently turned to the innermost being of man, religion and conscience, and from here it strengthened the isolation, and the separation of the exterior as states appeared only as a consequence of this'.[34] This directly touched the field of imperial public law as it had developed since the Peace of Augsburg and the *ius reformandi*, the religious conscience of the ruler that was synonymous with the internal space of the territorial state, as well as modern ethical life and the constitutional monarchical state.[35]

An analysis from the mature *Rechtsphilosophie* demonstrated the extent to which the Germanic World represented this turning point in world history. It resulted in the principle of the constitutional state, where the rationality of justice, law and truth replaced every form of otherworldliness – reconciling the rational subject with reality.[36] Hegel had long searched for a resolution – a way to integrate the inwardness of conscience and subjectivity into the political realm or substance of the state to produce a modern form of ethical life. The right to make reforms in religion had seemed to be the most natural basis from which to start.[37] This world history did not merely imply the judgement of power, but rather self-consciousness and freedom, what the theologians call providence: 'the interpretation and realization of universal spirit'.[38] Hence Schiller's words: 'Separate from the political realm, the German people established their own value, and even though the Empire may have perished, … German greatness endures. It is an ethical greatness … independent of its political fate'.[39]

4.0.6 Outline

In the first section (Section 4.1), I return once again to the issue of Roman law, which has recurred so frequently in this book. Yet, in this instance, I frame this jurisprudence within the historical context of the revolutionary Terror, in the despotism of freedom of Robespierre in which the individual, like the slave, was directly exposed to the power of the national state – producing radical equality and with an eye to Fichte's subjective idealism.

I demonstrate how Hegel directed his institutional concept of the state and the universal constitution of the estates against French centralization (both republican and Napoleonic). He also opposed those imperial estates that had successfully destroyed the subordinate systems and bodies through the application of aristocratic despotism, a topic we are now more than familiar with. Prussia, through its competitive regime that stood against the Empire, had most successfully carried this out. Prussia formalized the inheritance of Roman jurisprudence as it had been passed down in rational natural law, structuring it into a novel codification.[40]

In Hegel's affirmation of the subordinate systems and bodies, his relation to the existent institutions of the Empire becomes visible. These are an important source for his developing institutionalism. The fragments of the *Verfassungsschrift* provide substantive materials for understanding the structural organization of Hegel's political thought, which aims at a speculative unity in conceptual monistic form yet is rooted in an empirical and historical order of constitutions. Through his attack on the aristocratic despotism of the imperial estates and his affirmation of the Empire, Hegel's perspective aligns with reform absolutism. This also brings his thought into dialogue with the dualistic typology of despotism or the restricted form that Kant had translated into the dichotomy of despotism and republicanism. I thus demonstrate that Hegel's developing monism, his initial doctrine of political organism with its subordinate systems and bodies, was drawn from the sphere of imperial public law. Hegel's institutionalism belongs first and foremost to the German tradition and imperial constitutional context.[41]

The second section (Section 4.2) turns to absolute idealism and its particular analysis of the status quo of the state, differentiating it from government and constitution in the modern sense. This analysis decidedly followed the public law literature, most certainly Majer and perhaps also Pütter. Hegel adopted the division between the *Staatsverfassung* and government or administration through the estates and this complex arguably found its way into the mature *Rechtsphilosophie*.[42] I show how this led to a structured monism, where the *civitas composita* becomes part of a governmental architecture of the state, following the pre-critical metaphysics of Leibniz and Spinoza in *System der Sittlichkeit*. Such references provide immediate insight into Hegel's allegiance within German natural law. Historiography has emphasized a profound opposition between empirical (Pufendorf, Thomasius) natural law and metaphysical (Wolffian) approaches. This also includes the later critical methodology (Kant), which revised the entire history of the discipline yet was particularly related to the metaphysical school.[43] Hegel bridges the opposition, as we will see (Section 4.3).

At its most obvious level, Hegel's structured monism of the state was directed against the polarized transcendental idealism of Kant and Fichte. In the arguments of the period, these philosophies had reduced nature to an object. For Hegel, they had emboldened the concept of the machine state and mechanism, leading to the atomization of the individual; their varying conceptions of the organic were wholly insufficient. For Hegel, the machine state had direct historical equivalents in revolutionary French egalitarianism and Prussian absolutism, where the bourgeois principle had triumphed. I demonstrate how Hegel's institutionalism was opposed to ministerial centralization and mass democracy. These stand at the foundation of his alternative political conception, which connects to the monadic doctrine of simple substances – Leibniz's revision of Spinoza's single substance. This results in a highly idiosyncratic conception of the corporate territorial state, even of the imperial state, given Hegel's historical context.

In the final section (Section 4.3), I resume the discussion on the crisis above. I turn to Hegel's conceptualization of the turning point, of world history, focusing particularly on the Germanic World and its relation to the Empire. This involves examining the theorizations of public law, conscience and the right to make reforms in religion as successively established in the great treaties. On the one hand, I demonstrate how Hegel developed a decisive eschatology that sought to fill the void left after the collapse of imperial public law. On the other hand, I show how this involved a distinctive theory of conscience and consciousness that led directly to the modern constitutional state.

4.1 The machinery of enlightened revolution

4.1.1 Roman law and revolution

I have already analysed the issue of Roman law and aristocratic despotism in Hegel's early political thought. Yet, as I emphasized at the outset of that section,[44] there was another, and indeed perhaps far more obvious, object to consider in Hegel's critique of the decadence of ancient imperial Rome and the political vapidity of its jurisprudence. This was present, on the one hand, in Fichte's philosophy (from which Hegel's understanding of Roman law was derived to a certain extent, according to the critical literature);[45] on the other hand, the overwhelming importance of the political and historical context of the French Revolution cannot be denied.[46]

For Hegel, Roman law prized above all the property relation and the contract. It introduced an abstract equality and structured the basis of a formal legal personhood irrespective of the organic hierarchy of estates. With its destruction of the estates and the introduction of the *Code Civil* (1804) that in part reflected Roman jurisprudence, the French Republic during both the revolutionary and imperial periods was emblematic in this respect. A similar legal machinery could be identified in the enlightened Prussian state represented by the *Allgemeines Landrecht für die Preußischen Staaten* (1792) that, in its very organizational structure, followed the Justinian system of institutions. Procedure and method might have diverged, but there could be little talk of a real philosophical foundation. Thus, the expectation that legal provisions, concepts and materials would be drawn from nature and the 'innermost sanctity of philosophy' remained unfulfilled. Roman law provided the *Allgemeines Landrecht* with its legal substance.[47]

4.1.2 The minimal state

Before examining such things directly, Hegel's minimal concept of the state must be considered. Doing so will better position us to observe the distinction he was drawing between the imperial order – and how it could possibly be formed into a real state – and the form of political modernity to which he was wholly opposed.

Hegel gave the Empire a speculative dimension which mirrored existing structures, bringing his institutionalism into closer proximity with imperial publicism. The fact that the Empire with its distinct corporate forms could be viewed as an important source for Hegel's institutionalism has never been analysed in the critical literature – or at least never beyond Rosenzweig's initial intuitions. This observation has most likely gone unnoticed because it has been overshadowed by the overwhelmingly negative conclusions Hegel was forced to draw with respect to the Empire, given the increasingly evident historical consequences of the wars with revolutionary France. Beyond this, we must consider the publication history of the *Verfassungsschrift* and *System der Sittlichkeit*.[48]

It is worth emphasizing just how minimal Hegel's concept of the political really was. Whereas he indeed viewed power as a necessary attribute to public authority and government, it cannot be claimed that he went much further than this self-evident requirement. Indeed, this is precisely how he was able to affirm the imperial corporate system to structure his idea of the state, not to mention his attempt to develop a working federal model. In other words, he drew directly from the political *adiaphora* of the Empire. The free scope given to the citizen in the sphere of government or administration, in justice or civil law – whatever was left outside of the fixed quantum of a public authority – lent power if not fundamental organization to the state.[49] Even the contemporary liberal state, as Walter Jaeschke has so accurately emphasized, has further reach into the lives of its citizens.[50]

There are two things worth considering in this context. The first is that the alternative Hegel proposed, which drew on the prevailing structures of the Empire, cannot be separated from what he was opposing. Thus, his early institutionalism was emboldened by his political opposition to the Prussian power state and French centralization. Secondly, there is the intellectual lineage to consider. This drew Hegel to the history of German public law as well as to the systems of idealism to which his speculative theorizations equally belonged: his engagement with and transformation of Kant, Schelling and Fichte into his own system of absolute idealism, which we will study in the next section.

Beyond the necessity of establishing a supreme power and public authority – sovereignty in the classical understanding of the term, fundamentally defining the state as state – and thus ensuring internal and external security and collective defence against threats from other states, the imperial *adiaphora* prevailed. Conversely, these had been destroyed or brought under the control of a centralized power in republican France and in the aristocratic despotism of the electorate and imperial estate of Brandenburg-Prussia, which had introduced an artificial system of legislation with the *Allgemeines Landrecht*. Like France, Prussia too was based on the bourgeois principle, having undermined or created a feigned system of representation. This monocratic state was truly *the* power state in Germany. Hegel's analysis of Prussian aristocratic despotism, viewed in terms of its position as a citizen of the Empire, thus corresponded in its lineaments to Pütter's examination. This is to say nothing of the fact that it mirrors to a large extent what has been elaborated in the contemporary historiography. Absolutist Brandenburg-Prussia has been identified as the emblematic power state that used its military for domestic political purposes.[51]

In stark contrast to Prussian aristocratic despotism, the different corporate structures of the Empire provided Hegel with a variety of organic forms that could be used against what he identified as the mechanization of the state. His own view of the one and the many suggested that diversities contained elements of value and that without embracing diversity the larger whole would lack something. Of course, it was not enough to simply have a diversity of forms. In the worst case, in the absence of public authority – the larger whole – they produced little more than anarchy. Yet their destruction in the name of territorial consolidation undermined the very foundations of civic freedom. What was required was their organization in a legal constitution.

At times Hegel came very close to Pütter's comprehension of the objective legal connection. This was certainly the case if we consider his reflections in terms of one of the categories of his later concept of absolute spirit – religion. This will be explored in depth in the final section of this chapter. What is worth noting here, however, is just how strongly Hegel drew on the *adiaphora* or rather separated their freedoms from the need for a unified public authority. In this way, they did not come into conflict with the organization of sovereignty: 'the institutions of the magistrates, the rights of the cities and estates, etc., all these circumstances are only relatively important for the state and the form of their organization is indifferent to its true nature'.[52]

Philosophically, these structures were akin to ethical life or custom and habit. They thus contributed to the way in which the people were organized. For Hegel, the concern was to shape an objective legal connection through positive constitutional law whereby government could be established and a system of legislation realized that would form an object of speculative identity in complete accordance with such institutions – an organic outgrowth of the free activity of the subordinate systems and bodies.

4.1.3 Form against formlessness

State constitution and government must not come at the cost of sacrificing custom. On the contrary, they must emerge out of it. Thus, Hegel saw how the *adiaphora*, broadly interpreted in the historical development of the legal character of representation in the Empire, had contributed their freedom to modern European constitutionalism. In periods when culture had become formal by contrast, the separation of law and custom became fixed. In this context, crudeness in relation to the constitution became the norm while the machinery of legislation was directed against the single individual or corporate entity. The former was overwhelmingly prevalent in systems in which 'compulsion, conceived as a reality, i.e. presented in a system and in totality, immediately cancels itself and the whole'.[53] This coercive machinery was identified with Fichte's idealism and revolutionary fanaticism in which 'the absolute concept, the direct opposite of itself, is real, because the product is not an identity of the subjective and the objective, but pure objectivity, formlessness'.[54]

Hegel's denunciation of formlessness in this instance, unlike Majer, was not directed against the Empire which in fact had an almost infinite diversity of institutions but rather condemned the machinery of legislation that followed the 'pedantic desire to determine every detail, the unfree eagerness to order and administer an estate, corporation, etc., oneself, clothed in the garb of rational principles'.[55] It was accompanied by an axiomatic form of individualism stripped of any reference to the corporative universality of the inegalitarian system of estates.

Hegel's alternative model was obvious. In contrast to such formlessness, the constitution of '*freedom is in the form, and in the fact that the individual part, acting for itself and its own determinateness, is a subordinate system of the whole organism*'.[56] On the other hand, he saw the rigidly formal as destructive of the individual and the lower spheres or institutions of the state: 'the absolute government is not formal only because it presupposes the distinction of the estates and is thus truly supreme'.[57] In other words, the corporate elements common among the territorial states in the Empire could decisively shape an institutional idea and play a central role in the conception of political organism. The same assertion can be observed in a much later reference to the centralization of the French state under the ministerial dictates of Napoleon, detailing the importance of the corporation and communities as principles of balance and organic structuration.[58] For Hegel, in the fragments of the *Verfassungsschrift*, the legislative absolutism of the French and Prussian models was to be rejected outright. By contrast,

> a state power, without fear or jealousy, freely leaves to the subordinate systems and bodies a great part of the relations which arise in society, and their maintenance according to the laws; and every estate, town, village community, etc., may enjoy the liberty of doing and executing for themselves what lies within their districts. As the laws concerning this have gradually emerged directly from the customs themselves as sacred conventions [*Herkommen*], so has the legal constitution [*Rechtsverfassung*], the institutions of the lower courts and the rights of citizens developed within them.[59]

This reinforces the central importance of Hegel's relationship to the diverse institutions of the Empire and, arguably, how they, along with the legal constitution, form the later spheres of civil society. It is already clear that Hegel does not identify this legal constitution directly with the supreme point of union, the sovereignty of the state.[60] Rather, the legal constitution is the domain of freedom. Whereas these 'subordinate systems of rights and privileges' must not hinder the main activity of the state which can act against them in pursuing its objectives, it still represents

> a great advantage of the ancient states of Europe that, by securing the state power for its needs and its operation, it leaves a free scope for the citizens' own activity in the individual administration of justice, administration, etc., partly with regard to the appointment of the necessary officials, partly to the management of current business and the administration of laws and customs.[61]

This is a tradition that is also most strikingly evident in the mature *Rechtsphilosophie*: 'where Hegel still remained wedded to this ideal of a corporate society organized into "estates" with distinct functions.'[62]

The various forms of *adiaphora* did not, however, alter Hegel's insight into the necessity of the state. Grasping the single substance structured through the simple, he was able to circumvent the individualism at the basis of the modern revolution in which 'the separate energies of the ethical must be conceived in the state of nature or in the abstraction of man as in a mutually annihilating war'.[63] This proved how an abstract natural jurisprudence, whether empirical or formal, was ensnared in the threads of fate that finally resulted in the Reign of Terror.[64] It also reflected the equality introduced in the bourgeois state that had destroyed the system of estates and followed the dictates of a centralized mechanism, the social mechanics identified by Emmanuel Joseph Sieyès (1748–1836) observable in the *Déclaration des droits de l'homme et du citoyen* and Articles 1, 3 and 6 of the French constitution of 1791.[65] In such formal systems, the estates along with the provinces, parishes and corporations had lost all authority.[66]

For Hegel, the legal condition of abstract equality, leaving all anachronism aside, was particular to the introduction of a formal legal personhood that had historically emerged with Roman law that he identified strikingly with this levelling of the estates.

Roman law was at one with the enlightened machinery of revolution and the new gospel of universal equality. The problem remained everywhere one and the same: the destruction of the institutions exposed the single individual directly to a despotic power, slavery and equality triumphant: 'the deserted territories, deprived of political strength or unity, sank imperceptibly into the languid indifference of *private life*'.[67]

How, then, was it possible to affirm the higher ethical reality of the state without effacing the individual? Strikingly, Hegel's solution exhibited a structure remarkably similar to the conceptual differentiation between a superordinate state constitution with universal public law and a territorial government law subordinate to the overall system. This was organized structurally for Hegel in *System der Sittlichkeit* through the universal constitution of the estates:

> According to power, the universal is in its reality superior to the particular, for in whatever potentiality it may be, governing is formally, the absolute universal, the power of the whole is attached to it; but the government must at the same time be the *positive* absolute universal, thereby it is absolute potentiality; and the question is everywhere in the difference, that the government is truly potentiality against the particular, that the individuals are necessarily in the universal and the ethical.[68]

For Hegel, the individual was integrated through the custom of corporate belonging into the totality of the state through the estates: 'The relation of the different estates is not a relation of individual to individual; but each individual, by belonging to an estate, is a universal.'[69] This formed a direct contrast to the natural law individualism at the foundations of the revolutionary state and, to a much lesser extent, the theorizations of German natural law that always began with the house community. Hegel explicated his ideal through state constitution and government, effectively leveraging divisions that had been introduced to explain the diverse jurisdictions in the Empire. The Empire and Austria appeared in a far more positive light than either revolutionary France or the aristocratic despotism of Prussia as the territorial estates, the subordinate systems and bodies – and thus the representative principle – had been preserved in an organic fashion. What was needed was a positive system, a constitution that secured the universal corporate individual in public laws.

> The contradiction that the state is the supreme power, and that individuals are not oppressed by it, is resolved by the power of the laws; it is the disbelief in the power of the laws [*Gesetze*] that stems from the lack of wisdom, which oscillates between the necessity of giving the state the supreme power and the fear that the individual will be oppressed by it. All wisdom in the organization of states rests on the solution of this problem; the first thing, however, is that there should be a state, the first thing, therefore, that the power of the state should be supreme; but directly in this also lies the fact that there are laws [*Gesetze*].[70]

This description from the *Reinschrift* coincides with the idea from *System der Sittlichkeit* that government is the absolute universal but that it simultaneously must be *positive*: that is, that there are laws. This 'positive absolute universal' corresponds to 'the power of the laws' in the *Verfassungsschrift* and illustrates Hegel's consistent notion that the state's highest vitality lies in positive public legislation; that *Staatsgesetze* embody a concrete, active universal, mediating between the state's supreme power and individual freedom. This active universal is further articulated in the monarch's role alongside the estates:

> In an educated state the laws, or universality, stand between the personality of the monarch and the individuals; the single act of the monarch affects all, harms or injures all, or benefits all. But that the monarch is at the same time the power of the state, or that he has the supreme power, that there is a state at all, is equivalent.[71]

Elsewhere, Hegel had nuanced this position:

> The monarch is in charge of national affairs, especially insofar as they concern external relations with other states; he is the centre of state power, from which everything emanates that requires coercion according to the laws; the legal power is thus in his hands; the estates have a share in the legislation and they provide the means by which power is maintained.[72]

This concrete manifestation of the universal, embodied in the power of laws, necessarily implies the institutional forms through which it operates. This legal universality, a cornerstone of Hegel's modern state, thus found both its historical precursor and ongoing embodiment in the estates. These had evolved from the system of fiefs which had grown from a personal relation between vassal and prince to an objective legal relationship in the Empire. Like Pütter before him, Hegel had recognized how personality in the constitution of fiefs had transformed historically with the imperial constitution into an objective (impersonal) legal form.[73]

This laid the foundations for modern representation and constitutionalism, rather than their destruction. In stark contrast to the relation of mastery and slavery in Roman law, Germanic law demonstrated, as I already quoted in another context, how 'the status relationship was that of a free man, whose status, through voluntary subordination to a military chief, who looked out for his livelihood, was not lowered but raised'.[74] Hegel grasped this historically: 'These contradictory characteristics of a freeman and a vassal are united in the fact that the fiefs are not fiefs of the person of the prince, *but of the Empire*'.[75] The same evolution had first taken place territorially: 'this separation of the person of the prince and his subjects had already been constituted by the territorial estates'.[76] Moreover, 'the separation by territorial estates had already become legal'.[77] Hegel saw clearly where constitutional development had taken place and also how these organic forms were at once abolished by and preserved in modern representation. They constituted *impersonal* institutions, the absolute individuals of the territorial estates and imperial estates or the universal estates as constructed in *System der Sittlichkeit*.

That being said, we must also recognize Hegel's later differentiation between the territorial estates and the corporate structure of the estates as a form of social and political organization. Even if their function remains similar in both cases as a 'guarantee against arbitrariness', a 'universal constitution of the estates' is 'not the territorial estates'.[78]

This nuanced understanding of corporate structures, refined by Hegel, nonetheless builds upon and further articulates the insights of earlier publicists. In large part, this confirmed and extended Pütter's concept of impersonal, objective legal connection. This can be observed further in Hegel's concept of individualism and legal personhood, specifically the corporate belonging to an estate: 'the connection of the individual with the whole people now takes the form of duty, and his possession of a fief and a power is not dependent on the prince's will but is *legal*'.[79] Nonetheless, this positive development was threatened by how 'the disproportionate aggrandisement of individual estates has destroyed the very principle of the constitution of fiefs and the existence of Germany as a state'.[80] This was nowhere more evident than with the consolidation of the power state in Prussia and the destruction of the ancient constitution in France. These developments essentially undermined the organic corporate structures that had originally made an objective legal connection possible. Hegel denounced these absolutistic systems as formal structures that crushed the individual. He set them in opposition to the freedom that was possible in the Germanic World. All that was lacking was the appropriate political organization:

> The fact that in Germany there is no fulfilment of the unjust demand that laws, the administration of justice, the levying and collection of taxes, etc., language, customs and religion be regulated and governed by a single centre, but rather that the most disparate diversity takes place, would not prevent Germany from constituting a state; if it were organized otherwise as a public authority.[81]

All these *adiaphora* stood in sharp contrast to what we must now consider in detail: the machinery of enlightened revolution that, in affirming 'the supreme power of the state', had undermined 'all the institutions which the nature of a society entails' – regulating, ordering, supervising and directing them in every way.[82] This was a formal absolute universal without any true positivity, structurally governing in direct opposition to the individual. Its legal condition might have been universal, but it possessed the character of slavery, of formal equality leading to complete submission:

> The state of nature and the majesty and divinity of the whole of the legal condition, which is alien to the individuals and therefore itself individual and particular, as well as the relation of the absolute submissiveness of the subject to that supreme power, are the forms in which the fragmented moments of organic ethical life are fixed as particular essences and, like the idea, consequently distorted.[83]

This striking passage from Hegel's *Naturrechtsaufsatz* powerfully encapsulates his critique: a state defined solely by its abstract, supreme power, divorced from the organic ethical life of its citizens, inevitably leads to a distorted reality where universality becomes a tool of oppression, not liberation. It is a form of universality that paradoxically fragments the individual, rather than integrating them into a truly ethical whole.

4.1.4 Robespierre's despotism of liberty

For the Göttingen public lawyers, the contractual, voluntary and unequal society of lordship and bondage could degenerate into slavery, resulting in an ownership society that was strictly despotic. The lord of a slave was an owner, the obligation of slaves, slavery.[84] Hegel had surveyed the same sequence with the destruction of Greek ethical life in Roman antiquity, a movement that had entirely prepared the foundations for 'the ethical life of the *bourgeois* or of the private person'.[85]

With their abolition of representation and the estate of the free, both Prussia and the French Republic re-enacted the tragedy of the ethical, which had resulted in the mass legislation of Roman private law, raising private property and the contract to an absolute and thus equalizing freedom and slavery in turn. The people had become an anomalous mass: 'If at its apogee ancient civilization failed altogether to produce the category of popular representation, then the institution of slavery surely had a large share in this.'[86] By destroying the separation of powers and dissolving the legal connection to the constitution of fiefs, and by introducing an abstract legal equality, the single individual was exposed directly to formal (despotic) authority in France and Prussia. The creation of artificial systems of representation and legislation was sown on this fallow ground, upon the destruction of the very corporate structures that had historically given representation its original meaning.

It proves helpful to recall the words of Walter Benjamin (1892–1940): 'to Robespierre Ancient Rome was a past charged with the time of the now which he blasted out of the continuum of history. The French Revolution viewed itself as Rome reincarnate.'[87] In this way, the French Republic, both Robespierre's despotism of liberty as well as the imperial ambitions of Napoleon, was the object of Hegel's considerable scorn. If we consider this alongside Montesquieu's diagnosis, attributed to the age of absolutism, then France forms in a relatively rapid pace the historical transitions of Roman antiquity: from monarchy to republic and empire. To this we would do well to add that *System der Sittlichkeit* was designed as a critique of Fichtean natural law.[88] Part of Villey's frustration about Hegel's analysis of Roman law was that the most important sources for his understanding of it he claimed came from philosophy, from Fichte's *Grundlage des Naturrechts* (1796) (Foundations of Natural Right) and Kant's *Metaphysik der Sitten* (1797) (The Metaphysics of Morals).[89] The legal condition introduced in Roman antiquity had led to formal legal personhood that Hegel, arguably following Kant, equated with a state of nature or *status iuridicus*, abstract right:[90] 'The universal fragmented into the atoms of the absolute many individuals, this dead spirit is an *equality* in which *all* are considered as *each*, as *persons*.'[91]

For Robespierre – not unlike Kant in his way – there were only two types of government: freedom, embodied in the people, and the despotism of tyranny.[92] Consequently, he demonstrated how justice and human reason were corrupted by despotism. The latter followed a logic made only for its own self-serving ends, which in turn debased the thoughts, feelings and morals of people. For Robespierre, the *ancien régime* served as the historical model that he weighed against virtue as 'principe fondamentale du gouvernement démocratique ou populaire'.[93] This was identical to 'vertu publique' that was nothing less than love for the nation and its laws.[94] By contrast, the immoral was the 'contre-révolutionnaire' that conformed in every way with the weakness, errors and prejudice that were the calling cards of absolutist monarchy.[95]

Nonetheless, as Robespierre conceded, in order to realize public virtue a form of radical enforcement or coercion was necessary. This was the significance of terror, of 'justice prompte, sévère et inflexible' without which virtue was bereft of all power.[96] It was in this context that he argued that revolutionaries could learn from despots: 'Le gouvernement de la révolution est le despotisme de la liberté contre la tyrannie'.[97] At its most extreme, terror was even considered a form of mercy – the punishment meted out to oppressors equivalent to clemency. By contrast, to forgive them for their infractions was pure barbarism.[98]

At the foundation of the revolutionary French state stood the rational individual. The *Déclaration des droits de l'homme et du citoyen* made the dictates of natural jurisprudence positive in its deduction of the innate human rights that preceded the political order. The state of nature had become identical with a condition of absolute positive legal freedom, abstract equality. Yet, for Hegel, this represented an entirely formal individualism and an illogical form of reasoning a priori. It was an anomaly discoverable not only in the French Revolution and in the introduction of a legal equality in Roman law but also in the upheavals of German idealism or classical German philosophy.

Hegel sought to critique these streams of thought and action simultaneously, activities which had been pursued 'by would be philosophers and teachers of human rights'.[99] Based on the particular will of citizens, Fichte's organic central authority, for example, grasped how 'the individual, according to the contract of union, becomes part of an organized whole and thus merges with it into one'.[100] The axiomatic individualism of formal natural law was thus abolished in the state. Following the ancient Aristotelian tradition in which an individualism pre-existing the state was utterly alien, Hegel inverted the Kantian and Fichtean logic and thus also the rational individualism operative in the French revolutionary state. In this way, the *polis* – or Hegel's *Volk* – was ontologically prior (*physei proteron*): the whole far greater in order of importance than the part.[101] Preceding any notion of the individual, the people similarly was also organized for the final cause of its own perfection – the origin of all law and legislation lay in its customs: 'there is no reason and common sense *a priori*, nor any experience *a priori*, which would be an absolutely universal one, but only the living individuality of a people, an individuality whose highest determinations are again to be comprehended from a universal necessity'.[102]

Without its ethical world of institutions that brought about the very possibility of reason and language, the spirit of its laws in Montesquieu's sense, the individual must remain a pure abstraction. Hegel weighed this against the structured monism of the estates, denying the validity of the contract for political organization, which was common to the reception of Roman law that had undermined the imperial constitution through the *cives imperii* as well as rational natural law and Fichte's concept of the state.

Hegel's interpretation of Roman law is clearly marked by eclecticism. In actual fact Roman antiquity, like ancient Greece, had similarly presupposed the existence of the whole, the *civitas* – the state of nature completely unknown. In his revolutionary political immanentism that saw the individual citizen as the raw material of the state, Fichte's organism was structurally similar to the French revolutionary state, Prussian absolutism and the private legal world of Roman jurisprudence as Hegel had interpreted it: 'The same relationship existed between the isolated human being and the citizen.'[103] Where were the estates? Fichte constructed them artificially, mirroring the Prussian system of legislation:[104] 'There are, however, by nature only two different estates: one that only trains its body for mechanical labour and one that trains its mind exquisitely. Between these two estates there is a true mésalliance; and apart from this there are none.'[105]

Obviously with such a rigid opposition, organic unity was hardly conceivable – let alone the connection between landed property and the peasantry it had under its command or the nobility organized for war, preserving the ethical order.

4.1.5 The Roman World and political modernity

From the perspective of a wide-ranging historical and comparative constitutional analysis, for Hegel the political relationship to the constitution of fiefs, which provided representation with an original objective legal basis, distinguished the particular character of differentiated modern state constitutional development. In reference to England, the constitution of fiefs had evolved in a conservative-liberal direction, into parliament and its subsequent division into the House of Lords and the House of Commons. In France, the antagonism between the estates had dissolved the very structure – eventually producing a legal equality without status. Absolutism, however, had already destroyed the constitution of fiefs in transforming the nobility into uniform court functionaries. The Empire, for its part, through the extension of the constitution of fiefs to a system of states had foundered on the shores of its manifold polities.

For Montesquieu, Roman law had a role to play in the development of French absolutism. With the French Revolution, the political impotency of the nobility was democratized in an egalitarian fashion, resulting in a system of artificial representation.[106] Thus, for Hegel 'France's misfortune must be sought solely in the complete degeneration of the constitution of fiefs and the loss of its true character as a result of the assemblies of the Estates-General that were formed, the high and low nobility no longer appeared in the character in which its main strength lies in political organization, namely to be representative.'[107]

This is a more or less exact parallel to the discussion from the *Naturrechtsaufsatz* that saw the absolute estate, the estate of the free, become synonymous with the formal property-owning estate, the bourgeoisie – the sole people in the empirical phenomenon of the decline of Greek ethical life in Ancient Rome.[108] The main difference lies in the emphasis on the representative function that the governing estate ought to serve and how instead of being situated historically in antiquity, it was directed more emphatically at the modernity of the French Revolution that had clothed itself in Roman republican ideals.

Under the power of royal authority and the introduction of a new artificial system of taxation, Prussia, just like France, had utterly destroyed its corporate system of representation – the systems and bodies that made up the 'true constitution' in *System der Sittlichkeit* which had precise empirical equivalents in the description of the diversity of corporate forms existent in the Holy Roman Empire of the German Nation.[109]

Without exception, the centralized French Republic and absolutist Prussia are the enemies of the *Verfassungsschrift* – not only theoretically but also practically on the battlefield.[110] Such states followed 'the fundamental prejudice that a state is a machine with a single spring, which imparts motion to all the rest of the infinite mechanism'.[111] For the prophet of revolution Sieyès, this social mechanics was identified with 'the true means to provide for the great needs of political societies'.[112]

For Hegel, the regime of Terror and Virtue, the 'blind clamour for so-called freedom' of the French Revolution, signified just how necessary an organized structured form of government and constitution through the universal system of the estates really was.[113] Otherwise, 'in this bloody game the cloud of freedom has melted away'.[114] The corporate differentiation between the estates delineated in *System der Sittlichkeit* was directed against the despotism of liberty of a Robespierre in which the single individual, just like the slave, was immediately exposed, with the destruction of the estates, to the master: 'The answer that *Robespierre* gave to everything – here someone had thought this, done that, wanted this, or said that – was: **la mort**! Its uniformity is utterly boring, but it fits everything.'[115]

Robespierre was the master of the revolutionary state that produced an equality of slavery: 'the whole power of reality falls into one lump and the crudeness of this lump would have its equally crude and reckless power undivided at its apex'.[116] Similarly, Fichte's organism of the state was 'something hovering above [the] individual, something formal, for the formal is precisely the unity which is not in itself an absolute concept or absolute movement'.[117] The latter, we would do well to recall, was how government was structured through the estates as an organic principle. Robespierre and Napoleon were latter-day Neros. Like necromancers, they had revived the rotten corpse of imperial Rome: 'The mankind of late antiquity, having been reduced to the existence of a colorless mass, begins for a while to revere its lost self in the divine emperor. But the Caesars are no less people of the masses than their subjects are.'[118]

Ethical life became real when the individual in belonging to every estate belonged to none. This placed an emphasis on parity, participation and representation. The destruction of individual particularity took on a legal form through the knowledge of the universality of the law.[119] The universal legal person effaced the single individual, the slave in relation to the master, and thus the legislative rationalism of the machine state. Under the second form of government, the system of justice, the legislative power, this lent further significance to the idea that 'the organic principle is the freedom that the ruler himself is the ruled'.[120] A constitution must have this legal form, must be composed of universal *Staatsgesetze*, otherwise it is a despotism, as Kant had highlighted in the problem of mass revolutionary democracy. Equivalent to despotism, the relationship of mastery and slavery, a constitution without representation either followed the unorganized power of a revolutionary democracy or the condescension of the Roman *paterfamilias*. In mass democracy everyone wished to be sovereign. Thus, by *legerdemain*, all were slaves to the governing power: 'all the citizens may make decisions about (and indeed against) the single individual without his consent, so that decisions are made by all the people and not yet by all the people'.[121] Hegel followed

Kant, believing a constitution without representation to be unthinkable, an anomaly – essentially *without form*.[122]

4.1.6 From Kant's separation of powers to Fichte's Ephorate and the constituent power of the French revolutionary state

Without the separation of powers, for Kant neither form nor representation existed, but an absurd identification of one and the same person as legislator and executor of his own will: '*Republicanism* is the political principle whereby the executive power (the government) is separated from the legislative power. Despotism prevails in a state if the laws are made and arbitrarily executed by one and the same power.'[123] The French political system had attacked the venerability of the separation of powers, the freedom of Montesquieu's scheme.[124] This led to 'crudeness in relation to a constitution, in which nothing is separated but rather the whole as such moves directly against every individual characteristic of the determination, is a formlessness and the abolition of freedom'.[125] To counter this, Hegel took up the organic movement of ideal and real subsumption from Kant's syllogism and the freedom that existed in the form, the institutionalism of the subordinate systems and bodies.[126]

If this was not a direct critique of Robespierre and his rejection of the separation of powers in the name of the Roman people that leveraged the tribunate against the aristocracy and patricians, it was certainly an assault on the likeminded Fichte. Hegel's interest in the *Allgemeines Landrecht* had focused on the contributions of Ernst Ferdinand Klein (1744–1810) that were primarily concerned with penal law and the prison system. Importantly, Klein had attacked Kant's separation of powers. Fichte was also known for his engagement with the Prussian code.[127] And he had similarly questioned the applicability of the separation of powers to taxonomically distinguish republicanism from despotism, breaking with Kant and the reigning theorizations of the Göttingen School, which the Königsberg philosopher had appropriated: 'I have been led to other thoughts about the assumption that it is conducive to the security of law in the state to separate the legislative and executive powers, as Kant seems to assume.'[128] Still, as he later added, 'a constitution where the administrators of public power have no responsibility is a *despotism*'.[129] To resolve this issue, Fichte famously appealed to the Ephorate.

While resonating with the early modern Monarchomachism of Johannes Althusius (1563–1638), Fichte's Ephorate, as the critical literature has highlighted, may have much more in common with the tradition of the Roman tribunes than Sparta, an equation Cicero had already employed to advantage in republican antiquity.[130] Given the epoch in which Althusius was writing, a period when the *translatio imperii* was a living reality, this Roman legacy was probably no less true. From Fichte's historical context, we can add that Cicero was one of the principal authors the French revolutionaries and Robespierre drew on in their understanding of the Roman Senate as a central institution of public life, translated into the controversies surrounding the revolutionary state. Such perceptions betrayed a strong senatorial bias in which the decline of the Roman Republic was directly linked to the loss of power of the Senate.[131]

The question as to how Fichte was led to other thoughts about the separation of powers in *Grundlage des Naturrechts* might perhaps be most adequately situated in this context. Robespierre had turned to Roman history and the idea of the tribunate to counter aristocracy and nominally the Senate. Eventually, this took on the form of the National Convention and Committee of Public Safety as dictatorial organs in which executive and legislative power were united and that further suppressed every form of local government, having ultimate plenary control akin to the Senate of Roman antiquity.[132] For Hegel, the Fichtean and French republican notions, theory and reality, were dangerously equivalent. Indeed, it is a short step to see his early systematic political conceptions as responding to what he considered common to both – fanaticism:

> A formal idea of absolute government is to be found in all systems of theory, as well as of reality, namely, of an organic central authority, and indeed one which preserves the constitution; but α) such an idea as Fichte's Ephorate is in its negative attitude quite formal, and empty, ß) and since all possible supervision of government in all particulars is ascribed to it, thus a crude mixture of the universal and the individual [exists] in it; it is supposed to be a power over everything, thus to have a commanding, overpowering effect; and yet at the same time, as a power, it is supposed to be nothing.[133]

Hegel, then, viewed the organic central authority of Fichte as a very precise equivalent to the revolutionary French state and its formal idea of constituent power: a non-institutionalized source of all institutions, a formless formalism, *the* principal organizing element that defies the very idea of organization. After the fall of Robespierre, this parallelism even took a more pronounced form in the 'commission des lois organiques', tasked with implementing the constitution. Such organic laws are 'laws that concern the matter of the constitution as the basic organization of the body politic, that supplement and elaborate it and are therefore not normal laws, but laws that further shape the organization or (later) the organism of the constitution'.[134] Eventually, this implied that a constitution must find the rule for its organization within itself.[135] A form-giving power that saw the mutual co-dependent genesis of constitution and organization was immanent to the idea. This raised the spectre of the status of such laws. Were they legislative or constituent?

Sieyès had analysed this issue incisively. There were essential constitutional laws, those concerning the organization of legislative and executive bodies, which could only be decided by the nation as a constituent power. Every corporate body was subject to the possibility of becoming unjust, of separating its interests from the universal. Only the nation was incapable of this insofar as its interests were identical with the universal as such.[136] This was the crude mixture Hegel identified in Fichte's Ephorate, a formal power over everything but a nothing at the same time.

The nation so considered was a will without an organization, even though all organization contradictorily proceeded from it. Thus, what had applied to the constituted did not apply to the constituent: 'It is impossible to create a body for an end without giving it the organization, forms, and laws it needs to fulfil the functions for which it has been established. This is what is meant by the *constitution* of that body.'[137] By contrast, the nation was form giving without form, even though a very close relationship existed between organization, constitution and the exercise of constituent power. When Sieyès had identified the third estate with the nation, the destruction of the system of estates was at hand as well as the separation of powers tied to it. For Hegel, this could only lead to a formal idea of government, a fanaticism that destroyed the freedom of the form – the revolutionary constituent power of the nation, a pure abstraction: 'Just as the third estate no longer has its own representation in execution, no gradual transition from the hard form to a suitable one had taken place in the new Etats Generaux.'[138] What the system of ethical life offered, by contrast, was a *reality* by which a state organization could be grasped; it was only through historicity of customs and institutions that the political had an organization and this was made real through the system of estates.

4.2 The division between constitutional law and government law: Political metaphysics and the structured monism of the state

4.2.1 Leibniz and Spinoza in Hegel's early absolute idealism

In *Elementa iuris publici Germanici*, Pütter had made passing reference to Ludolph Hugo's work when analysing the peculiarity of the imperial *forma Reipublicae*, noting how it consisted not only of a single state but of many particular states that were subordinate to the emperor.[139] This observation, for Pütter, was definitive. What set Pütter apart from Hugo's classification, however, 'was mainly conditioned by his different approach, which resembled that of Leibniz. He concentrated on the historical process by which several independent states amalgamate into a larger whole.'[140] This methodology, even when leaving specific historical accounts aside, found a striking parallel in Hegel's early absolute idealism. Indeed, if Pütter's *civitas composita* can be described as an amalgamated complex state of states, the political organism with its absolute individuals in *System der Sittlichkeit* can be classified as a substantial state of simple estates.

This classificatory parallel firmly positioned Hegel's thinking within the metaphysical tradition of German natural law or the philosophical idealism of universal public law, distinguishing his approach from prevalent empirical and formal methodologies. Hegel detailed the divisions in the discipline of natural law, speaking of the empirical approach (Pufendorf, Hobbes, Grotius and Thomasius) of self-preservation, love and hatred, sociability and the like and 'the more scientific empiricism' of Wolff that differed from pure empiricism as the relationship between quality and object had become fixed in a conceptual form, natural law strictly deduced from higher axioms. Ultimately, this led to the formal approach championed by Kant and Fichte.[141] Hegel condemned the pure abstraction of this formal approach, which, for him, reduced empiricism and nature to dead matter. It was precisely to overcome this formalism that he turned to several sources, most pre-critical but not all metaphysical (Aristotle, Montesquieu, Spinoza and Leibniz).

Hegel's philosophy radically affirmed a systematic approach to science and philosophy, directly following Leibniz and echoing his call for a new method of learning and teaching jurisprudence.[142] Still, in the mature *Rechtsphilosophie* Hegel critically distinguished his philosophical method from the merely formal consistency of the *Corpus iuris civilis* that Leibniz had praised when he called for its logical restructuring, stating: 'That consistency praised by Leibniz is certainly an essential property of legal science, as of mathematics and every other intelligent science; but this consistency of the understanding has nothing yet to do with the satisfaction of the demands of reason and with philosophical science.'[143] In other words, the *novo methodus* Hegel set out to develop would also be distinguished from the Leibnizian approach. Still, in his commitment to system and a rational and deductive methodology, he followed Leibniz and Wolff whose ideal of philosophy as 'the science of all possible things' or *Weltweisheit* made it possible to construct a system of the world on the basis of a single principle.[144] For Hegel, this culminated in his own entirely 'new treatment of philosophy' that presented a method 'identical with its contents'.[145] His speculative logic, designed as a bridge between the rational (metaphysical) and the real (empirical), thus conserved and transformed previous logical and metaphysical forms of thought by incorporating further categories, embracing empiricism within a comprehensive system. His dialectic was thus designed as a bridge between the rational and the real.[146] Hegelianism as a movement occupied a similar position in the university, for however brief a period, as Wolffian civil religion.[147]

The pre-critical metaphysics of Leibniz had played a central, even leading, role in the theoretical context of Hegel's early absolute idealism. On the one hand, alongside the ultimately more important Spinoza, it was used as a way to structure the objective pole of subject-object identity. Leibnizian metaphysics thus served an organizational function which allowed Hegel to further grasp the single substance yet structured through the simple which was irreducible: 'In contrast to this principle of absolute unity [of Spinoza], Leibniz made the absolute multiplicity, the individual substance, the principle, which, however, is unified in God, the monas monadum.'[148] This confection of pre-critical substance metaphysics eventually led Hegel to his own speculative language or philosophical science of reason, liberated from Schelling and entailing a rapprochement to Fichte, who structured the subjective pole of subject-object identity.[149]

The genesis of Hegel's idealistic philosophy goes beyond our present concerns. Rather, what is important to highlight is how he used the theoretical insights of Leibniz in *System der Sittlichkeit* to organize the substance metaphysics of Spinoza 'according to which all things are in God and there is nothing singular'.[150] This led to a very distinct idea of the state that mirrored the discussion on the imperial constitution to a large extent through the introduction of its characteristic division between the *forma imperii* and the *forma regiminis*, which, with Majer, became state constitution and government, the constitution in the modern sense as the legal norms governing state power.

In the *Differenzschrift*, Spinoza was identified as *the* philosopher of union. He had solved a problem intrinsic to early modern metaphysical dualism, reinterpreting the Cartesian doctrine of *res cogitans* and *res extensa*: 'thinking substance and extended substance are one and the same substance, comprehended now under this attribute, now under that. So, too, a mode of extension and the idea of that mode are one and the same thing, expressed in two ways.'[151] Moreover, Spinoza had denounced teleology and the notion of final causes that he attributed psychologically to an all-too-human narcissism.[152] This was isolated in the context of a critique of Kant's idea of organism in *Glauben und Wissen* (1802).[153] Hegel demonstrated that this notion too belonged to human psychology; an illusory abstract pre-existent unity, wholly subjective, although Kant had identified it with a supreme and transcendent principle of reason, the unity of particular and universal. The simple avoidance of the concept of mechanism could not avert the reduction of nature to the purely human mode of observation, of limited discursive human understanding 'in whose general concepts the particular phenomena of nature are not contained'.[154]

For Hegel, Spinoza's pre-critical substance metaphysics got around this problem of metaphysical dualism that had been reintroduced in Kantian critical philosophy, only to be radicalized by Fichte and particularly the romantics who followed in his footsteps. From the standpoint of Hegel's early absolute idealism 'nothing is to be said about the reality of nature by this human mode of observation'[155] in which a systematic totality of knowledge became nothing more than an 'aggregation of facts'.[156]

Hegel deplored the way in which Kant's 'authentic idealism' had degenerated from the true principle of speculation, which attained the identity of subject and object with the transcendental deduction of the categories, to a dogmatic philosophy of the thing in itself: 'whereby nothing but the empty form of opposition is objectively expressed – again hypostasized and posited as absolute objectivity, like the things of the dogmatist'.[157] For Hegel, Kant had thus committed the age-old sin of treating the abstract as something real which then comes to lord itself over reality. This reasserted the Newtonian understanding of nature and the human world, having reduced them to the dictates of mechanism. Derived from a strict understanding of natural laws, fixed movement was prioritized in contrast to a concrete unity or organic whole – such as Hegel's system of the sun or system of ethical life. Similarly, the human subject was degraded to a cog or wheel in a state machine.[158] This political metaphor begs to be explored in greater detail; it forms the core of Hegel's critique of Fichte's organic central authority as well as the concentration of political power in revolutionary France and enlightened Prussia in the fragments of the *Verfassungsschrift*.[159]

If Spinoza answered the problem of metaphysical dualism, Leibniz provided the essential material by which this single substance could be conceptualized as *structured*: 'The monad … is nothing other than a simple substance which enters into compounds, "simple" meaning "without parts".'[160] To this end, Leibniz similarly introduced a principle of organism that was opposed to classical mechanics, widely criticizing Cartesianism and Newtonian physics: 'where there are no parts, neither extension, nor shape, nor divisibility is possible. And these monads are the true atoms of nature and, in a word, the elements of things.'[161] Leibniz's approach was an initial answer to Hegel's later critique of Spinoza's system: 'It lacked infinite form, spirituality, freedom. I have already stated earlier that to set up a system of form is to grasp the organism of the One. Spinoza has renounced this.'[162] As we know, such form was identified with the organization of freedom in *System der Sittlichkeit*.[163]

Fundamentally, Leibniz separated the monad as the true atom from the false atomism of physics, the artificial mechanism from the divine machine. The human connection to God functioned as a simple substance, an organic whole that simply could not be further divided by means of empirical-numerical determination. This flew in the face of the strictly external reproducible relationship of action and reaction that took place under the covering laws of the artificial machine. Leibniz distinguished the latter from the complexity of 'living bodies, [which] are still machines in their smallest parts, to infinity'.[164] He even spoke of an organic mechanism, organic machine and organic molecule. In this way, mechanism was not yet directly opposed to organism as such. Hegel drew a similar equation when speaking of how the ideas of philosophy governed the world, spirit – not bayonets, troop movements or cannons: 'just as a clock has gears, but its soul is time'.[165] Consequently, 'life was no longer to be explained by a certain arrangement of matter':

> but by animate substances from the outset, which act through a corresponding 'organization' of the body. This was influenced by Leibniz's concept of monads, which, as corporeal and at the same time animated substances, were to be the basic components of the natural bodies still called 'mechanisms' or 'machines.' This meant that the idea of the universal mechanism had basically already been abandoned.[166]

The divinely animating substance of Hegel's political thought in *System der Sittlichkeit* was identified with ethical life as such. Fundamentally, this outstripped the (Kantian) morality of individualism that could only be grasped as a separate part, an atom alienated from the whole as well as any apriorism. This is how we ought to understand the words from *System der Sittlichkeit* that, through the virtues that are the appearance of ethical life, 'the difference between morality and natural law is established, not as if it were separate, excluded from the latter, but its content is entirely in natural law, the virtues appear in the absolutely ethical, but only in their transience'.[167] In this way, Hegel appropriated the finite idealism of Kant and Fichte, their formal natural law and doctrines of morality, and incorporated them into the absolute idealism of the system of ethical life as moments.

So it happened that Hegel's absolute idealism overcame the dogmatism of the understanding which could only view things as separate or sundered. This was surpassed by means of the concepts of a unique practical philosophy (ethics), firstly through natural law, then in his mature work through objective and absolute spirit – on artistic, religious and philosophical planes.[168] Whereas Hegel indeed appropriated the concept of organism from Kant, for whom the organized essence had taken up a leading role, unlike the critical philosopher, Hegel disavowed the teleological dimension, the causality of the whole, as insufficiently liberated from the notion of mechanism.[169] For Hegel, this was evident in the Kantian attempt to grasp nature by means of the understanding: 'the way of looking at things thus remains a thoroughly subjective one, and nature a purely objective, a merely thought one'.[170]

It has been claimed that if ever there were an author who could have come to terms with the complexity of imperial and territorial jurisdictions, reconciling the existence of the Empire and the imperial estates without dissolving all distinctions of substance, it would have been the author of the *Monadology* (1714).[171] The fact remains, however, that Leibniz's metaphysical treatise appeared somewhat late in the day. He died within two years of its completion. His political writings on the Empire in any case contain little explicit trace of the metaphysics for which he later became famous. Even so, a generation later his pre-critical philosophy, as we have just seen, could be leveraged to elucidate a developing doctrine of the state. As we will now see, Hegel deployed it in a particular way with a view to elaborating a system of estates. This gave a corporate structure to the absolute, the single substance or Spinozistic God of the people in *System der Sittlichkeit*. At another level, pre-critical metaphysics more generally shaped his approach to the complex of opposites entailed in the division between government and constitution.

4.2.2 Irreducible simple substances in contrast to composite parts

While much of Hegel's metaphysics was developed on largely incommensurable foundations, namely those of Kantian critical philosophy and its reception in Fichte and Schelling, the results of his assessment of the state in *System der Sittlichkeit* are strikingly similar to how imperial public law had conceived simple states amalgamating into a larger complex whole. It might be helpful to recall that Pütter was a student of Wolff's and Wolff a student of Leibniz. For Leibniz, the very existence of simple substances could further be proven on the basis of the compound or the composite that was 'nothing but an accumulation or aggregate of simples'.[172] Evidently, Hegel aimed at a higher systematic conception of the state, at an organic unity that stood in contrast to any mechanical harmony produced by a mere aggregate. That being said, composition took place through the system of estates that had two forms, at rest and in movement, the state constitution (*forma imperii*), government (*forma regiminis*) and the true constitution.[173]

The separation of the status quo of the state from the constitution as government, in an organizational sense reserved for the legal norms connected to state authority, had begun to assume more and more influence with the spread of this division in the last phase of imperial public law. As we now know Majer was entirely representative of this shift, identifying constitution in the second sense as stemming from revolutionary modernity. Yet, as Gertrude Lübbe-Wolff has so accurately perceived, 'any hint of an endeavour to cast such contents in the legal form of constitutionally guaranteed individual rights – in short: fundamental rights – which are generally regarded as so essential' is missing from the Hegelian position.[174] She was referring to the mature *Rechtsphilosophie*, but the same was no less true of *System der Sittlichkeit*.

The rejection of fundamental rights as a creed to be positively codified at the basis of the modern constitutional state followed Hegel's institutionalism. In a similar way, Kantian formal moral autonomy must be subordinate to a higher principle.[175] Law and morality were subordinate categories of the organic state. We have already seen that Hegel had levelled the same critique at the *leges fundamentales* in the Empire.[176] The Leibnizian notion of simple substances was put to work in Hegel's hands to pursue a comparable logic. Thus, if the estates were simple substances, they could not be composed of parts: 'monads can only begin and end at once, that is, they can only begin by creation and only end by annihilation, whereas that which is composite begins or ends by part'.[177] In this way, the corporate bodies that made up the system of estates were irreducible. Hence, the individual did not participate in the universal *as* an individual – but only through a given estate in which they received a type of equality and became 'a true individual and a person'.[178] Thus, 'every citizen must think of himself as an "organ of a living whole"'.[179] Additionally, '"German freedom" properly restored, would be the most rational, and hence the stablest form of popular sovereignty.'[180] In *System der Sittlichkeit*, this was developed through the corporate distinctions between the estates that made up the true constitution.

Ultimately, equality did not exist on the basis of a bourgeois legal culture. Following the modern revolution, this would have secured fundamental individual constitutional rights as the basis of the state. Although these did indeed appear in some form or fashion under the second system of government, the system or administration of justice in which the individual was treated as a completely indifferent universal person, the estates were given primacy – even the administration of justice fell under the dictates of a particular estate.[181] The state was structured through the distinct estates, each of which taken collectively was the people. Thus, a type of democracy existed. Just as with the administration of justice in which legal personhood took on the form of an abstract universal, all determination or distinct qualities were ultimately reduced to indifference.

The state constitution realized the positive unity of form and essence in *System der Sittlichkeit*. Spinoza's single substance was set alongside the simple substances of the estates, which, like Leibniz's monads, did not begin or end with parts (the individuals of revolutionary liberalism). Every determination or difference was a negation (*Nam omnis determinatio est negatio*)[182] that was carried to and abolished in the absolute. The fact that the ethical 'can only organize itself in individuals as its substance'[183] reveals a Leibnizian modification of the substance metaphysics of Spinoza: Leibniz 'takes individuality, the opposite mode, as his principle, so that the Spinozistic system is thus outwardly integrated'.[184] This cannot conceal the fact, however, that these very individuals were not atoms but corporations or estates – simple substances not parts. The truth resided only in the *system* of ethical life as a structured whole: 'The people as an organic totality is the absolute indifference of all determinations of practical and ethical life; its elements as such are the form of the identity of indifference; then that of difference, and finally that of absolute living indifference; and none of these elements is an abstraction, but a reality.'[185] This already demonstrates the three different logical stages: the movement of the concept and its realization which taken together form the idea. The organic totality of the people was a sovereign power indifferent to the differences that it nonetheless preserved and maintained. This was a logic that could later produce a concept of the state as the guardian of civil society.

With the idea that the substance of the state constitution was realized through a corporate structure of different estates as simple substances, Hegel's conceptualization had a striking similarity to the imperial state as a membered body of absolute individuals. The secondary corporate systems also mirrored the difference between a subordinate government law and universal public law. Further, Pütter's idea of the *populus* in the 1770 edition of *Institutiones juris publici Germanici* reflected a similar idea of the '"people" [which] does not mean – in modern democratic terms – the sum or totality of individuals, but a structured unit of families and corporate entities (commonalities)'.[186] Everywhere, the German tradition – which Hegel clearly inherited in *System der Sittlichkeit* – following the Aristotelian tradition began with the house community before political association in the state.[187] Under the influence of modern rational jurisprudence, for Pütter *populus* represented this pre-political unity. Hence, even if the people cannot be reduced to the state of nature or to individual human beings, 'the *suprema potestas*, which is what makes the mere "tribe" a state, is separated from and contrasted with the people'.[188]

The metaphysics of Hegel's structured monism got the better of rational jurisprudence at every turn. Still, the organization of the people was the mere appearance of ethical life, its particularity: 'the subsumption of all under a universal which would have reality for their consciousness, would be one with them, and would have power and authority over them'.[189] The *Staatsverfassung* or *forma imperii* was a body politic in stasis while the unity of form and essence was grasped through the absolute movement in government and the true constitution, a speculative *civitas composita* of members and estates: 'ethical life, as this living, independent spirit, which appears as a Briareus of myriads of eyes, arms and the other members, each of which is an absolute individual, is absolutely universal'.[190] Here again we see how the estates as simple substances were irreducible – further, how Hegel deployed both the older concept of the body politic alongside organism and organization.[191] In another respect, Hegel had given an idealistic twist here to Pufendorf's 'irregulare aliquod corpus et monstro simile'.

4.2.3 The doctrine of organism within the single substance of the state

Hegel's political organism in *System der Sittlichkeit* demonstrates an internal order distributed over the simple substances of the estates, conceived as individual potentialities. This is not an external relationship between distinct parts; rather, it suggests that even complex compounds can, in certain respects, be analogous to these simples.[192] Hegel described this in basic logical-dialectical terms – through the concept, its movement and realization in the idea. The criterion of the system was the organic unity that unfolded according to individuality, particularity and universality. Each estate (the bourgeoisie, the peasantry and the nobility) was involved as a simple substance in the structuration of the Spinozistic single substance: 'the God of the people' which was no 'multitude without relation or mere plurality'.[193] In this way, every estate was a corporate universal in parity with another corporate universal, *not* 'a relationship of individuals to individuals'.[194] Moreover, through the diversity of these estates, government – as a structure of power – was conceived as equivalent to the *status mixtus*, which Hegel described in detail:

> Monarchy is the representation of the absolute reality of ethical life in one individual; aristocracy in several; it differs from the absolute constitution, by heredity, still more by property; and because it has the form and not the essence of the absolute,

> it is the worst. – Democracy is the representation in all, thus mixing property with it, and not separating the absolute estate. For the absolute constitution the form of aristocracy or monarchy is indifferent; it is also democracy in the estates.[195]

Once again, Majer's influence resonates here. For Hegel, the mere *subjective* organization of sovereignty, or the particular *forma Reipublicae*, was inconsequential compared to its *objective* organization – the state's structure as a security complex for private freedom and collective property.[196] The only fundamental crux, as fragments from the *Verfassungsschrift* made perfectly clear, was that 'the whole power of the state exists in a supreme point of union'.[197] Beyond this, 'the manner in which the particular effects and sides of the union flowing from this are present, or the particular constitution is *indifferent* to the fact that a multitude forms a power'.[198] Put differently, so long as sovereignty existed – as long as the people appeared in the form of ethical life as a membered and organized totality – the contention over the *forma Reipublicae* was completely irrelevant.

Translated into the similar conceptual language of the *Differenzschrift*, Hegel drew on absolute idealism to forge his understanding of sovereignty and the state, in which 'the principle of identity is the absolute principle of the whole'.[199] Perhaps not by chance, and under Schelling's influence, this political metaphysics of sovereignty was also termed the 'absolute indifference point'[200] – an undifferentiated unity of identity between the subjective and the objective, representing absolute reason as the 'total indifference of the subjective and objective'.[201] Yet, the supreme point of union from the *Verfassungsschrift* was also a modification of Fichte's concept. Unlike the dictates of rational jurisprudence, the people were not pre-political but emerged simultaneously with the state's structured monism: 'In that the people is the living indifference and all natural difference is annihilated, the individual sees itself in everyone as itself; it arrives at the highest subjectobjectivity.'[202] Thus, by aligning with Schelling's 'absolute indifference point' – where the subjective and objective coalesce – Hegel developed a conceptual framework that resonated with Majer's insight: that the particular *forma Reipublicae* ultimately dissolved into the state's deeper, undifferentiated unity of sovereignty.

The instrumentalization of a Leibnizian metaphysics of simple substances or irreducible monads alongside the Spinozistic-inspired idea of the single substance of 'the divinity of the people' were developed not only to overcome the increasing dogmatism of the critical philosophy and its radicalization in Fichte but also to address political events and developments of Hegel's own time.[203] Since 1798, Hegel had considered how 'the separate finds its union only in One Being'.[204] This took on the name of the absolute in the *Differenzschrift* that he directly identified with the substance of Spinoza.[205] On the other hand, in contrast to Kantian reflection and the understanding that had reduced nature to an object through the abstraction of reality, *reason* became a speculative (dialectical) methodology that pursued the unity of the finite with the infinite and thus retained a unique correspondence to the absolute, maintaining an immanent connection to the totality as its structuring logic.[206] Philosophy had developed to answer a pressing need, systematic philosophy in particular: 'When the power of unification disappears from human life, and the opposites have lost their living relationship and interaction and gain independence, the need for philosophy arises. In this respect it is a coincidence; but under the given division there is a necessary attempt to abolish the opposition between established subjectivity and objectivity.'[207]

This can be construed as a political metaphysics that became far more emphatic when Hegel turned to criticize the machinery of the purely rational state, the state of the understanding (*Verstandes-Staat*), *not* reason. This 'is not an organization, but a machine; the people are not the organic body of a common and rich life, but an atomistic multiplicity poor in life, the elements of which are absolutely opposed substances, partly a set of points, through the understanding, modifiable matter'.[208]

Everywhere, Hegel had opposed this atomism with an institutional logic or his system of estates. On the one hand, Leibniz had counterbalanced the simple substance of the monad to the false mechanism of modern physics and science that explained things strictly mechanically. This much we have seen. On the other hand, 'Leibniz seems to have been the first to have labelled the theories of Descartes, Spinoza and Malebranche, which competed with his *Monadology*, as "systems"'.[209] This approach thoroughly structured the opening of the *Differenzschrift* and Hegel's initial understanding of the history of philosophy.[210]

To critique the dogmatic position, Hegel at first followed Fichte's three principles at the beginning of the *Wissenschaftslehre* (1794), but these were 'obviously reshaped by motives of Leibnizian philosophy'.[211] If the genuine speculation of Kant's transcendental deduction had disappeared through the abstraction of the thing in itself, Fichte's radicalization of absolute subjectivity similarly destroyed true organism. All of this resulted only in the 'science of the subjective subject-object'[212] that could 'only construct a mechanics'.[213] It thus unavoidably reified the purposiveness of nature. In this way, the One Being identified with the philosophy of union was subordinated to the artificial mechanism of the machine state, to the understanding that could never move beyond mere opposition to grasp the speculative logic of reason.

4.2.4 The philosophy of union

Systematic philosophy, as Hegel had conceived it in the *Differenzschrift*, was aimed at the construction of a subjective subject-object that would discover its corollary in a science of the objective subject-object, with transcendental philosophy and natural philosophy eminently unified.[214] Whereas in transcendental philosophy subjectivity was the principle, in natural philosophy objectivity was: 'in transcendental philosophy, the subject, as intelligence, is the absolute substance, and nature is object, an accident; in natural philosophy, nature is the absolute substance, and the subject, intelligence, only an accident'.[215] This dichotomy was the result of a misunderstanding of the substance metaphysics of Spinoza that grasped the opposite as its principle, the absolute object, which seriously misconstrued his philosophy.[216] On the contrary, the single substance of the *Ethics* (1677) was elaborated firstly as nature (*de natura*) then as mind or reason (*de mente*). Hence, for the young Hegel, the first two parts of Spinoza's book had already overcome the presumed opposition between natural philosophy (allness) and transcendental philosophy (Kant's formalism and Fichte's I or ego).[217] It was following this Spinozistic model that the philosophy of union in *System der Sittlichkeit* aimed at the highest subjectobjectivity.

Nature, like God, denoted 'a unity which everywhere contains both the universal and the particular, unity and multiplicity'.[218] In Hegel's own words, it was 'a single organized separate and united whole'.[219] Thus, he essentially followed an organological idea:[220] 'The higher point of view is neither one in which the one or the other science is cancelled, and either the subject or the object alone is asserted as absolute, nor one in which the two sciences are mixed up.'[221] By combining the strengths of pre-critical substance metaphysics with the genuine insights of transcendental idealism, Hegel sought to overcome the contradictions of an absolute that tottered between a science of the subjective and the objective and which had insufficiently overcome the mechanical idea of the state.

All of this led to a very peculiar political alternative that we have tentatively observed through the corporative absolute of *System der Sittlichkeit* in which the empirical body politic of the imperial publicist tradition had been transformed through a decisive process of philosophical speculation. The state had become a speculative *civitas composita* of estates, analysed in the structured corporative unity of the absolute constitution and government. This was an objective political and legal order in which the contract – and thus the capitulation – played little to no role outside of the formation of a nascent service society based on the universality of legal personhood.[222] It followed the idea already present in the *Differenzschrift* of how the 'totality of knowledge becomes a system, an organic whole of concepts whose highest law is not *understanding* but reason'.[223] Hence, any division between the state constitution and government was eclipsed by the organized character of the absolute that, as a system of freedom, structurally contained both rest and movement. Hegel's systematization of Majer's status quo or *Staatsverfassung* (*forma imperii*) and government (*forma regiminis*) or the true constitution thus contained its own principle of self-organization – it went against any idea of external constraint. The true constitution was a philosophical, internal and actualized concept of the state.

The speculative state of Hegel's early absolute idealism was no aggregate, but a single substance organized through absolute individuals or estates. This model of explanation followed the idea of a system of monads that could not be further divided but which nonetheless made up the monad of monads (*monas monadum*), God. This came in the paradoxical form of the unity of the people in God that nonetheless sundered itself into an infinite multiplicity of things, each of which itself was absolute, the influence of one monad over the other merely ideal – the whole, a plenum:[224] 'every part of the subject, and every part of the object itself in the absolute, is an identity of subject and object; every cognition is a truth, just as every speck of dust is an organization'.[225] For Hegel, losing oneself was akin to finding oneself, the pain of separation undone.[226] Like the concept of the monad, this entailed '"disappearing in the active chain"':[227] 'Each individual is a blind link in the chain of absolute necessity that forms the world. Each individual can only elevate themselves to mastery over a greater length of this chain if they recognize where the great necessity is going and from this recognition learn to utter the magic words that evoke its form.'[228] Or, as he put it even more memorably, murder negates the life of the individual but so too does absolute ethical life. If the first destroys the individual objectively as a physical person, the second does so subjectively, spirit becoming one with the objective:[229] 'In ethical life, then, the individual is in an eternal mode; his empirical being and doing is absolutely universal; for it is not the individual that acts, but the universal absolute spirit in him.'[230] This is also how Hegel understood Montesquieu: 'All the parts of the constitution and legislation, all the determinations of ethical relations, are determined as such by the whole, and form an edifice in which no connection and no ornament has existed *a priori* ... In this sense, Montesquieu founded his immortal work on the contemplation of the individuality and character of peoples.'[231]

4.2.5 The eclecticism of *System der Sittlichkeit*

From the vantage point of Hegel's completed absolute idealism, the Leibnizian solution to the single Spinozistic substance must be cast aside; it failed to differentiate itself sufficiently from abstract atomism and the aggregate: 'The principles of the composite must be the simple. – Bad enough. For at that moment when the composite is spoken, the unity is only an external, accidental one; what is true in it is a multiple.'[232] Interpreted politically, this echoes a denunciation of the idea of the composite state. What was true was the multiple. The once integrated parts disintegrated the whole, themselves becoming independent states. Rather than the unity of form and essence, the multiple was an essence without form. Similar to the later critique of Spinoza, this dismissal of Leibniz most likely demonstrates an anxiety of influence – both having been so pertinent to the development of the objective side of subject-object identity or what in Hegel's maturity went by the name objective spirit.

Still, the fact remains that Leibniz was also less successful than Spinoza in overcoming the Cartesian dualism that awoke the need for philosophy in the first place. Hegel had rediscovered this dichotomy in his own time with transcendental idealism. Importantly, this division was identified in the *Differenzschrift* with a 'form of fixed reflection, as a world of thinking and imagined being, in opposition to a world of reality, [that] falls ... in the Western North.'[233] This would eventually become the Nordic principle of the Germanic World, which similarly sought the reconciliation of opposites. This represented philosophically what had already taken place theologically with the Lutheran Reformation, then with the *Frühaufklärung* and *Aufklärung* – the internalization of conscience.

Rather than seeing Leibniz's *Monadology* as a solution to Cartesianism, Hegel condemned it for reintroducing its problems on a different plane. This came in the form of 'the definition: *the absolute is the object*' in which the monad, as a simple totality, disintegrated into a multiplicity of differences, which are themselves monads, *ad infinitum*.[234] The introduction of God in no way solved this problem: 'Nothing comes into the monad from without; it is in itself the whole concept, distinguished only by its own greater or lesser development. In the same way, this simple totality disintegrates into the absolute multiplicity of differences in such a way that they are independent monads.'[235] Thus, Hegel considered Leibnizian philosophy to have fully developed the object as a contradiction; it was something thought but determined by a pre-established harmony: God as the *monas monadum*: 'When the monad is supposed to be self-determining, it is still a receptacle which passively reflects relations which have been predetermined by God. … Leibniz's *apperceptio*, like Descartes' *cogito*, is a species of *external reflection*.'[236] Yet this cannot alter the fact that without structured monism the organized multitude of *System der Sittlichkeit* would have been impossible.[237] The diverse systems of estates gave body to the Spinozistic absolute. Moreover, this always remained the institutional solution to the revolutionary state:

> The potencies of ethical life in this reality, representing themselves within the perfect totality, are the *estates*. … According to the true concept of an estate, it is not a universality that lies outside of itself and is something thought; rather, the universality is real in it; it recognizes itself in its equality and constitutes itself as universal against universals.[238]

The eclecticism of *System der Sittlichkeit* presents a fascinating scheme in which the depth and conceptual range of the imperial public law tradition is worked out within the framework of absolute idealism. The truth for Hegel resided in the *system*, as we have seen, which was nothing more than the organization of absolute ethical life into an indifferent totality of estates: 'an absolute people; its concept is the absolute oneness [*Einsseyn*] of individualities'.[239] The subordinate systems, the political *adiaphora*, then became integrating parts of government and state constitution in the form of the estates. This was how the membered corporate whole became a people in which the separation of powers could be maintained. This was an organized structure, the unity of essence and form realized through the absolute concept or absolute movement by which 'the intuition of ethical life, which is a people, becomes a manifold reality'.[240]

Through this concept of the people, the division between the state constitution and government had been vanquished. The people were neither a formal absolute nor a formless mass, but a reality that involved the conceptual unfolding of consciousness in the structured organization of both the true constitution and government, through the estates that traversed these systems of ethical life in movement. Hegel opposed such organic structures to abstract formal absolutes, those of the French revolutionary state and enlightened Prussian centralization, which could only ever produce formless masses arrayed against the state through their introduction of legal equality and destruction of the corporate system of the estates and representation. These were machines of legislation, not organisms. Crime and punishment were thus tradable goods: 'the state, as a judicial power, holds a market with well-defined terms that are called crimes and that are traded to it for other well-defined terms, and the legal code is the list of current prices'.[241]

4.2.6 The historical context of late imperial patriotism

Through the separation of powers into different moments, into a complex system of systems that followed the organization into diverse estates, Hegel set out to demonstrate how, in the organic movement, the individual and the universal were one and the same.[242] The absolute warring estate, the Germanic estate of the free, theorized in both the *Naturrechtsaufsatz* and *System der Sittlichkeit*, established 'the necessity of philosophy in a people as the ideal *compliment to war*. … The *absolute labour* is *death* alone, because it abolishes specific individuality, which is why *bravery* in the state brings absolute *sacrifice*.'[243]

Given the historical context of Hegel's early political thought, what this shows is how imperial patriotism intensified in the wars against revolutionary France.[244] First, we have to remember that Hegel's patriotism looked to the Empire for as long as conceivably possible – only once all hopes at reform were dashed did revolution make its appearance and even then German freedom through a corporate system of estates remained the ideal. Second, if we accept the interpretation of *System der Sittlichkeit* I have put forward, the radical transformation of the Empire does not imply its overthrow. Third, the minimal idea of the state was indifferent to the differences that made up the Empire. The collective defence of property and the organization required to that end were universal. Obviously, Hegel had recognized the necessity of military organization in the imperial opposition to the French Republic and to the threatening neutrality of Prussia, equally conceived as a foreign power after the Peace of Basel, if not before.

Hegel's absolute warring estate as well as the peasantry, connected to the nobility through the bearing arms and legal jurisdiction in *System der Sittlichkeit*, was perhaps best figured empirically in the imperial armies of Archduke Karl (1771–1847) or those which he sought to reform and raise in a more modern fashion against the French aggressor. Just like Leibniz before him, Hegel had been drawn to Mainz.[245] The biographical literature has often pointed to the possible republican influence through the Jacobin Club and the fact that Mainz had been annexed to France in 1798. From this perspective, Hegel's two visits to the famed imperial city were thought to have been undertaken to experience revolution first hand.[246] Yet Mainz had long remained the centre of imperial reform politics, safeguarding the constitutional integrity of the Empire and the rights of the smaller imperial estates. This had been obvious with the League of Princes (1785–90) but was actually already the case much earlier – throughout the late seventeenth and early eighteenth centuries. Mainz continued to be central in the later politics of the *Rheinbund*.

Long ago, Wilhelm Dilthey (1833–1911) made the connection between the *Caesarinus Fürstenerius* (1677) written in Mainz under Johann Christian von Boineburg (1622–72) and the archbishop elector Johann Philipp von Schönborn (1605–73) and the *Verfassungsschrift*.[247] He claimed that Hegel – whether he knew the *Caesarinus Fürstenerius* or not – theoretically restored and further developed Leibniz's political thought in the fragments.[248] This came down to the issue of power that was strewn throughout as a way of determining the central attribute of the state alongside a historically realistic approach to politics. For Dilthey, Leibniz had identified power as the essential marker of sovereignty, which involved the realization of political will, both internally and externally, without being limited by the lower levels of the corporations, estates and privileges and at the higher levels by federations and political associations. Beyond Dilthey's insights, the comparable intentions of reform could be evaluated as well as the strikingly similar historical contexts – each framed by a predatory France. Like Hegel, Leibniz too wished 'to strengthen the imperial union, and it is not surprising that he strongly deplored the signs of disintegration in the Empire, which he saw as being caused above all by the particular interests of the imperial estates'.[249]

From these perspectives, Hegel's connection to Mainz might have been decidedly different. Thus, other scholars have connected Hegel to Dalberg, Pütter's student, imperial patriot and archbishop, even arguing that he might be the possible patron of the *Verfassungsschrift*.[250] In a very similar fashion to Hegel, Dalberg had sought to galvanize the political torpor of a self-divided Empire into an effective central government without sacrificing the smaller estates.[251] He had first turned to Archduke Karl. All else failing, however, by drawing on a mythology of the Carolingian renaissance that saw the Franks and the French as a Germanic people, Napoleon could also be figured as a possible saviour of the Empire.[252]

This form of imperial patriotism continued unbroken into the Napoleonic period, just as did the methodology of imperial public law that was communicated to the *Rheinbund*. Hegel's Germanic World began with the Franks and Charlemagne.[253] Even if he believed that an entirely new political system was necessary, it still ought to be based on Germanic freedom. The supreme point of union, the absolute indifference point of sovereign power, was the guardian of the political *adiaphora*, the institutionalism of the subordinate systems and bodies. What is true of the fragments of the *Verfassungsschrift* is equally true of the Berlin lectures on world history. As we know, Hegel alternated in his usage speaking of *Germanisches Weltreich*, *Das germanische Reich*, *Das Germanische Princip und Reich* and *Das germanische Reich*. What would be in any case clear to the audience listening to these lectures would be the associations with imperial publicism and the last of the four kingdoms that had been identified with the end of history in the early modern imperial patriotic literature for which the transfer of Empire from Rome to Germany remained real.

For Hegel, the Göttingen taxonomy of the constitutional state and its opposition to despotism could equally be transferred to the novel confederation of sovereign states – the *Rheinbund*. He had long identified, as we have seen, the disappearance of the principle of representation as the essential evil. His conception already recognized the need for a federalist structure in the fragments of the *Verfassungsschrift*.[254] Patriotism would only be able to develop if cooperation for the common good was recognized, rather than the particularistic interests that were so characteristic of the territorial estates and imperial estates: 'The territories would have to be provided with a form of collaboration for the common good.'[255]

The fact that 'in the first years of the Confederation of the Rhine, the new "sovereignty" of the princes was associated with the expectation that it would be used as a liberal reform dictatorship,'[256] however, verged dangerously upon the aristocratic despotism that threatened the abolition of the territorial estates and thus representation in the first place.[257] On the other hand, it was also strikingly similar to the semantic shift that had been introduced by Robespierre's revaluation of values, in which despotism was an essential part of the realization of law and freedom.[258] When the Württemberg territorial estates were abolished, as Hegel recounted during his time in Bamberg as a newspaper editor, 'Napoleon said in anger to the Württemberg minister: I made your master a sovereign, not a despot!'[259] As Hegel further lamented, 'the German princes have not yet grasped the concept of a free monarchy and have not attempted to implement it – Napoleon will have to organize all of this.'[260] In the second *Ständeschrift* everything in this world is turned upside down, but at that moment in time Hegel obviously sees the Württemberg Constitution (1815) as a thoroughly rational piece of legislation. He thus places the principle of free constitutional monarchy in the hands of the king. This is directed against the good old law, the entrenched ancient privileges of the Württemberg estates.

Before these later political realities had made their appearance, however, Hegel's early speculative system of absolute idealism had sought a definitive structure for the imperial constitution and the territorial corporate state through a structured organization. With this regulative ideal for contemporary application, the subjective and the objective, as opposite poles, were drawn together by an unyielding magnetism – into the philosophy of union that we have now so thoroughly seen.[261] This provided the foundation not only for the imperial state but also for a distinct form of constitutional universality that could be transferred to other political and historical contexts. Our study of *System der Sittlichkeit* has filled a gap in the scholarship. To date, too little attention has been paid to the fact that this manuscript belongs to contemporary publicist interpretations of the German corporative state and reform absolutism. It is a model that in large part is carried over to Hegel's maturity.

4.3 Toleration and religion: From the imperial constitutional context to the philosophical eschatology of world history

4.3.1 The integration of the *ius internum* into the *ius externum*

Already in *System der Sittlichkeit*, Hegel argued that 'the *conscience* ... was only something inner, not inner and outer simultaneously, something subjective not objective'.[262] It was thus deficient in comparison to an idea of consciousness in which 'the individual subsumes absolute ethical life under himself, and it appears to him as his individuality'.[263] In the form of the ethical disposition of the individual towards the state, this was present, however fleetingly, in the virtues. Hegel sought a solution, through a modern ethical life of institutions, to the introduction of dichotomy into history with the *ius internum* and the *ius externum*. This division between the inner realm of conscience and the external order of politics had been raised by Protestantism and incrementally resolved by imperial public law in the great treaties from the Peace of Augsburg onwards. Still, Hegel also identified the idea of the Empire as an empty word due to the fact that subjective freedom was as yet disconnected from ethical life.[264] Reflection on this problem led Hegel to a dialectical concept of consciousness as a form of mediation explicitly related to laws and customs. By means of the idea of conscience becoming consciousness, the isolated individual was to be reconciled – or 'educated' – to the objectivity of the political.[265]

The inner principle or conscience was the philosophical principle as such for Hegel. It actually first awoke with Socrates's *daimon*, that 'divine something' that alienated the Greek philosopher from the *polis* – the individualism which Plato's *Republic* could not absorb. The latter was a perfect substance that was, however, devoid of subject, the inner individual principle of the free subjective spirit that appeared initially with Socrates and then with Christianity to continue its long sojourn up into the modern period: to the casuistry of Jesuitism and Luther's personal faith, to the French Revolution and the rights of man: 'This is the *higher principle of modern times*, which the *ancients*, *which Plato* did not know.'[266] Since the outbreak of the Reformation freedom of conscience had become a central aspect of German imperial public law, which was extended to every dominant denominational creed after the Westphalian treaties. Imperial public law consequently produced a relativistic juridical framework in which the varieties of confession coexisted. In this rather limited sense, it could also be considered secular.[267]

The political order of the Greeks, which for Hegel found expression representatively in Plato's thought, was an ethical substance, the being and doing of the individual identical with the customs and habits of the political community: 'Anyone unfamiliar with the history, education and legislation of the city of Athens who lived within its walls for a year could get to know them through the festivals.'[268] This stood in graphic contrast to Germany: 'We are thus without religious imagination, which would have grown on our soil, and would be connected with our history, and certainly without all political imagination.'[269]

Admittedly, *System der Sittlichkeit* had directed the main part of its theoretical energies to the construction of an ethical order on the Greek model. That being said, as we have seen, it too recognized the problematic dimension of conscience that had introduced dichotomy into history. Identical to Christianity and the later Protestant personal relationship with God for Hegel, the inwardness of the individual was alienated from the political community. As Hegel glossed in his handwritten notes to mature *Rechtsphilosophie*, 'the ancients knew nothing of conscience'.[270] Aristotle's practical philosophy was thus concerned with nothing other than the customs and mores, the habits of the individual, which were equivalent to the institutions of the political community – its *ethos*. Hegel recognized that the Greeks were an *ethical* but in no form or fashion a *moral* people.[271] They were not Kantians.

By contrast, the novel dimensions of subjectivity had to be taken into account in any discussion of the modern state. Reconciliation was only possible if the free subjective spirit, taken on its own terms, was preserved within the objective. Thus, Hegel set out to elaborate a dialectical theory that was both subjective and objective at the same time. This was part of his attempt to answer the complex problem he had long identified with the Reformation, to provide a customary or ethical foundation for the *ius reformandi*:

> The Reformation, and the bloody assertion of the right to make reforms in religion, is one of the few events in which a part of the nation took an interest, an interest which did not evaporate with the cooling of the imagination, but in which the feeling of a permanent right, the right to follow in matters of religious opinion one's own self-wrought or acquired conviction, was active.[272]

This issue was also something intrinsic to German public law and the juridical framework it produced that preserved an exclusive space for subjective freedom and conscience in the great treaties that surrounded it, not to mention the later German enlightened tradition. For Hegel, as he put it in *Glauben und Wissen*, the *Aufklärung* was simply a cultural inflection of Protestantism a 'religion [that] builds its temples and altars in the heart of the individual'.[273] This isolation of the individual or the separation of its subjectivity from the outer order of the state, as we are already familiar from the *Differenzschrift*, was 'the source *of the need for philosophy*', a philosophy that was thus tasked with re-establishing a harmony that had been rent.[274] Thus, the failures of the Empire to reconcile free subjectivity with an ethical life of laws and institutions were the object of Hegel's philosophical exploration. This became part of the sphere of absolute spirit: art, religion and philosophy *and* essential to the dimension of world history or Hegel's philosophical eschatology: 'The element of the existence of the *universal spirit*, which in art is intuition and image, in religion feeling and imagination, in philosophy pure, free thought, is in *world history* the spiritual reality in its whole range of inwardness and outwardness.'[275]

In Germany the struggles of inward life and conscience had been at the forefront of the new definition of religion and personal faith. Even so, it would be incorrect to see this as a problem for Protestantism alone. Already with the Peace of Augsburg, the *ius reformandi* belonged to the Catholic faith as well. As historians have understood it, the Peace of Westphalia resolved the ambiguities regarding the freedom of religion and conscience that had undermined the Peace of Augsburg.[276] Whereas the prince's territorial right to determine religious confession in accordance with his own inner conscience and conviction was reaffirmed a final time in 1648,[277] it had now largely become a secular right. More importantly, the plurality of confessions and their (private or public) practice was explicitly recognized. Essentially, the Peace of Westphalia reaffirmed the freedom of belief of the two predominant confessions as well as accepting the reformed (Calvinist) faith and expanded this right beyond the princes to the individual subjects of a given principality. It firmly established religious division in the imperial constitution, providing safeguards for religious minorities, while simultaneously granting rights of property, conscience and religion to every individual.[278]

It is worth noting that both the fragment 'Religion' and the Jena draft 'kan, wodurch die Freyheit' (can, whereby the freedom) analysed the *itio in partes* (*I.P.O.* Article V §52) – the principle of confessional antagonism that divided the Imperial Diet into religious parties (a phenomenon not mirrored in the Territorial Diet). In these earlier manuscripts, Hegel viewed the rights of conscience as detrimental to the Empire, seeing them as a ruse for princes to alienate their subjects from the imperial state, with religion itself becoming factious. However, the dialectic functions here as well: 'By tearing the state apart, religion has, however, helped to promote another division, at least some parts of it, and has thus given strength to some basic principles that are necessary conditions for the existence of a state.'[279] The separation implied in this early context is that of church and state, which becomes quite a different matter from the perspective of his mature political Protestantism.[280] Hans Maier, a very important Catholic political thinker in Germany, appreciated the earlier position much more than what he termed Hegel's later 'Reformation pathos'.[281]

4.3.2 Law as a doctrine of the state

In Hegel's later thought, law had formed into a doctrine and object of consciousness. It moved beyond what still remained *mechanical* in civil legislation in *System der Sittlichkeit* in which the constitution of the courts stood opposite the organic constitution.[282] It was in this sense that Hegel seemed 'to claim everything scientific in jurisprudence for philosophy and to leave the subaltern technique and formalism to the jurists and their faculty'.[283] Further, in being an inward object of conscience and then self-consciousness, law was also more than simply the practical philosophy of custom and habit identified with the Greeks. Hegel, as we have seen, identified the break in antiquity with Socrates's *daimon*. It led to the Greek philosopher's condemnation by his own city as well as the ethical disposition that rendered him willing to die for its laws. A similar tragic fate was recognized in the actions of Antigone whose ethical disposition followed 'the unwritten and infallible law of the gods' by committing a crime against what was contingent in existing law and power.[284]

For Hegel, modernity was to be identified with such higher principles, the free subjective spirit. This was no longer restricted to conscience and the subjectivity of feeling and representation (religion), the good and conscience as they appeared in the final section on morality in the mature *Rechtsphilosophie* before the development of consciousness in ethical life. What had become ethical and customary was what imperial public law had sanctified as the freedom of conscience as such. By permitting the free practice of religion and the extension of toleration, a higher ethical relationship to the state could develop. This was the historical importance of the Germanic World. As far as it protected religious communities, preserving the inner space for religious freedom, religious doctrine and the right to make reforms in religion, public law could affirmatively dispose individuals uniquely towards the institutions of the state, opening the space for constitutional patriotism and a modern form of ethical life.[285] Thus, like religion, 'the state also has a doctrine, since its institutions and what applies to it in general in terms of the law, constitution, etc. is essentially in the form of *thought* as law'.[286] This involved self-conscious freedom – an ethical or customary disposition towards the laws, not mechanism.[287] As Ernst-Wolfgang Böckenförde (1930–2019) has correctly highlighted: 'This state is not a product of religion generally, but in its characteristic unity of universality and particularity, which is the recognition of subjectivity, it is a product of the *Christian* religion.'[288]

We might further note in this context just how particular Hegel's perspective was to the evolution of imperial public law that even after its demise it essentially shaped his reflections on the relation of religion to the state, the incorporation of conscience and morality into an ethical life of consciousness in institutions and laws. This complex issue had already been theoretically framed in 1795–6 when Hegel identified the right to make reforms in religion as a potential basis for ethical life, albeit limited to the Protestant confession.[289] Obviously, at that stage, the notion of law as a conscious doctrine had not yet developed. This still had to wait for the most hallowed adage of his early absolute idealism in *System der Sittlichkeit* a few years later: 'right in the form of consciousness is law'.[290]

Hegel, while in Bern, lamented the absence of a shared religious and political imagery. Christianity had 'cut down the sacred groves' or, as he later repeated in *Glauben und Wissen*, treated 'the sacred grove as timber'. With romanticism, it fled beyond the boundaries of reason.[291] This was immediately opposed to another form of movement in which 'the inner must also become external, intention must attain reality in action, the immediate religious feeling must express itself in external movement, and the faith that flees the objectivity of knowledge must become objective in thoughts, concepts and words'.[292] In Bern, Hegel referred to the dull readings of the Augsburg Confession (1530), repeated annually in Protestant churches.[293] The unity of the *sacrum imperium* was no longer possible due to the division between faiths but a renascent philosophy of union was through the doctrine of universal public law. This seems nowhere more evident than in the fragments of the *Verfassungsschrift*. The Christian religion generally, irrespective of creed, was intertwined with the potential formation of the state and formed the basis of a pluralistic society:

> in that religion has completely torn the state asunder, it has at the same time, in a wondrous manner, given an idea of some principles on which a state can be founded; in that its division has torn men apart in their innermost being, and yet should still remain a union, it must unite them externally through other things, warfare, etc.; a union which is the principle of modern states.[294]

Another form of union mentioned in this context was tellingly public law, precisely what had legalized the division that had grown from religious civil war. The fact that religious separation and its sanction in imperial public law were so closely woven together still represented a paradox. That religion was a part of constitutional law contradicted the concept of the state for the early Hegel; a state should be based on its separation from the church.[295] After the resolution of the *Normaljahr*, the denominational question had ultimately been settled. The same could be said about the important restriction in *I.P.O.* Article V, which referred back to it. Through these sources, the imperial constitution had nothing to say about the inward dimension of conscience, the practice of adherents to a particular religious denomination, but only concerned the external character of religion if it happened to impact or threaten the status quo. In other words, the stability of the constitutional compromise, present in the extension of the freedom of conscience and its sanctity in public law, was everywhere given primacy.

Imperial public law set out to safeguard religious communities in the Empire in order to prevent the recurrence of a calamity such as the Thirty Years' War. In this way, law and the constitution could provide an external connection – a separate and distinct doctrine. It is very difficult to imagine that Hegel's interpretation of the complex relationship between church and state would have been possible without his direct engagement with the imperial constitution or the German historical context more generally. Save the existence of imperial public law, it could hardly have become a subject of consideration. After all, the freedom of conscience and religion that imperial public law permitted allowed for the flourishing of organic religious communities and such religious freedoms were an integral part of how the free subjective spirit could develop a patriotic relationship to the constitution and its laws.

What all of this makes clear is that it was not religion as such which was the realm of freedom but rather public law and the state that gave free scope to it; conscience and the pluralistic practice of confession were *adiaphora* for the supreme point of union. In legally permitting confessional differences and subjective conviction, the state in the process had developed the space for a higher ethical relation, establishing the *external* connection: 'the principle of its form, as universal, is essentially thought, it is also *from the state* that *freedom of thought* and *science* has proceeded'.[296] In Hegel's maturity, this resulted in a universal doctrine of institutions and laws he termed objective spirit: 'State and laws, like duties, receive in this relationship the highest corroboration and the highest obligation for consciousness.'[297] This was directly related to the expansion of the freedom of conscience, which was initially provided by imperial public law: 'The form of reality of religion in the broad sense, which manifests itself in the state, is that of the thinking consciousness, of *the universality that forms itself externally as law*.'[298]

Philosophically speaking, Hegel had resolved the earlier paradox in his interpretation of imperial public law. The fact that freedom of religion and conscience were intertwined with constitutional law was no longer a problem. Precisely because of the indifference of the state towards confession, inner disposition and external action could be aligned. In the state, as he construed it, action was conditioned not by constraint but by freedom. It established a framework of right which protected the interests and property of its citizens and in the process provided the foundation of ethical life – foundation because regulation still needed to be married harmoniously to the inner disposition to meet Hegel's objectives. This would happen because the state and its doctrine of law had a character that could inspire love. Human disposition would accord with following state laws, which would appear not as regulations but as issuing from an entirely human source that could be conceived subjectively – legislation becoming an expression of the thinking will. The state, as Hegel conceptualized it, fitted this specification.

4.3.3 The *Aufklärung*, conscience and religion

Hegel's understanding of conscience and religion is distinctive, yet profoundly rooted in the imperial publicist tradition and the perspectives developed in its public law. This section will explore how his views, particularly in comparison to thinkers like Hobbes, Pufendorf and Thomasius, shaped his vision of a modern ethical state where religious freedom fosters political unity. If imperial public law progressively established the freedoms of conscience and faith through the juridification of the religious schism, the *Aufklärung* and natural law contributed theoretically as well to its endeavours.

The historiography of the *Aufklärung* had received renewed impetus in the work of Taddäus Anselm Rixner (1766–1838). In his last series of Berlin lectures on the history of philosophy (1825–6), Hegel directly followed the three volumes of Rixner's *Handbuch der Geschichte der Philosophie* (1822). He recommended this work, with minor reservations, to his audience.[299]

Most noteworthy for our concerns here is the inclusion of Pufendorf in Hegel's interpretation which followed Rixner's analysis. The natural lawyer did not appear in the earlier surviving lecture manuscripts and Hegel situated him importantly in the passage between Hobbes, Issac Newton (1643–1727) and Leibniz. Hegel had praised Hobbes's correct assessment of the state of nature as one of equality and thus, correspondingly, of lawlessness. Yet he pointed out that the legal condition Hobbes had established to take its place led to a system of mere passive obedience. While it was indeed necessary to exit the state of nature so that the natural will could be educated to the general will and the laws of reason, the fear that lay at the basis of the Hobbesian description, no less than the subordination to the single will of the monarch, was irrational and consequently despotic.[300]

Still, Hobbes separated conscience from political jurisdiction. This was due not only to the fact that the machinations of power cannot truly know and control the inner thoughts of human beings. It was also a question of recognizing the minimal requirements for salvation and the origins of religious civil war. Hence, as Hobbes famously stated in *Leviathan* (1651), the law erred when it extended beyond 'the Rule of Actions … to the very Thoughts and Consciences of men by Examination and Inquisition of what they Hold, not withstanding the Conformity of their Speech and Actions'.[301] When it came to religion, Hobbes stated that everybody believes or doubts at his own peril. There is the external cult, the realm of speech and action, the public religion dictated by the sovereign, and there was private worship, free in secret, that belonged to the internal dimension of conscience.[302] This is what Hobbes discussed in *De cive* (1642) as the 'internal court' and the 'external court' of obligation.[303] This was not an aspect of his supposed liberalism, but rather a consequence of his realism.[304] For Hegel, the legal condition must be differentiated from the pure subjection to the law that he saw operative in Hobbes's political thought.[305] That conception was simply too one-sided; it was an example of the most perfect despotism: 'The English have much struggled with this principle of passive obedience, according to which it is said that the kings have their power from God, which is quite true on one side, but it is understood to mean that they have no responsibility, that their blind will, their mere subjective will, is that which must be obeyed'.[306]

The importance of Rixner's interpretation of Pufendorf is that it pointed to the other side of the equation, which had been shaped by imperial public law and the German historical context. The German natural lawyer thus emphasized '"the peace and security of social life by *transforming the inward duties of conscience into external duties of compulsion*"'.[307] By contrast, Hobbes had placed priority on the state: 'The definition offered by Hobbes is fundamentally an *exterior* one that does not proceed from the subject himself, or a fortiori from his consciousness, but from the way he is described by a juridical system lying outside of him.'[308] Hence, the *Frühaufklärung* and *Aufklärung* more generally stressed the inner life of conscience that had come to prominence with the Reformation and only then subsequently deduced the external realm of law and politics. This directly followed the contours of imperial public law in the great treaties, but it was also integral to the pietism that Pufendorf and Thomasius (Hegel and Schelling) partly followed.[309] Thomasius supported the later radical anti-clericalism of *Leviathan* and *Historia Ecclesiastica* (1668), but – tellingly – disagreed with Hobbes on the extent of the sovereign's jurisdiction over his subjects in religious matters.[310] Hence, 'Thomasius not only wants to protect the inner conviction as such, but also to exclude all external attempts that impair the freedom of individual choice.'[311] Yet Thomasius's understanding of ethics is that it only binds internally in conscience which made it impossible for the law of reason to generate a civic ethos as Wolff had done. This transformed law into external coercion, even if it ought to be reasonable and agreeable to conscience, destroying the metaphysical foundations of the older natural law. Kant reopened the possibility of the consonance between the prescriptions of law and morality by recognizing the inner compulsory force of natural law.[312] In this way, he had revived issues that had been laid to rest with the metaphysical tradition. Hegel had already begun to fuse the dimensions of morality and natural law in *System der Sittlichkeit*, precisely through the ethical disposition.[313]

For Hegel, Pufendorf demonstrated how 'in the struggle to establish the legal conditions in the state and to establish a juridical constitution [gerichtliche Verfassung], the reflection of thought emerged and played a significant role'.[314] In identifying sociability – a form of love – as a basis, a more worthy human motive than fear had been recognized. As Hegel further noted, this was a vital ingredient of natural law discourse and its definition of the purpose of the state that then decidedly took leave of pure constitutional law and history. Repeating a variation of Rixner's quote from Pufendorf, Hegel emphasized natural jurisprudence rather than the sanctification of conscience: 'the drives of men, which nature had implanted in their hearts, were regarded as the source of what existed. Sociality was man's instinct for sociability; constitutional law was thus conceived according to universal determinations.'[315] Still, Pufendorf's efforts remained deficient, due to their lack of precision. While individual motives were at the foundation, there remained little to no detail about 'what the citizen is entitled to demand from the state authority for his preservation. Also, not what he is entitled to demand from state authority for his submission and his taxes for himself and the common welfare of the whole.'[316] Pufendorf thus fell short of providing a fully articulated framework for the ethical integration of the individual into the state: a task Hegel would later pursue more completely which relates him more closely to the metaphysical (Wolffian) tradition.

The principles Pufendorf developed grew out of a sustained reflection on the causes of the Thirty Years' War and the compromises that concluded it which were threatened in an insurmountable way by the Revocation of the Edict of Nantes (1685).[317] With respect to creedal conflict, Pufendorf plainly saw the merits of leniency. He recognized that reconciling differences between religions was not well left to the clergy. This is because 'they grow warm with Dispute' and 'cherish the Strife'.[318] Hence, 'the Judgement in Matters of Faith does not belong to the Ministry alone'.[319] An effect of religious civil war was to open the door for Protestant lay theologians to try their hand.[320] Pufendorf was one of many.[321] Yet lay theology too could be a misnomer: 'in Protestantism there is also no clergy that would be the exclusive depositary of church doctrine, because there are no *lay* people in it'.[322] For Hegel, it was this that made a reconciliation possible between the inner life of conscience and modern ethical life, the freedom of consciousness in the institutions of the state and its public law: 'Precisely because in Lutheran Protestantism, unlike in medieval Catholicism, Christianity is not taken as a *polis* religion, it enables a rehabilitation of the political in the sense of a political ethics.'[323]

Although Pufendorf accepted the confessional schism as a permanent part of imperial political reality, he lamented the fact from early on.[324] Toleration was simply a lesser evil. If the cost of religious unity was persecution and political instability, it could not be promoted. French domestic policy seemed to simply prove this reality. It produced a new wave of Huguenot immigration to Brandenburg-Prussia where Pufendorf was employed for the last years of his life by the Calvinist and Great Elector Friedrich Wilhelm (1620–1688). The Edict of Potsdam (1685) offered refuge and a new home to some 20,000 Protestant refugees from France. The Great Elector was the first ruler to establish religious toleration as a legal principle of public law, which he did as early as 1645. This encompassed even fringe sects. Toleration restored the population of Prussia and improved its economic situation after the devastation of the Thirty Years' War.[325]

Pufendorf's point of view readily accommodated Lutheranism, a religion that supported monarchical power.[326] It was in the best interests of the ruler, so Pufendorf supposed, to promote the unity of religion and thus 'subordinate the church to the secular power of the state'.[327] Yet the unity of religion in no way applied to the Holy Roman Empire as a whole. The laws that the great treaties set down did not permit a repetition of the calamity that had partly caused the wretched religious civil war in the first place when Ferdinand II had attempted to impose the Catholic confession by force of arms.[328] This bitter experience certainly played a role in Pufendorf's description of toleration. Stripped bare, as he put it, it was nothing more than 'of the Nature of a Truce in War, which suspends the Effects of it, and the actual Hostilities, while the State and Cause of the War do remain'.[329]

For Hegel, the fact that religion could not play the role of a civil religion any longer in the Empire is what had opened up the potential for ethical life to develop as a secular disposition, between the individual, the state and its laws. Modern ethical life was a product of the Christian religion in general and Lutheranism in particular. The Germanic peoples had inherited the principle of inner conscience, which the Jewish people had also carried earlier within the absolute loss represented by the abstract universality of the Roman World, its legal formalism and equality.[330] Initially this path inward led to abstraction, to a formal God and a rote law. Jesus had answered this crisis through a love, which overcame abstract legal order.[331] The Lutheran Reformation too had initially led to an abstract form of inwardness; it raised the suspicion of evil and persecuted on the basis of possible guilt as the inner disposition of the accused remained outside of the reach of the state. Such trials of conscience resulted in allegations of heresy and the burning of witches: 'It was not until the beginning of the eighteenth century that Thomasius, Professor at Halle, resisted this pervasive superstition with the greatest success.'[332] Hegel ran the epochs together: 'The main reason was suspicion. This principle of suspicion appears in equal dreadfulness under Roman imperial rule and under Robespierre's Reign of Terror at the time of the French Revolution: the disposition as such was to be punished.'[333] Hegel's linkage of these seemingly disparate historical moments underscores his argument about the persistent danger of unmediated inwardness when it becomes subject to external political control.

By contrast, if freedom of conscience and religion were secured in the public laws of the state, the soul of the individual could be once again related to the *polis* or political community as it had been in antiquity.[334] Hegel's position on Pufendorf and Thomasius demonstrates how antagonism towards eclecticism and empiricism is not necessarily a norm of the metaphysical approach, as has been described in the historiography of German natural law.[335] Indeed, Hegel seems to be as equally concerned with a public order as Thomasius was, delimiting the province of the state over religion, morality, law and politics, and it was precisely in this sense that the free ethical disposition could develop. Crucially, Kant's recognition that natural law fundamentally binds inwardly in conscience provided the key for absolute idealism to develop. This recognition by Kant overcame Thomasius's sharp division between morality and law, a division that had initially put an end to the metaphysical tradition.[336]

The division between the *ius internum* and the *ius externum* is part of the history of the modern state. Historically speaking, as the state came into prominence so too did the concept of politics as a distinctive discipline freed from the constraints of theology and jurisprudence. The Edict of Nantes (1598) provided the first real evidence of a separation of church and state in which 'the "government of God" is relegated to the realm of morality and remains without any tangible meaning for politics'.[337] In depriving both conscience and individual judgement of their political effects, they had been functionally reinterpreted: 'The neutralization of conscience by politics assisted with the secularization of morality. … A morality striving to become political would be the great theme of the eighteenth century.'[338]

In Germany, however, conscience was never neutralized; it remained an object of legislation, decisively a part of constitutional law. In a similar way, the *Frühaufklärung* and *Aufklärung* were theological and institutional. They were identified with the state and non-polemical in orientation. In the fragments of the *Verfassungsschrift*, Hegel began to pluck the first fruits of years of study of ecclesiastical and constitutional law that stretched back to his doctorate. He saw the *itio in partes* as particularly detrimental to the union required for a state.[339] Religion, which ought to belong to the political *adiaphora*, had actually become an essential political matter.[340] Hegel referred to an outlandish comparison, one that undoubtedly he himself had drawn rhetorically.[341] He ironically compared the *itio in partes* to the right of insurrection of the French constitution of 24 June 1793, radical ideals which were immediately set aside in favor of the very terror and centralized power of Robespierre: 'The difference is that the German Empire has governments in its various parts independent of the whole; but if the state and the government and laws were based on the decisions of the Emperor and the Empire, then both would have to be considered the same.'[342] The *itio in partes* was a right of insurrection for the imperial estates. Further, it meant that 'the separation of the minority from the majority is legitimized in every matter of state that has nothing to do with religion'.[343] Echoing perspectives common to the *Frühaufklärung* and *Aufklärung*, Hegel stated that 'the separation of religion and politics is necessary; it is not a power over religion that is required for the supreme power, God forbid, but precisely no power over it, no rights in regard to it; only then is the supreme power for the defence of the internal and external possible'.[344]

The gulf between this position and that of Hobbes is worth noting. That said, it reflects the more proximate context of confessional pluralism in the Empire and the compromise that brought an end to the religious and political conflict.[345] The logic of Hegel's argument is that if religion is made a nonissue, if it truly becomes part of the *adiaphora*, the realm of freedom and the state can emerge. This is a far cry from giving leeway to a civil religion or significance to an external cult. While it still conveys the characteristics of a separation of church and state, it is important to recognize how the freedom of religion and conscience, the right to make reforms in religion, the individual choice of faith and confession, were part of that form of consciousness that could eventually be identified with legal right, the doctrine of laws and institutions in the state. Hegel had turned the right to make reforms in religion into an instance of custom, convention and habit that no longer destroyed the unity of the state but – sanctioned by it – developed into a pluralistic society that could lead to constitutional patriotism. In this way, 'the principle of religious and ethical conscience ultimately becomes one and the same, in the Protestant conscience – the free spirit knowing itself in its rationality and truth. The constitution and legislation as well as their activities have as their content the principle and the development of ethical life, which emerges from the truth of religion.'[346]

4.3.4 Philosophical eschatology: The theodicy of world history

What can be seen from the foregoing is that 'state and religion (church) are different actual and actualizing forms of the same and indeed unified substance'.[347] The perspective of religion's relation to the state as one of coordination, superordination or subordination and the related view of a politics of conscience as a conflictual field that ends in neutrality is not Hegel's view: 'For him it is a question of a relationship of *parallelism*.'[348] Yet this also involved an historical process which Hegel depicted as integral to absolute spirit, 'the immense transition of the inner into the outer, of the imagination of reason into reality, on which the whole history of the world has laboured, and through which labour educated mankind has gained the reality and consciousness of rational existence, of state institutions and laws'.[349] This section will explore how Hegel's philosophy of world history functions as a philosophical eschatology, reconciling inner conscience with external law, culminating in the 'Germanic World' as the ultimate expression of modern ethical life.

In a profoundly comprehensive way, Hegel grasped world history as a philosophical eschatology; it was a history of salvation or healing (*Heilsgeschichte*), even in its development of secularity.[350] This followed Schiller's idealism. The point worth stressing is that it was a question of coming to understand world history and the evolution of law, which became an object of conscious thought at one with the free being and activity of the individual in constitutional monarchy. It is in this context that we find the full flowering of Hegel's historical conception and the eschatological end it implied. Spirit had been undergoing a process of intensive labour. Hegel's ambition to reconcile inner spirit with outer reality, culminating an epoch, is sharply illuminated by the following observation:

> Hegel's completion becomes ambiguous when he changes Virgil's '*romanam condere gentem*' into '*se ipsam cognoscere mentem*'. This change means: The original

> foundation of the Roman world-empire, this basis of Europe, required the same effort as was ultimately necessary for a final self-exploration of spirit. To the extent that, with knowing and willing, Hegel ended an epoch which lasted two and a half millennia and precisely thereby opened up a new epoch, he in fact brought to an end the history of the Christian *logos*. A whole world of concepts, of language and edification, came to an end with Hegel's history of European spirit.[351]

This 'completion' marked a pivotal shift, signalling both an end to the history of the Christian logos and the dawn of a new era of self-exploration for spirit.

Two central issues are connected with this quote. First, the founding of the Roman Empire as a basis of European history. Second, the shift towards the intellectualization of its concept, which was indeed Schiller's contribution to the conceptualization of the Holy Roman Empire of the German Nation that was akin to Hegel's thinking on the Germanic World – the turning point, the crisis of world history as world-historical judgement that directly followed Schiller. Under the guise of the *translatio imperii*, according to the earlier tradition of imperial patriotism, this Roman Empire had come to Germany and it was one that would last until the end of time. The fact remains, however, that for Hegel the end of time had arrived. According to the traditional doctrine, God's empire or kingdom was ushered in after the collapse of the final empire. For Hegel, however, 'the kingdom of God' (*das Reich Gottes*) was a symbol for the reconciliation of the worldly and the divine. It stood for an abolition of the separation between this world and the next: 'The fact that his philosophy of history makes use of an older, biblically based schema to describe this development fits symbolically and in an aesthetically satisfying way with the programme of a philosophy that has set itself the task of recognizing not only history but also revealed religion as rational and true.'[352]

Hegel's understanding of the kingdom of God was also referred to in the last paragraph of *System der Sittlichkeit* where it stood in direct opposition to Greek conceptions of religion. Unlike the Greeks, whose religion remained tied to nature and was not yet *absolutely* ethical, this new spiritual realm demanded a fundamental separation. This separation, for Hegel, was not merely a weakness but a necessary, even 'absolute crime' or 'death' – a profound break required for the absolute ethical movement of God's kingdom on earth to emerge: 'This separation must be complete; the ethical movement of God absolute, not crime and weakness [like the Homeric gods] but absolute crime, death.'[353] Jesus in dying an earthly death had overcome human subordination to nature and reconciled man to the absolute, God. Protestantism belonged to a similar movement as it had denounced the edifice that came to stand between human beings and the absolute with the positivity of the Christian religion in the Catholic Church. This historical development culminated in a new religious consciousness – one that sought a deeper, ethical reconciliation:

> Infinite pain is permanent in sanctification, and reconciliation itself a sigh for heaven. Now that Protestantism has cast off alien consecration, the spirit can venture to sanctify itself as spirit in its own form and to restore the original reconciliation with itself in a *new religion*, in which the infinite pain and the

> entire burden of its contradiction are absorbed, yet dissolved unclouded and pure, namely, when there will be a *free people* and reason will have been reborn into its reality as an ethical spirit, which is bold enough to take on its pure form *on its own ground and in its own majesty*.[354]

A core aspect of absolute idealism was the theology of this modern Christian spirit, as Hegel grasped it: 'That the true is real only as a system, or that substance is essentially subject, is expressed in the conception which expresses the absolute as *spirit*, – the most sublime concept, one which belongs to the modern age and its religion.'[355] This understanding of the absolute as spirit, as the coincidence of substance and subject, a hallmark of the modern age and its religion, found its ultimate political expression in Hegel's conceptualization of the Germanic World as the final apotheosis of world history. In this historical-philosophical vision, the *ius internum* (the internal moral and spiritual principle of the modern subject) was effectively incorporated into the *ius externum* (the external, public law of the state). This crucial synthesis opened up the possibility for a renascent model of ethical life, one where *nomos* and *ethos* could finally be unified, mirroring, yet transcending, the immediate (natural) unity of the Greeks. Indeed, as Joachim Ritter (1903–1974) explains of this concept in antiquity, for the Greeks, '*nomos* is law in its association with politics and legislation, but at the same time it belongs to *ethos* and is a custom legitimized by tradition and sanctified from time immemorial'.[356] Hegel thus envisioned a modern state where inner and outer reality, individual freedom and universal law, were one and the same.

For Hegel, this time immemorial could be traced to the initial path inwards of early Christianity which grew under a despotic empire and coincided with the formalism of Roman law. This beginning of a true reconciliation between the *ius internum* and the *ius externum*, however, had only been made possible in the custom of the right to make reforms in religion, secured in imperial public law since 1555. The intertwining of religion and politics dominated the Holy Roman Empire, essentially shaping the structure of imperial public law, from the legalization of the denominational schism to the subjective rights of conscience that became part of a positive system of public law: 'Religion, instead of separating itself from the state by its own division, has rather brought this division into the state, and most of all contributed to the abolition [*aufzuheben*] of the state, and has so interwoven itself into what is called the constitution that it is a condition of constitutional laws.'[357]

The reason why religion was so fatal to the Empire, as Hegel saw it, was compounded by the fact that the connection to the imperial constitution was already so tenuous in Germany.[358] With the loss of the universal salvation-historical character of the *sacrum imperium* that predominated in the Middle Ages and even after the Peace of Augsburg, an empirical secularization of sorts took place.[359] This was carried forward in public law.

For Hegel, the Germanic World of his philosophy of world history was a constitutional monarchy in which the free conscience of the monarch, his free thinking subjectivity mirrored that of his subjects: 'princely power concerns what is in and of itself universal, which in subjective terms consists in the *conscience of the monarch*, and in objective terms in the *whole of the constitution* and in the *laws*'.[360] There was thus the free subjective spirit of conscience, the *ius internum*, and its correspondence with the public laws in which such freedom was guaranteed, the *ius externum*. The summation of this history was a theodicy: 'The development of the principle of the spirit is the true theodicy; the concept has been accomplished in history, and this is the glory of God, for God has realized and revealed himself in it.'[361] The contours of Hegel's argument become increasingly apparent. The very evolution of the modern ethical disposition was a history peculiar to the Christian religion that was revealed in world history but also in imperial public law in which freedom of conscience and religion had played such a central role.

Modern industrial society and scientific cognition were results of the spiritual world of Lutheranism, which, slowly liberating itself from an abstract inwardness, was eventually reconciled with the world. This also encompassed the morality of truthfulness of Jesuitism, its casuistry and the quest for certainty that led to the scientific subject.[362] The cleft between religion and politics, the exclusion of theological truth and judgement from public law, had emerged from a thoroughly Christian history: the conflict over confession.[363] The same was true for the very nature of the modern constitutional state that secured the rights of freedom of conscience. Without European Christianity, such events were incomprehensible. Yet under this eschatological end – this theodicy of world history with its phenomenology of the spirit of the modern Christian religion – nihilism, atheism, materialism and revolution were lurking. It was in this precise way that the break with Hegel's philosophy of spirit, not unlike Napoleon's earlier destruction of the Holy Roman Empire, could itself be considered world historical. It was the end of the history of the European spirit and at the same time the last gasp of imperial public law that Hegel had incorporated into his idea of the Germanic World with constitutional monarchy and the peculiar relation of religion to the state.[364]

From here one need only refer alternately to the young Hegelians, Karl Marx (1818–83) and Friedrich Nietzsche (1844–1900). For Marx, Hegel's logical mediations, indeed tied in a particular way to the institutionalism of his legal philosophy, represented an 'uncritical spirit, this mysticism, is the enigma of modern constitutions (κατ' εξοχήν the estate-constitution) as well as the mystery of the Hegelian philosophy, especially the *Philosophy of Right* and the *Philosophy of Religion*'.[365] Speaking of the eventual triumph of atheism, Nietzsche saw how the Germans had delayed this 'most dangerously for the longest time. Hegel in particular was its delayer par excellence, with his grandiose attempt to persuade us of the divinity of existence, appealing as a last resort to our sixth sense, "the historical sense"'.[366] Both views agree with and are confirmed by an understanding that 'Hegel's system is fundamentally the philosophy of religion, the depiction of the self-revelation of God'.[367]

Understood in this fashion, Hegel's philosophy of world history that concluded in the Germanic World opened up the possibility for a new *ethos*, but one for its own time. Religion had become a secular right. The higher conceptual unity of consciousness in contrast to the inwardness of conscience was made possible through the pure free will that was a product of thought thinking itself.[368] This stemmed from both the modern revolution identified with philosophy,[369] but also with the idea of religion that had grasped the innermost being of man.

Since *I.P.O.* Article V, freedom of conscience had been anchored in imperial public law. With the denominational question largely to be settled by individual conscience, the freedom of the churches and sects, an affirmative relation to the modern constitutional state could evolve, one that assured such rights in its public law. So conceived, the modern constitutional state must allow a plurality of different confessions being indifferent to the differences occurring in civil society, even if it itself was historically a product of the modern Christian religion in general. For example, by granting civil rights to Quakers and Anabaptists, as purely private persons and Jews as a foreign people because of the fact 'that they are first and foremost *human beings*', a type of 'self-esteem, as *legal* persons in civil society' could develop.[370] This might then lead to the ethical disposition, a form of patriotism towards the modern constitutional state and its doctrine of public law.

The peculiarity of Hegelian philosophy was that it contained nihilism, atheism, materialism and revolution incipiently, in seed. It had grown in a very particular way from imperial public law, having spiritualized a dead Empire and made it into an object of conscious thought through the progress of the European spirit in the diversity of its forms. All other efforts to shore up the break that had been introduced by the French Revolution were half-measures by comparison, mere restorations of an epoch that had decidedly passed. In this fundamental way, Hegel's philosophy was '"a coming to terms with corruption." Its highest manifestation is simultaneous with the beginning of a decline, at "a time when everything is understood to be in a state of dissolution"'.[371]

No doubt, it was the passage from Nietzsche on sixth sense, the historical sense that Carl Schmitt (1888–1985) had in mind when he referred to Hegel, alongside his Berlin colleague and antipode Friedrich Carl von Savigny (1779–1861), as a great restrainer (*Katechon*).[372] For Schmitt, Hegel, like Savigny, was *Epimethean*. On the one hand, this seems to be readily confirmed if we consider Hegel's particular view on the untimeliness of philosophy that, unlike Nietzsche's perspective, was retroactive *not* future oriented – it always arrived too late.[373] On the other hand, Hegel's thought had grasped world history as an eschatological end that had concluded with the Germanic Empire or World of which the Carolingian was a part. The Napoleonic legislation that had been introduced everywhere in the Rhineland could also be viewed against the same horizon within the same organizing frame.[374] Hegel was largely silent about the migration of the European spirit. As Napoleon put it: *cette vieille Europe m'ennuie*. America was the land of the future, the Slavic World a point of mediation in the struggle of Christian Europe with Asia.[375]

This intricate historical-philosophical synthesis reveals Hegel's remarkable ability to integrate the history of Christianity, the imperial public law that sanctioned confessional schism and thereby transformed religious divisions into secular political rights and the modern revolution into a totalizing philosophy or theodicy of world history, wherein all contradictions of spirit were resolved in the absolute, God. Unlike Savigny, as Schmitt conceded, Hegel 'was also able to recognize, acknowledge and comprehend the Promethean direction of his present'.[376] This made his eschatological construction of the Germanic World uncertain; the premise of every absolute end was a radical break or new beginning. Hence, little more was required than to liberate the dialectic from the system in order to end in materialism, atheism, nihilism and revolution.

4.4 Epilogue

4.4.1 Codification, the universal estate and civil society

Rather than summarizing the material I have analysed in this chapter (which I will do more fully in the Conclusion) I want to use this section to discuss the historical fate of Hegel's doctrine of right in the form of consciousness is law, the Hegelian School and the erosion of the reform during the *Vormärz* that shaped his later philosophy and its legacy.

If Hegel's system of mediations opened the door to a conception of the state based on officialdom rather than Savigny's *Juristenstand*, this is because 'Hegel's state was a legal state, and his jurisprudence was no longer a separate profession, but a state civil service'.[377] He had been critical of positive legislation in *System der Sittlichkeit* and the *Naturrechtsaufsatz* in which he balanced the mechanical character of a code with ethical life and the organic constitution.[378] Yet the most hallowed adage – that right in the form of consciousness is law – completed what still remained mechanical in the code. Thus, positive codification in *System der Sittlichkeit* was already a necessary stage on the way to the organic constitution. The actual writing of reason was no longer mechanical but had become a source of conscious knowledge, the spirit of the form. This is confirmed above all by Hegel's later conception: 'What right is *in itself* is *posited* [*gesetzt*] in its objective existence, i.e. determined by thought for consciousness, and *known* as what is right and is valid – *law* [*Gesetz*]; and right is *positive* right in general through this determination.'[379]

Hegel's explicit defence of codification had already begun in Heidelberg. He sided with his then colleague Anton Friedrich Justus Thibaut (1772–1840) in favour of maintaining the *Code Civil* that had been introduced by the French in the Rhineland in opposition to Savigny and the Historical School of Law.[380] The privileging of custom or customary law, while also being something thought and thus an object of possible knowledge remained, however, the provenance of a lucky few. It led to an elitist *Juristenstand* as the unique repository of legal knowledge. By contrast, the publishing of private law in a code or public law in a constitution which all could *know* – thereby becoming objects of conscious knowledge – was a step towards freedom.[381] Indeed, Hegel's opposition to Savigny's conception of the continued derivation of law from the sepulchre of custom could be read back into the fragments of the *Verfassungsschrift* – of those spheres of power and chance in which acquisition by force was gradually fixed and made legal through the passage of time.[382] Hegel attacked this obscure Germanic power that eventually became a system of private law through the reception of Roman law. This positivized the very oblivion of custom that the Historical School espoused as the central source of all law, permitting it to lord over the present. There was simply no universal public law or natural law. Rather, there were particular laws that differed from one country to the next that were above all private *not* public. Natural law had collapsed entirely into a philosophy of positive law and in so doing came to an end.[383] Exercising a monopoly over custom from which law indeed genetically emerged, the jurist of the Historical School guarded an exclusive store of arcane knowledge. This was a far cry from the right of reason or 'the great systems of German idealism [that] contain "philosophies of law" whose origins in the textbooks of the older natural law and the *ius publicum universale* are obvious'.[384]

The view that custom as such was to be esteemed as higher than law, according to Eduard Gans, threatened the very autonomy of jurisprudence by strictly emphasizing the power of the past over the present. Perhaps nowhere was the opposition more incisively drawn than in Altenstein's advisory opinion on the matter that defended his appointment of Gans to the professorship at the Faculty of Law in Berlin to the crown prince who weighed in on Savigny's side as part of the romantic reaction against Hegel and the Hegelian School.[385] As minister of education, Altenstein was the most important supporter of Hegel and Hegelianism in Berlin. Hegel and Altenstein were friends of some standing.[386] What Altenstein had to say on the matter of the Historical School and Gans not only touches all of the important distinctions between their approaches but also clearly favours Hegelianism as the more encompassing scientific perspective – inclusive of the advances in historical method made by Savigny in jurisprudence:

> The Historical School considers custom, not statute law, to be the main source of law. It only recognizes statute law as having a supplementary effect. Professor Gans believes that this is certainly the case in all original and initial states, but that as soon as the states become more developed, statute law becomes not only the main source, but almost the sole source of law, and custom recedes in law as much as in mores and language. An impartial glance at the present state of all European countries confirms this opinion, and legislation appears to be active everywhere, while custom receives no further growth.[387]

This point of view clearly mirrors Hegel's perspective on the progress made in legal science from custom to code to the central contribution of philosophy *to* law: 'When the customary laws come to be collected and compiled, which must soon happen with a people who have only reached a certain degree of education, this collection is then the *code of law*, which, because it is a mere collection, will of course be characterized by its *formlessness*, indeterminacy and incompleteness.'[388]

The language here curiously reflects that of the fragments of the *Verfassungsschrift* in which Hegel identified the imperial constitution with a multitude of rights devoid of unity and principle, more a collection than a system.[389] Formlessness was overcome – a code was completed – *once right ruled in the form of consciousness to become law*. Laws by becoming positive were a step in the direction towards becoming a universal object of thought, becoming *form* – the principle of right and knowledge. Part of Hegel's argument against the Historical School was also that 'the valid laws of a nation, by the fact that they are written and collected, do not cease to be its customs'.[390] By denying an educated nation and its *Juristenstand* the right to make a legal code 'would be one of the greatest reproaches that could be inflicted on a nation or that estate'.[391] This is due to the fact that 'what is right only acquires not only the *form* of its universality but also its true definiteness when it becomes law'.[392] Otherwise, law threatens to become the 'accidental property of a few'.[393]

The debate over codification became a central issue in the polemics between Hegel, Gans and the Hegelian School against Haller, Hugo, Savigny and the Historical School.[394] In Berlin, Hegel identified the *Allgemeines Landrecht* with the enlightened epoch in which 'the laws of nature and justice have been called reason'.[395] With this, he followed an emphasis on the philosophical discipline that had been established already by Leibniz and Wolff and the *Aufklärung* that had a direct institutional presence (in the universities) and had led to the codification movement.[396] Would law or philosophy be tasked with training the civil service or universal estate? Gans also took up the struggle against Savigny and the Historical School from within the law faculty. His appointment by Altenstein to the professorship in Berlin represents a crucible.[397] Gans rightly saw that there was a direct continuity between the *Allgemeines Landrecht*, the reform movement and Hegel.[398] In the compelling *Critique* (1841–2), Marx saw the same: 'what Hegel says about "the Executive" does not merit the name of a philosophical development. Most of the paragraphs could be found verbatim in the Prussian *Landrecht*.'[399]

However, what this perspective overlooks is that the reform under Hardenberg and Stein had since the beginning directed its energies against the *Landrecht* and the pluralism of the estates that had been sanctioned by this code.[400] The aim must be to establish a unitary state, *not* the almost endless description of orders and functions of the *Sattelzeit*.[401] The rights of an estate 'ceased to be personal rights and became property rights'.[402] The *Landrecht*, by contrast, attempted to transform German rank society into a service society but was still based on the social conditions at the end of the eighteenth century.[403] Its principal focus was certainly not the free individual, alienated from the family, who had become the child of civil society.[404] For Altenstein, 'above all, it is important to break the legislative monopoly of lawyers. The judicial system, he explained, has gained a "harmful preponderance over the whole" in recent decades'.[405] Hegel and the philosophy faculty served his turn. Yet the *Landrecht* must be abandoned. On the one hand, the reaction made sure it preserved ancient privileges maintaining hereditary serfdom and patrimonial jurisdiction;[406] on the other hand, it was akin to an artificial system of representation long recognized in the scholarship as the first model of the Prussian constitution:[407] 'The state as guardian and servant of civil society – this is the theoretical concept of the Prussian constitution of 1791/94.'[408] Arguably, the importance of the *Landrecht* for Hegel lay in the fact that it was a positive code that he later considered had formalized the dictates of enlightened natural law and right reason.

Hegel was offered a professorship in Berlin by Altenstein because the then Prussian minister of education sought '"to rid himself of the arguably very cliquish scholarly aristocracy of Berlin (v. Savigny, Schleiermacher etc.), i.e. to find a scientific counterpoise on which he could rely"'.[409] A glance at the correspondence between the minister and Hegel over his appointment, Hegel and the ministry, and Hegel's surviving draft letter to Hardenberg that accompanied a copy of the *Grundlinien* confirms this in every way.[410] The reformers had all been shaped by the last epoch of imperial public law, the *mos Gottingensis*. They were all students of Pütter's reform absolutism. Hegel's philosophy was its inheritor. Far more so than the romanticism that inspired Pütter's student Hugo.

His innovations led to the Historical School of Law that looked to the unification of throne and altar and eulogized the mysticism of custom and the Middle Ages over law and legislation. Hegel had been opposed to Hugo since 1802.[411] To this we can add that Hegel's conceptualization of the universal estate coincided in a very particular way with the legal reality that had come to the fore with Hardenberg's legislation that separated civil society and the state, having decisively transformed the status of the estates.[412]

Hegel's philosophy and that of the Hegelian School were the philosophies of enlightened reform, of natural law, codification and constitutionalism, not the reaction that came to usurp them in the decade after his death with Friedrich Julius Stahl (1802–1861), Savigny and Schelling; they also involved (passive) revolution (revolution from above). As Hegelianism developed historically, as an institutional force of the reform, it was directed towards the legitimization of a transitional regime. The enlightened rule of officials did not necessarily permit political freedom but opened the door to it with the expectation of the introduction of a constitutional system and of written public law: 'The reform wanted to catch the revolution and point its social movement in a planned direction. Thus, all the laws of the reform work itself were designed for movement, the goal of which was understood in the sense of idealistic philosophies of history as the fulfilment of the world plan in general human freedom and ethical life.'[413]

The faith in this bureaucratic system and its corresponding Hegelianism had been shattered by 1847. With each passing year the demand for estate representation increased against the officialdom, which guarded the reform.[414] This demonstrated how the estates, as a parliamentary body or in their political capacity, could potentially develop a hostile opposition to the state.[415] This idea went against the very principle of the organic state in which the estates were to be incorporated into the totality as a *mean* following the principle of *logical* mediation: 'It is one of the common but most dangerous prejudices to conceive of estates chiefly in terms of their opposition to the government, as if that were their essential position.'[416] By 1829, however, the hope in the reform was already rapidly beginning to wane. In his lectures, Gans even developed a Hegelian doctrine of opposition; he argued that this was in no way *contingent* but 'a *necessary* element of *every* state'.[417] In the face of the continued failure of the monarch to enact the promised constitution of Prussia, Gans turned away from the language of reconciliation that had presented the rational as that which was in the process of being realized. He was led in turn to develop a novel taxonomy: Prussia was a tutelary state (*ein vormundschaftlicher Staat*), distinguished from the absolute and the despotic.[418]

In *System der Sittlichkeit* Hegel had used the estates as part of a structured monism that saw the people at one with the absolute or God. Such an institutional solution shows a substantial degree of consistency throughout his political thought. Thus, in the mature *Rechtsphilosophie*, he sought to use the estates as both a social and political order to dissolve the opposition between the government and the people, the isolated individuals and spheres of modern civil society. Importantly, in this scenario he gave primacy to the civil service or bureaucracy, the universal estate since it had the general interest as its explicit objective.[419] Further, in this capacity it responded to the problematic separation between civil society and the state that had become a novel legal and political reality.[420] However much it proved difficult 'the civil service had an advantage inherent in its very status in bringing together the particular interests of the various estates into a necessarily common decision-making body in the legislature, the civil service had an advantage here that was inherent in its very status'.[421]

The hostility that Hegel had expressed against the machinery of enlightened revolution and Fichtean idealism in Jena was in fact linked to the historical fate of his philosophy. The subordinate systems and bodies of the organic state had failed as an institutional compromise once entrenched oligarchical privileges frustrated any potential universality of the state and the promised Prussian constitution failed to materialize. This mirrored the contradiction that developed between the bureaucracy as an active force of reform and the provincial estates in Prussia and also in the Rhineland.

For Marx writing in the 1840s, the bureaucracy defended an imaginary universality – simply pursuing its own particular end. Hence, the universal estate had become 'a tissue of practical illusion, or the illusion of the state'.[422] Elsewhere, representative of the executive power, it was considered simply the civil society of the state: 'In actuality, the bureaucracy as civil society of the state is opposed to the state of civil society'.[423] Hence, the concentration of power in the universal estate aided and abetted the alienation of state from society as self-government through the estates and institutions was blocked. There was no longer any room for the principle of subsidiarity as its very existence aimed at subverting a state that was no longer reformist but restorationist and reactionary in character. What Marx diagnosed as emblematic of the Hegelian concept of the state was in fact drawn directly from the historical and political context, of the corruption of legislative power in the hands of a bureaucracy blocking the material forces of society:[424]

> Hegel has the state proper, the executive, move into the management of the state's universal interest and of legality, etc. within civil society via the holders [of the executive power]; and according to him these executive office holders the executive civil servants are really the true representation of the state, not 'of' but 'against' civil society. The opposition between state and civil society is thus fixed; the state does not reside within but outside of civil society; it affects civil society merely through office holders to whom is entrusted the management of the state within this sphere.[425]

The identification of Hegelianism with the reform bolstered the growing division between the alternatives of liberalism, a constitutional development towards communism and the rising legitimacy of a theocratic (Christian) restorative state in the *Vormärz*. The slow death of the reform ended rather suddenly once Friedrich Wilhelm IV (1795–1861) assumed the throne in Prussia. The entrenched conservative circles were victorious along with the Historical School of Law.

4.4.2 Consciousness and revolution

The doctrine of law in the state identified with a universal phenomenological consciousness that had progressed through all of the different spheres, from abstract law, morality, civil society and ethical life to the absolute spirit of world history, had dissolved. Philosophy was its own time grasped in thought and its time had passed. As Marx stated in the famed eleventh thesis of his *Theses on Feuerbach* (1845): 'The philosophers have only *interpreted* the world in different ways; the point is to *change* it.'[426] Hegel had simply failed to draw out the logical conclusions of his own philosophy: 'The critique of heaven is transformed into the critique of the earth, the critique of religion into the critique of law, the critique of theology into the critique of politics.'[427] The history of freedom that the philosopher had sought in the Germanic World where the system of representation and European parliamentarianism had first emerged and became the basis of all modern constitutional monarchical states did not escape the young Marx's criticism which foamed with indignation and denunciation of everything existing: 'What is shouted into the forests echoes back from the forest. So peace to the primeval Teutonic forests! But war upon the conditions in Germany!'[428]

The premise of any critique, as the young Marx recognized, was the critique of religion. This was intimately tied to the break with Hegel's philosophical eschatology that had determined every aspect of his system, particularly the estates constitution as well as any given mode of knowing – the final step before a radical shift.[429] The *Promethean* dimension of a dialectic liberated from the system became absolute criticism with the young Marx. History, freed of its theodicy, became an historical materialism that set out 'to establish the truth of this world'.[430] Yet presumably this dimension was present in seed in Hegel's conception of public law. As György Lukács (1885–1971) recognized perceptively, the emerging universal class of the proletariat equally implied a distinct theory of consciousness, one that led back to Hegel.[431] Even if Hegel's philosophy of law became too closely associated with Hardenberg's reforms in which the civil service was meant to represent the entirety of civil society, this dimension of its universality could not be ignored. Furthermore, the education of consciousness in the public laws of the state was identical with the universal estate and the power of its rationality:

> When Hegel described the administrative bodies as the battlefield between social interests and state structures (§289), when he regarded the civil service as the 'universal estate' whose personal commitment coincided with the interests of the general public (§291), when he described it – more sociologically – as the 'main part of the middle estate', in which the educated intelligentsia and the legal consciousness of the mass of the people coincided (§297), when, finally, he granted the civil service an independent intermediate position between the people and the authorities – with all these statements he not only painted the picture that Prussian civil servants had of themselves, but largely the reality itself.[432]

There was something anachronistic and modern in Hegel's universal estate and the doctrine of legal consciousness. On the one hand, the rationality of the civil service, the bureaucracy open to talent through the examination, could be viewed as a stabilizing element in the state. Inasmuch as the barriers to access to the civil service had disappeared, it looked less and less like an estate in the traditional understanding of the term. It was a universal. Here the divide between living from and for politics had largely dissolved, even though Hegel continued to favour landed property and the independence of the nobility.[433] On the other hand, inasmuch as the authority of office and the state opposed the unorganized mass of people, this demonstrated another aspect of Hegel's political Aristotelianism, a doctrine opposed to the idea that the people should rule: 'Such a democracy is fairly open to objection that it is not a constitution at all; for where the laws have no authority, there is no constitution. The laws ought to be supreme over all, and the magistracies should judge the particulars, and only this should be considered a constitution.'[434]

The development that led to the formation of the proletariat cannot be exclusively discovered in the idea of Hegel's rabble, as it also implied a discrete organizational form.[435] This has been rightly related to Hegel's concept of the universal estate as a principal instrument of rationality, notwithstanding Marx's opposition to the dwindling reform bureaucracy in the historical context of the 1840s: 'Marx described the proletariat as a "universal class", a mass situated virtually beyond the condition of class, the particularity of that mass being denied in its very conditions of existence. But he could not have formulated that idea if Hegel had not, in his *Philosophy of Right* of 1821, developed a theory of the "universal *Stand*".'[436] But beyond the proletariat, 'the Hegelian civil servant (conceived as the main instrument of rationality)' even more decisively points to the professional revolutionary: 'Hegel's view that the people was unable to rule may have suggested to Lenin the idea that the proletariat, left to itself, would never go beyond trade unionism and would never seize power unless organized by revolutionary leaders.'[437]

This dimension to Hegelianism has long been identified with a doctrine of consciousness that had been decidedly opposed, with the Prussian reform and particularly Altenstein, to the mysticism of Savigny and the Historical School of Law. This was even before Marx went on the attack denouncing that the Historical School of Law justified 'the infamy of today by the infamy of yesterday'.[438] In contrast to every restorationist theocratic philosophy, Marx recognized that Hegel's solution to revolutionary modernity – the cleft between civil society and the state – his organic or institutional ideal of the state 'was the most successful attempt yet "to look upon the state from the perspective of human eyes and to develop its natural laws [*Naturgesetze*] on the basis of reason and experience"'.[439] Hegel's organic state was a continuation or completion of rational natural law and the philosophy of universal public law: 'This perspective regards the state as a great organism in which legal, ethical, and political freedom are to find their actualization, and in which the individual citizen of the state obeys in the laws of the state [*Staatsgesetze*] only the natural laws [*Naturgesetze*] of his own reason, of human reason.'[440]

What Marx perceived here was precisely Hegel's idea that right in the form of consciousness is law. The crux of the problem lay in the fact that the Prussia reform had faltered; the reaction had firmly taken hold of the steering of the state – the Historical School of Law triumphant alongside Schelling and Stahl. In such a context, a radical right in the form of consciousness could develop in the absence of – even in dialectical opposition to – any corresponding law. It was no longer possible to reconcile rationality with reality.

Conclusion

The development of Hegel's legal and political thought represents a profound synthesis of diverse intellectual and historical currents. At its core, it was deeply rooted in the imperial public law tradition, which had developed terms like *forma imperii* and *forma regiminis* to articulate the legal complexities of a composite state. This inheritance was significantly augmented by Kantian legal philosophy and Fichtean idealism that Hegel critically transformed. Hegel clearly appropriated Majer's crucial innovations, particularly his rigorous concept of the state and his thorough division between private and public law, government and constitution, as evident in the *Verfassungsschrift* and *System der Sittlichkeit*. The Tübingen professor himself had been shaped by the prevalent imperial public law conceptions of the *mos Gottingensis*. These key elements, set against the backdrop of the transformative events of the French Revolution, were meticulously brought together by Hegel to forge his unique and totalizing philosophy of modern ethical life.

For Hegel, constitution and government converged in a monistic state concept, which found its expression in the multiplicity of estates. This echoes the public law tradition's development of a *civitas composita* – a structure whose persistence, albeit speculatively realized, I have demonstrated in Hegel's early absolute idealism. Unlike the absolutist state machine, Hegel rejected the rigid opposition of the understanding, envisioning a state where the system of estates, as government and constitution, formed the objective organization of sovereignty. For him, the freedom of these seemingly subordinate spheres, the political *adiaphora*, was not distinct from, but integral to, the state's supreme unity, demonstrating a complementary and homologous relationship between organization and form – the architectonic or hieroglyph of reason.

When Hegel spoke of 'the organization of this body which is called the German state constitution', he firmly situated himself within the imperial public law tradition.[1] Yet, eschewing empirical description, he deployed philosophical speculation drawing on pre-critical substance metaphysics to unify diverse imperial and territorial structures within an absolute idealism. He recognized the imperial state as a theoretical state (*Gedankenstaat*) where individual power and private concerns had permeated the public sphere.[2] As he decisively remarked, titles and patriotic glorifications could no longer mask the decomposition of the body politic, revealing Germany's reality as a collection of independent states rather than a united whole.[3] Hegel's observation underscored the renewed urgency of classifying the imperial constitution. The revolutionary wars and French ambitions made the former luxury of indecision about the *forma Reipublicae* or the locus of sovereignty untenable as the ground had irrevocably shifted.

Political deterioration rooted in developments like armed neutrality led Hegel to a crucial realization. Aligning with the patriotic publicists of the Third Germany of the smaller estates, he concluded that the traditional balance of power was untenable, highlighting the impossibility of a unified imperial union and the need for new political safeguards: 'with regard to a danger for the German estates, Austria and Prussia are on the same level. What used to be called German freedom would have to take precautions against both.'[4] Such insights solidified Hegel's conviction regarding the Empire's inevitable dissolution, ending his earlier indecision. The widespread practices of territorial cessions and secularizations, historically common since the Reformation, were now dramatically applied as war reparations.[5] Hegel's study of these processes, particularly through works like Pütter's, starkly illustrated the Empire's dismemberment, compelling him to actively 'update' contemporary public law discourse and forge new conceptual tools for a collapsing order.[6]

Hegel's emphasis on 'concepts' over 'titles' reflected his engagement with the Aristotelian tradition of *politica*, through which he critiqued the *simulacra imperii* and a hollow imperial patriotism that idealized the emperor who, as Pütter put it famously, was 'the only completely independent person in Germany, even the first in rank of all of the crowned heads of Europe'.[7] Hegel understood Napoleon's destruction of this *Realverbindung* – Pütter's objective legal connection – as the dismantling of the old feudal order (*nexum*) of allegiance. In its place, Hegel posited a concept of monarchy as the true embodiment of state power, a limited monarch bound by the estates, foreshadowing his mature understanding of sovereignty.[8]

Amidst rapid historical developments, Hegel continually refined his definition of the state, transcending both empirical and formal natural law, as well as contractual theories. His political Aristotelianism offered a conservative response to the individualistic 'heresies' of Fichte and the French Revolution. He argued that natural law's emphasis on individual rationalism contradicted the concept of an ethical life and the state as a pre-existing totality, describing such fragmented understandings as distorting organic ethical life into the individual and the particular.[9] This critique further informed his view of the Empire as merely a theoretical state, devoid of real political power, which had devolved into the private law leveraged by the imperial estates.

The Empire's unique trajectory saw the ascendency of *Fürstenrecht* and Roman private law.[10] Just as the king was conceived to have two bodies, the territorial prince wielded two legal persons – 'persona publica sive Principis' (public character or rather character of the ruler) and 'persona privata seu hominis privati' (private character or rather character of the private man).[11] Majer's crucial contribution was delineating these, separating *dominium* from the public legal order and identifying its public exercise as despotism. For Hegel, this marked a turning point: the pervasive application of Roman private law and exclusive property rights had dissolved the Empire. This also clarified the conceptual distinction between private and public law, which became definitively established with the post-1806 emergence of the state's legal personality following Napoleon's destruction of the Empire and its complimentary concept of *Landeshoheit*.

In the *Reinschrift* Hegel's chapter 'Begriff des Staats' showcased Majer's influence,[12] while 'Rechtmäßigkeit, dass die Ausübung der Staatsgesetze nicht zu Stande kommt' (Legality is such that the Exercise of the Laws of the State does not come about) – addressed the failure of a true state in Germany. If the former outlined the abstract requirements for unity, the latter stressed the monarch's personality. This led Hegel to the stabilization of the monarchical principle through positive public law, which shares a striking continuity with Pütter's objective legal connection. Hegel's key insight was that the seeming contradiction between supreme state authority and individual freedom is only resolved by the power of laws. This principle of universality mediates between the personality of the monarch and the individual. He argued that true political prudence lies in this balance, where the sovereignty of the state is intrinsically linked to a robust system of public law and a constitution.[13]

This equilibrium, rooted in *Staatsgesetze*, prefigures Hegel's mature concept of the constitutional state and the unique Germanic contribution to world history. His critique of the Empire, influenced by Majer's private princely law, stemmed from the insight that a particular legal power, not true public law, had dissolved it. As Hegel argued, when 'opposition to the decisions of state authority has itself been elevated to the form of law', the state is fundamentally undermined for 'it is a legal act if the state is prevented from being a state in which the power that can oppose it is lawful'.[14] This reflected the contractual nature of the imperial state, where private property and the particularism of the *cives imperii* effectively privatized the public order, driven by the unique reception of Roman private law and contract law writ large in the electoral capitulations, peace treaties and house contracts.[15]

Hegel, writing in a distinct epoch, drew different conclusions than Moser and Pütter. While Moser's empirical method for Hegel described the Empire in decline, Hegel's analysis confronted its consequences directly. Pütter's foundational *Realverbindung* had effectively vanished and, following Majer, the imperial structure had become a *Privatum Imperium Romano-Germanicum* – an aristocratic collective of increasingly consolidated states. Hegel's emphasis on state sovereignty and the Empire's disintegration aligned with Pufendorf's *systema civitatem* concept, which similarly grappled with the Empire's ambiguous status as neither a limited monarchy nor a true federation.[16] Ultimately, however, Majer and Hegel's convergence on the concept of the state stemmed from their shared urgency in confronting a singular historical and theoretical crisis. Considered historically and contextually, however, Hegel was as profoundly influenced by Pütter's legacy and the reform movement that he essentially founded through his students who became the principal architects of the developing constitutional state.

Hegel argued that the progress of public law was impeded by Roman private law and private princely law, mirroring a historical disjunction between convention and law. Overcoming this required a real idea of universality embodied in a system of *Staatsgesetze*. In contrast to Fichte's organic central authority and Robespierre's despotism of freedom, Hegel embraced Kant's separation of powers, arguing that a 'true ethical totality must have entered into this separation'.[17] This was structurally realized through the estates, where the monarch as 'the centre of state power from which everything emanates that requires coercion according to the laws' was balanced by 'the estates [that] have a share in legislation, and they provide the means by which power is maintained'.[18] His philosophy of union, rooted in organic ethical life, thus harmonized custom and law, fusing the particular and the universal through the real-existing institutions of the state.

Hegel's *System der Sittlichkeit* captured 'the oneness of the universal and the particular' under absolute ethical life, seeking to establish public law through reason and consciousness, with supreme power in a revised *Realverbindung* of absolute identity in the system of estates.[19] This regulative ideal directly addressed the empirical insights of the *Verfassungsschrift*. For Hegel, the monarch embodying state sovereignty reconciled supreme power with individual liberty through the power of the laws.[20] This 'third option' – a constitutional rule of law holding sovereignty in check – represented his organic principle, defining the modern constitutional state and implicitly incorporating the idea of subsidiarity. Laws, therefore, were not based on individualism, but rather individualism and private law emerged as products of the objective public legal order that sanctioned such private rights in the freedoms of conscience and religion.

Through meticulous analyses across its four chapters, this book has established an innovative framework for studying the formation of Hegel's legal, political and historical thought. It has demonstrated how Hegel critically appropriated methodological insights from Moser, transformed natural law and universal public law through Pütter and, most crucially, absorbed Majer's modern and shrewd division of private and public law – a conceptualization central to the young Hegel's understanding of the state. By tracing these intellectual lineages, this study reveals how Hegel integrated elements of imperial public law into his critique of Roman law and the French Republic, shaping his speculative concept of the state as a structured monism that valued corporate belonging over radical legal egalitarianism. This approach is further exemplified in Hegel's *System der Sittlichkeit*, which developed a structured monism and an unequal system of cooperative contraries. Ultimately, the book illuminates how the structures of public law, the constitutional compromise of the Empire and the medieval doctrine of the four empires or monarchies continued to shape Hegel's thinking into his philosophical maturity, leading to his reconceptualization of the world-historical Germanic Empire as the final moment of imperial public law, and explaining why the subsequent break with his philosophy itself became world historical. This work also precisely shows how the transformation of conscience into a doctrine of legal consciousness, an ethic of institutions and laws, became central to his doctrine of the universal estate and was transferred to the revolutionary epoch, rooted in imperial public law guarantees of freedom of conscience and religion.

This study stands as a testament to the crucial role of imperial public law in shaping Hegel's thought, revealing the historical roots of his state theory and its profound implications for modern political philosophy and the history of German public law. By unearthing this complex intellectual lineage, the book provides a fundamentally new lens through which to understand the genesis of Hegel's modern constitutional state and its enduring legacy in European history.

Notes

Foreword

1. Karl Marx, *Capital. A Critique of Political Economy, Volume One*, trans. Ben Fowkes (London: Penguin Books, 1976), 103.
2. Hence Moser's dictum 'Teutschland wird auf teutsch regiert'. Johann Jacob Moser, *Von Teutschland und dessen Staats-Verfassung überhaupt* (Stuttgart: Metzler, 1766), 550.
3. Georg Wilhelm Friedrich Hegel, 'The German Constitution', in *Political Writings*, ed. Laurence Dickey and trans. Hugh B. Nisbet (Cambridge: Cambridge University Press, 1999), 6.

Introduction

1. Henning Ottmann, 'Ein philosophisches Finale: Hegels Verfassungsschrift (1799–1803)', in *GpD*, 395–7.
2. Michel Villey, 'Das römische Recht in Hegels Rechtsphilosophie', in *Materialien zu Hegels Rechtsphilosophie. Band 2*, ed. Manfred Riedel (Frankfurt am Main: Suhrkamp, 1974), 131–51.
3. Franz Rosenzweig, *Hegel and the State*, trans. Josiah Simon and Jules Simon (London: Routledge, 2024), 128–207.
4. *GW5[RV]*, 1–219. I rely on the critical edition, published in 1998.
5. Michael Stolleis, *Geschichte des öffentlichen Rechts in Deutschland, Erster Band: Reichspublizistik und Policeywissenschaft 1600–1800* (Munich: C. H. Beck, 1988), 296; Knud Haakonssen, 'German Natural Law', in *The Cambridge History of Eighteenth-Century Political Thought*, ed. Mark Goldie and Robert Wokler (Cambridge: Cambridge University Press, 2006), 251–90.
6. Michael Stolleis, *Public Law in Germany 1800–1914* (Oxford: Berghahn, 2001), 19.
7. Rosenzweig, *Hegel and the State*, 128–9.
8. See *GW15[FsG]*, 231–2.
9. Rosenzweig, *Hegel and the State*, 128.
10. See the first of the two identically titled but very different studies by Hans Maier, 'Hegels Schrift über die Reichsverfassung', *Politische Vierteljahresschrift*, 4, no. 4 (1963): 349. For an earlier study in which I link this directly to Hegel's political Aristotelianism, see Nathaniel Boyd, 'The Constitution of Crisis: Politics, Decline and Decision in Hegel's *Verfassungsschrift*', in *Crisis and Renewal in the History of European Political Thought*, ed. Cesare Cuttica and László Kontler (Leiden: Brill, 2021), 280–302.
11. Notker Hammerstein, 'Das Römische in der Lehre der Reichs-Publicisten', in *Res publica litteraria Ausgewählte Aufsätze zur frühneuzeitlichen Bildungs-, Wissenschafts- und Universitätsgeschichte*, ed. Ulrich Muhlack and Gerrit Walter (Berlin: Dunker & Humblot, 2000), 153.

12. See Mathias Pape, 'Revolution und Reichsverfassung – Die Verfassungsdiskussion zwischen Fürstenbund und Rheinbund', in *Verfassung und Revolution. Hegels Verfassungskonzeption und die Revolution der Neuzeit, Hegel-Studien Beiheft 42*, ed. Elizabeth Weisser-Lohmann and Dietmar Köhler (Hamburg: Felix Meiner, 2000), 68; compare Rosenzweig, *Hegel and the State*, 198 n. 107.
13. See Friedrich Schiller, 'Deutsche Größe. Zur Feier der Jahhundertwende'. Available online: www.normannia-winterberg.de/mediapool/56/565510/data/Schiller_-deutsche_Groesse.pdf (accessed 30 April 2025). The precise date of composition has never been established; it could also have been written in 1801.
14. I draw each of these titles from the final parts of the four Berlin lectures on the philosophy of world history (see *GW27,1–4[VWG]*).
15. Samuel von Pufendorf, *The Present State of Germany*, trans. Edmund Bohun, ed. Michael J. Seidler (Indianapolis: Liberty Fund, 2007), 28–31; *HD1*, 25–106.
16. See *GW27,2[VWG]*, 755–60.
17. Hans Maier, 'Hegels Schrift über die Reichsverfassung' in Georg Wilhelm Friedrich Hegel, *Über die Reichsverfassung*, ed. Hans Maier (Hamburg: Felix Meiner, 2004), 196, 214 n. 7 rightly emphasizes that the four realms of world history (the Oriental, Greek, Roman and Germanic) were originally three in the fragments of the *Verfassungsschrift*. Henceforth, I will cite Maier's two identically titled essays followed by 1 (early version) or 2 (later version).
18. *GW5[RV]*, 115.
19. See Gertrude Lübbe-Wolff, 'Die Bedeutung der Lehre von der vier Weltreichen für das Staatsrecht des Römischen-Deutschen Reichs', *Der Staat*, 23, no. 3 (1984): 369–89.
20. Jean Bodin, *Methodus historica: duodecim eiusdem argumenti scriptorium tam veterum quam recentiorem commentariis adaucta* (Basel: Officina, 1576), 299.
21. See Philipp Melanchthon, *Chronicon carionis latine ex positum et auctum multis et veteribus et recentibus Historiis, in narrationibus rerum Graecarum, Germanicarum et Eccleisiasticarum* (Frankfurt: Zepffelii, 1559), 22, 33, 53, 353, 354–96 on the fourth monarchy, Rome 1335 and where he directly takes over the translation theory 1331–77.
22. See Dieter Grimm, *Constitutionalism: Past, Present, and Future* (Oxford: Oxford University Press, 2016), 98.
23. The *Reinschrift* is the clean copy that Hegel reworked in late 1802, perhaps early 1803, before abandoning the manuscript unpublished (see *GW5[RV]*, 161–202). This was around the same time *System der Sittlichkeit* (*GW5[SdS]*, 277–361) was composed. For details on the composition of the *Reinschrift* and the surrounding historical events, I rely on Kurt Rainer Meist, 'Editorischer Bericht', in *GW5*, 590–5. The pertinent sections in Majer are *ATSK*, 9–24; *TSK1*, 13–16.
24. *ATSK*, 21–4; *GW5[SdS]*, 277–36; Rosenzweig, *Hegel and the State*, 163.
25. Dieter Henrich, 'Logical Form and Real Totality: The Authentic Conceptual Form of Hegel's Concept of the State', in *Hegel on Ethics and Politics: The German Philosophical Tradition*, ed. Robert B. Pippen and Otfried Höffe (Cambridge: Cambridge University Press, 2004), 241–2.
26. Nathaniel Boyd, 'Pufendorf on Confessional Strife and Interstate Relations', in *Pufendorf's International Political and Legal Thought*, ed. Peter Schröder (Oxford: Oxford University Press, 2024), 28–32.
27. See Kersten Krüger, *Die Landständische Verfassung: Enzyklopädie deutscher Geschichte, Band 67* (Munich: Oldenbourg, 2003), 1. With its legal complexity, its problems of unity in diversity, of local autonomy and integration, the Empire even

brings up associations with the European Union. The principle of subsidiarity became essential to the Treaty of the European Union (Article 5 (§3)).

28. *GW5[SdS]*, 340. Hegel firmly belongs to a tradition of corporate reflection. Under the influence of Friedrich Wilhelm Schelling (1775–1854), Otto von Gierke (1841–1921) revived this for the Germanic division of the Historical School of Law in his association theory of the state in the late-nineteenth and early-twentieth centuries (see *Der Staat als Genossenschaft. Zum rechtshistorischen und politischen Werk Otto von Gierkes*, ed. Peter Schröder (Baden-Baden: Nomos, 2021)). For a fine interpretation of Hegel's corporatism that uses Gierke's scholarship, see George Heiman, 'The Sources and Significance of Hegel's Corporate Doctrine', in *Hegel's Political Philosophy: Problems and Perspectives, A Collection of New Essays*, ed. Zbigniew Pelczynski (Cambridge: Cambridge University Press, 1971), 111–35.
29. The Latin terms are generally interchangeable, as form of state (*reipublicae*) or sovereignty (*imperii*) in contrast to its administration (*de administratione reipublicae*) or the mode of the exercise of sovereignty, its government (*modo regiminis imperii*). Compare Pütter's first edition of the *Elementa* (*EG[1754]*, 52–64) with the third edition (*EG[1760]*, 49–58). The first uses *forma Reipublicae*, the second *forma imperii*.
30. *GW20[E1830]*, 536–7 (§552).
31. Hanns Gross, *Empire and Sovereignty: A History of the Public Law Literature in the Holy Roman Empire, 1599–1804* (Chicago: University of Chicago Press, 1973).
32. Martti Koskenniemi, *To the Uttermost Parts of the Earth: Legal Imagination and International Power (1300–1870)* (Cambridge: Cambridge University Press, 2021), 795–967.
33. This is most obviously the case with respect to Pufendorf (see Gross, *Empire and Sovereignty*, 311–28). But he is also inaccurate when it comes to Hegel's biographical details.
34. See ibid., 476–9; Koskenniemi, *To the Uttermost Parts of the Earth*, 939–49.
35. Heinz Kimmerle, 'Zur Chronologie von Hegels Jenaer Schriften', *Hegel-Studien*, 4 (1967): 125–76.
36. Meist, 'Editorischer Bericht', 549–745.
37. Kurt Rainer Meist, 'Anmerkungen', in *GW5*, 746–825. I also follow his commentary in the paperback edition that is not as extensive, see Kurt Rainer Meist, 'Zur Textedition der Verfassungsschrift', in Georg Wilhelm Friedrich Hegel, *Über die Reichsverfassung*, ed. Hans Maier (Hamburg: Felix Meiner, 2004), vii–lxxxi. In English, H. S. Harris, *Hegel's Development: Towards the Sunlight (1770–1801)* (Oxford: Clarendon Press, 1972), 434–77 remains unmatched.

1 Imperial public law in *statu cadentis imperii*: Johann Jacob Moser

1. Harris, *Towards the Sunlight*, 11.
2. For critical remarks on Moser's supposed positivism, see Horst Dreitzel, *Absolutismus und ständische Verfassung in Deutschland. Ein Beitrag zu Kontinuität und Diskontinuität der politischen Theorie in der frühen Neuzeit* (Mainz: Philipp von Zabern, 1992), 109 n. 22.
3. Heinz Mohnhaupt, 'Verfassung I', in *GG6*, 855.

4. In an early definition of territorial supremacy, Moser appealed, however, to natural law, divine law and the law of nations (see *CJP*, 449) which he also reasserted in *NtSR14*, 9, 11.
5. *NtSR1*, 549.
6. Moser is referred to directly in the most recently discovered fragment, 'Der Nahme für die Staatsverfassung' (The Name for the State Constitution) (see *GW5[RV]*, 56); Meist, 'Anmerkungen', in *GW5*, 750, 759, 760, 767, 768, 771, 772, 777 has analysed Moser's impact on numerous fragments. 'Der Nahme für die Staatsverfassung' was accompanied by a note by Hegel's protégé Eduard Gans (1797–1839) confirming its authenticity (see Meist, 'Editorischer Bericht', 580–1).
7. For the older literature, which assessed the relationship hypothetically, see Rosenzweig, *Hegel and the State*, 547 listing *NtSR1* and *NG*; Rolf K. Hočevar, *Stände und Repräsentation beim jungen Hegel: Ein Beitrag zu seiner Staats- und Gesellschaftslehre sowie zur Theorie der Repräsentation* (Munich: C.H. Beck, 1968), 212 cites *PJP* and *GhSv*. Neither Rosenzweig nor Hočevar were privy to 'Der Nahme für die Staatsverfassung'.
8. Mack Walker, *Johann Jakob Moser and the Holy Roman Empire of the German Nation* (Chapel Hill: University of North Carolina Press, 1981), 237–45.
9. Gross, *Empire and Sovereignty*, 444.
10. *BtS-FR1*, 19.
11. *NtSR1*, 27.
12. See *GW5[RV]*, 108–9.
13. Ibid., 109.
14. Ibid., 52, 56.
15. Mohnhaupt, 'Verfassung I', 857.
16. *GW5[RV]*, 12.
17. For Hegel's perception on the workings of the Imperial Cameral Court (*Reichskammergericht*) the Aulic Council (*Reichshofrat*) and the burden of cases, see ibid., 183.
18. Ibid., 44.
19. Ibid., 61 (italics added). A register of fief ownership, an *urbarium* or rent roll consisted of the rights and benefits a fief holder possessed over his serfs and peasants.
20. *NtSR1*, 456.
21. *GW5[SdS]*, 328. Hegel translates Aristotle's *polis* with people (*Volk*).
22. *GW5[RV]*, 12.
23. Ibid., 79. This perspective is actually confirmed by Pufendorf's analysis in the *Monzambano* (1667) which fundamentally involved a rejection of the Aristotelian typology.
24. See Pape, 'Revolution und Reichsverfassung', 52.
25. *NtSR1*, 184.
26. See Wolfgang Burgdorf, 'Proto-Constitutionalism: The Imperial Constitution in the Electoral Capitulations and Basic Law Guarantees', *German History* 36, no. 3 (1994): 415–31.
27. *GW15[VL]*, 30–125; *GW26,1[VPR]*, 1–225.
28. Ibid., 151 (§125) (original italics). No doubt Hegel takes aim in this context at *NtSR14–16* which detailed territorial supremacy in all of its forms.
29. See *GW5[RV]*, 52–7.
30. See Rosenzweig, *Hegel and the State*, 143, 195–6 n. 54. True, Moser here is only referenced in passing. Rosenzweig rather gives priority to Majer's influence.

31. *GW5[RV]*, 5–14. As Meist, 'Editorischer Bericht', 563–4 has reported the fragment was taken up at a later stage and reworked by Hegel as can be seen by the additions that are distinct from the original that is dated to 1799. It is the original outline for the introduction.
32. See *GW5[RV]*, 111.
33. *GW26,1[VPR]*, 218 (§164); *GW14,1[PdR]*, 273 (§340).
34. *GW1[FSI]*, 145.
35. See *GW5[RV]*, 201–2, 111; *GW14,1[PdR]*, 274–5 (§343).
36. Schiller, 'Deutsche Größe'.
37. 'Sollte das politische Resultat' already had the phrasing in the margins, a later addition. Its initial conceptualization, however, occurred in the body of the text: 'daß Deutschland, gar kein Staat mehr ist' (see *GW5[RV]*, 6). This was tied to a discussion of the Aristotelian typology, which directly raises the issue of the synonymity of the concept of the state with the traditional categories of constitution Hegel discusses – bringing him firmly into the tradition of *politica*.
38. Ibid., 10.
39. Ibid., 161. For details on the *Reinschrift*, see my Introduction.
40. Walker, *Johann Jakob Moser*, ix.
41. *NtSR1*, 550. Undoubtedly, 'Schulwort' is a reference to the Aristotelian constitutional typology.
42. *GW5[RV]*, 196.
43. See Hočevar, *Stände und Repräsentation*, 165–8.
44. *PJP*, 4.
45. Ibid., 14–15.
46. Ibid.
47. Gross, *Empire and Sovereignty*, 403, 401.
48. Walker, *Johann Jakob Moser*, 283–95.
49. Horst Dreitzel, *Protestantischer Aristotelismus und absoluter Staat. Die 'Politica' des Henning Arnisaeus (ca.1575–1636)* (Wiesbaden: Franz Steiner, 1970), 1.
50. *PJP*, 7.
51. Harris, *Towards the Sunlight*, 417–18. Hegel most likely followed Pütter (see *HD3*, i–vi, 1–71).
52. See Johan van der Zande, 'Statistik and History in the German Enlightenment,' *Journal of the History of Ideas* 71, no. 3 (2010): 411–32. August Ludwig Schlözer (1735–1809), the more radical younger colleague of Pütter and Gottfried Achenwall (1719–1772) and the first to theorize the cleft between civil society and the state that Hegel made famous, developed the discipline further (see Martin Peters, *Altes Reich und Europa: der Historiker, Statistiker und Publizist August Ludwig (v.) Schlözer (1735–1809)* (Munich: LIT, 2003); Martin Peters, 'Das Verhältnis von Staat und Gesellschaft im Werk A. L. Schlözers', in *Souveränitätskonzeptionen. Beiträge zur Analyse politischer Ordnungsvorstellungen im 17. bis zum 20.* Jahrhundert, ed. Martin Peters and Peter Schröder (Berlin: Duncker & Humblot, 2000), 109–30). For the limitations of Schlözer's distinction between civil society and the state, 'which only hints at the Hegelian "difference"', see Manfred Riedel, *Between Tradition and Revolution: The Hegelian Transformation of Political Philosophy*, trans. Walter Wright (Cambridge: Cambridge University Press, 2011), 140.
53. Mohnhaupt, 'Verfassung I', 855. The italics are quotations taken from Johann August Eberhard, *Abhandlung von dem Begriffe der Bearbeitung der Deutschen Staatsklugheit* (Wittenberg: Zerbst, 1768), 61, 38.

54. Merio Scattola, 'Scientia Iuris and Ius Naturae: The Jurisprudence of the Holy Roman Empire in the Seventeenth and Eighteenth Centuries', in *A Treatise of Legal Philosophy and General Jurisprudence Volume 9, A History of the Philosophy of Law in the Civil World, 1600–1900*, ed. Damiano Canale, Paolo Grossi and Hasso Hofmann (Dordrecht: Springer, 2009), 3–4.
55. *PJP*, 14–15.
56. *NtSR1*, 544–7.
57. *GW5[RV]*, 56 (original italics). This comes from 'Der Nahme für die Staatsverfassung'.
58. Ibid., 5.
59. Ibid., 161.
60. Rosenzweig, *Hegel and the State*, 132.
61. Maier, 'Hegels Schrift 1', 337 n. 11 (original italics). The Latin can be translated as 'the state of a crumbling empire'.
62. *GW5[RV]*, 9.
63. See *BtS-FR1*, 19 – already quoted in Section 1.0.2.
64. Mohnhaupt, 'Verfassung I', 855.
65. Hippolithus à Lapide, *Dissertatio de ratione status in imperio nostro Romano-Germanico* (1640). The publication date has never really been established; it could also have been published in 1647. Conring was the first to identify the author as Bogislaw Philipp von Chemnitz (1605–1678). *GW31,2[ABH]*, 1021–3 has 1647 as the listed date of publication for the two Latin editions Hegel owned. In all likelihood these travelled with him from the late Frankfurt or early Jena periods up until his death – one of the editions is also listed in the original estate sale (see *Verzeichniss der von dem Professor Herrn Dr. Hegel und Dr. Herrn Seebeck hinterlassene Bücher-Sammlungen* (Berlin: C.F. Müller, 1832), 51, entry number 1266). This means that these editions are not the rare quarto edition but the duodecimo edition, which was printed in Holland. Fixing the actual date of publication 'is not arbitrary. In the first case, the writing would be a five-year delayed reaction to the Peace of Prague of 1635, in the second case a propaganda document to strengthen the anti-Habsburg forces in the run-up to the Peace of Westphalia' (Stolleis, *Geschichte des öffentlichen Rechts*, 204). The latter perspective is reflected in Hegel's interpretation of its idea of German freedom as particularization. Meist cites the German translation published during the Seven Years' War, seemingly unaware that Hegel owned two original Latin copies (Meist, 'Anmerkungen', 760).
66. See Gross, *Empire and Sovereignty*, 408–10.
67. Walker, *Johann Jakob Moser*, 66–7.
68. *NtSR3*, 27.
69. The beginning of this debate started with the application of the Bodinian concept to the level of territories that favoured the development of a theory of *superioritas territorialis*. This began with the German jurist Andreas von Knichen (1560–1621). The full sovereignty of the territories in an imperial union was never completely achieved.
70. Walker, *Johann Jakob Moser*, 297.
71. *NtSR14*, 16–18, 27.
72. Walker, *Johann Jakob Moser*, 296.
73. *NtSR13*, 1150; *NtSR14*, 25, 242.
74. *GW5[RV]*, 70.
75. *NtSR14*, 295.
76. Some imperial estates were ecclesiastical territories (Trier, Mainz, Cologne).

77. Gross, *Empire and Sovereignty*, 418. Moser must have taken his lead from Ludolph Hugo (see Section 1.2.5).
78. See Mohnhaupt, 'Verfassung I', 856.
79. *NtSR1*, 183–4.
80. *NtSR14*, 26.
81. *NtSR3*, 32.
82. *NtSR14*, 27.
83. Walker, *Johann Jakob Moser*, 297.
84. Stolleis, *Geschichte des öffentlichen Rechts*, 258–70.
85. See Mohnhaupt, 'Verfassung I', 856. On this development, see Hegel as well (*GW5[RV]*, 61).
86. Mohnhaupt, 'Verfassung I', 857.
87. Ibid.
88. Ibid., 856.
89. Of the thirty-one volumes of *Neues teutsches Staats-Recht*, a total of ten, if we include the eight sub-volumes of *NtSR16*, cover the diverse subjects of territorial supremacy. Pütter's two-volume *Beyträge zum teutschen Staats- und Fürsten-Rechte* (1777–79), appearing shortly thereafter, covers the subject as well. This attests to the rising import of *Landeshoheit* in the disquisitions of German imperial public law that it had begun to transform into a quasi-federal discipline.
90. This is taken from the early fragment 'über ihre Entstehung' (on their emergence) (*GW5[RV]*, 15).
91. Ibid., 8–9.
92. Ibid.
93. For this analysis in connection to Majer, see Sections 3.2.1–3.2.5.
94. *GW5[RV]*, 13.
95. Ibid.
96. *NtSR16*.
97. *GW5[RV]*, 9, 12–13.
98. Ibid., 10. Note here the use of the concept of German public law. The legal thinker of Roman law Gustav Hugo (1764–1844), a student of Pütter's and a recipient of Hegel's enduring scorn, believed that public law as a term supplanted the previously used state law at the end of the eighteenth century (see Stolleis, *Public Law in Germany, 1800–1914*, 31 n. 83). Although I have not been able to locate a direct reference to the German term in the works of Moser, Pütter or Majer that I have consulted, the spread of the way in which a vernacular, Germanized form was used to convey concepts was taken over directly from the Latin (Roman) sources (see *AEP-Fr*, 86–93, for example). The dichotomy between private and public law, attributed to Ulpian (*c.* 170 BCE–223 (or 228) CE) (*Digest* I.I.1.2.), slowly took hold in the context of the revolutionary emergence of a modern (depoliticized) civil society distinct from the strictly political state. In the fragments of the *Verfassungsschrift*, Hegel used the term public law sparingly and far more frequently employed the older concept of state law. Yet this seems to attest precisely to the interchangeability of the concepts, reflecting a period of semantic change.
99. *GW5[RV]*, 12.
100. The Peace of Westphalia consisted of two treaties: the Peace of Osnabrück signed between the emperor, the imperial estates and Sweden (*Instrumentum Pacis Osnabrugensis*) and the Peace of Münster signed between the emperor, the imperial estates and France (*Instrumentum Pacis Monasteriensis*). The treaties of Münster

and Osnabrück were not only international peace settlements and imperial laws but also part of the constitution (see Randall Lesaffer, 'The Westphalian Peace Treaties and the Development of the Tradition of Great European Peace Settlements Prior to 1648', *Grotiana* 18 (1997): 71).

101. *GW5[RV]*, 12.
102. Ibid., 13–14, 29–37, 48–50, 64–5, 91–2, 108–9, 126–31, 136–7, 140–2, 151–4, 187–90, 205 and 206–7.
103. See Helmut Quaritsch, *Souveränität. Entstehung und Entwicklung des Begriffs in Frankreich und Deutschland vom 13. Jahrhundert bis 1806* (Berlin: Dunker & Humblot, 1986), 108.
104. Gross, *Empire and Sovereignty*, 294.
105. Quaritsch, *Souveränität*, 113–14.
106. Peter Schröder, 'Reich versus Territorien? Zum Problem der Souveränität im Heiligen Römischen Reich nach dem Westfälischen Frieden', in *Altes Reich, Frankreich und Europa Politische, philosophische und historische Aspekte des französischen Deutschlandbildes im 17. und 18. Jahrhundert*, ed. Olaf Asbach et al. (Berlin: Dunker & Humblot, 2001), 142.
107. *NtSR14*, 25, 242. These original formulations are owed to Ludolph Hugo, *De statu regionum Germaniae liber unus* (Frankfurt: Zunerri, 1689), 13 which examined the imperial form of government as a state composed of states. Although it was not the first to investigate the concept of the quasi-federal state, it was one of the earliest prized for its precision and systematicity. Originally a dissertation Hugo defended (20 August 1661), it was only later published by the Gießen professor and natural lawyer Johann Nicholas Hert (1651–1710). On Hert, see Stolleis, *Geschichte des öffentlichen Rechts*, 241–2.
108. On Moser's imprisonment, see Walker, *Johann Jakob Moser*, 226–45.
109. *NtSR3*, 13.
110. Ibid. Compare 29, however, where it is clear that Moser could have also taken this idea from the *Hippolythus*, certainly when speaking of the head of the Empire.
111. Ernst-Wolfgang Böckenförde and Gerhard Dohrn-van Rossum, 'Organ, Organismus, Organization, politischer Körper', in *GG4*, 562.
112. See Rudolf Hoke, 'Bodins Einfluss auf die Anfänge der Dogmatik des deutschen Reichsstaatsrechts', in *Verhandlungen der internationalen Bodin Tagung*, ed. Horst Denzer (Munich: C.H. Beck, 1973), 325.
113. Ibid., 323–8. See *LtSR1*, 198–9.
114. Hoke, 'Bodins Einfluss', 328.
115. Ibid., 327.
116. Ibid., 328.
117. *NtSR3*, 15.
118. Ibid., 13–14.
119. Ibid., 13.
120. See *NtSR1*, 19 where Moser cited from an imperial commission decree from 17 March 1727 issued by the imperial court that denounced a French policy brief that sought to treat the imperial estates alone under the title *Corpus Germanicum*: 'From which one can clearly deduce with what further manner and cunning, and for what reason one endeavours to separate the supreme head of the Roman Empire from its members, under a never before used, indecent, metaphorical name and unusual style: to bring about a separation of *Corps Germanique* from *Caesarea Majestate*' (original italics). Moser went on to add that drawing a direct equation between

Empire and imperial estates was not in itself condemnatory. Rather, it was the intentions of the French which were problematic. This is why emperor and Empire were to be favoured, as this made it impossible to think of the head without the members and vice versa (see ibid., 20).

121. See *LtSR1*, 264, 280, 375–7 for accounts of these lawyers.
122. *NtSR3*, 14 (original italics). The imperial commission decree cited above attested to this usage in referring to 'das allerhöchste Oberhaupt'.
123. See Karl Otmar von Aretin and Notker Hammerstein, 'Reich', in *GG5*, 470.
124. Ibid.
125. *NtSR3*, 15.
126. For these details and on the publication history of this edition, see Stolleis, *Geschichte des öffentlichen Rechts*, 175 citing Robert J. Evans, *The Wechel Presses: Humanism and Calvinism in Central Europe 1572–1627* (Oxford: Past and Present Society, 1975).
127. Jean Bodin, *De republica libri sex* (Frankfurt: Wechel & Fischer, 1591), 305.
128. Quaritsch, *Souveränität*, 53.
129. *NtSR3*, 15.
130. For a short biographical sketch, see Rudolf Hoke, 'Hippolithus a Lapide', in *Staatsdenker in der frühen Neuzeit*, ed. Michael Stolleis (Munich: C. H. Beck, 1995), 118–20. For details on the text see *LtSR1*, 207–13; *HD2*, 47–55. On the different French and German translations and their respective historical contexts, see Rudolf Hoke, 'Staatsräson und Reichsverfassung bei Hippolithus a Lapide', in *Staatsräson: Studien zur Geschichte eines politischen Begriffs*, ed. Roman Schnur (Berlin: Duncker and Humblot, 1975), 407–25.
131. Aretin and Hammerstein, 'Reich IV', 470 claim the *Hippolythus* had no influence, although admitting that it was used by both Pufendorf and Gottfried Wilhelm Leibniz (1646–1716). Hegel belonged to this tradition and identified the *Hippolythus* with the idea of German freedom during the Thirty Years' War. Pütter's account of the significance of the *Hippolythus* is markedly at odds with the historical revisionism of Aretin and Hammerstein (see *HD2*, 48–9).
132. *NtSR3*, 15.
133. Bodin *De republica libri sex*, 283 had stated that the empire 'may be a pure aristocracy'. It is worth noting that he used the subjunctive (*pura sit Aristocratia*), not the indicative. Thus, he was not as axiomatic as is often depicted. The *Hippolythus* used the subjunctive in a similar discussion as well, although recognizing a diversity of aristocratic forms (see Lapide, *Dissertatio de ratione status*, 36). This passage is analysed and translated in Section 3.4.2.
134. Ibid., 28.
135. *NtSR1*, 554; compare Lapide, *Dissertatio de ratione status*, 29.
136. Gross, *Empire and Sovereignty*, 235.
137. *NtSR3*, 15.
138. Marc Foster, 'The Edict of Restitution (1629) and the Failure of Catholic Restoration' in *The Ashgate Research Companion to the Thirty Years' War*, ed. Olaf Asbach and Peter Schröder (London: Routledge, 2014), 205–15.
139. *NtSR3*, 16.
140. Ibid.
141. *GW5[RV]*, 65.
142. The issue is picked up neither by Maier, 'Hegels Schrift 2' nor by Meist, 'Anmerkungen', 771.
143. For the historical details, see Dreitzel, *Absolutismus und ständische Verfassung*, 20.

144. Ibid.
145. Bodin, *De republica libri sex*, 190–1, 283.
146. See Dreitzel, *Absolutismus und ständische Verfassung*, 20 n. 10 where the precise conceptual lineage of the idea is shown. Bodin took it from the historian Johannes Sleidanus (1506–1556).
147. Bodin, *De republica libri sex*, 348, 362–3, 369–79; compare, Lapide, *Dissertatio de ratione status*, 77 where a similar perspective on the capacity of the Count Palatine to judge the emperor appears.
148. Stolleis, *Geschichte des öffentlichen Rechts*, 184.
149. *NtSR3*, 28.
150. Julien H. Franklin, 'Sovereignty and the Mixed Constitution: Bodin and his Critics', in *The Cambridge History of Political Thought 1450–1700*, ed. James Henderson Burns (Cambridge: Cambridge University Press, 2006), 311.
151. *NtSR3*, 28.
152. *LtSR1*, 189.
153. The French translation had been used for similar ends during the Spanish War of Succession (1701–14). The title was more forthright about the real intentions of the book (*Interêts des princes d'Allemagne*). It appeared in two volumes in 1712.
154. *NtSR3*, 47.
155. Ibid., 29.
156. The debate over the author of the remarks or translator of the German edition has never been definitively settled. Pütter states that the famous cameralist Johann Heinrich von Justi (1717–1771) is both the author of the remarks and translator (*HD2*, 49). Other possibilities have been put forward: Johann Philipp Carrach (1730–1769) (as translator) and Johann Friedrich von Troeltsch (1728–1793) (author of the remarks) (see Hoke, 'Staatsräson und Reichsverfassung', 409 n. 11). Moser's polemic seems at some points rather misplaced. The remarks maintain the pre-eminence of the emperor as supreme head. Moreover, the author went out of his way to distinguish *Landeshoheit* from sovereignty and makes the case for the subordination of the imperial estates to emperor and Empire as a political system. Yet the precision with which they followed the *Hippolythus* is impossible to deny, specifically in terms of the marks of sovereignty which are discussed as an outward appearance and shadow of former majesty (see *Unpartheyische Gedanken über die Anmerkungen des teutschen Hippolithus a Lapide* (Cologne: Peter Marteau, 1762), 21–32 on the imperial *forma Reipublicae* and 60–7 on the rights of sovereignty).
157. *HD2*, 49.
158. See Hoke, 'Staatsräson und Reichsverfassung', 412.
159. Lapide, *Dissertatio de ratione status*, 538 (original capitalization).
160. Ibid., 520 – Niccolò Machiavelli, *Florentine Histories*, trans. Laura F. Banfield and Harvey C. Mansfield Jr. (Princeton University Press, 1988), 105–45. The precise reference is obscure. The *Hippolythus* cites the entire third book.
161. Lapide, *Dissertatio de ratione status*, 521.
162. *GW5[RV]*, 7.
163. *NtSR3*, 15–16.
164. For Bodin, there could only be three different types of constitution: monarchy, aristocracy and democracy. To a large extent, the purity of these Bodinian concepts produced novel typological categories. This has been noted in the critical literature which registers a total of twenty-seven new types of constitution that could all be

correlated with each other (see Horst Denzer, 'Bodins Staatsformenlehre', in *Bodin Tagung*, ed. Denzer, 241).

165. *GW5[RV]*, 64–5. This goes back to 'Sollte das politische Resultat' which set out from the failure to classify the imperial constitution. Hegel also indicated there that the reason why this was impossible was because of the variety and diversity of German rights and freedoms (ibid., 6–7).
166. Ibid., 64–5.
167. Ibid., 10.
168. See Boyd, 'The Constitution of Crisis', 280–302. For detailed histories, see Friedrich Meinecke, *Die Idee der Staatsräson in der neueren Geschichte* (Munich: Oldenbourg, 1929); Noel Malcolm, *Reason of State, Propaganda, and the Thirty Years' War: An Unknown Translation by Thomas Hobbes* (Oxford: Oxford University Press, 2007). For the reception of Tacitus in the sixteenth and seventeenth centuries, compare Richard Tuck, *Philosophy and government, 1572–1651* (Cambridge: Cambridge University Press, 1993); Kenneth C. Schellhase, *Tacitus in Renaissance Political Thought* (Chicago: University of Chicago Press, 1976); Michel Senellart, *Machiavélisme et raison d'état: XIIe-XVIIIe siècle* (Paris: Presses Universitaires de France, 1989). This reception is intimately linked with the rise of the so-called 'reason of state' literature and the complicated reception of Machiavelli's works.
169. See Lapide, *Dissertatio de ratione status*, 151–203, 390–404.
170. *Annals* I.6, II.36, II.59; *Histories* I.4.
171. *Politics* 1309b35–36. See Horst Dreitzel, 'Reason of State and the Crisis of Political Aristotelianism: An Essay on the Development of 17th Century Political Philosophy', *History of European Ideas* 28, no. 3 (2002): 163–87.
172. See Meist, 'Anmerkungen', 775–7 where he demonstrates that Hegel could have lifted these concepts from *Der neue Teutsche Merkur* 1 (1790): 48–58 from a fictional dialogue entitled 'Über reelle und persönliche Majestät', which was followed by a short gloss 'Ein Wort über Machiavellis Fürsten', 59–60. However, it is equally probable that Hegel drew these concepts directly from his own copies of the *Hippolythus*. For instance, it explicitly discusses the Empire and the collectivity of its imperial estates as possessing *maiestas realis*, while attributing only *maiestas personalis* to the emperor. It also famously portrayed the emperor as a mere *simulacrum* or *umbra* (shadow) of power (see Lapide, *Dissertatio de ratione status*, 515–20, 520–43, 544–9).
173. *GW5[RV]*, 129.
174. Stolleis, *Geschichte des öffentlichen Rechts*, 205.
175. For the actual complexity of this relation and the argument that the *Hippolythus* rather follows the anti-Machiavellian doctrine of Christian reason of state, see Hoke, 'Staatsräson und Reichsverfassung', 412.
176. *GW5[RV]*, 132. True, the context here is specifically framed with respect to Italy. However, this cannot detract from the fact that Hegel is attacking the German mirror of princes and the hypocrisy of the anti-Machiavellism of Friedrich II (1712–1786). Hence, the overarching context involved the breaching of treaties, the invasion of Silesia (1740) and the Seven Years' War which were further reflected by Hegel into his own time.
177. See Philipp Melanchthon, *Commentarii in aliquot politicos libros Aristotelis* (1530), paragraphs 18, 19, 20.
178. See Hella Mandt, 'Tyrannis, Despotie', in *GG6*, 667.
179. Ibid.

180. Aristotle identified despotism with 'the fourth sort of oligarchy' that 'approaches a monarchy' and it was 'analogous to the last sort of democracy' (*Politics* 1293a13–34). Despotism was an extension of household rule or the *oikos* and was thus private rather than political; it was similar to tyranny, but on the contrary 'hereditary and legal' – 'a sort of monarchy not uncommon among foreigners' (1285a18–28). It was most likely with respect to the latter opinion that Melanchthon mentioned how despotism had been equated with the Ottoman Empire: 'Formerly the kind of authority of kings there was among the barbarians, people also now assert such is the model of power among the Turks where the sultan independently does everything and, cowed as cattle, the population is forced to obey whatever the tyrant commands.' Melanchthon then identified this with a royal and democratic despotism determined by law – thus paraphrasing Aristotle (see Melanchthon, *Commentarii*, paragraph 19). Luther stopped short of characterizing the Ottoman Empire as despotic. He termed it, perhaps even more derogatorily, as 'Müntzerisch' – thus referencing Thomas Müntzer (1489–1525) and the recent Peasants' War (1524–5) (see Mandt, 'Tyrannis, Despotie', 668).
181. See *GW5[RV]*, 6.
182. Ibid., 64–5; for a comparable statement, see Franz Wieacker, *A History of Private Law in Europe: With Particular Reference to Germany*, trans. Tony Weir (Oxford: Clarendon, 1995), 72.
183. *GW5[RV]*, 64. This point regarding Hegel's nuanced engagement with the historical tradition is further illuminated by figures like Pufendorf. For Pufendorf, the inquiry into the Empire's status (its condition or state-like quality), as exemplified by the German title of the *Monzambano, Bericht Vom Zustande des Teutschen Reichs* (Dresden: 1667), could not be fully equated with the modern concept of the 'state'. This 'status' or 'condition' discourse, prevalent in the eighteenth century, provided the backdrop for later constitutional and state-form discussions (see Mohnhaupt, 'Verfassung I', 853–4). Hegel's analysis, as discussed in the main text, marks a crucial semantic development where 'condition' and 'constitution' evolve, and 'state' emerges as a distinct and independent concept, a conceptual change fundamentally shaped by figures like Majer (see Sections 3.0.1 and 3.4.1).
184. *GW5[RV]*, 92.
185. Johann Christoph Krause, *Abhandlungen aus dem deutschen Staatsrechte, mit beständiger Rücksicht auf das teutsche Herkommen, Band I* (Regnerische Buchhandlung, 1797), 53 (original italics). A second volume never appeared. On the possible relation between Krause and Hegel, see Meist, 'Anmerkungen', 759–64, 772. I argue against any direct influence (see Section 3.4.2).
186. See *GW5[SdS]*, 309–27 for this historical transition.
187. *GW5[RV]*, 93.
188. To translate the constitution of fiefs (*Lehensverfassung*) with the seemingly more apt feudal constitution is a mistranslation, see Otto Hintze, 'The Preconditions of Representative Government', in *The Historical Essays of Otto Hintze*, ed. Felix Gilbert and Robert Berdahl (Oxford: Oxford University Press, 1975), 310:

> Feudalism is a concept that still needs to be clarified and is rather complex. One must … distinguish it from the genuine system of fiefs. The system of fiefs is a clearly definable *legal* concept, whereas feudalism is a more sociological type or the collective term for such a type. The system of fiefs is the narrower, feudalism

> the broader concept … *there is no general connection between the feudal system and the system of estates.* (italics added)

Hegel himself stressed that a fief was a legal concept (see *GW5[RV]*, 100–1).

189. Ibid., 93–4.
190. Ibid., in the margins.
191. Max Weber, *Economy and Society: An Outline of Interpretive Sociology*, ed. Guenther Roth and Claus Wittich (Berkeley: University of California Press, 1978), 1079 (translation modified).
192. Heinz Eulau, 'Theories of Federalism under the Holy Roman Empire', *The American Political Science Review* 35, no. 4 (1941): 643.
193. *GW5[RV]*, 93, in the margins.
194. Ibid., 105.
195. Ibid., 147–53.
196. Hans-Christoph Kraus, *Das Ende des alten Deutschlands. Krise und Auflösung des Heiligen Römisches Reiches Deutscher Nation 1806* (Berlin: Dunker & Humblot, 2007), 27–8.
197. *GW5[RV]*, 107. This notorious passage cannot be isolated from its historical context as a universal principle for state behaviour. Only historical criticism – and *not* moral indignation – is sufficient to disprove it, assessing whether other motives drove the political interests Hegel was analysing. None of Hegel's Weimar critics made this attempt (see Walter Jaeschke, *Hegel-Handbuch: Leben-Werk-Schule* (Stuttgart: Metzler, 2016), 94–5).
198. *GW5[RV]*, 103. Hegel draws his analysis from Machiavelli, although on this occasion he goes uncited (see Niccolò Machiavelli, *Discourses on Livy*, trans. Harvey C. Mansfield and Nathan Tarcov (Chicago: University of Chicago Press, 1999), I.25, 60). The reference is used somewhat more explicitly in the second *Ständeschrift* (see *GW15[VL]*, 33). This shows a broader range in Hegel's reading of the Florentine than the more obvious citation from an outdated French translation of *The Prince* (1532) (see *GW5[RV]*, 205–6).
199. Ibid., 103–4. See Barbara Stollberg-Rilinger, *The Emperor's Old Clothes: Constitutional History and the Symbolic Language of the Holy Roman Empire*, trans. Thomas Dunlap (Oxford: Berghahn, 2015), 1–14. The starting point of her study is precisely Hegel's analysis of imperial symbol and ritual.
200. See *GW4[NR]*, 456–7. I examine this sequence at a far greater length in 2.3.1–2.3.6. Hegel's study of Gibbon goes back to his stay in patrician Bern (1793–6) where his republicanism of that period was frustrated at the utter corruption of the aristocratic form of government.
201. There is little real evidence of a reception or understanding of Roman *public* law until the beginning of the nineteenth century.
202. Rudolf Hoke, 'Die Emanzipation der deutschen Staatsrechtswissenschaft von der Zivilistik im 17 Jahrhundert', *Der Staat* 15, no. 2 (1976): 224. That Roman public law was never received was already the opinion of early modern German publicists, such as Limnaeus. This was another way to break with Roman law in general as it would be entirely false to treat the German constitution through the lens of a jurisprudence that had never even been present.
203. *GW5[RV]*, 6–7.
204. Ibid., 64.
205. *GW5[SdS]*, 361.

206. *GW14,1[PdR]*, 228 (§273).
207. *GW5[RV]*, 6. This misinterprets Aristotle's view of despotism as a private legal form, an extension of household rule. Hegel, by contrast, sees tyranny as the establishment of legal force, historically replacing private power. The tyrant, in this view, educates and shapes a culture of obedience, thereby laying the groundwork for public state law. This leads to the stark conclusion that since the Germans 'could not tolerate a tyrant, they have disappeared as a people' (*GW8[JSIII]*, 259). Similarly, revenge, once rationalized, becomes the administration of justice: the blood feud, historically supplanted by warfare between states (see *GW5[SdS]*, 320–3).
208. *GW5[RV]*, 44–5.
209. See *GW26,1[VPR]*, 165–8 (§135).
210. Ibid., 168. Compare *GW5[JN]*, 492: 'Germany is not a monarchy, etc., not a *state*, but an *Empire*. "Empire" is *meant* to be a concept, or rather, if it is to be a state, an empty notion.'
211. *GW26,1[VPR]*, 223 (§168).
212. Ibid., 222. It is worth also noting in this context that the Roman World with its abstract legal formalism and equality coincides for Hegel with the French Republic under Robespierre. This dimension is analysed in 4.1.1–4.1.6.
213. *ATSK*, 1–2 (original italics). Majer references the *Hippolythus*.
214. *GW5[RV]*, 111.
215. See Maier, 'Hegels Schrift 2', 214 n. 7.
216. I operate under the assumption that Hegel already assimilated Rousseau's thought largely to Fichte in his early Jena period (1801–3). This is the reason why he is scarcely discussed in this book.
217. For the first thesis, see Ludwig Siep, 'Deutscher Idealismus: G.W.F. Hegel', in *Politischer Aristotelismus. Die Rezeption der aristotelischen Politik von der Antike bis zum 19. Jahrhundert*, ed. Christoph Horn und Ada Neschke-Hentschke (Stuttgart: Metzler, 2008), 283; for the second, see Lübbe-Wolff, 'Die Bedeutung der Lehre von der vier Weltreichen', 369–89. That the two approaches are intrinsically related has been shown in the classics Jacob Taubes, *Occidental Eschatology*, trans. David Ratmoko (Stanford: California University Press, 2009); Karl Löwith, *Meaning in History: The Theological Implications of the Philosophy of History* (Chicago: University of Chicago Press, 1957).
218. *GW26,1[VPR]*, 218 (§164). This is a quote from the final line of the second last stanza of Friedrich Schiller, 'Resignation'. Available online: http://www.michaelbryson.net/academic/schiller-resignation.pdf (accessed 27 May 2025). Hegel's use of this dictum at the transition to the philosophy of world history strangely goes unmentioned in Reinhart Koselleck, 'Crisis', trans. Michaela Richter, *Journal of the History of Ideas* 67, no. 2 (2006): 371 where Schiller is discussed.
219. *GW14,1[PdR]*, 281 (§358). For my discussion, see Sections 4.0.5 and 4.3.4.
220. *GW5[RV]*, 111–12.
221. See Chistoph Link, 'Dietrich Reinkingk', in *Staatsdenker*, ed. Stolleis, 82; Melanchthon, *Chronicon carionis*, 1331–77.
222. *NtSR1*, 20. Moser levelled this critique at the Wittenberg state law teacher Caspar Heinrich Horn (1657–1718) who made his name in part by sticking to the idea that Germany was a unitary state against the compelling conclusions of the *Monzambano*. Horn followed the idea of the *translatio imperii*; the emperor was a Roman king and imperial vicar, the imperial estates akin to the Roman *collegio* (see *LtSR1*, 355–8). For

Pütter's denunciation of the *translatio imperii* from a legal-historical perspective, see *BtS-FR2*, 34–8.

223. See Melanchthon, *Commentarii*, paragraph 48.
224. *GW26,1[VPR]*, 219 (§165).
225. Ibid., 219–25 (§§165–70)
226. *GW14,1[PdR]*, 274 (§343).
227. *GW5[RV]*, 157.
228. *Politeia* is at once a 'generic name – a constitution' and a particular type of rule (*Politics* 1279a38).
229. See Meist, 'Anmerkungen', 750.
230. *GW14,1[PdR]*, 226–9 (§273). For reference to another set of lectures on the philosophy of law expressing the same idea, see Lübbe-Wolff, 'Die Bedeutung der Lehre von der vier Weltreichen', 388.
231. *GW5[RV]*, 111.
232. Ibid., 115.
233. Schiller, 'Deutsche Größe'.
234. See *GW5[RV]*, 203–19.
235. Maier, 'Hegels Schrift 1', 336 n. 11 (original italics).
236. *GW5[RV]*, 13–14. This passage from 'Sollte das politische Resultat' is later reworked in 'Diese Form des deutschen Staatsrechts' (This Form of German Constitutional Law) (see ibid., 63).
237. Ibid., 161.
238. Ibid., 202.

2 The Empire as the impersonal legal connection of the composite state: Johann Stephan Pütter

1. Notker Hammerstein, *Jus und Historie. Ein Beitrag zur Geschichte des historischen Denkens an deutschen Universitäten* (Göttingen: Vandenhoeck, 1972), 309 (original italics).
2. Martin Otto, 'Pütter, Johann Stephan', *Neue Deutsche Biographie* 21 (2003): 1–2.
3. Pütter's contributions were rather limited to the first two chapters of the third book, only a sixth of the total work. His name did not appear in later editions, there were a total of eight between the 1750s and 1780s (see Jan Schröder, 'Gottfried Achenwall, Johann Stephan Pütter und die "*Elementa Iuris Naturae*"', in *AN*, 334). Still, this is enough to even cursorily prove the influence of natural jurisprudence on Pütter's thinking. The framework of those two chapters details the origin of the state in a contract of association of families in the state of nature who then enter into the contract of submission for security, ease and the pursuit of the common welfare. Pütter then deduces that this is the origin of constitutional law or universal political law that he subsequently divides into the relation between citizens and the sovereign (public law) and the relation among citizens themselves (private law). Clearly, the influence of Roman law is evident in this taxonomy (see ibid., 211, 213). It is also noteworthy that Pütter distinguishes here between constitutional law and public law. For an analysis of the book in English but principally concerning Achenwall's contribution, see Koskenniemi, *To the Uttermost Parts of the Earth*, 884–91.

4. See Schröder, 'die "*Elementa Iuris Naturae*" ', 335; compare Haakonssen, 'German Natural Law', 251–90, on Kant in particular and his relation to Achenwall, Pütter and the earlier metaphysical and empirical traditions of natural law, 279–90.
5. Meist, 'Editorischer Bericht', 664.
6. See Kurt Rainer Meist, 'Zur Textedition der Verfassungsschrift', in Georg Wilhelm Friedrich Hegel, *Über die Reichsverfassung*, ed. Hans Maier (Hamburg: Felix Meiner, 2004), lxiv.
7. Meist, 'Anmerkungen', 753; compare the even more succinct comments in Meist, 'Zur Textedition', lxxviii.
8. The dissertation, by the Tübingen theologian Johann Friedrich Le Bret (1732–1807), was entitled *De ecclesiae Wirtembergicae renascentis calamitatibus* (1793) (On the Calamities of the Reborn Church of Württemberg). It was defended by both Hegel and Friedrich Hölderlin (1770–1843).
9. Meist, 'Zur Textedition', lxxviii.
10. See Rosenzweig, *Hegel and the State*, 163.
11. Meist, 'Anmerkungen', 753; Meist, 'Zur Textedition', Lxxviii.
12. Rosenzweig, *Hegel and the State*, 163. In the first year of Hegel's studies in Tübingen (1788–9), Majer, for example, lectured on *ius publicum imperiale* and *ius publicum territoriale Imperii Statuum*, thus on imperial public law and the constitutional law of the entire imperial territories (*Staatsrecht der gesammten Reichslande*). This was followed in 1789–90, 91–2, 92–3 by similar offerings (see *Ordo praelectionum cum publicarum tum privatarum in perantiqua studiorum Universitate Tubingensi habendarum*). Available online: http://idb.ub.uni-tuebingen.de/opendigi/LXV11_qt (accessed 26 April 2025).
13. Johannes Daniel Hoffmann (1740–1814) and Friedrich Wilhelm Gottlieb Tafinger (1760–1813) also delivered lectures on Pütter's public law (see *Ordo praelectionum cum publicarum tum privatarum*).
14. Carl Friedrich Häberlin, *Handbuch des teutschen Staatsrechts. Band 1* (Berlin: Vieweg, 1794), preface.
15. From the 1790s onwards, Hugo delivered lectures on Pütter's *Juristischen Encyclopädie und Methodologie*. This had tremendous impact, presumably because it accommodated the predisposition to specialization that was already occurring at that time (see Stolleis, *Geschichte des öffentlichen Rechts*, 313–14).
16. Otto, 'Pütter, Johann Stephan', 1.
17. See Christoph Link, 'Johann Stephan Pütter', in *Staatsdenker*, ed. Stolleis, 315.
18. *LtSR1*, 444. In the late 1730s, Pütter attended Wolff's lectures as a student in Marburg while Wolff was exiled there from the University of Halle. See Heinz Mohnhaupt, 'Pütter, Johann Stephan', in *Juristen. Ein biographisches Lexikon. Von der Antike bis zum 20. Jahrhundert*, ed. Michael Stolleis (Munich: C.H. Beck, 2001), 519. Gross, *Empire and Sovereignty*, 443 cites Pütter's systematic approach as the only possible evidence of the influence of Wolff. I follow Link, 'Johann Stephan Pütter', 315–16 who is far more assertive when he states that Pütter sought to reform the existence of the norms of legal and political practice according to a rationalist natural law methodology.
19. Ibid., 316.
20. See Dreitzel, *Absolutismus und ständische Verfassung*, 111–20.
21. Link, 'Johann Stephan Pütter', 317.
22. *AN*, 213–15, 225.
23. Link, 'Johann Stephan Pütter', 318.

24. *GW5[RV]*, 202.
25. *AN*, 215.
26. See Dreitzel, *Absolutismus und ständische Verfassung*, 128 n. 17; compare Reinhard Blänkner, 'Der Absolutismus war ein Glück, der doch nicht zu den Absolutisten gehört. Eduard Gans und die hegelianischen Ursprünge der Absolutismusforschung in Deutschland', *Historische Zeitschrift* 256, no. 1 (1993): 31–66.
27. *AN*, 183 (original italics).
28. Immanuel Kant, 'Perpetual Peace: A Philosophical Sketch', in *Political Writings*, ed. Hans Reiss, trans. Hugh Barnett Nisbet (Cambridge: Cambridge University Press, 2006), 100–1.
29. See *GW5[RV]*, 152; compare *HD2*, 291.
30. On the *ius publicum universale*, see *AN*, 223–63. Natural law is the general orientation of the textbook, the sections on universal public law included.
31. The relation to Dalberg remains hypothetical. For Maier, 'Hegels Schrift 2', 213, Dalberg might have been the patron of the *Verfassungsschrift*; for Rosenzweig, *Hegel and the State*, 197–8 n. 106, 107, Hegel's esteem for Archduke Karl (1771–1847) and later Napoleon shares striking similarities with Dalberg; and, finally, Meist, 'Zur Textedition', lxii, lxviii, lxxx has explored the relation in a general contextual way. Dalberg was also a member of the Schiller circle in Jena. Hegel sent a copy of the *Rechtsphilosophie* to Hardenberg with a letter extolling the position of philosophy and its agreement with the rational (reforming) state (only his draft letter survives) (see *Briefe von und an Hegel. Band II (1813–1822)*, ed. Johannes Hoffmeister (Hamburg: Felix Meiner, 1969), 241–2).
32. See Michael H. Hoffheimer, *Eduard Gans and the Hegelian Philosophy of Law* (Dordrecht: Springer, 1995), 19–22. The real question of whether Savigny belonged to romanticism or classicism has been studied critically by Wieacker, *A History of Private Law in Europe*, 286–92.
33. Paolo Becchi, 'German Legal Science: The Crisis of Natural Law Theory, the Historicisms, and "Conceptual Jurisprudence"', in *A Treatise of Legal Philosophy*, ed. Damiano Canale, Paolo Grossi and Hasso Hofmann (Dordrecht: Springer, 2009), 187–8; Kurt Rainer Meist, 'Altenstein und Gans. Eine Frühe politische Option für Hegels *Rechtsphilosophie*', *Hegel-Studien* 14 (1979): 39–72. I elaborate more on these issues in the final chapter.
34. Hermann Conring, 'Exercitatio de Germanici imperii civibus', in *Opera Vol. I*, ed. Johann Wilhelm Göbel (Helmstedt: Meyer, 1730), 516. See Dietmar Willoweit, 'Kaiser, Reich und Reichsstände bei Hermann Conring' in *Hermann Conring (1606–1681): Beiträge zu Leben und Werk*, ed. Michael Stolleis (Berlin: Duncker & Humblot, 1983) 321–34 at 325.
35. See Christian Thomasius, *Institutes of Divine Jurisprudence with Selections from Foundations of the Law of Nature and Nations*, ed. and trans. Thomas Ahnert (Indianapolis: Liberty Fund, 2011), 492.
36. Samuel Pufendorf, 'De systematibus civitatum', in *Dissertationes academicae* 226–83. This shift in Pufendorf's perception of the Empire has been the subject of a recent insightful study, see Ben Holland, 'De Systematibus Civitatum: Pufendorf on Confederations and Composite Kingdoms', in *Pufendorf's International Political and Legal Thought* (Oxford: Oxford University Press, 2024), 41–57.
37. See *GW31,2[ABH]*, 1211. This Thomasius edition was published first in 1695. Meist seems to have been unaware that Hegel owned a copy of the *Monzambano* as he cites the second edition translated from Latin into German. Moreover, he mistakenly raises

the issue of how monstrosity appeared as a central concept there (see 'Anmerkungen', 767–8), when in fact Pufendorf had removed the reference due to controversy. For Meist, it was in no way necessary to consider that Hegel consulted the *Monzambano*. The discussion was so general that it could have been gleaned from any number of contemporary sources. Indeed, I would add that the reference was to either Majer or Moser, *not* Pufendorf (see *GW5[RV]*, 52). 'Der Nahme für die Staatsverfassung' practically paraphrases Majer (*TSK1*, 58–9). Majer also introduced the idea of a nameless form (ibid., 51). The first chapter of Moser's *NtSR1* was entitled 'Von Teutschland und dessen verschiedenen Namen'. The conception of sovereignty in Pufendorf and Hegel has been explored comparatively. The point being to bring to light the theoretical foundation of Hegel's concept of sovereignty as it was established in the Frankfurt and Jena periods within the context of a similarly fragmented imperial reality (see Akira Hayase, 'Die Frage nach der Souveränität, die sich durch die Verfassungsschrift Hegels zieht: Bodin, Pufendorf und Hegel', *Kenkyu-ronso* 85 (2015): 97–114).

38. Horst Dreitzel, 'Samuel Pufendorf', in *GGP*, 757–812, 773.
39. *GW5[RV]*, 6.
40. *BtS-FR1*, 20.
41. *AN*, 255.
42. Bodin, *De republica libri sex*, 273. See Franklin, 'Sovereignty and the Mixed Constitution', 302–9.
43. Pufendorf, *The Present State of Germany*, 173; Thomasius, *Institutes of Divine Jurisprudence*, 492.
44. Peter Schröder, 'The Constitution of the Holy Roman Empire after 1648: Samuel Pufendorf's Assessment in His Monzambano', *Historical Journal* 42, no. 4 (1999): 961–83.
45. Holland, 'De Systematibus Civitatum', 46.
46. *AN*, 257 (original italics).
47. *BtS-FR1*, 31.
48. Gross, *Empire and Sovereignty*, 447.
49. See the pathbreaking analysis by Karl-Heinz Ilting, 'Hegels Auseinandersetzung mit der Aristotelischen Politik', *Philosophisches Jahrbuch* 71 (1963): 38–58. More recently, Siep, 'Deutscher Idealismus: G. W. F. Hegel', 276–96. For an analysis in English, see H. S. Harris, *Hegel's Development: Night Thoughts (Jena 1801–1806)* (Oxford: Clarendon Press, 1983), 102–43. Once again, I disagree with Meist, 'Anmerkungen', 750 who has under-emphasized the extent of this Aristotelianism that he believes Hegel is simply caricaturizing. For another discussion of this, see Section 1.4.4.
50. *GW5[RV]*, 6. For statistics, see Section 1.1.1. A lectern statistician was a political scientist who followed a comparative approach to constitutions based on Aristotelian method. This originates with Conring and was revived by Achenwall.
51. Ibid., 161 (original italics).
52. Ibid., 62. This comes from the Jena fragment 'Diese Form des deutschen Staatsrechts', but it is reworked material of ideas that go back to 'Sollte das politische Resultat' (ibid., 8).
53. Ibid.
54. Johann Heinrich Gottlob von Justi, *Natur und Wesen der Staaten als die Quelle aller Regierungswissenschaften und Gesezze* (Mitau: Steidel, 1771), 117 – cited in Dreitzel, *Absolutismus und ständische Verfassung*, 105.
55. *EG*, 55.

56. Ibid., 53–4 and, more generally 52–64.
57. Eulau, 'Theories of Federalism', 663.
58. *KB*, 14–15 (original italics).
59. *BtS-FR1*, 22; compare Hugo, *De statu regionum Germaniae*, 33–4; also Gottfried Wilhelm Leibniz, *Political Writings*, ed. Patrick Riley (Cambridge: Cambridge University Press, [1972] 1988), 118: 'for, just as there are certain things in which the bond of our Empire is more strict, so there are others in which the power of the princes seems greater'.
60. *BtS-FR1*, 53–4.
61. Ibid., 36, 31.
62. *KB*, 14 (original italics).
63. Stolleis, *Geschichte des öffentlichen Rechts*, 313.
64. Ibid. Stolleis is referring to *Elementa iuris publici Germanici* (1754).
65. *EG*, 53.
66. *IG*, 35 (original italics and capitalization). This chapter (28–36) is on the *forma imperii Germanici*.
67. See Rosenzweig, *Hegel and the State*, 132. Though he did not cite the precise source, he quoted from this later edition published in 1802. This can be gleaned from the fact that he mentioned erroneously that Pütter formulated this idea at the same time as the *Verfassungsschrift* critically assessed the question of political alliance in the Empire or the reality of its state connection. After 1770, *Elementa iuris publici Germanici* was entitled *Institutiones juris publici Germanici*.
68. Rosenzweig, *Hegel and the State*, 132.
69. Ibid.
70. The theoretical conception of the composite state had first been popularized by the Tübingen jurist and political Aristotelian Christoph Besold (1577–1638). It found its way into the public law of Limnaeus that Pütter held in very high esteem. Limnaeus probably stands at the origin of Pütter's appropriation of the concept.
71. *BtS-FR1*, 20.
72. *GW5[RV]*, 62.
73. See Pape, 'Revolution und Reichsverfassung', 53.
74. Kraus, *Das Ende des alten Deutschlands*, 27–8.
75. *GW27,1[VWG]*, 459.
76. *GW5[RV]*, 109.
77. Ibid., 138. This quote comes from 'kan, wodurch die Freyheit' (can, whereby the freedom), a manuscript that has the character of a transcription that has not been precisely dated. It could be either after 1799 or 1801. In this way, it could refer either to the First Coalition War or the Second Coalition War (see Meist, 'Editorischer Bericht', 584). Hegel's perspective confirms the insight about the *systema civitatem* made by Rosenzweig, *Hegel and the State*, 132 discussed above.
78. *AN*, 257.
79. Ibid.
80. *BtS-FR1*, 57. Hegel also held the view, but only in terms of the original German state (see *GW5[RV]*, 129). Pütter's doctrine of parallel is already evident here that was such a subject of contention for Majer. It shows how Pütter derived the imperial status from the districts or imperial estates.
81. Pufendorf, *The Present State of Germany*, 173. The brackets identify editorial emendations to the original translation, for the details see ibid., xxxii. Pütter favoured the position of Damian Ferdinand Haas, *De monarchia S.R.I. Limitata*

contra Hippolytum a Lapide, Severinum Monzanbanum* (Giessen: Brown, 1750). It seems Hegel used Haas (1726–1805) as well in his study of the imperial financial system (see *GW5[RV]*, 43), as he cites from *Vorschläge, wie das Justizwesen am Kammergerichte* (1786–8). Yet as Meist, 'Anmerkungen', 767, has so astutely proven this was copied verbatim from Moser. This adds to the evidence of Moser's impact and revises Rosenzweig, *Hegel and the State*, 194 n. 9 who highlighted Haas's influence and did not see the more direct connection to Moser.

82. *KB*, 21.
83. Ibid., 16.
84. Ibid., 21.
85. *AN*, 255.
86. *BtS-FR1*, 42.
87. Ibid., 53.
88. See Gross, *Empire and Sovereignty*, 451.
89. *BtS-FR1*, 53.
90. *GW5[SdS]*, 340.
91. *GW5[RV]*, 173 – that is, note that the terms are the same.
92. Ibid., 153.
93. See Joachim Whaley, *Germany and the Holy Roman Empire, Vol. II: The Peace of Westphalia to the Dissolution of the Reich 1648–1806* (Oxford: Oxford University Press, 2012), 616; Wolfgang Burgdorf, 'Imperial Reform and Visions of a European Constitution in Germany Around 1800', *History of European Ideas* 19 (1994): 406. Even Rousseau belonged to the publicist current through his project for perpetual peace that saw the Empire as crucial for maintaining the balance of power. He also lavished praise on the study of German public law. The latter, in its final phase with Nikolaus Thaddäus Gönner (1764–1827), incorporated Rousseau's republican ideas on popular sovereignty to comprehend the political position of the emperor (for these details on Rousseau, see Peter Schröder, *Trust in Early Modern International Thought, 1598–1713* (Cambridge: Cambridge University Press, 2017), 181–3, 194–5, on German public law 3 n. 9; for Rousseau's incorporation into late imperial public law, see Gross, *Empire and Sovereignty*, 468).
94. *GW5[RV]*, 124, 126–8, 137, 145, 157. For example, Hegel took his interpretation of Cardinal Richelieu (1585–1642) from Johannes von Müller, *Darstellung des Fürstenbunds* (Leipzig: Weidmanns, 1787), 63. This hinged on Müller's (1752–1809) analysis of the French statesman who he viewed as fortifying the laws of the Germans and thus what he referred to as European freedom. For a treatment of Hegel and Müller and their connection to publicism and the imperial constitution, see Pape, 'Revolution und Reichsverfassung', 45–52; Meist, 'Anmerkungen', 772–3, 777–8 has also analysed the connection.
95. Maier, 'Hegels Schrift 2', 213.
96. *GW5[RV]*, 152–3.
97. *GW5[JN]*, 505. The reference is to Heinrich Luden, *Hugo Grotius nach seinen Schicksalen und Schriften dargestellt* (Berlin: Unger, 1806), 231 n. *).
98. Rosenzweig, *Hegel and the State*, 163.
99. Harris, *Night Thoughts*, 140–3.
100. *GW4[NR]*, 455.
101. Ibid.
102. *GW5[RV]*, 19. This comes from the short Frankfurt fragment 'Im Deutschen Reich' (In the German Empire) which tersely dealt with the fact that the Empire had no

state officials, subjects were primarily interested in minimal taxation, security of property and a functioning system of justice.

103. *GW4[NR]*, 455.
104. *KB*, 14–15 (original italics).
105. *GW4[NR]*, 454–5.
106. Ibid., 457.
107. Ibid., 456.
108. Ibid., 455.
109. *GW5[RV]*, 167–7.
110. *AN*, 257.
111. *GW5[RV]*, 173.
112. See ibid., 166.
113. *AN*, 249.
114. Gross, *Empire and Sovereignty*, 412.
115. *AN*, 249.
116. Ibid.
117. See Meist, 'Anmerkungen', 758.
118. Mohnhaupt, 'Verfassung I', 857.
119. See *GW14,1[PdR]*, 78 (§75); this appeared already in *System der Sittlichkeit* (see *GW5[SdS]*, 308–9).
120. The reception of contract law which was part of the Roman law doctrine of obligations – although the Romans had neither an explicit technical name nor theory of the contract – stretches back to the infiltration of this jurisprudence in the early modern period in Germany (see Max Kaser, *Roman Private Law*, trans. Rolf Dannenbring (Pretoria: Gutenberg, [1965] 1984), 42; Peter Stein, *Roman Law in European History* (Cambridge: Cambridge University Press, 2004), 90). See Section 1.2.3 where I have discussed similar issues with respect to contract law and the capitulations.
121. *GW5[RV]*, 166.
122. See the remarkable analysis by Gertrude Lübbe-Wolff, 'Über das Fehlen von Grundrechten in Hegels Rechtsphilosophie. Zugleich ein Beitrag zum Verständnis der historischen Grundlagen des Hegelschen Staatsbegriffs', in *Hegels Rechtsphilosophie im Zusammenhang der europäischen Verfassungsgeschichte*, ed. Hans-Christian Lucas and Otto Pöggeler (Stuttgart: Frommann-Holzboog, 1986), 425.
123. *GW14,1[PdR]*, 238 (§281) – also referred to in Lübbe-Wolff, 'Über das Fehlen von Grundrechten', 437.
124. Ibid., 436–7, 432.
125. Ibid., 436 n. 43.
126. See *GW5[RV]*, 19.
127. *AN*, 249.
128. Ibid., 239.
129. For Hegel's discussion on these questions, see *GW14,2[PdR-Beilagen]*, 285–6.
130. *AN*, 239 (original italics). I have added the original Latin to stress the continuity between Pütter and Bodin in this instance in which fundamental laws (*leges imperii*) similarly flout positive law which he discussed in precisely the same way with periods of interregnum and the Salic law (see Bodin, *De republica libri sex*, 740, 745, 767–8).

131. *EG*, 55 (original capitalization, italics added). This bond is thus the objective legal connection. *Nexum* could be one of several things, all interrelated: 'a form of binding obligation'; 'bondsman'; 'the action of binding or plaiting together', 'something that fastens, a bond, joint, etc. (natural or artificial)', 'a tie (kinship…)', 'any legal obligation', 'an intertwined or entangled formation, interposition', 'a combination' (*The Oxford Latin Dictionary*, ed. Peter G. W. Glare (Oxford: Clarendon, 2012), 1327). The implied semantic field perfectly elucidates the legal relations of subordination and superordination in an imperial hierarchy based on fiefs.
132. See *KB*, 14–15.
133. *BtS-FR1*, 60.
134. Bodin, *De republica libri sex*, 283.
135. *BtS-FR1*, 60 – Dietrich Reinkingk (1590–1664) inverted Bodin's characterization of the imperial constitution, from a pure aristocracy into a pure monarchy. The political Aristotelians and the most fervent followers of the Dutch jurist Dominicus Arumaeus (1579–1637) who stood on the ideological side of the imperial estates, such as the *Hippolythus*, produced conceptions that contained a monarchical element – thus reintroducing the mixture that Bodin had utterly scorned. See Sections 1.3.2 and 3.4.2 where I have translated the pertinent passages.
136. *BtS-FR1*, 57. See Pütter's distinction between despotic and political rule in *AN*, 243.
137. *BtS-FR1*, 125.
138. Dreitzel, *Absolutismus und ständische Verfassung*, 128–9.
139. See Lübbe-Wolff, 'Über das Fehlen von Grundrechten', 425–6.
140. See Mandt, 'Tyrannis, Despotie', 655.
141. *AN*, 198. The *societas herilis* was the name given to the society between lord and bondsman in late Latin Aristotelian Neo-Scholastic philosophy (see Günther Bien, Ulrich Dierse and Johannes Winckelmann, 'Despotie, Despotismus', *HWPh2*, 133). The idea goes back to Luther and Melanchthon. They had conceptualized a division between kingdom (*regnum*), tyranny and herile imperium (despotism) or the household rule of the head of the family (*herilis*) that differentiated structurally between autocratic monarchy and a kingship bound by written laws (see Dreitzel, *Absolutismus und ständische Verfassung*, 19). Aristotle had discovered the two types of *imperia* and *dominia*, the regular and the corrupt. For Melanchthon, 'the body-politic is an association of citizens arranged by law' (see *Commentarii*, paragraph 40). Drawing on Aristotle and the Christian tradition, however, he also praised despotism, the rule of the *paterfamilias* over his children that preceded law, as the most civilized, albeit rare, form of rule (ibid., paragraph 68, 49).
142. *AN*, 217, 239.
143. Link, 'Johann Stephan Pütter', 319.
144. *AN*, 243. I translate civil (*bürgerlich*) as political following the point made by Schröder, 'die "*Elementa Iuris Naturae*"', 334 that the authors did not yet distinguish between civil society and the state.
145. *AN*, 241 (original italics).
146. Ibid., 243.
147. *BtS-FR1*, 20 – quoted fully at the outset of 2.1.1.
148. Denzer, 'Bodins Staatsformenlehre', 241.
149. See Link, 'Johann Stephan Pütter', 320.
150. *AN*, 255 (original italics).
151. See *BtS-FR1*, 53 as well as the praise lavished on Limnaeus in *LtSR1*, 199: 'the first who undertook to develop constitutional law in the German Empire to its full

extent, and with great effort provided his countrymen with a reference library in this science. He has surpassed all his predecessors, and his successors have copied from him for quite some time'.

152. See Stolleis, *Geschichte des öffentlichen Rechts*, 224.
153. Pufendorf, *The Present State of Germany*, 173.
154. Stolleis, *Geschichte des öffentlichen Rechts*, 313.
155. *Digest* I.III.31; Bodin, *De republica libri sex*, 123: 'Sovereignty is the highest power over citizens and subjects and unbound by laws' – see also 129, 132. Again, the influence of Limnaeus, who had confessed that he was never fond of the formula, may be evident on Pütter here (see Johannes Limnaeus, *Juris publici Imperii Romano-Germanici I* (Strasburg: Spoor, 1628), 100).
156. *AN*, 239.
157. See Bodin, *De republica libri sex*, 275 on indivisibility, 305 on the division between *Reipublicae statum* and *imperandi ratione* or *gubernatio*. The *status mixtus* had already been rejected earlier in his *Methodus historica*, 177. For a reassessment of Bodin that deemphasizes his absolutism, see Daniel Lee, *The Right of Sovereignty: Jean Bodin on the Right of State and the Law of Nations* (Oxford: Oxford University Press, 2023).
158. Hugo, *De statu regionum Germaniae*, 7, 20.
159. Ibid., 13, 26. This argument reappears in *BtS-FR1*, 218, 217–23.
160. Hugo, *De statu regionum Germaniae*, 147 (original capitalization, italics added).
161. *BtS-FR1*, 192. Compare Hugo, *De statu regionum Germaniae*, 149. He had already pointed to the parcelling out of the *regalia* to the imperial estates and similarly identified *Landeshoheit* as diminutive when compared with the highest power of the state (*summa potestatis civilis*) (ibid., 19–20).
162. Harris, *Night Thoughts*, 140.
163. Ibid., 140–3.
164. *GW5[SdS]*, 334.
165. See *GW4[NR]*, 458.
166. *GW5[SdS]*, 326.
167. Ibid., 344; see Frederick C. Beiser, 'Fichte and the French Revolution', in *The Cambridge Companion to Fichte*, ed. David James and Günter Zöller (Cambridge: Cambridge University Press, 2017), 38–64.
168. Gottlieb Fichte, *Grundlage des Naturrechts nach Prinzipien der Wissenschaftslehre. Zweiter Teil oder Angewandtes Naturrecht* (Hamburg: Felix Meiner, 2013), 51 (original italics).
169. *GW4[NR]*, 455.
170. Ibid., 456.
171. Ibid.
172. For my discussion, see Sections 4.1.1–4.1.6.
173. *GW5[RV]*, 194.
174. See Gross, *Empire and Sovereignty*, 361–2.
175. Otto, 'Pütter, Johann Stephan', 1.
176. The beginnings of a distinction between a sovereign and a private legal sphere of the ruler can already be found in the Middle Ages, but the discipline of private princely law only began to emerge in the eighteenth century. Its first theoretical conceptualization can be traced to Grotius and Pufendorf, however. This was then passed on to *Reichspublizistik* (see Dietmar Willoweit, 'Privatfürstenrecht', in *HRG4*, 791).

177. Hugo, *De statu regionum Germaniae*, 215 (original capitalization). Hugo must be considered the source of the popularization of this theory of the *cives imperii*, of Roman private law applied to the political relations between the imperial estates and the Empire, though, as we saw in Section 2.2.4, his teacher Conring had first made it possible.
178. *GW5[RV]*, 194.
179. Wieacker, *A History of Private Law in Europe*, 143–55.
180. Stein, *Roman Law in European History*, 39.
181. Charles de Montesquieu, *The Spirit of Laws*, trans. and ed. Anne M. Cohler et al. (Cambridge: Cambridge University Press, 1989), 547. See the penetrating analysis by Myriam Bienenstock, 'Die "Ungeschicklichkeit, die wahrhaften Sitten in die Form von Gesetzen zu bringen", ist "das Zeichen der Barbarey": Hegels Kodifikationsforderung um 1802', in *Verfassung und Revolution*, ed. Weisser-Lohmann and Köhler, 94.
182. See *GW27,1[VWG]*, 320, 365. This perception goes back to Hegel's earliest period. In Rome, obedience to a despot had been turned into a system (see *GW1[FSI]*, 202).
183. *GW5[RV]*, 157.
184. See Hugo, *De statu regionum Germaniae*, 218 – he follows an argument made by Grotius.
185. Kaser, *Roman Private Law*, 115–18.
186. *The Oxford Latin Dictionary*, 626 offers as its primary definition of *dominatio*: 'The position or authority of a *paterfamilias*.' The secondary definition: 'The position of an absolute or arbitrary ruler, dominion, despotism.' This accords with Melanchthon's statement in the *Commentarii*: 'the head of the family domineers the slaves "despotically"' which he then proceeds to identify with the best rule of the state (paragraph 20, 54, 68).
187. For Hegel's discussion of the issue, see *GW5[RV]*, 198.
188. *AN*, 201 – Achenwall's contribution, not Pütter's.
189. See *HD2*, 288–94.
190. *GW5[RV]*, 152–8.
191. Weber, *Economy and Society*, 973–8.
192. *LtSR1*, 43. For Pütter's most extensive treatment, however, see *BtS-FR2*, 30–47.
193. Stein, *Roman Law in European History*, 91.
194. Thomas A. Brady Jr., *German Histories in the Age of Reformations, 1400–1650* (Cambridge: Cambridge University Press, 2009), 98.
195. *GW5[RV]*, 152.
196. *HD2*, 297.
197. Ibid., 295–6.
198. Hintze, 'The Preconditions of Representative Government', 332.
199. Maier, 'Hegels Schrift 2', 213. I resume this discussion in Sections 3.1.3–3.1.4.
200. *GW5[RV]*, 152. Of all of the imperial estates, Prussia was the most successful in implementing the aristocratic despotic form, which essentially entails a territorial lord wielding autocratic power.
201. Ibid. 111.
202. Ibid., 149. Hegel directly follows Kant, 'Perpetual Peace', 100.
203. *GW5[RV]*, 202.
204. See Bien, Dierse and Winckelmann, 'Despotie, Despotismus', 137.
205. August Wilhelm Rehburg, *Über die Staatsverwaltung in Monarchien und die Dienerschaft des Regenten* (Hahn, 1807), 226. Hegel owned the book (see

GW31,2[ABH], 1242) and had been analysing and excerpting Rehberg's work since his earliest period (see GW1[FSI], 357; GW3[FE], 191–200).

206. See Villey, 'Das römische Recht in Hegels Rechtsphilosophie', 133.
207. Kant, 'Perpetual Peace', 100–1.
208. See Bien, Dierse and Winckelmann, 'Despotie, Despotismus', 133.
209. *GW5[SdS]*, 338 (italics added). The contract applies only to the abstract relations of private law, to the relations of service and labour in the house community but not to the family as such or marriage (see ibid., 308). This critique is levelled at Immanuel Kant, *The Metaphysics of Morals*, trans Mary Gregor (Cambridge: Cambridge University Press, 1991), 96–7. Hegel's differentiation between political rule from that of the family, whose economic functions are taken over by modern civil society in his mature thought, demonstrates another aspect of his Aristotelianism as does his preference for political over despotic rule. Yet the *societas herilis* is no longer appropriate to the family either insofar as the character of rule everywhere must be over the free, the Roman principle of *dominium* is excluded. Christian love structures the family relation which leads to a true union that can only exist between beings of equal power (see *GW2[FSII]*, 84).
210. *GW5[RV]*,148.
211. See Stolleis, *Geschichte des öffentlichen Rechts*, 203–7.
212. *LtSR1*, 207.
213. *HD2*, 48–9; compare *LtSR1*, 207–213.
214. Gross, *Empire and Sovereignty*, 481.
215. Hermann Conring, *Der Ursprung des deutschen Rechts*, ed. Michael Stolleis, trans. Ilse Hoffmann-Meckenstock (Frankfurt am Main: Insel, 1994), 18–20, 173–80.
216. Montesquieu, *The Spirit of Laws*, 545.
217. See Wieacker, *A History of Private Law in Europe*, 132–42.
218. *GW5[SdS]*, 285.
219. *GW5[RV]*, 50–1.
220. Ibid., 63.
221. *Politics* 1285a18–28.
222. Ibid., 1292a32–4.
223. See Bienenstock, 'Hegels Kodifikationsforderung', 89–92.
224. Roderich von Stintzing, *Geschichte der deutschen Rechtswissenschaft. Zweite Abteilung* (Munich: Oldenbourg, 1884), 1–6.
225. For a *Reichspublizistik* perspective on the introduction of Roman law completely reliant on Conring's innovations, although with no explicit reference to them, see *BtS-FR2*, 30–47.
226. Conring, *Der Ursprung des deutschen Rechts*, 160–5; compare *BtS-FR2*, 41–6.
227. Willoweit, 'Kaiser, Reich und Reichsstände', 321. For the most comprehensive assessment of Conring's thought, see Constantin Fasolt, *The Limits of History* (Chicago: University of Chicago Press, 2004). Until Fasolt, Gross, *Empire and Sovereignty*, 255–92 remained the only thorough analysis in English.
228. Ibid., 281.
229. Krause, *Abhandlungen*, 52–5, 58.
230. Ibid., 52.
231. Ibid., 10.
232. See Aretin and Hammerstein, 'Reich IV', 471.
233. Conring, *Exercitatio de Germanici imperii civibus*, thesis viii.
234. For the *locus classicus* on these issues, see Hoke, 'Die Emanzipation', 211–30.

235. *LtSR1*, 39–44.
236. Ibid., 151.
237. Gross, *Empire and Sovereignty*, 281.
238. *LtSR1*, 77. Andlau's zeal for Roman law was based on the *translatio imperii*. A modern Latin/German edition of Andlau's contribution to imperial public law has appeared, see *Kaiser und Reich (Libellus de cesarea monarchia)*, ed. Rainer A. Müller (Frankfurt am Main: Insel, 1998). As can be observed with the pseudonym *Caesarinus Fürstenerius*, Leibniz played on Andlau's title. For an analysis of the *caesariner* and *fürstenianer* see Krause, *Abhandlungen*, 67–8.
239. *LtSR1*, 87–8 and, more generally, 77–88.
240. *GW5[RV]*, 37.
241. Hugo, *De statu regionum Germaniae*, 7; Volker Sellin, 'Regierung, Regime, Obrigkeit', in *GG5*, 403.
242. See Villey, 'Das römische Recht in Hegels Rechtsphilosophie', 142–3.
243. *GW5[RV]*, 126.
244. See Villey, 'Das römische Recht in Hegels Rechtsphilosophie', 133. I am of the opinion that such preservation is far more realistically considered an intelligent use of *simulacra* – to employ the very fitting Tacitean language to this context. Hegel had seen clearly 'how the Roman Emperors, who put an end to the anarchy of the Roman Republic and reunited the Empire into one state, preserved all the *external* forms of the Republic intact' (*GW5[RV]*, 103 (italics added)). Hegel followed Machiavelli (see Section 1.4.2). For the gradual evolution of Roman public law from the Republic to the Principate and beyond, see the nuanced discussion by Adriaan Sirks, 'Public Law', in *The Cambridge Companion to Roman Law*, ed. David Johnson (Cambridge: Cambridge University Press, 2015), 332–52.
245. See Villey, 'Das römische Recht in Hegels Rechtsphilosophie', 133.
246. Ibid., 144, 150 n. 71, 142–3. This disagrees with Kaser's account. Already in the early agricultural period, as he indicates, a distinction existed between power over things and power over persons (see Kaser, *Roman Private Law*, 116).
247. Villey, 'Das römische Recht in Hegels Rechtsphilosophie', 142–3.
248. See *LtSR1*, 100–1.
249. Gross, *Empire and Sovereignty*, xvi, xv.
250. *Politics*, 1255b16–23.
251. See Hugo, *De statu regionum Germaniae*, 13, 19.
252. *HD2*, 291.
253. *LtSR1*, 198.
254. Ibid.
255. *GW5[RV]*, 201–2.
256. Rudolf Hoke, 'Johannes Limnaeus', in *Staatsdenker*, ed. Stolleis, 109.
257. Ibid.
258. *GW5[RV]*, 167. For a fuller discussion of this issue, see Section 3.4.1.

3 The twilight of German imperial public law: Johann Christian von Majer

1. Rosenzweig, *Hegel and the State*, 128–207. For Hočevar, *Stände und Repräsentation*, 170 Majer's probable influence on Hegel ultimately remains improvable. I disagree.

Majer became full professor for constitutional and feudal law in his homeland Württemberg at Tübingen in 1778. He was an advisor to the supreme court (*Ober-Tribunalrath*) in Württemberg and was the rector of the University of Tübingen five times 1783, 1790–1, 1795–6, 1802–3 and 1806–7 (see Manfred Friedrich, 'Majer, Johann Christian von (württembergischer Personaladel 1808)', in *Neue Deutsche Biographie* 15 (1987): 717–18.

2. See Rosenzweig, *Hegel and the State*, 196 n. 55. I can find no evidence of such lectures, however, in the list of courses offered by Majer during Hegel's time spent in Tübingen.
3. Hegel had made a translation of the *Agricola*; it is presumed to be from the Stuttgart period, but it was undated and has been lost (see Karl Rosenkranz, *Hegels Leben* (Berlin: Duncker & Humblot, 1844), 12; compare Harris, *Towards the Sunlight*, 48).
4. Johann Christian Majer, 'Beyträge zur Geschichte der Menschheit aus den Annalen der Teutschen', *Der Teutsche Merkur* 2, no. 1 (1773): 30–44, 136–49; 3, no. 1 (1773): 39–63; 4, no. 2 (1773): 195–244; 6, no. 1 (1774): 76–112. It is possible Hegel consulted the review during his study of the imperial constitution (see Meist, 'Anmerkungen', 775–7). I already discussed this in Section 1.3.5.
5. Ernst Landsberg, *Geschichte der deutschen Rechtswissenschaft. Dritte Abtheilung* (Munich: Oldenbourg, 1898), 454–5. Majer taught Pütter's *Elementa iuris publici Germanici*, imperial public law according to the *mos Gottingensis* (see *Ordo praelectionum cum publicarum tum privatarum*).
6. *TSK1*, 16.
7. Rosenzweig, *Hegel and the State*, 163.
8. Grimm, *Constitutionalism*, 98. Majer is important also as the principal author of private princely law of the eighteenth century (see Willoweit, 'Privatfürstenrecht', 791–4). He divided the prince into two distinct legal persons, governed respectively by public and private law. Princely constitutional law (*Staatsfürstenrecht*) involves all of the rights and obligations the prince accrues with respect to the public order of the state, as its representative. Private princely law involves all the rights and obligations to which a prince, as an (individual) person, is entitled in the furtherance of his own individual interests that arise from the entirety of his private rights (see *AEP-Fr*, 163, 167–8).
9. *GW5[SdS]*, 327.
10. Ibid., 339 (original italics). Ibid., 340.
11. See *TSK1*, 57 – Majer followed Moser in identifying the *forma imperii* with the state constitution.
12. Rosenzweig, *Hegel and the State*, 163 (translation modified).
13. See ibid., 181, 206 n. 296; compare *GW5[RV]*, 165–78.
14. See *ATSK*, 85.
15. Ibid., 1–2. I already quoted this passage in Section 1.4.4.
16. See Akira Hayase, 'Hegel und das alte Reich – Kontinuität der politischen Tradition', in *Logik und Realität: Wie systematisch ist Hegels System?*, ed. Yohichi Kubo and Christoph Jamme (Leiden: Brill, 2019), 283–4.
17. Harris, *Towards the Sunlight*, 58. The reason for the interest in law was apparently the threat to reform the Tübinger Stift that came from Duke Karl Eugen (1728–1793). Hegel was not successful in his pleas with his father to shift disciplines (ibid., 60). Law, however, was a respected discipline in the family. Hegel's mother, Maria Magdalena Louisa (1741–1783) (née Fromm), was the daughter of a lawyer at the High Court of Justice at the Württemberg court. Hegel's unrequited desire to graduate with a master's in law, not theology, beyond mere illness, accounts also for the long stays in Stuttgart

away from Tübingen and the rather disapproving remarks by a certain professor (see Jaeschke, *Hegel-Handbuch*, 5).

18. I have already cited the details in Section 2.0.2.
19. Robert von Mohl, *Enzyklopädie der Staatswissenschaft. Zweite umgearbeitete Auflage* (Tübingen: Laupp, 1872), 182, 397. See Jaeschke, *Hegel-Handbuch*, 65–7 and the discussion of the transformation of the legal condition of the early Christian church into a spiritual state or its political organization.
20. These lectures were delivered by Majer in 1787–8, 1788, 1789, 1790 (see *Ordo praelectionum cum publicarum tum privatarum*).
21. *ATSK*, 153–85.
22. *GW5[RV]*, 175 – see also Hayase, 'Hegel und das alte Reich', 286; Ottmann, 'Ein philosophisches Finale', 397.
23. *GW5[RV]*, 15, in the margins.
24. This general rule did not apply, however, to the ecclesiastical imperial estates, the prince bishoprics and prince abbots. They were awarded the full protection of the Empire in both secular and clerical rights. Hence, the 'Clerical Reservation' (*Geistlicher Vorbehalt*) denied them the *ius reformandi* (see Martin Heckel, *Deutschland im konfessionellen Zeitalter* (Göttingen: Vandenhoeck, 1983), 47 – referring to the Peace of Augsburg §§16 and 18.
25. *GW5[RV]*, 99.
26. See Boyd, 'Pufendorf on Confessional Strife and Interstate Relations', 23–8.
27. *GW5[RV]*, 103.
28. *GW4[DS]*, 13–14.
29. *GW5[RV]*, 15.
30. *GW4[DS]*, 13.
31. Ibid.
32. See Meist, 'Anmerkungen', in *GW5*, 746–825.
33. Ibid., 754, 770–1, 815. With a single exceptional reference to *TSK1*, 197 Meist's citations are restricted to *TwSR2*. It seems that he did not consult Rosenzweig's discussion of Majer when carrying out his research.
34. See Hayase, 'Hegel und das alte Reich', 283–4. I say 'arguably' because Rosenzweig is not cited.
35. Ibid., 283. Hayase is not alone among contemporary Japanese scholars in his interest in Hegel's concept of sovereignty and its relation to the imperial constitution. This has also been treated systematically by Takeshi Gonza, 'Reichsauflösung, Rheinbundreformen und das Problem der Staatssouveränität. Die Entstehung der Hegelschen Souveränitätstheorie und ihr geschichtlicher Hintergrund', *Hegel-Studien* 41 (2006): 113–48.
36. *TSK1*, 5 – I am literally paraphrasing here.
37. *ATSK*, 2.
38. Just as these concepts were synonyms for Pütter, as we saw in the previous chapter, the same held for Majer (see *TSK1*, 56–7).
39. See *ATSK*, 3, 4.
40. See ibid., 2 where Schöpflin is mentioned; for *Unformlichkeit* see ibid., 172–3.
41. Ibid., 174.
42. *LtSR2*, 219. Majer cites this passage as well in *TSK1*, 63–4.
43. *GW5[RV]*, 153.
44. Ibid., 103; compare, however, *GW5[SdS]*, 314–15 where Majer's neologism indeed does appear. I analyse Hegel's use of formlessness in Sections 4.1.3 and 4.4.1.

45. Hayase, 'Hegel und das alte Reich', 277.
46. Stolleis, *Public Law in Germany, 1800–1914*, 19 (original italics).
47. Ottmann, 'Ein philosophisches Finale', 396.
48. *GW5[RV]*, 201–2.
49. See *GW14,1[PdR]*, 226–9 (§273). I have discussed this in Section 1.4.4.
50. *GW5[RV]*, 201. This is actually the chapter title Hegel gave to the last pages of the *Reinschrift*.
51. Hayase, 'Hegel und das alte Reich', 282.
52. Stolleis, *Public Law in Germany, 1800–1914*, 18.
53. *TSK1*, 29 (original italics).
54. Dreitzel, *Absolutismus und ständische Verfassung*, 130.
55. See Harris, *Towards the Sunlight*, 426 n. 1.
56. Barbara Stollberg-Rilinger, *Vormünder des Volkes? Konzepte landständischer Repräsentation in der Spätphase des Alten Reiches* (Berlin: Duncker & Humblot, 1999), 267. In Majer's case, this approach was used not only critically but also apologetically and restoratively. On constitutional relativism more generally as the legislative enactment of laws tailored to the type of regime, see George Duke, *Aristotle and Law: The Politics of Nomos* (Cambridge: Cambridge University Press, 2019), 63–84.
57. We are thus in a position to slightly revise the point made by Harris, *Towards the Sunlight*, 416 n. 2 – referencing Rosenzweig: 'I think it is not unlikely that Hegel began studying Pütter, Moser, and the rest as soon as he set *Der Begriff der Positivität* (the revised introduction of the "Positivity" essay) aside.'
58. *ATSK*, 133 n.*) (original italics).
59. *GW2*, 101–9.
60. See Heinrich Scheel, *Süddeutsche Jakobiner. Klassenkämpfe und republikanische Bestrebungen im deutschen Süden Ende des 18. Jahrhunderts* (Berlin: Akademie Verlag, 1962), 291–353 in which the writings of both Majer and Hegel are treated, albeit separately.
61. See Stollberg-Rilinger, *Vormünder des Volkes?*, 270 n. 137.
62. Sinclair, who had seen in the Jacobin dictatorship a necessary phase of the French Revolution, was the radical – *not* Hegel (see Scheel, *Süddeutsche Jakobiner*, 454).
63. Jaeschke, *Hegel-Handbuch*, 75.
64. See Stollberg-Rilinger, *Vormünder des Volkes?*, 274.
65. For a fine sketch of the pamphlet war and the historical context, see Harris, *Towards the Sunlight*, 416–34 in which he also situates Hegel's Jean-Jacques Cart (1748–1813) translation (ibid., 419) (see *GW2[FSII]*, 395–581).
66. Harris, *Towards the Sunlight*, 429–30 n. 2, 425–6.
67. Scheel, *Süddeutsche Jakobiner*, 329.
68. Gonza, 'Hegelschen Souveränitätstheorie', 121. The quotes are from Rosenkranz, *Hegels Leben*, 91.
69. Harris, *Towards the Sunlight*, 432.
70. *ATSK*, 100.
71. *SSrG*, viii–ix.
72. See Stollberg-Rilinger, *Vormünder des Volkes?*, 270.
73. Jaeschke, *Hegel-Handbuch*, 75.
74. Hegel owned the works of Jakob Friedrich Gutscher (1761–1834) who was less conservative than Majer but still sought to temper demands for reform by arguing that they had already taken place historically. Like Hegel's, the demands were aimed at putting an end to the oligarchic character of the estates. On the other hand, Hegel

also had works by the Göttingen professor Ludwig Timotheus Spittler (1752–1810) who had been appointed by the duke to strengthen the Privy Council in Stuttgart (see *GW31,2[ABH]*, 1076–7, 1291–4; Scheel, *Süddeutsche Jakobiner*, 316, 307). Spittler published a pamphlet primarily aimed at preserving the traditional constitution. He considered the territorial estates as empowered by national representation. Majer attacked him on these grounds. Prioritizing the immediacy of rule, the property owners and landlords decided for themselves and in their own name. By contrast, the idea of representation for Majer followed what he termed the mandate fiction, that the people 'mandated' their original sovereignty to the representatives of the state (*TSK2*, 556).

75. Majer discusses several principles. The Empire was based on the religious principle; the revolutionary state on the national principle; the German territorial states on the predial principle (manorial property). This led further to two distinct types of territorial constitution: the patrimonial and the freeholder.
76. For the notable exceptions, see Horst Dreitzel, *Monarchiebegriffe in der Fürstengesellschaft: Semantik und Theorie der Einherrschaft in Deutschland von der Reformation bis zum Vormärz. Band 2* (Cologne: Böhlau, 1991), 765, 803; Dreitzel, *Absolutismus und ständische Verfassung*, 121–9; Hasso Hofmann, *Repräsentation. Studien zur Wort- und Begriffsgeschichte von der Antike bis ins 19. Jahrhundert. 4. Auflage mit einer neuem Einleitung* (Berlin: Duncker & Humblot, 2003), 393–5; Stollberg-Rilinger, *Vormünder des Volkes?*, 267–75.
77. Gross, *Empire and Sovereignty*, 455–85 covers some of the publicists of the last generation. Dreitzel's claim that he breaks off where Pütter ended in *LtSR2* is erroneous (see Dreitzel, *Absolutismus und ständische Verfassung*, 125 n. 9) as Gross examines Gönner and concludes his study with Hegel.
78. *LtSR2*, 91–4.
79. Robert von Mohl, *Die Geschichte und Literatur der Staatswissenschaften in Monographieën dargestellt. Zweiter Band* (Erlangen: Enke, 1856), 288–9.
80. Landsberg, *Geschichte der deutschen Rechtswissenschaft*, 454–5.
81. Ibid., 454.
82. See *LtSR2*, 93.
83. Landsberg, *Geschichte der deutschen Rechtswissenschaft*, 454.
84. For the possible relationship between Häberlin's textbooks on Pütter's public law and Hegel, see Meist, 'Anmerkungen', 759–60, 768–9, 803–4.
85. Mohl, *Die Geschichte und Literatur*, 289.
86. *TSK1*, 24–5.
87. *NtSR14*, 311.
88. See *LtSR1*, 241–3.
89. Krause, *Abhandlungen*, 53.
90. Hugo, *De statu regionum Germaniae*, 13. The source quote is unidentified, and I have been unable to locate it in Mevius's work. Pütter cites the source in *EB1*, 16 but it remains fragmentary. Majer quotes Latin and German variations of the passage as do Pütter and Hugo. This testifies to the fact that it had become a catchphrase and had long left the realm of exact citation.
91. *TSK1*, 29.
92. Brady, *German Histories*, 99.
93. See Johann Nicholas Hert, 'Lectori', in Hugo, *De statu regionum Germaniae*, unpaginated.

94. *TSK1*, 51. Majer disagrees with Hert's interpretation of the *Hippolythus* (ibid., 52 n. 16) and with his characterization of the state form (ibid., 54–5 n. 17), however.
95. *ATSK*, 135–9.
96. Ibid. 135.
97. Hugo, *De statu regionum Germaniae*, 143.
98. Ibid. 142.
99. Eulau, 'Theories of Federalism', 650 n. 27 (original italics) – referencing Moser and the constitutional historian Eichhorn. Indeed, Hugo's very title pinpointed the dichotomy between government or administration (*regimine*) and the form of constitution or state (*Reipublicae*). Hence, the after-effect of Hugo's ideas cannot be underestimated – even on the history of German Idealism, given that Kant and Hegel took over the characteristic division.
100. Landsberg, *Geschichte der deutschen Rechtswissenschaft*, 40 (italics added).
101. Hugo, *De statu regionum Germaniae*, 75.
102. See Quaritsch, *Souveränität*, 110 – referencing articles I: 17–20, 22, 23; II: 21, 23, 24, 25 of the *Rheinbunds-Akte* (12 July 1806). For a comparative discussion, see Section 1.2.5.
103. See *GW5[RV]*, 169.
104. *TSK1*, 57–8. This material finds its way into Rosenzweig, *Hegel and the State*, 143, 195–6 n. 54. 'Der Nahme für die Staatsverfassung' is also worth comparing on this point: 'The name for the state constitution of Germany always causes trouble for constitutional law theory' (see *GW5[RV]*, 52).
105. Ibid., 161.
106. Ibid., 6–7. Hegel decides, initially following Voltaire, that the imperial *forma Reipublicae* should be considered an anarchy but immediately added that this name no longer applied 'because Germany can never be regarded as One state' (ibid., 7 (Hegel's capitalization)).
107. *ATSK*, 177.
108. *GW5[RV]*, 96–7.
109. *ATSK*, 168–71.
110. Ibid. 174.
111. For my discussion, see Section 2.2.1.
112. *ATSK*, 180.
113. *GW5[RV]*, 64–5. For my foundational discussion on this passage, see Section 1.3.3.
114. *ATSK*, 173; compare *GW5[RV]*, 128–9.
115. *ATSK*, 171–7.
116. See *BtS-FR1*, 66–8.
117. *TwSR2*, 147.
118. *ATSK*, 131. The *Hippolythus* had been popularized in the Dalberg reform circle in Mainz to which Hegel might have been connected (see Section 4.2.6). Nicolaus Vogt (1756–1836) had dramatized the *Hippolythus* in the play *Gustav Adolph König in Schweden als Nachtrag zur europäischen Republik* (Varrentrapp and Wenner, 1790). Chemnitz was envisioned as having drafted a European World Republic (see ibid., vol. 2, 5–13). Hegel initially praised the Swedish king as the saviour of German freedom of conscience, of the Protestant cause, but also more critically in terms of his ambitions (*GW5[RV]*, 106, 126, 214). The *Hippolythus* was also favourably cited in *Darstellung des Fürstenbunds*. We know Hegel had Müller's elaborate piece of political journalism in hand while composing his fragments (*Darstellung des Fürstenbunds*, 74 n. 1, 121–2, 220 n. 9, and 296 n. 4; compare *GW5[RV]*, 119). Müller

was also a member of the Dalberg circle. Universal monarchy, balance and *teutsche Libertät* were the catchwords, all of which found their way into Hegel's fragments. These references to the *Hippolythus* have not been taken into account by Meist, 'Anmerkungen', 759–64.

119. *ATSK*, 172–3 (original italics).
120. Ibid., 177.
121. Ibid., 179–82.
122. See Sections 2.3.1–2.3.6.
123. *ATSK*, 131.
124. Ibid., 181 (original italics).
125. *GW5[RV]*, 129.
126. See ibid., 64–5. Meist, 'Anmerkungen', 770–1 considers the concept of the body politic discussed in 'Der Nahme für die Staatsverfassung' as stemming from *TwSR2*, 93, 95–147 in which Majer uses it as a substitute for the imperial association when he discusses the imperial circles (*Reichskreise*) or districts. This earlier usage is very similar to how Moser and Pütter employed the concept. For this reason, I think the extended theoretical discussion we find in *ATSK*, 126–32 and the notable shift in Majer's thought towards an explicit affirmation of this aristocratic form in *TSK2*, ii, 265–6 appear to be far more probable sources for Hegel's analysis in general, certainly insofar as Majer considers it within the context brought about by the Peace of Basel and the wars with revolutionary France (*ATSK*, 175–82).
127. *ATSK*, 181 (original italics); compare *GW5[RV]*, 62, 71–2, 108, 111, 115, 129, 137, 167, 170, 173, 175, 178.
128. Ibid., 182–5; Meist, 'Anmerkungen', 754–9. Hegel's Voltaire reference belongs to the same context insofar as he also isolates anarchy in the same way, connected to the aristocratic principle and private law in the transfer of empire from Rome to Germany as we saw in Sections 2.3.4–2.3.6.
129. *ATSK*, 126.
130. Ibid., 130.
131. Ibid., 130, 129, 123.
132. Ibid., 171–3.
133. *GW5[RV]*, 153.
134. *ATSK*, 173.
135. Ibid. The uniform and homogeneous application of *Landeshoheit* was responsible for the destruction of the hierarchical form (see ibid., 174).
136. *GW5[RV]*, 110.
137. Ibid., 124–5 (original boldface type).
138. *GW5[RV]*, 65.
139. *ATSK*, 112 (original italics).
140. *GW5[RV]*, 161.
141. See ibid., 65.
142. *ATSK*, 130.
143. Ibid. (original italics).
144. *GUrV*, 167.
145. *ATSK*, 175.
146. *GUrV*, 167–8.
147. *GW5[RV]*, 8. Majer's book appeared in 1798, Hegel began working on 'Sollte das politische Resultat' in 1799.
148. *ATSK*, 120–1.

149. Ibid., 181, 182 – I say Majer, but it is actually Müller's anonymous excerpt. For Hegel's discussion on the issue following Pütter (see *GW5[RV]*, 152).
150. Ibid., 148.
151. *GUrV*, 167–8.
152. *ATSK*, 181.
153. Ibid., 171 (original italics).
154. *GW5[RV]*, 105.
155. Stolleis, *Geschichte des öffentlichen Rechts*, 185.
156. See *EB1*, 16; *BtS-FR1*, 218 – another variation of the formula also appears in ibid., 188.
157. Hugo, *De statu regionum Germaniae*, 147; *ATSK*, 174.
158. *BtS-FR1*, 218.
159. See Hugo, *De statu regionum Germaniae*, 13. The argument reappears more generally in *BtS-FR1*, 217–23.
160. *TSK1*, 31 n. 7.
161. *EB1*, 15–16. Pütter cites the original quote by Mevius. Thus, his reversal of the formula is intentional.
162. Gross, *Empire and Sovereignty*, 444.
163. *TSK1*, 32.
164. Hugo, *De statu regionum Germaniae*, 52.
165. *TSK1*, 32 (original italics).
166. Gross, *Empire and Sovereignty*, 452. For my initial discussion, see Sections 1.2.1–1.2.5.
167. *TSK1*, 30.
168. Ibid., 28.
169. Ibid., 29 (original italics).
170. Ibid., 65.
171. Ibid., 28.
172. Ibid., 60.
173. Ibid., 32.
174. Mohl, *Die Geschichte und Literatur*, 289.
175. Ibid.
176. *TSK1*, 29 (original italics).
177. Ibid., 28; Dreitzel, *Absolutismus und ständische Verfassung*, 124.
178. Hugo, *De statu regionum Germaniae*, 147 (original italics) – the reference is to Dietrich Reinkingk, *Tractatus de regimine seculari et ecclesiastico* (Gießen: Nicola Hempeli, 1618).
179. *TSK1*, 37.
180. *TSR2*, 241. See Stollberg-Rilinger, *Vormünder des Volkes?*, 240 n. 27 where other examples from Moser are cited.
181. Or at least this is what he argued in *TSK1*, 55 n. 17.
182. *GW5[RV]*, 13.
183. See Stollberg-Rilinger, *Vormünder des Volkes?*, 240.
184. *TwSR2*, 93–4, 96–8. This early publication was immediately preceded by Majer's initial excursuses on Tacitus in *Der Teutsche Merkur*.
185. See, for example, *ATSK*, 174.
186. Bienenstock, 'Hegels Kodifikationsforderung', 93 has connected Hegel's approach also rightly to Voltaire's critique of Montesquieu's naïve enthusiasm for Tacitus in *Essai sur les moeurs* (1756).

187. *TwSR2*, 98. Such insights correspond with the historical scholarship. The jurists and judges appointed to the Imperial Cameral Court were to ideally be trained in Roman law following the imperial edict of 1495 in which it was accepted as the *ius commune*. Yet the imperial estates reserved the right to appoint the judges and notaries, assuring their own interests (see Harold Joseph Berman, *Law and Revolution II: The Impact of the Protestant Reformations on the Western Legal Tradition* (Cambridge, MA: Belknap Press, 2003), 36; compare Wieacker, *A History of Private Law*, 71–7).
188. See *GW5[RV]*, 88–90.
189. See ibid., 64–5; compare *ATSK*, 173.
190. *GW5[RV]*, 115.
191. Ibid., 110.
192. Ibid., 94.
193. Meist, 'Anmerkungen', 771. It should be noted that Meist is referring to the fragment 'Der Nahme für die Staatsverfassung' and not the Jena outline 'kan, wodurch die Freyheit' from which the previous quote is taken.
194. Rosenzweig, *Hegel and the State*, 196 n. 55. Hočevar, *Stände und Repräsentation*, 170 follows Rosenzweig in making the case for the possible impact of *Germaniens Urverfassung*. Meist is the only scholar to consider the very early works. For a recent reassertion of the importance of Tacitus – although with no mention of Majer – see Richard Bourke, *Hegel's World Revolutions* (Princeton, NJ: Princeton University Press, 2023), 124:

    > Hegel traced this to the 'German' idea of freedom. The concept had its origins in accounts of the German (or Teutonic) tribes as variously relayed by Boulainvilliers, Montesquieu and Tacitus. Tacitus was most likely Hegel's immediate source: in his *Germania*, he had drawn a picture of tribal society in which authority was controlled from the bottom up and participation in affairs was widespread.

195. *ATSK*, 13 (original italics).
196. *BtS-FR1*, 186.
197. See *LtSR1*, 29–30.
198. *BtS-FR1*, 119. Compare Wieacker, *A History of Private Law*, 73 who pinpoints a similar genealogy. In contrast to Pütter, however, for Wieacker this was part and parcel to the collapse of the Empire: 'This definitive transfer of powers to the great feudal lords explains why constitutional and legal development in Germany from the late Middle Ages centres on the territorial states.' For all of his imperial patriotism, the logic remains comparable. Why else would Pütter revert so frequently, as we have seen, to the territories to interpret and supplement imperial public law?
199. *TSK1*, 63–4; compare *LtSR2*, 219.
200. *TSK1*, 66.
201. *GUrV*, 16.
202. *TSK1*, 65; compare *ATSK*, 54.
203. *TSK1*, 16.
204. See Stolleis, *Geschichte des öffentlichen Rechts*, 299–305.
205. Stollberg-Rilinger, *Vormünder des Volkes?*, 270–2.
206. *GW5[RV]*, 60. This passage from 'Diese Form des deutschen Staatsrechts' is a reworking of the original ideas from 'Sollte das politische Resultat' (compare ibid., 8–9).
207. *GUrV*, 167.

208. For an older study of Möser in English, see Klaus Epstein, *The Genesis of German Conservatism* (Princeton, NJ: Princeton University Press, 1966), 297–338. For an excellent revisionist approach, see Frederick C. Beiser, 'Justus Möser and the Roots of Historicism', in *The German Historicist Tradition*, ed. Frederick C. Beiser (Oxford: Oxford University Press, 2011), 63–97; compare Jan Schröder, 'Justus Möser', in *Staatsdenker*, ed. Stolleis, 294–309.
209. *GUrV*, 24, 30–1. These are the pages where Majer cites from Möser's *Osnabrückische Geschichte*. In his discussion of serfdom, Majer refers to Möser's *Patriotische Phantasien* (Patriotic Fantasies) (*GUrV*, 66).
210. Friedrich Meinecke, *Die Entstehung des Historismus*, ed. Carl Hinrichs (Munich: Oldenburg, 1959), 344. Hegel owned a copy of *Osnabrückische Geschichte, Patriotische Phantasien* and other works, see *GW31,2[ABH]*, 1185–98 Möser's influence on Pütter, Müller and Johann Gottfried Herder (1744–1803) has been established, all fundamental references for Hegel's early political and legal thought. Moreover, Möser was central for Johann Wolfgang von Goethe (1749–1832), a principal figure for Hegel's early development and lifelong acquaintance.
211. Maier, 'Hegels Schrift 1', 349.
212. Ingmar Kurt Ahl, 'Möser, Justus', in *Juristen*, ed. Stolleis, 446.
213. Landsberg, *Geschichte der Deutschen Rechtswissenschaft*, 455; compare Stollberg-Rilinger, *Vormünder des Volkes?*, 267; Dreitzel, *Absolutismus und ständische Verfassung*, 123.
214. Schröder, 'Justus Möser', 296–7.
215. Dreitzel, *Absolutismus und ständische Verfassung*, 123–6.
216. For a concise overview, see Alexandra Gajda, 'Tacitus and Political Thought in Early Modern Europe', in *The Cambridge Companion to Tacitus*, ed. Anthony J. Woodman (Cambridge: Cambridge University Press, 2009), 253–68. For the largely still authoritative interpretation, Schellhase, *Tacitus in Renaissance Political Thought*, 31–100.
217. Stolleis, *Geschichte des öffentlichen Rechts*, 93.
218. Ibid.
219. This type of approach is perhaps exemplified best in Germany by the professor of history and politics at Altdorf, Arnold Clapmar (1574–1604). He was the first to give lectures on public law (see Tuck, *Philosophy and Government*, 124–8).
220. Arnaldo Momigliano, *Studies in Historiography* (London: Weidenfeld & Nicolson, 1966), 122. This outdated view is assessed critically in what follows.
221. Stollberg-Rilinger, Vormünder des Volkes?, 234–5; see ibid., 235 n. 3 for reference literature on the German Tacitus reception.
222. Ronald H. Martin, 'From manuscript to print', in *Companion to Tacitus*, ed. Woodman, 241–52.
223. Richard F. Thomas, 'The Germania as a literary text', in *Companion to Tacitus*, ed. Woodman, 59–72.
224. Ibid., 60–1.
225. Strangely the earlier prefaced editions by Hermann Conring, 'Praefatio de historiarum, Germanorum imprimis, studiis' to C. Tacitus, *De moribus Germanorum* (1635, 1678) are not cited (see *GUrV*, 25–6). Even so, Majer's relation to Hert keeps his spirit alive (see Stolleis, *Geschichte des öffentlichen Rechts*, 241–2). In his efforts to discover what was Germanic in the imperial constitution, Conring had turned to Tacitus. He set the standard of the Tacitus reception in separating the Germanic Empire from the Roman Empire in an attempt to work out its originally federative

character. Both the *Reichstag* and the *Landtag* were considered remnants of the original Germanic constitution (see Willoweit, 'Kaiser, Reich und Reichsstände', 325).
226. Stolleis, *Geschichte des öffentlichen Rechts*, 94.
227. *GUrV*, 23.
228. Ibid.
229. Ibid., 23–4 (original italics).
230. Ibid., 24.
231. On the manuscript tradition of the *opera minora*, see Martin, 'From Manuscript to Print', 245–8.
232. This point has been answered thoroughly in the negative: 'The *Germania* is far from reliable as a historical, anthropological or sociological work, however important it has been in the realm of reception' (see Thomas, 'The Germania as a Literary Text', 59–60).
233. *GUrV*, 24.
234. Majer's citation is much more extensive than what I quote here, see ibid., 30–1 n. ***). Justus Möser, *Osnabrückische Geschichte allgemeine Einleitung* (Schmid, 1768) (unpaginated). I have quoted from Möser directly. Majer is true to the text but changed the spelling in places.
235. Ibid., 1–2. Möser cites Tacitus directly. The city of Osnabrück cannot be ancient as the Germanic tribes did not live in cities or villages (see *Germania*, 16).
236. Ibid., 2.
237. Möser, *Osnabrückische Geschichte*, 2.
238. *GW1[FSI]*, 359.
239. *GUrV*, 29.
240. *Germania*, 28–46. Thomas, 'The Germania as a literary text', 60–1; the same point is recognized by Majer (see *GUrV*, 165).
241. Ibid., 29, 30.
242. *GW5[RV]*, 8.
243. *GUrV*, 167.
244. *GW5[RV]*, 7.
245. Ibid., 10.
246. Ibid., 61.
247. *GUrV*, 30.
248. Ibid., 32–3.
249. *The Gallic War*, iv.1.
250. Ibid., vi.22.
251. *GUrV*, 34 (original italics).
252. Ibid., 39.
253. See Thomas, 'The Germania as a Literary Text', 59–61.
254. *GUrV*, 39.
255. Ibid., 40.
256. *GW5[RV]*, 9.
257. *GUrV*, 30 (original italics).
258. *TwSR3*, 113–17.
259. See Wieacker, *A History of Private Law*, 72.
260. Stein, *Roman Law in European History*, 39.
261. Montesquieu, *The Spirit of Laws*, 547.
262. *GW5[RV]*, 63, 10–11 (original italics).
263. Möser, *Osnabrückische Geschichte*, preface (unpaginated).

264. See Schröder, 'Justus Möser', 301, 302, 303.
265. *GW5[RV]*, 60.
266. Hugo, *De statu regionum Germaniae*, 222.
267. Justus Möser, *Sämtliche Werke, neu geordnet aus dem Nachlass. Band 6*, ed. Bernhard R. Abeken (Nicolai, 1842), 12 – henceforth cited as *SW* followed by volume number.
268. *GW5[RV]*, 198.
269. Hugo, *De statu regionum Germaniae*, 221–4.
270. *GW5[RV]*, 58.
271. Ibid., 64–5.
272. Ibid., 37.
273. Ibid., 60–1.
274. Schröder, 'Justus Möser', 297. For the historical and sociological character of Möser's conception, see Dreitzel, *Absolutismus und ständische Verfassung*, 123.
275. Möser, *SW5*, 191. Manse, from medieval Latin *mansus*, the principal house or dwelling of an estate.
276. See Möser, *Osnabrückische Geschichte*, preface (unpaginated).
277. Möser, *SW9*, 241.
278. See Montesquieu, *The Spirit of Laws*, 653, 709, 712.
279. *TSK2*, 556 (original italics). We are in some way unable to escape the polemics of *Landtagspublizistik* as this belongs to Majer's attack on Spittler who had considered the territorial estates as empowered by national representation. Majer's later shift in position was part of his reaction against the reform debates and the French Revolution. For that analysis, see Stollberg-Rilinger, Vormünder des Volkes?, 267–75.
280. *ATSK*, 61–4, 115.
281. See *GW5[RV]*, 110–11.
282. For the imbrication of natural law and public law, see *AN*, 223–63.
283. *ATSK*, 99.
284. Ibid., 45.
285. Ibid., 69.
286. See Scattola, 'Scientia Iuris and Ius Naturae', 1–41 who has shown how German natural law led to a redescription of the state of nature, which became a nascent society, laying the basis for the emergence of sociology. This had grown out of the natural law practised by the Göttingen School in particular (ibid., 26–8).
287. *ATSK*, 64. Compare ibid., 69 where philosophy and the facts of history are once more set in stark contrast.
288. See *TSK2*, 556.
289. *ATSK*, 48 (original italics).
290. *Digest* I.I.1.2:

> There are two branches of legal study: public and private law. Public law is that which respects the establishment of the Roman commonwealth, private that which respects individuals' interests, some matters being of public and others of private interest. Public law covers religious affairs, the priesthood, and offices of state. Private law is tripartite, being derived from principles of *ius naturale*, *ius gentium*, or *ius civile*.

291. Karl Salomo Zachariae, *Der Geist der deutschen Territorialverfassung* (Leipzig: Gerhard Fleischer, 1800), 203 – cited in Dreitzel, *Absolutismus und ständische Verfassung*, 124. Hegel owed numerous works by Zachariae, for example, *Vierzig Bücher vom Staate* (Stuttgart and Tübingen: Cotta, 1820–32 (four volumes))

that dealt with the German federal state system and the doctrine of government (see *GW31,2[ABH]*, 1329–39).

292. For a sketch of Böhmer's thought, see Gross, *Empire and Sovereignty*, 386–91, 402, 417, 441–3.
293. Justus Henning Böhmer, *Introductio in Ius Publicum Universale ex Genuinis Iuris Naturae Principiis Deduatum et in Usum Iuris Publici Particularis Adornatum* (Magdeburg: Orphanotropheum, [1710] 1726), 54, 55 n. (o) (italics added).
294. *The Oxford Latin Dictionary*, 1607 offers the following definition for *privata*: 'a person who holds no public office', 'a person who is not a ruler, a subject'. Most likely it was to this extent that the earlier tradition argued that princes had much in common with their subjects under the *ius privatum principum*, which concerned the private benefit and not the public order. Contracts of sale and loan, marriages, wills and similar issues were considered here (see Willoweit, 'Privatfürstenrecht', 791–2).
295. *AEP-Fr*, 86 (italics added).
296. Krause, *Abhandlungen*, 5. I give priority to the Latin, using state for public society (*öffentliche Gesellschaft*).
297. *ATSK*, 47.
298. *AEP-Fr*, 258.
299. Stolleis, *Public Law in Germany, 1800–1914*, 11. Even modern civil society is of Roman origin. This was observed incisively by Haller: '"the mother and root of all the errors" of the revolutionary period was solely "the unfortunate idea of a Roman *societas civilis*, which was transferred to all other social relationships' (Manfred Riedel, 'Gesellschaft, bürgerliche', in *GG2*, 773 – citing from Ludwig von Haller, *Restauration der Staatswissenschaft. Band 1* (Stein, 1816), xxvi).
300. *ATSK*, 55 (original italics).
301. Ibid., 54.
302. Ibid.
303. *AEP-Fr*, 19 (original italics).
304. Ibid., 102.
305. *ATSK*, 47.
306. *AEP-Fr*, 80.
307. For a still unsurpassed analysis of Haller in English, see Robert M. Berdahl, *The Politics of the Prussian Nobility: The Development of a Conservative Ideology 1770–1848* (Princeton, NJ: Princeton University Press, 1988), 231–63.
308. Jan Frederik Niermeyer, *Mediae Latinitatis Lexicon Minus: A Medieval Latin French/English Dictionary* (Leiden: Brill, 1954), 487.
309. *ATSK*, 55.
310. *Politics* 1285a18–23.
311. Villey, 'Das römische Recht in Hegels Rechtsphilosophie', 142–3.
312. Mandt, 'Tyrannis, Despotie', 694–5.
313. Ludwig von Haller, *Handbuch der allgemeinen Staaten-Kunde, des darauf gegründeten allgemeinen Staatsrechts und der allgemeinen Staatsklugheit nach den Gesetzen der Natur* (Winterthur: Stein, 1808), 33. These ideas find their way into Haller's mature work which stands at the centre of Hegel's reflections (see *GW14,1[PdR]*, 182–3 (§219), 201–7 (§258)).
314. Haller, *Handbuch der allgemeinen Staaten-Kunde*, 73.
315. See *TSK2*, 556 quoted in Section 3.2.5 above. The accepted historical formula of Otto Brunner (1898–1982) of how the estates had nothing to do with representation but rather ruled immediately thus did *not* have its origin in the early modern period

but in the patrimonial theory of Majer and Haller (see Dreitzel, *Absolutismus und ständische Verfassung*, 126).

316. Maier, 'Hegels Schrift 1', 349.
317. *GW14,1[PdR]*, 183 (§219).
318. *AEP-Fr*, 80.
319. Ibid., 36.
320. Ibid., 36–7.
321. On Ulpian, see ibid., 133.
322. Ibid., 82.
323. Ibid., 80.
324. See Schröder, 'Johann Stephan Pütter', 318–19.
325. *AEP-Fr*, 85–6.
326. Ibid., xvi.
327. I thus agree with Stollberg-Rilinger, *Vormünder des Volkes?*, 267 who criticizes Dreitzel and Hofmann on this point.
328. See *GW5[RV]*, 116–17.
329. *AEP-Fr*, 225.
330. Ibid., 162.
331. Ibid., 163.
332. Ibid., 227. See *AF-As*.
333. *AEP-Fr*, 163–4. See my discussion in 3.4.1.
334. See Koskenniemi, *To the Uttermost Parts of the Earth*, 930–9, in particular 939 who establishes a different genealogy, stating that Hegel lifted his terminology from Georg Friedrich von Martens (1756–1821).
335. See Riedel, 'Gesellschaft, bürgerliche', 742–6.
336. See Ada Neschke-Hentschke, 'Frankreich im Zeitalter der Religionskriege: Jean Bodin', in *Politischer Aristotelismus*, ed. Horn and Neschke-Hentschke, 201.
337. Ibid., 199.
338. See Riedel, 'Gesellschaft, bürgerliche', 738–42.
339. *AEP-Fr*, 77–9.
340. Ibid., 79 (italics added).
341. See *BtS-FR2*, 48–52.
342. Stein, *Roman Law in European History*, 62.
343. Ibid. For Hegel's analysis of these concepts, see *GW14,1[PdR]*, 67–8 (§62).
344. See Hofmann, *Repräsentation*, 394.
345. *GW5[RV]*, 194.
346. Hintze, 'The Preconditions of Representative Government', 333.
347. *GUrV*, 44 n. *).
348. *Germania*, 25.
349. *GUrV*, 65; for a similar discussion, compare Möser, *Osnabrückische Geschichte*, 103 n. (a).
350. See *GW5[SdS]*, 334 – I quoted the passage in Section 2.3.1.
351. Thomas, 'The Germania as a literary text', 71 – citing *Agricola* 1.4.39.2.
352. *Institutiones*, 1.iv.
353. Möser, *Osnabrückische Geschichte*, 103 n. (a).
354. Riedel, *Between Tradition and Revolution*, 115.
355. *GW27,3[VWG]*, 1073.
356. *GW14,1[PdR]*, 54 (§40) (original italics and boldface type).

357. *GW14,2[PdR-Beilagen]*, 295. In §89 Heineccius is obviously citing directly from the *Institutiones*, 1.iv – as quoted above. The German 'und doch konnte er verkauft werden vom Vater – früher getötet werden' is Hegel's gloss on the Latin text.
358. *GUrV*, 45.
359. Ibid.
360. Montesquieu, *The Spirit of Laws*, 547.
361. *GUrV*, 45.
362. Weber, *Economy and Society*, 1081.
363. *GUrV*, 56 (original italics).
364. Ibid. (original italics).
365. *LtSR2*, 219.
366. Stollberg-Rilinger, *Vormünder des Volkes?*, 271–2.
367. *ATSK*, 87 (original italics). Weber later repeated similar arguments against the Soviet revolutionary state. The supposed abolition of private property would only exacerbate centralized bureaucratic rule by officials (see Weber, *Economy and Society*, 1453).
368. *ATSK*, 100 (original italics).
369. Ibid., 100–1 (original italics). Majer's thoughts may tell us much about his thinking of the German territorial states and why representation need not necessarily apply, many of them were small. Patrimonial states were even more restricted in size; they never contained a large population and worked best as an integrating part of a larger state system such as the Holy Roman Empire (see ibid., 56).
370. See *GW5[RF]*, 157. Hegel directs this critique against the idea that the democracy established by Theseus for the Greeks could be applied in modern times and for large states.
371. *GUrV*, 64 (italics added, original underlining).
372. *Germania*, 25.
373. *GW5[SdS]*, 338.
374. Weber, *Economy and Society*, 1082.
375. *GUrV*, 65.
376. Ibid., 64 (original italics and capitalization). Majer references *Germania*, 25 where Tacitus describes the different forms of servitude among the Germans. They do not have slaves in the Roman sense, but an unfree population tied to the land and obligated to pay tribute in grain, cattle or cloth.
377. Möser, *Osnabrückische Geschichte*, 103 n. (a).
378. Ibid.
379. *GUrV*, 63.
380. Thomas, 'The Germania as a literary text', 64.
381. Moses Finley, *The Ancient Economy* (London: Hogarth Press, 1985), 181.
382. Ibid.
383. The English word 'loan' has its roots in Middle English as a gift from a superior and is related to the Dutch 'leen' and the German 'lehn' – thus to the system of fiefs (*Lehenswesen*).
384. *GUrV*, 66 – referring to Möser's notorious defence of serfdom, 'Etwas zu Naturgeschichte des Leibeigenthums' in *Patriotische Phantasien* (see *SW4*, 297–302).
385. *GUrV*, 65 (original italics).
386. *Germania*, 20.
387. *GW5[SdS]*, 305.
388. See ibid., 359.

389. This is the difference between the vocation of living 'for' politics and the profession of living 'from' politics, although not entirely mutually exclusive (see Max Weber, 'The Profession and Vocation of Politics', in *Political Writings*, ed. Peter Lassman and Ronald Spiers (Cambridge: Cambridge University Press, 2010), 318).
390. *GW4[NR]*, 455.
391. Ibid.
392. See my discussion in Sections 4.4.1–4.4.2.
393. *Germania*, 13.
394. *GUrV*, 67–8.
395. *Germania*, 13.
396. Ibid.
397. *GUrV*, 166.
398. Ibid.
399. Stollberg-Rilinger, *Vormünder des Volkes?*, 241 – citing Möser's correspondence.
400. *LtSR2*, 93.
401. *TSK1*, 19 (original italics).
402. See *TwSR1*, 7–8.
403. *TSK2*, 553.
404. *ATSK*, 20 (italics added).
405. Ernst-Wolfgang Böckenförde, *Der Staat als sittlicher Staat* (Berlin: Dunker & Humblot, 1978), 16.
406. For my initial discussion, see Section 3.0.1.
407. *ATSK*, 20 (original italics).
408. *GW5[RV]*, 132.
409. Ibid., 116.
410. *TSK1*, 14 (original italics).
411. *GW14,1[PdR]*, 269 (§330).
412. Ibid. (§331).
413. *GW5[RV]*, 166.
414. Ibid.
415. *ATSK*, 54 (original italics).
416. *GW5[RV]*, 167.
417. *TSK1*, 13 (original italics).
418. *GW5[RV]*, 165. Compare Rosenzweig, *Hegel and the State*, 206 n. 296 where he connects this formulation to *AF-As*, 137: 'since it was precisely for the sake of this (property) and its security that the state union was established'.
419. See Maier, 'Hegels Schrift 2', 202; Maier, 'Hegels Schrift 1', 349 n. 63. Earlier in the first version of this essay, Maier indicated how the collective defence of property demonstrated Hegel's connection to the German Enlightenment and natural law, particularly to Carl Gottlieb Svarez (1746–98), the principal architect of the *Allgemeines Landrecht für die Preußischen Staaten* (1792).
420. Harris, *Towards the Sunlight*, 432, 436–7; Pinkard, *Hegel: A Biography*, 74, 78–81.
421. *ATSK*, 10.
422. Ibid., 9.
423. *GW5[RV]*, 166.
424. For a critical discussion on Hegel's assessment of polyarchy within the context of the imperial constitution in contrast to constitutional monarchy, see Bourke, *Hegel's World Revolutions*, 175.
425. *GW5[RV]*, 166–7.

426. *TSK1*, 13
427. *ATSK*., 12 (original italics).
428. *TSK2*, 265–6.
429. See *ATSK*, 131.
430. Ibid., 92, 126–31.
431. *TSK1*, 79–120; *TSK2*, 265–85.
432. See my discussion in 3.0.3 and quote from *ATSK*, 2.
433. See Hoke, 'Hippolithus a Lapide', 120–1.
434. Lapide, *Dissertatio de ratione status*, 36–54, 306–17.
435. Rosenzweig, *Hegel and the State*, 195–6 n. 54 considers Majer as the source for Hegel's discussion of the *Reichsoberhaupt*.
436. Lapide, *Dissertatio de ratione status*, 36.
437. See Meist, 'Anmerkungen', 759–64.
438. *TSK1*, 35–66.
439. Meist, 'Anmerkungen', 760. See the citation from Häberlin which is also very convincing (ibid).
440. Rosenzweig, *Hegel and the State*, 143, 196 n. 58.
441. *TSK1*, 51 (original italics).
442. See my initial analysis in Sections 2.3.3–2.3.6.
443. *GW5[RV]*, 37.
444. *GUrV*, 178.
445. Ibid., 176.
446. *GW5[RV]*, 202.
447. See ibid., 105.
448. See Willoweit, 'Privatfürstenrecht', 791–4.
449. *GW5[RV]*, 116–17.
450. See *ATSK*, 174.
451. For a particular clear assertion of his adoption of Möser's methodology, see *TSK2*, ii, iii, v.
452. Ibid., 279.
453. Ibid.
454. Ibid., 277. For the glory and sovereignty thesis linked intricately to landlordship, see ibid., 553.
455. Aretin and Hammerstein, 'Reich IV', 471.
456. *GW5[RV]*, 15.
457. For an overview of the period focusing on the opposition of the Holy Roman Empire to the French Revolution in Hegel's thought, see Bourke, *Hegel's World Revolutions*, 105–30.
458. *TSK2*, 280 (original italics).
459. See *GW27,1[VWG]*, 453.
460. Ibid.
461. Ibid., 453–4.
462. Ibid., 453. That Hegel used his earlier fragments on the imperial constitution as a basis for his later lectures on the Germanic World seems obvious. The Berlin lectures, transcribed by Griesheim, took up the same analysis. The *Hippolythus* had the same central role as does the discussion of internal or constitutional war.
463. *GW5[RV]*, 25.

464. *HD2*, 48–9; *LtSR1*, 207–13.
465. See *GW5[RV]*, 63, 78, 79–80, 102, 106–7, 115–20.
466. *ATSK*, 171–5.
467. *GW5[RV]*, 166.
468. Ibid., 64–5.
469. Ibid., 187–8.
470. *ATSK*, 15.
471. *GW5[RV]*, 79.
472. *ATSK*, 173 (original italics).
473. *TSK1*, 13 (original italics).
474. *Germania*, 11; Majer makes a similar point with respect to marriage (see *GUrV*, 146–7 n. *), for the pagan Germanic peoples indissoluble. What the Christians had committed to religion for the pagans had been constitutional.
475. *GW5[RV]*, 202.
476. *ATSK*, 172–3.
477. Ibid., 177.
478. *GW5[SdS]*, 330.
479. See ibid., 359.
480. *GW5[RV]*, 117.
481. Maier, 'Hegels Schrift 1', 349.
482. *GW5[RV]*, 165–6.
483. Maier, 'Hegels Schrift 1', 349.
484. Hans Medick, *Naturzustand und Naturgeschichte der bürgerlichen Gesellschaft: die Ursprünge der bürgerlichen Sozialtheorie als Geschichtsphilosophie und Sozialwissenschaft bei Samuel Pufendorf, John Locke und Adam Smith* (Göttingen: Vandenhoeck, 1967).
485. Weber, *Economy and Society*, 212–45.
486. Ibid., 1006–69, 1092–1130.
487. *ATSK*, 9–17; compare Weber, *Economy and Society*, 901–4.
488. Ibid., 54.
489. See Landsberg, *Geschichte der deutschen Rechtswissenschaft*, 454.
490. Catherine Colliot-Thélène, *Le Désenchantement de l'État. De Hegel à Max Weber* (Paris: Les éditions de minuit, 1992).
491. *GW14,1[PdR]*, 204 n. 1 (§258).
492. Maier, 'Hegels Schrift 1', 344 n. 38 – referencing *GW14,1[PdR]*, 201–7 (§258). The argument is repeated with nuance in 'Hegels Schrift 2', 216 n. 42: 'In the philosophy of law, the protection of property through the administration of justice is still an element in the formation of civil society, but no longer of the state; in the philosophy of history, the need for security of property is described as a "principle of opinion".'
493. See Böckenförde, *Der Staat als sittlicher Staat*, 21.
494. *GW14,1[PdR]*, 201 (§258).
495. Böckenförde, *Der Staat als sittlicher Staat*, 21.
496. *GW26,1[VPR]*, 233. In 1818–19.
497. Ibid., 102 (§92) (original italics).
498. Ibid., 511. In 1819–20.
499. Ibid., 77.

4 The Empire of ethical life: Georg Wilhelm Friedrich Hegel

1. Hegel to Windischmann 27 May 1810, in *Briefe von und an Hegel. Band I (1785–1812)*, ed. Johannes Hoffmeister (Hamburg: Felix Meiner, 1969), 314 (italics added).
2. Rosenzweig, *Hegel and the State*, 128–9. For a rejection of the ideas surrounding this crisis and the supposed revolution they had on Hegel's thought in Frankfurt, see Harris, *Towards the Sunlight*, 258–70. Harris deflects the issue to Hölderlin's mental state through discussing later letters between Hegel and Sinclair. No mention is made of the historical context, however, in which Hegel, Sinclair and Hölderlin found themselves in Frankfurt and Jena nor of the personal nature of the crisis so described by Hegel.
3. See *GW15[FsG]*, 231–2.
4. Maier, 'Hegels Schrift 1', 349.
5. *GW2[FSII]*, 141.
6. Koselleck, 'Crisis', 358, 377.
7. See *GW2[FSII]*, 395–581.
8. See Harris, *Towards the Sunlight*, 419–34.
9. *GW2[FSII]*, 569.
10. Harris, *Towards the Sunlight*, 428.
11. *GW2[FSII]*, 103.
12. See *GW8[JSIII]*, 181–2.
13. Ibid., 179; *GW15[FsG]*, 207–49.
14. *GW5[RV]*, 216.
15. Ibid.
16. For some suggestions, see Rolf-Peter Horstmann, 'Anmerkungen', 343 in *GW8[JSIII]*.
17. Koselleck, 'Crisis', 358.
18. See *GW8[JSIII]*, 179 (original italics and capitalization).
19. Ibid. (in the margins, original italics).
20. Ibid., 179–80.
21. Ibid., 180 (in the margins, original italics).
22. See my discussion in Section 1.4.4.
23. *GW5[RV]*, 157–8.
24. Ibid., 158.
25. Ibid.
26. See *GW2[FSII]*, 141. Ian Harris, 'Hegel, Jesus, and Political Theory', *Leicester University Discussion Papers in Politics* 92, no. 10 (1992): 1–21.
27. See *GW2[FSII]*, 125–6.
28. Dieter Henrich, 'Einleitung des Herausgebers: Vernunft in Verwirklichung', in *Hegels Philosophie des Rechts. Die Vorlesung von 1819/20 in einer Nachschrift* (Frankfurt am Main: Suhrkamp, 1983), 17.
29. *GW14,1[PdR]*, 280 (§357).
30. Ibid., 280–1 (§358) (original italics).
31. Ibid. (original italics).
32. See *GW2[FSII]*, 125–6; Henrich, 'Logical Form and Real Totality', 242.
33. See *GW1[FSI]*, 374–5.
34. *GW5[RV]*, 95.
35. For my analysis, see Sections 4.3.1–4.3.4.

36. See *GW14,1[PdR]*, 281 (§360).
37. See *GW1[FSI]*, 359–60; compare ibid., 3. Hegel's first entry in his diary (26 July 1785) recounting the facts he had learnt from a sermon delivered on Melanchthon's Augsburg Confession (1530).
38. *GW14,1[PdR]*, 274 (§342).
39. Schiller, 'Deutsche Größe'.
40. See Carl Gottlieb Svarez, 'Kurze Nachricht von dem neuen Preussischen Gesetzbuche und von dem Verfahren bey der Ausarbeitung desselben', *Annalen der Gesetzgebung und Rechtsgelehrsamkeit in den preussischen Staaten* 8 (1791): xxii–xxiv.
41. For the institutionalism debate, see Henrich, 'Einleitung des Herausgebers', 30–8; Jean-François Kervégan, *The Actual and the Rational: Hegel and Objective Spirit* (Chicago: University of Chicago Press, 2018), 279–330; Terry Pinkard, *Hegel's Phenomenology: The Sociality of Reason* (Cambridge: Cambridge University Press, 1994), 269–343; Robert B. Pippin, *Hegel's Practical Philosophy* (Cambridge: Cambridge University Press, 2008), 239–72; Benno Zabel, 'The Institutional Turn in Hegel's Philosophy of Right', *Hegel Bulletin* 31 (2015): 80–104.
42. See *GW14,1[PdR]*, 226–9 (§273), already analysed in the first chapter in which each of the regular Aristotelian *forma Reipublicae* is sublated in constitutional monarchy as the final historical form. There is an obvious parallel between this discussion and *System der Sittlichkeit* in which the aristocratic and democratic forms are present in the organization of the estates and where monarchy appears as the reality of ethical life.
43. See Wieacker, *A History of Private Law*, 249–56; Haakonssen, 'German Natural Law', 260–78, 279, 283. Thomasius and his school represented a historical and relative form of natural law, Wolff a metaphysical antagonism to the eclectic and empirical paradigm.
44. See Section 2.3.1.
45. Villey, 'Das römische Recht in Hegels Rechtsphilosophie', 134.
46. For a similarly critical appraisal of the French Revolution in Hegel's thought, see Bourke, *Hegel's World Revolutions*, 131–62. Bourke has displaced the older literature, most notably Joachim Ritter, *Hegel and the French Revolution* (Cambridge, MA: MIT Press, 1984).
47. Svarez, 'Kurze Nachricht', xxiv.
48. Both were published by Georg Mollat (1863–1947) during the Second Empire (1871–1918), as a type of eulogy to Otto von Bismarck (1815–98) which made imperial patriotism and lack of nationalism laughable. The manuscripts were thus central to the political imagination of the unified German nation state under Prussia and consequently had an important role to play in the mythology of the Bismarck Hegelians. For a study of the most notorious of the Bismarck Hegelians, see Nathaniel Boyd, 'Erich Kaufmann et la théorie hégélienne du droit international', in *Hegel et le droit*, ed. and trans. Élodie Djordjevic (Editions Panthéon-Assas), 147–70. Rosenzweig also fell prey to this conception. He thus traced an underground line of development from the *Verfassungsschrift* through to the *Paulskirche*, the failure of the 1848 revolution, and then to 18 January 1871, the *Reichsgründung* when King Wilhelm II (1859–1941) was declared German emperor in the *Galerie des glaces* (Versailles) (see *Hegel and the State*, 163). Still, in Hegel's recognition that the power of a conqueror (Archduke Karl) was necessary to unite the common people with their territorial estates into a state, Jaeschke, *Hegel Handbuch*, 96 has considered that this was 'a perhaps unpopular but nevertheless clairvoyant prognosis' which, some seventy

years later, became true with Bismarck. Although far more historically and critically nuanced, the connection thus remains.

49. *GW5[RV]*, 169–70.
50. See Jaeschke, *Hegel Handbuch*, 97.
51. Krüger, *Die Landständische Verfassung*, 28.
52. *GW5[RV]*, 169.
53. *GW4[NR]*, 474. See Heinz Kimmerle, 'Die Staatsverfassung als "Konstituierung der absoluten sittlichen Identität" in der Jenaer Konzeption des "Naturrechts". Der Spekulative Charakter von Hegels politischer Philosophie', in *Hegels Rechtsphilosophie*, ed. Lucas and Pöggeler, 137.
54. *GW5[SdS]*, 314–15. For Majer's coinage of the neologism *Unformlichkeit* to describe the evolution from the simple to the complex to the dissolutive and its derivation from the earlier public law literature, see Section 3.0.3.
55. *GW5[RV]*, 174.
56. *GW5[SdS]*, 340 (italics added).
57. Ibid., 345.
58. See *GW26,3[VPR]*, 1442–3.
59. *GW5[RV]*, 173.
60. Ibid., 167. See *GW26,1[VPR]*, 233. I have discussed this in Section 3.5.3 in reference to Majer's raw concept of the state as a defence structure for private property and freedom.
61. *GW5[RV]*, 172.
62. Harris, *Towards the Sunlight*, 426; see *GW26,3[VPR]*, 1442–3.
63. *GW4[NR]*, 425.
64. See Dan Edelstein, *On the Spirit of Rights* (Chicago: University of Chicago Press, 2018), 172–91.
65. Hegel owned an edition of Sieyès's collected works (see *GW31,2[ABH]*, 1290). He had documents related to the French Revolution, including the constitutions of 1795, 1797, 1797–8 (see ibid., 1341–3). He also owned works by the liberal revolutionary, historian of the French Revolution and biographer of Sieyès Konrad Engelbert Oelsner (1764–1828) (ibid., 1201–8). Hegel had personally met Oelsner – considered the most important German eyewitness to the French Revolution – while in Bern during the latter's exile from the Reign of Terror. See Hegel to Schelling (24 December 1794) in *Briefe. Band I*, 11–12.
66. Riedel, 'Gesellschaft, bürgerliche', 763.
67. *GW4[NR]*, 457 (original italics).
68. *GW5[SdS]*, 339–40 (italics added). Hegel took this language of *Potenzen* from Friedrich Wilhelm Joseph von Schelling, *Einleitung zu seinem Entwurf eines Systems der Naturphilosophie oder Ueber den Begriff der speculativen Physik* (Leipzig: Gabler, 1799), 38–83, 190–5, 236–42. It referred to a dynamic sequence of steps or interrelated levels in his philosophy of identity and nature. Evidently, Hegel is using it as a type of structuring principle for the power of the public laws (see Wolfgang Förster, 'Potenz, Potenzen', in *HWPh7*, 1167–9).
69. *GW5[SdS]*, 334.
70. *GW5[RV]*, 202.
71. Ibid.
72. Ibid., 111.
73. See my discussion in Sections 2.1.3 and 2.2.6.
74. Hintze, 'The Preconditions of Representative Government', 333.

75. *GW5[RV]*, 112 (italics added).
76. Ibid., 100.
77. Ibid., 101.
78. *GW8[JSIII]*, 264, in the margins.
79. *GW5[RV]*, 112 (italics added).
80. Ibid., 102.
81. Ibid., 178.
82. Ibid., 174.
83. *GW4[NR]*, 427.
84. *AN*, 201.
85. *GW4[NR]*, 468 (original italics).
86. Hintze, 'The Preconditions of Representative Government', 339.
87. Walter Benjamin, 'Theses on the Philosophy of History', in *Illuminations: Essays and Reflections*, ed. Hannah Arendt, trans. Harry Zohn (New York: Schocken, 1969), 261. This position is confirmed in the recent literature: 'Antiquity, particularly Roman antiquity, was a living, breathing, visceral world for many of the Revolutionaries' (see Beatrice da Vela and Benjamin Earley, 'Senatus and Sénat: the Reception of the Roman Senate during the Radical Stage of the French Revolution (1792–4)', *Classical Receptions Journal* 7, no. 1 (2015): 47). By contrast, Greek antiquity was Hegel's model (as well as Hölderlin's in *Hyperion* (1797–9)).
88. For the details and genesis of the manuscript, see Meist, 'Editorischer Bericht', 662–70. Early in 1802, Hegel had announced he would deliver free lectures on Fichte's natural law.
89. Villey, 'Das römische Recht in Hegels Rechtsphilosophie', 134.
90. Immanuel Kant, 'On the Common Saying: "This May Be True in Theory, but It Does Not Apply in Practice', in *Political Writings*, 76.
91. *GW9[PdG]*, 260 (original italics).
92. Maximilien Robespierre, *Oeuvres de Maximilien Robespierre*, ed. Albert Laponneraye and Armand Carrel (Paris: Faubourg Saint-Denis, 1840), vol. 1, 46, 51.
93. Ibid., vol. 3, 544.
94. Ibid.
95. Ibid., 545.
96. Ibid.
97. Ibid., 550.
98. Ibid., 553.
99. *GW5[RV]*, 172. Meist, 'Anmerkungen', 781–2 isolates some of the possible sources of Hegel's polemic – notably Rousseau, Fichte and Robespierre.
100. Fichte, *Grundlage des Naturrechts*, 198.
101. See *Politics* 1253a.
102. *GW4[NR]*, 481.
103. Fichte, *Grundlage des Naturrechts*, 202.
104. See Reinhart Koselleck, *Preußen zwischen Reform und Revolution. Allgemeines Landrecht, Verwaltung und soziale Bewegung von 1791 bis 1848* (Stuttgart: Klett, 1975), 108.
105. Fichte, *Grundlage des Naturrechts*, 329. The *Allgemeines Landrecht* artificially reproduced the system of estates in which the protection of the nobility was viewed in similar terms, with privileged access to education (see Koselleck, *Reform und Revolution*, 108).
106. See *GW5[RV]*, 112–14; Maier, 'Hegels Schrift 2', 208–9.

107. *GW5[RV]*, 113.
108. The precise wording and conceptuality of both discussions are also strikingly similar to those of Sieyès. On this connection specifically with relation to constitutional monarchy, see Guy Planty-Bonjour, 'Du Régime représentatif selon Sieyès à la monarchie constitutionnelle selon Hegel', in *Hegels Rechtsphilosophie*, ed. Lucas and Pöggeler, 13–35.
109. *GW5[RV]*, 173.
110. Ibid., 174, 140.
111. Ibid., 174. For possible sources (Herder, Schlözer, Justi), see Meist, 'Anmerkungen', 782–3.
112. Emmanuel Sieyès, 'Views of the Executive Means Available to the Representatives of France in 1789', in *Political Writings: Including the Debate between Sieyès and Tom Paine in 1791*, ed. and trans. Michael Sonenscher (Indianapolis: Hackett, 2003), 5; compare Sieyès, 'What Is the Third Estate?', in *Political Writings*, 134. In the latter instance, this demonstrates the reliance on the method of rational natural law. For Böckenförde and Rossum, 'Organ', 568 n. 289, Sieyès's social mechanism was an exact continuation of the clockwork metaphor comparison begun by Hobbes.
113. *GW5[RV]*, 131.
114. Ibid., 149.
115. *GW5[JN]*, 493 (original italics and boldface type).
116. *GW5[SdS]*, 345.
117. Ibid., 280.
118. Taubes, *Occidental Eschatology*, 65 – the reference is not to Hegel but to the Tübingen dialectical theologian Ferdinand Christian Baur (1792–1860).
119. See *GW5[SdS]*, 341.
120. Ibid., 358.
121. Kant, 'Perpetual Peace', 101.
122. Ibid.
123. Ibid.
124. See da Vela and Earley, 'Senatus and Sénat', 51.
125. *GW5[SdS]*, 340.
126. Ibid., 348–9 – the reference is to Kant, *The Metaphysics of Morals*, 124–5.
127. See Bien, Dierse and Winckelmann, 'Despotie, Despotismus', 141–2.
128. Fichte, *Grundlage des Naturrechts*, 13.
129. Ibid., 157–8 (original italics).
130. *De legibus*, II.33 and *De republica* III.16. See Marco Rampazzo Bazzan, 'Das Ephorat bei J.G. Fichte', *Fichte-Studien* 27 (2006): 122 also with critical reference to the older literature on the origin of the Ephorate in Fichte and its possible assonance with Althusian Monarchomachism.
131. See da Vela and Earley, 'Senatus and Sénat', 52.
132. Ibid., 50–2.
133. *GW5[SdS]*, 344–5.
134. Böckenförde and Rossum, 'Organ', 571.
135. Ibid.
136. See Sieyès, 'Views of the Executive Means', 24–5.
137. Sieyès, 'What Is the Third Estate?', 135 (original italics).
138. *GW5[RV]*, 113, in the margins.
139. See *EG*, 53–4 and, more generally 52–64.

140. Eulau, 'Theories of Federalism', 662. This might be another way Wolff influenced Pütter.
141. *GW5[NR]*, 420. See Wieacker, *A History of Private Law in Europe*, 254.
142. *GW4[DS]*, 9–12; *GW13[E1817]*, 19–20 (§§7–8). This followed Leibniz's famous treatise *Nova methodus discendae docendaeque jurisprudentiae* (1667).
143. *GW14,1[PdR]*, 30 (§3).
144. See Christian Wolff, *Vernünftige Gedanken von dem gesellschaftlichen Leben der Menschen, und insonderheit dem gemeinen Wesen, 'Deutsche Politik'*, ed. Hasso Hoffmann (Munich: C.H. Beck, 2004), 57.
145. *GW13[E1817]*, 5.
146. *GW19[E1827]*, 36 (§9), 55–7 (§§37–9).
147. See John Edward Toews, *Hegelianism: The Path Toward a Dialectical Humanism (1805–1841)* (Cambridge: Cambridge University Press, 1980), 1–9.
148. *GW30,3[VGP]*, 1296.
149. See Heinz Kimmerle, *Das Problem der Abgeschlossenheit des Denkens. Hegels 'System der Philosophie' in den Jahren 1800–1804* (Bonn: Grundmann, 1982), 120–2, 126, 127. Kimmerle is referencing the 1804 Jena system outline (see *GW6[JSI]*, 264). Both authors are central to the objective logic (see, for example, *GW11[WLI]*, 88–9, 95–6, 246–9, 376–9). For Leibniz in this context, see David Ingram, 'Hegel on Leibniz and Individuation', *Kant-Studien* 76 (1985): 420–35.
150. *GW5[SdS]*, 325. This is a rewording of Baruch Spinoza, 'Ethics', in *Complete Works*, ed. Michael L. Morgan and trans. Samuel Shirley (Hackett, 2002), I, Proposition 15, 224: 'Whatever is, is in God, and nothing can be or be conceived without God. Now modes (Def. 5) cannot be or be conceived without substance; therefore, they can be only in the divine nature and can be conceived only through the divine nature. But nothing exists except substance and modes (Ax. I).'
151. Ibid., II, Proposition 7, 247.
152. Ibid., I, Appendix, 239.
153. *GW4[GW]*, 342.
154. *GW4[DS]*, 69.
155. Ibid.
156. See Immanuel Kant, *Metaphysical Foundations of Natural Science*, ed. and trans. Michael Friedman (Cambridge: Cambridge University Press, 2012), 33–92.
157. *GW4[DS]*, 5. This characterization was first Kant's which he contrasted with (Humean) scepticism. It was a way of describing a pre-critical metaphysics that was organized by a transcendent ground of identity (Cartesianism) that structured the phenomenal realm (see Immanuel Kant, *The Critique of Pure Reason*, ed. and trans. Paul Guyer and Allen W. Wood (Cambridge: Cambridge University Press, 1998), 653–8). Hegel's discussion follows Fichte and Schelling in particular where the opposition had become one between dogmatism and idealism (see Friedrich Wilhelm Joseph Schelling, 'Philosophische Briefe über Dogmatismus und Kritizismus', in *Werke 3*, ed. Hartmut Buchner, Wilhelm Jacobs, Annemarie Pieper (Stuttgart: Frommann-Holzboog, 1982), 66–75. For the debate with Fichte, where the opposition is most clearly stated, see Annemarie Pieper, 'Editorischer Bericht', 41–4.
158. Kimmerle, *Abgeschlossenheit des Denkens*, 139, 140.
159. See Barbara Stollberg-Rilinger, *Der Staat als Maschine. Zur politischen Metaphorik des absoluten Fürstenstaats* (Berlin: Dunker & Humblot, 1986), 227–9, 210–16, 224, 230. Johann Gottlieb Fichte, *Beitrag zur Berichtigung der Ortheile des Publikums über die französische Revolution. Erster Theil. Zur Beurtheilung Ihrer Rechtsmäßigkeit*

(1793), 91, 87, 100–2 had critiqued the metaphor as characteristic of monarchy. It led to the slavery of all and the freedom of one – reform absolutism did not exist. The tendency of every monarchy was internally to absolute rule or autocracy, externally to universal monarchy. His assertion of the culture of freedom directly implied a withering away of the monarchical state. Hegel owned the book (see *GW31,2[ABH]*, 1045–6). Dreitzel, *Absolutismus und ständische Verfassung*, 112 has rightly claimed that the earlier metaphor had nothing to do with authoritarian, military or disciplinary organization, but belonged to reform absolutism and was actually much closer to the later idea of organism with its conception of the monarch as guardian of the constitution.

160. Gottfried Wilhelm Leibniz, *Monadology: A New Translation and Guide*, ed. and trans. Lloyd Strickland (Edinburgh: Edinburgh University Press, 2014), 14 (§1).
161. Ibid. (§3).
162. *GW30,3[VGP]*, 1282.
163. *GW5[SdS]*, 340.
164. See Leibniz, *Monadology*, 27 (§64).
165. *GW5[JN]*, 503.
166. Böckenförde and Rossum, 'Organ', 559.
167. *GW5[SdS]*, 328.
168. See Kimmerle, 'Die Staatsverfassung', 132.
169. Immanuel Kant, *The Critique of the Power of Judgement*, ed. and trans. Paul Guyer (Cambridge: Cambridge University Press, 2000), 244–7, also see 234.
170. *GW4[DS]*, 69.
171. Gross, *Empire and Sovereignty*, 335.
172. Leibniz, *Monadology*, 14 (§2).
173. *GW5[SdS]*, 339–40.
174. Lübbe-Wolff, 'Über das Fehlen von Grundrechten', 425.
175. Henrich, 'Einleitung des Herausgebers', 17.
176. See Section 2.2.6.
177. Leibniz, *Monadology*, 15 (§6).
178. *GW5[SdS]*, 334. Hegel is still operating under a 'Platonic inspired' concept of the *polis* of the Germanic *Volk* made up of families, groups and estates. Only after *System der Sittlichkeit* will he take up the Aristotelian critique of Plato's 'unitary state' (see *GW8[JSIII]*, 233–4, in the margins).
179. Harris, *Towards the Sunlight*, 426.
180. Ibid., n. 1.
181. *GW5[SdS]*, 357–9.
182. Yitzhak Y. Melamed, "Omnis determinatio est negatio" – Determination, Negation and Self-Negation in Spinoza, Kant, and Hegel', in *Spinoza and German Idealism*, ed. Eckart Forster and Yitzhak Y. Melamed (Cambridge: Cambridge University Press, 2012), 175–96.
183. *GW5[SdS]*, 333.
184. *GW30,3[VGP]*, 1278.
185. *GW5[SdS]*, 327.
186. Böckenförde and Rossum, 'Organ', 562. The reference is to a later edition of the *Elementa* (see *IG*, 1).
187. See *GW5[SdS]*, 338.
188. Böckenförde and Rossum, 'Organ', 562 (italics added).
189. *GW5[SdS]*, 325.

190. Ibid., 328.
191. Ibid., 314, 327, 331–5, 339, 340. The exact genealogy is insufficiently traced in Böckenförde and Rossum, 'Organ', 584–6. Preference there is given strictly to the *Rechtsphilosophie* which is contrasted rather simplistically to the *Verfassungsschrift*, with little or no attention paid to the actual merging of the concepts in the same period as Hegel works his way towards his fully fledged idea of organism. Aside from the reference to *System der Sittlichkeit*, see *GW4[ÜaI]*, 151, 159, 163; *GW4[GW]*, 342, 361 and *GW4[NR]*, 478.
192. Leibniz, *Monadology*, 26 (§61).
193. *GW5[SdS]*, 326, 325.
194. Ibid., 334.
195. Ibid., 361.
196. For my extended discussion, see Section 3.4.1.
197. *GW5[RV]*, 167.
198. Ibid., 166 (italics added).
199. *GW4[DS]*, 63 (original italics).
200. Ibid. Hegel followed Friedrich Wilhelm Joseph von Schelling, 'Darstellung meines Systems der Philosophie' in *Sämtliche Werke, Erste Abtheilung, Vierter Band*, ed. K. F. A. Schelling (Stuttgart: Cotta, 1856–61), 115–212.
201. Ibid., 115.
202. *GW5[SdS]*, 325–6.
203. Ibid., 326.
204. *GW2[FSII]*, 11. See also Henrich, 'Logical Form and Real Totality', 241–67.
205. See *GW4[DS]*, 5.
206. Ingram, 'Hegel on Leibniz and Individuation', 427:

> Hegel returns to Leibniz in abolishing the distinction between sensibility and understanding and, in effect, reproaches Kant for grounding real identity in spatio-temporal location, how does he circumvent the Leibnizian *aporia* [of pre-established harmony]? He does so by conceiving reason dialectically. Stated differently, he retrieves those concepts of reflection which Kant transfers from pure understanding to the *jenseits* of sensibility, namely, difference, opposition, matter, etc., and extends their range of application to include the very reason which grounds reality as such. (original italics)

207. *GW4[DS]*, 14.
208. Ibid., 58.
209. Manfred Riedel, 'System, Struktur', in *GG6*, 303 (italics added).
210. See *GW4[DS]*, 9–12.
211. Kimmerle, *Abgeschlossenheit des Denkens*, 122.
212. *GW4[DS]*, 68.
213. Ibid., 69.
214. Ibid., 68.
215. Ibid.
216. See Birgit Sandkaulen, 'Die Ontologie der Substanz, der Begriff der Subjektivität und die Faktizität des Einzelnen. Hegels reflexionslogische "Widerlegung" der Spinozanischen Metaphysik', in *Internationales Jahrbuch des Deutschen Idealismus*, ed. Karl Ameriks and Jürgen Stolzenberg (Berlin: de Gruyter, 2008), 243.
217. See *GW4[ÜaI]*, 135.
218. Kimmerle, 'Abgeschlossenheit des Denkens', 138.

219. *GW2[FSII]*, 342.
220. Kimmerle, 'Abgeschlossenheit des Denkens', 140.
221. *GW4[DS]*, 68.
222. See *GW5[SdS]*, 334.
223. *GW4[DS]*, 23 (italics added).
224. Leibniz, *Monadology*, 24, 27 (§§51, 62).
225. *GW4[DS]*, 65.
226. *GW5[SdS]*, 326.
227. See Kimmerle, *Abgeschlossenheit des Denkens*, 126 – this is a quote from Leibniz's correspondence. The source is apparently Neo-Platonic (see ibid., n. 183).
228. *GW5[VNR]*, 465.
229. See *GW5[SdS]*, 311.
230. Ibid., 325.
231. *GW4[NR]*, 481.
232. *GW30,1[VGP]*, 172.
233. *GW4[DS]*, 14.
234. *GW19[E1827]*, 157 (§194) (original italics).
235. Ibid.
236. Ingram, 'Hegel on Leibniz and Individuation', 430, 427.
237. *GW5[SdS]*, 325.
238. Ibid., 334 (original italics).
239. Ibid., 279; compare 289 where this is developed in the natural relations of the house community.
240. Ibid., 280.
241. *GW4[NR]*, 449.
242. Ibid., 348.
243. Rosenkranz, *Hegels Leben*, 132 (original italics).
244. Stolleis, *Geschichte des öffentlichen Rechts*, 318.
245. For the earlier importance of Mainz and Leibniz's role, see Schröder, 'Reich versus Territorien?', 134–43, particularly 141; Schröder, *Trust*, 137–54.
246. The trips to Mainz took place in spring 1798 and September 1800 (see Harris, *Towards the Sunlight*, 431, 432 n. 1, 458, 475; compare Pinkard, *Hegel: A Biography*, 84).
247. Wilhelm Dilthey, 'Die Jugendgeschichte Hegels', in *Gesammelte Schriften. Band 4* (Stuttgart: Teubner, 1990 (sixth edition)), 127–9. For translated excerpts of the *Caesarinus Fürstenerius*, see Leibniz, *Political Writings*, 111–20.
248. Dilthey, 'Die Jugendgeschichte Hegels', 128.
249. Schröder, 'Reich versus Territorien?', 134.
250. See Maier, 'Hegels Schrift 2', 213; Meist, 'Zur Textedition', lii; Rosenzweig, *Hegel and the State*, 150, 198 n. 107.
251. Pape, 'Revolution und Reichsverfassung', 47–8.
252. Burgdorf, 'Imperial Reform', 404. For Napoleon's opinion of Dalberg, see Pape, 'Revolution und Reichsverfassung', 68; compare Rosenzweig, *Hegel and the State*, 198 n. 107. Even after the dissolution of the Empire, Dalberg played a central role in the *Rheinbund* as *Fürstprimas* (Prince Primate) (see *Rheinbunds-Akte*, Article IV). For a translation of Dalberg's work *Von der wahren Grenzen der Wirksamkeit des Staats* (1793) in English, see Douglas Moggach, *What Is a State For? Karl von Dalberg's Critique of Liberalism and the Defence of Enlightened Absolutism* (Anthem Press, 2026). Hegel's period in Bamberg (1807–8) as a newspaper editor reveals his

interest in Napoleon's cultural policy, but also his attempt to counteract mistrust in the confederation army which saw French troops once again deployed on German soil. Hegel weighed in against reactionary forces, like the Russian Cossacks. This would have aligned with the interests of both Dalberg and Napoleon. For Hegel's activity as newspaper editor, see Manfred Baum and Kurt Rainer Meist, 'Politik und Philosophie in der Bamberger Zeitung: Dokumente zu Hegels Redacktionstätigkeit 1807–1808', *Hegel-Studien* 10 (1975): 87–127.

253. See *GW27,2[VWG]*, 755–60.
254. See Maier, 'Hegels Schrift 2', 210.
255. *GW5[RV]*, 154.
256. Dreitzel, *Absolutismus und ständische Verfassung*, 121.
257. Harris, *Towards the Sunlight*, 429–30 n. 2 has argued that the first *Ständeschrift* provides evidence for a dictatorship of the bourgeoisie, Hegel the most radical of the pamphleteers. For a more critical position, see Scheel, *Süddeutsche Jakobiner*, 329. Hegel may have belonged to the left wing, but he was no radical.
258. See Mandt, 'Tyrannis, Despotie', 678.
259. Hegel to Niethammer (29 August 1807), in *Briefe. Band 1*, 185. The German theologian, philosopher and educational reformer Friedrich Niethammer (1766–1848) was a lifelong friend of Hegel's; they had first met as students at the Tübinger Stift.
260. Ibid.
261. For the regulative ideal thesis, see Harris, *Night Thoughts*, 139, 141 n. 4.
262. *GW5[SdS]*, 312–13 (original italics).
263. Ibid., 328.
264. See *GW27,2[VWG]*, 755–60; compare *GW5[JN]*, 492.
265. See Ernst-Wolfgang Böckenförde, 'Bemerkung zum Verhältnis von Staat und Religion bei Hegel', in *Staat, Recht, Freiheit*, 136–7.
266. *GW8[JSIII]*, 263 (original italics).
267. See Ian Hunter, 'Public Law and the Limits of Philosophy: German Idealism and the Religious Constitution', *Critical Inquiry* 44, no. 3 (2019): 529.
268. *GW1[FSI]*, 360.
269. Ibid.
270. *GW14,2[PdR-Beilagen]*, 721. Hegel is drawing on the work of Goethe's secretary Friedrich Wilhelm Riemer (1774–1845). I follow the analysis of Joachim Ritter, '"Politik" und "Ethik" in der praktischen Philosophie des Aristoteles', in *Metaphysik und Politik. Erweiterte Neuausgabe* (Frankfurt am Main: Suhrkamp, 2018), 111–12.
271. Ibid., 112; compare *GW14,1[PdR]*, 140–1 (§150).
272. *GW1[FSI]*, 360.
273. *GW4[GW]*, 316.
274. *GW4[DS]*, 12 (original italics).
275. *GW14,1[PdR]*, 274 (§341).
276. See Joachim Whaley, *Germany and the Holy Roman Empire, Vol. I: From Maximilian to the Peace of Westphalia 1493–1648* (Oxford: Oxford University Press, 2012), 625.
277. See Whaley, *Germany and the Holy Roman Empire, Vol. II*, 193.
278. Whaley, *Germany and the Holy Roman Empire, Vol. I*, 625.
279. *GW5[RV]*, 22.
280. See *GW20[E1830]*, 530–41 (§552).
281. Maier, 'Hegels Schrift 2', 212.

282. See *GW5[SdS]*, 359. Again, it is most likely that Hegel's engagement with the *Allgemeines Landrecht* shaped his perception. Crime and punishment are the core focus: the machinery of legislation in a machine state. Although his reflections in *System der Sittlichkeit* predate the *Code Civil*, the latter was published in 1804 so debates surrounding it too could have entered into his considerations on the subject.
283. Carl Schmitt, 'Die Lage der europäischen Rechtswissenschaft (1943/44)', in *Verfassungsrechtliche Aufsätze aus den Jahren 1924–1954. Materialien zu einer Verfassungslehre* (Berlin: Duncker & Humblot, 2003), 428. Schmitt is referring to the *Naturrechtsaufsatz*, but the same conditions apply to *System der Sittlichkeit*. These sections on Hegel are unfortunately not included in the English translation (see Armin von Bogdandy et al. (eds), *Carl Schmitt's European Jurisprudence* (Baden-Baden: Nomos, 2022), 9–47).
284. *GW9[PdG]*, 236. See also ibid., 255.
285. It is to this extent that I disagree with Hunter, 'Public Law and the Limits of Philosophy', 529, 542–4. The religious constitution, the relativistic juridical framework as he terms it, is Hegel's starting point in Bern, in the *Verfassungsschrift* and in his maturity. The fact that the formation of law developed into a separate (secular) doctrine, through bracketing religious civil war that led to toleration, was precisely part of the material – or 'philosophical foundation' – that shaped Hegel's concept of the state. Further, Hunter simplifies public law. It is practically impossible to separate the positive sources completely from philosophical doctrine – even though he rightly pinpoints the most successful author to do so: Moser (ibid., 537–9). While Moser indeed rejected the speculations of universal public law, he still employed natural law and the Bible. We have also seen the extent to which a purely positive analysis was practically unable to avoid the philosophical problems of the *forma Reipublicae* and sovereignty. In any case, Moser is the exception to the rule. Pütter already revived the issue of the *forma Reipublicae* and universal public law. It would seem rather artificial to separate the most famous public lawyer of the last generation and his methodological approaches from the collection of imperial positive laws he set out to systematize with them.
286. *GW14,1[PdR]*, 218 (§270) (original italics).
287. Ibid.
288. Böckenförde, 'Staat und Religion', 122–3 (original italics). He is referencing *Philosophie des Rechts* §261 addition and §260.
289. See *GW1[FSI]*, 360–1.
290. *GW5[SdS]*, 357.
291. *GW1[FSI]*, 359; *GW4[GW]*, 317.
292. Ibid.
293. See *GW1[FSI]*, 361. Perhaps there is some prescience to be noted here. In Berlin on 25 June 1830, Hegel delivered a speech on the three-hundredth anniversary of the Augsburg Confession (see *GW16*, 311–22). This could also cement his relation to Melanchthon's Protestant Aristotelianism.
294. *GW5[RV]*, 99.
295. Ibid.
296. *GW14,1[PdR]*, 221 (§270) (original italics).
297. Ibid., 214.
298. Böckenförde, 'Staat und Religion', 124 (italics added).
299. *GW30,3[VGP]*, 855. Hegel also endorsed Rixner in the lectures of 1822–3 (see *GW30,2[VGP]*, 517).

300. I have treated these issues extensively, see Nathaniel Boyd, 'Hegel's Hobbes: From the Historical Context of the Constitution to Conscience and Consciousness', *History of Political Thought* 40, no. 2 (2019): 327–56.
301. Hobbes, *Leviathan*, 471 (original emphasis).
302. Ibid., 249.
303. Thomas Hobbes, *On the Citizen*, trans. and ed. Richard Tuck and Michael Silverthorne (Cambridge: Cambridge University Press, 1998), 54, 55.
304. Boyd, 'Hegel's Hobbes', 333.
305. The argument is strikingly similar to his earlier opposition to Fichte. As Harris, *Night Thoughts*, 110 pointed out, in *System der Sittlichkeit* and the *Naturrechtsaufsatz* Hegel was determined to treat Hobbes and Fichte together.
306. *GW30,3[VGP]*, 1293. Hegel's views were in all likelihood drawn from the Earl of Clarendon (1609–1674) and his account of the English Revolution. Hegel owned the volumes of the *History of the Rebellion and Civil Wars in England* (1641) as well as Clarendon's autobiography (1660–7) (see *GW31,3[ABH]*, 1023–30). In his last years in exile before his death, Clarendon viciously attacked *Leviathan*.
307. Taddäus Anselm Rixner, *Handbuch der Geschichte der Philosophie. Dritter Band* (Seidel, 1823), 31 (italics added). This is presumably a quote from Pufendorf, but I have been unable to locate the source.
308. Étienne Balibar, *Identity and Difference: John Locke and the Invention of Consciousness*, ed. Stella Sanford, trans. Warren Montag (London: Verso, 2013), 104–5 (original italics).
309. See Martin Brecht and Jörg Sandberger, 'Hegels Begegnung mit der Theologie im Tübinger Stift. Eine neue Quelle für die Studienzeit Hegels', *Hegel-Studien* 5 (1969): 47–81. The evidence is critically assessed in ibid., 47–51.
310. Noel Malcolm, 'Hobbes and the European Republic of Letters', in *Aspects of Hobbes* (Oxford: Oxford University Press, 2002), 464, 532. Thomasius produced an abridged translation of the *Historia Ecclesiastica*.
311. Hinrich Rüping, 'Thomasius und seine Schüler im brandenburgischen Staat', in *Humanismus und Naturrecht in Berlin Brandenburg Preussen: Ein Tagungsbericht*, ed. Hans Thieme (Berlin: de Gruyter, 1979), 80.
312. Wieacker, *A History of Private Law*, 252–3.
313. *GW5[SdS]*, 328.
314. *GW30,3[VGP]*, 1293.
315. *GW27,4[VWG]*, 1557.
316. Rixner, *Handbuch*, 31.
317. See Boyd, 'Pufendorf on Confessional Strife', 23–32.
318. Samuel Pufendorf, *The Divine Feudal Law: Or, Covenants with Mankind, Represented*, trans. Theophilus Dorrington, ed. Simone Zurbuchen (Indianapolis: Liberty Fund, 2002), 26 (original capitalization).
319. Ibid., 27.
320. Ibid., 33.
321. Dreitzel, 'Samuel Pufendorf', 809.
322. *GW14,1[PdR]*, 220–1 (§270) (original italics).
323. Reinhart Maurer, 'Hegels politischer Protestantismus', *Der Staat* 10, no. 4 (1971): 467 n. 21.
324. Pufendorf, *The Present State of Germany*, 204.
325. See Boyd, 'Pufendorf on Confessional Strife', 24.
326. Pufendorf, *The Present State of Germany*, 225–6.

327. Simone Zurbuchen, 'Samuel Pufendorf's Concept of Toleration' in *Difference and Dissent: Theories of Toleration in Medieval and Early Modern Europe*, ed. Cary J. Nederman and John Christian Laursen (Maryland: Rowman and Littlefield, 1996), 170.
328. Foster, 'The Edict of Restitution (1629)', 205–15.
329. Pufendorf, *Divine Feudal Law*, 15.
330. *GW14,1[PdR]*, 280–1 (§§357–8).
331. See *GW2[FSII]*, 141. Harris, 'Hegel, Jesus, and Political Theory', 17.
332. *GW27,4[VWG]*, 1543.
333. Ibid., 1542.
334. *GW20[E1830]*, 530–41 (§552).
335. Haakonssen, 'German Natural Law', 260–78; compare Wieacker, *A History of Private Law*, 249–56.
336. Ibid., 252.
337. Ernst-Wolfgang Böckenförde, 'Die Entstehung des Staates als Vorgang der Säkularisierung', in *Staat, Recht, Freiheit*, 105.
338. Reinhard Koselleck, *Critique and Crisis: Enlightenment and the Pathogenesis of Society* (Cambridge, MA: MIT Press, 2000), 39.
339. *GW5[RV]*, 95–9.
340. Ibid., 21–2, 46, 98, 102, 199.
341. Meist, 'Anmerkungen', 752–3 notes the anomaly. Hegel's interpretation of the *itio in partes* in the early fragment 'Religion' is drawn from Pütter's *Historische Entwickelung*, but clearly there is no such discussion in that work about the revolutionary constitution in France.
342. *GW5[RV]*, 21–2.
343. Ibid., 98.
344. Ibid., 46.
345. See ibid., 126, 102. Hegel seems to run the *itio in partes* of *I.P.O.* Article V, §52 together with Article VIII.
346. *GW20[E1830]*, 541 (§552).
347. Böckenförde, 'Staat und Religion', 124 (original italics).
348. Ibid.
349. *GW14,1[PdR]*, 215 (§270).
350. This idea of a philosophical eschatology comes from Taubes, *Occidental Eschatology*, 125–94. Yet he constructs it on an entirely different, three-staged philosophy of history related to Joachim of Fiore (1135–1202).
351. Karl Löwith, *Martin Heidegger and European Nihilism*, ed. Richard Wolin trans. Gary Steiner (New York: Columbia University Press, 1995), 198 (original italics). The first Latin phrase means 'to found the Roman nation'. It comes from *Aeneid* 1: 33. The full line is 'Tantae molis erat Romanam condere gentem!' (So great a task it was to found the Roman nation!). The second Latin phrase means 'To know the spirit itself' and is reminiscent of an ancient Greek aphorism, inscribed at the Temple of Apollo in Delphi: 'know thyself'.
352. Lübbe-Wolff, 'Die Bedeutung der Lehre von der vier Weltreichen', 389. At the Tübinger Stift, *das Reich Gottes* was the watchword. In his philosophy of world history, Hegel directly connected this to the Christian idea that the human being, as free, was a moment of the divine idea (ibid.).
353. *GW5[SdS]*, 361.
354. *GW5[VNR]*, 465 (original italics).

355. *GW9[PdG]*, 22 (original italics and punctuation).
356. Ritter, '"Politik" und "Ethik"', 113.
357. *GW5[RV]*, 96.
358. Ibid.
359. Aretin and Hammerstein, 'Reich IV', 471.
360. *GW14,1[PdR]*, 239 (§285) (original italics).
361. *GW27,4[VWG]*, 1570.
362. See ibid., 1540–3. Conscience, certainty and science (*Gewissen*, *Gewissheit*, *Wissenschaft*) thus share a striking etymological consistency and are elements secured or promoted by the public law of the modern state.
363. Thus, the famous dictum from Böckenförde, 'Die Entstehung des Staates', 112: '*The liberal, secularised state lives from conditions that it cannot itself guarantee*' (original italics).
364. See Hunter, 'Public Law and the Limits of Philosophy', 547 who views this in terms of the collapse of imperial public law: 'What actually permitted the political activism of the philosophers during the *Vormärz* was not the truth of their philosophies, or a historical dialectic unfolding this truth in time, but something quite different – the suspension of the constitutional order that had previously maintained their rival truths in a condition of pluralistic equilibrium.'
365. Karl Marx, *Critique of Hegel's Philosophy of Right*, trans. Joseph O'Malley (Cambridge: Cambridge University Press, 1970), 83–4.
366. Friedrich Nietzsche, *The Gay Science: With a Prelude in Rhymes and an Appendix of Songs*, trans. Walter Kaufmann (New York: Vintage, 1974), 306–7 (§357).
367. Taubes, *Occidental Eschatology*, 155.
368. *GW27,4[VWG]*, 1560.
369. See *GW14,1[PdR]*, 201–4 (§258).
370. Ibid., 217 n. 1 (§270) (original italics). Similar ideas can already be found in *System der Sittlichkeit* where law treated the individual as an abstract universal, irrespective of particularity (see *GW5[SdS]*, 358).
371. Löwith, *European Nihilism*, 199–200 is quoting from Hegel's interpretation of Proclus (412–485 CE).
372. Schmitt, 'Die Lage der europäischen Rechtswissenschaft', 427–9.
373. *GW14,1[PdR]*, 16.
374. See Christoph Kletzer, 'Custom and Positivity: An Examination of the Philosophic Ground of the Hegel–Savigny Controversy', in *The Nature of Customary Law: Legal, Historical and Philosophical Perspectives*, ed. Amanda Perreau-Saussine and James B. Murphy (Cambridge: Cambridge University Press, 2007), 147:

    > Whereas Hegel sought to defend the status reached by the French Revolution, substantially expressed in Napoleonic codifications of private law, Savigny wanted to defend the old Roman law (the validity of which was founded on customary law) against revolutionary innovations like Napoleonic codes. Whereas Hegel wanted a conservation of the revolution, Savigny wanted a conservative revolution, a restoration of the pre-revolutionary order.

375. Löwith, *European Nihilism*, 200.
376. Schmitt, 'Die Lage der europäischen Rechtswissenschaft', 429.
377. Ibid.
378. See Bienenstock, 'Hegels Kodifikationsforderung', 85–9.
379. *GW14,1[PdR]*, 175 (§211) (original italics).

380. Becchi, 'German Legal Science', 185–224.
381. *GW14,1[PdR]*, 175–7 (§211).
382. *GW5[RV]*, 8–9.
383. Becchi, 'German Legal Science', 187–8 – in reference to Gustav Hugo.
384. Stolleis, *Geschichte des öffentlichen Rechts*, 296 (original italics). Stolleis singles out the *Grundlinien*.
385. See Meist, 'Altenstein und Gans', 44–5.
386. Ibid., 49–50.
387. Altenstein quoted in ibid., 49. The manuscript, its origin, purpose and the reworking of the drafts and long delay are described by Meist (see ibid., 44–5). It was a response to Savigny's threat to resign (29 December 1828) that had been made in view of Gans's appointment to the professorship in Berlin. The crown prince Friedrich IV (1795–1861) interceded on Savigny's behalf in an attempt to persuade Altenstein not to appoint Gans (8 July 1829). This required the minister to justify his position. Once Friedrich IV acceded to the throne (1840), Schelling and Friedrich Julius Stahl (1802–1861) were mobilized to bury Hegel and his legacy in Berlin. Gans had already passed away (see Berdahl, *The Politics of the Prussian Nobility*, 348–73).
388. *GW14,1[PdR]*, 174–5 (§211) (original italics).
389. *GW5[RV]*, 9.
390. *GW14,1[PdR]*, 176 (§211).
391. Ibid., 177.
392. Ibid., 175 (original italics).
393. Ibid., 176.
394. Ibid., 203–4 (§258). For the *locus classicus* on Hegel and Savigny, see Aldo Schiavone, *Alle origini del dritto borghese. Hegel contro Savigny* (Rome: Laterza & Figli, 1984). For a recent analysis that studies Schmitt's discussion in detail, see Reinhart Mehring, 'Savigny or Hegel? History of Origin, Context, Motives and Impact', in *Carl Schmitt's European Jurisprudence*, ed. Bogdandy et al., 65–86.
395. *GW27,4[VWG]*, 1557.
396. Damiano Canale, 'The Many Faces of the Codification of Law', in *A Treatise of Legal Philosophy*, ed. Canale, Grossi and Hofmann, 164–73.
397. See Meist, 'Altenstein und Gans', 44–5, 46–9. Compare Toews, *Hegelianism*, 111–12 who notes the underlying anti-Semitism involved which Gans complained about to Altenstein.
398. Koselleck, *Reform und Revolution*, 380; Norbert Waszek, 'Eduard Gans on Poverty and on the Constitutional Debate', in *The New Hegelians: Politics and Philosophy in the Hegelian School*, ed. Douglas Moggach (Cambridge: Cambridge University Press, 2006), 27–33.
399. Marx, *Critique*, 44. Marx probably took this knowledge directly from Gans. Aside from the lectures on criminal law (1836–7), he attended those Gans delivered on the *Allgemeines Landrecht* (1838) (see Waszek, 'Eduard Gans', 36 n. 48).
400. Koselleck, *Reform und Revolution*, 155.
401. See Berdahl, *The Politics of the Prussian Nobility*, 220–2, 97–106.
402. Ibid., 221. See the position taken by Gans, who considers that the estate concept itself dissolved through the ability to move between the estates (ibid., 222).
403. Canale, 'The Many Faces of the Codification of Law', 174.
404. Meist, 'Altenstein und Gans', 51. When the code was revised in the nineteenth century, the first part of it, which dealt with legal personality, survived in that it treated the condition of individuals as members of the state irrespective of status

and personal circumstance (see Canale, 'The Many Faces of the Codification of Law', 173).

405. Koselleck, *Reform und Revolution*, 155 – quoting the *Riga Memorandum* (1807).
406. Ibid., 156.
407. Canale, 'The Many Faces of the Codification of Law', 172.
408. Reinhart Koselleck, 'Staat und Gesellschaft in Preußen 1815–1848', in *Staat und Gesellschaft im deutschen Vormärz 1815–1848*, ed. Werner Conze (Stuttgart: Ernst Klett, 1962), 81.
409. See Kletzer, 'Custom and Positivity', 126 n. 6 quoting from Hegel's contemporary Heinrich Leo (1799–1878).
410. See the concerned correspondence in *Briefe von und an Hegel. Band II (1813–1822)*, ed. Johannes Hoffmeister (Hamburg: Felix Meiner, 1969).
411. See Bienenstock, 'Hegels Kodifikationsforderung', 85–9. This came in the form of his attack on Gustav Hugo and positive law in the *Naturrechtsaufsatz*.
412. See Koselleck, *Reform und Revolution*, 388.
413. Koselleck, 'Staat und Gesellschaft', 86.
414. Koselleck, *Reform und Revolution*, 381.
415. *GW14,1[PdR]*, 252–3 (§304).
416. Ibid., 251 (§302).
417. Waszek, 'Eduard Gans', 43–4.
418. Ibid., 44–5.
419. *GW14,1[PdR]*, 251 (§303).
420. See Koselleck, *Reform und Revolution*, 388.
421. Ibid., 389.
422. Marx, *Critique*, 46.
423. Ibid., 45.
424. Koselleck, *Reform und Revolution*, 384 n. 176.
425. Marx, *Critique*, 49–50.
426. Karl Marx, *Early Political Writings*, ed. and trans. Joseph O'Malley (Cambridge: Cambridge University Press, 1994), 118 (original italics).
427. Marx, *Critique*, 132 – from the 'Introduction' (1843–4).
428. Ibid., 133.
429. Löwith, *European Nihilism*, 199.
430. Marx, *Critique*, 132 – from the 'Introduction' (1843–4).
431. György Lukács, *History and Class Consciousness*, trans. Rodney Livingstone (London: Verso, 2023).
432. Koselleck, 'Staat und Gesellschaft', 88–9. Compare Meist, 'Altenstein und Gans', 53, however, where he speaks more critically. Even if Hegelian philosophy 'explicitly set out to teach the determination of socio-political reality by reason instead of a revolutionary negation of it and placed the administration of the realization of reason within the state in the hands of educated civil servants', this was never unproblematic. In favouring the middle estate, Hegel could have also been following *Politics* 1295b3–5: 'Now in all states there are only three elements: one class is very rich, another very poor, and a third is a mean. It is admitted that moderation and the mean are best.'
433. *GW14,1[PdR]*, 171–2 (§203), 253 (§305).
434. *Politics* 1292a32.
435. Frank Ruda, *Hegel's Rabble: An Investigation into Hegel's Philosophy of Right* (London: Continuum, 2011).

436. Étienne Balibar, *The Philosophy of Marx*, trans. Chris Turner (London: Verso, 2007), 51.
437. J. F. Suter, 'Burke, Hegel, and the French Revolution', in *Hegel's Political Philosophy*, ed. Pelczynski, 70.
438. Marx, *Critique*, 132 – from the 'Introduction' (1843–4).
439. Karl Marx, 'Der leitende Artikel in Nr. 179 der "Kölnischen Zeitung"', in *Marx-Engels-Gesamtausgabe*, vol. 1, 1 (Berlin: de Gruyter, 1975), 189 – quoted in Michael Wolff, 'Hegel's Organicist Theory of the State: On the Concept and Method of Hegel's "Science of the State"', in *Hegel on Ethics and Politics*, ed. Pippin and Höffe, 294.
440. Marx, 'Der leitende Artikel', 189.

Conclusion

1. *GW5[RV]*, 165.
2. Ibid., 202.
3. Ibid., 64.
4. Ibid., 148.
5. Meist, 'Anmerkungen', 754–8, 785–9, 794–5.
6. See Meist, 'Zur Textedition', lxiv.
7. *BtS-FR1*, 41.
8. *GW5[RV]*, 65.
9. *GW4[NR]*, 427.
10. *GW5[RV]*, 37.
11. See Willoweit, 'Privatfürstenrecht', 791 (original italics).
12. See *GW5[RV]*, 165–78. For my discussion Sections 3.4.1–3.4.3.
13. Ibid., 202.
14. Ibid., 201.
15. Ibid., 202.
16. Hayase, 'Die Frage nach der Souveränität, 107.
17. *GW5[SdS]*, 340.
18. *GW5[RV]*, 111.
19. *GW5[SdS]*, 325.
20. *GW5[RV]*, 202.

Bibliography

Primary sources

Achenwall, Gottfried, and Johann Stephan Pütter. *Anfangsgründe des Naturrechts*, edited and translated by Jan Schröder. Frankfurt am Main: Insel, 1995.

Andlau, Peter von. *Kaiser und Reich (Libellus de cesarea monarchia)*, edited by Rainer A. Müller. Frankfurt am Main: Insel, 1998.

Aristotle. *Politics*, translated by Jonathan Barnes. Princeton, NJ: Princeton University Press, 1985.

Bodin, Jean. *De republica libri sex*. Frankfurt: Wechel & Fischer, 1591.

Bodin, Jean. *Methodus historica: duodecim eiusdem argumenti scriptorium tam veterum quam recentiorem commentariis adaucta*. Basel: Officina, 1576.

Böhmer, Justus Henning. *Introductio in Ius Publicum Universale ex Genninis Iuris Naturae Principiis Deduatum et in Usum Iuris Publici Particularis Adornatum*. Magdeburg: Orphanotropheum, 1726.

Caesar, Julius. *The Gallic War*, translated by H. J. Edwards. Cambridge, MA: Harvard University Press, 1917.

Cicero, Marcus Tulius. *De republica, De legibus*, translated by Clinton Walker Keyes. Cambridge, MA: Harvard University Press, 1928.

Conring, Hermann. *Der Ursprung des deutschen Rechts*, edited by Michael Stolleis and translated by Ilse Hoffmann-Meckenstock. Frankfurt am Main: Insel, 1994.

Conring, Hermann. 'Exercitatio de Germanici imperii civibus'. In *Opera Vol. I*, edited by J. W. Göbel, 516–28. Helmstedt: Meyer, 1730.

Conring, Hermann. 'Praefatio de historiarum, Germanorum imprimis, studiis'. In Publius Cornelius Tacitus, *De moribus Germanorum, ex recensione Justi Lipsii*. Helmstedt, 1678.

Eberhard, Johann August. *Abhandlung von dem Begriffe der Bearbeitung der Deutschen Staatsklugheit*. Wittenberg: Zerbst, 1768.

Fichte, Johann Gottlieb. *Beitrag zur Berichtigung der Ortheile des Publikums über die französische Revolution. Erster Theil. Zur Beurtheilung Ihrer Rechtsmäßigkeit*. 1793.

Fichte, Johann Gottlieb. *Grundlage der gesammten Wissenschaftslehre*. Leipzig: Gabler, 1794.

Fichte, Johann Gottlieb. *Grundlage des Naturrechts nach Prinzipien der Wissenschaftslehre. Zweiter Teil oder Angewandtes Naturrecht*. Hamburg: Felix Meiner, 2013.

Fichte, Johann Gottlieb. *Reden an die deutsche Nation*, edited by Alexander Aichele. Hamburg: Felix Meiner, 2008.

Haas, Damian Ferdinand. *De monarchia S.R.I. Limitata contra Hippolytum a Lapide, Severinum Monzanbanum*. Giessen: Brown, 1750.

Haas, Damian Ferdinand. *Vorschläge, wie das Justizwesen am Kammergerichte*. Wetzlar, 1786–8.

Häberlin, Carl Friedrich. *Handbuch des teutschen Staatsrechts. Band 1*. Berlin: Vieweg, 1794.

Haller, Ludwig von. *Handbuch der allgemeinen Staaten-Kunde*. Winterthur: Stein, 1808.

Haller, Ludwig von. *Restauration der Staatswissenschaft. Band 1*. Winterthur: Stein, 1816.
Hegel, Georg Wilhelm Friedrich. 'The German Constitution'. In *Political Writings*, edited by Laurence Dickey and translated by Hugh B. Nisbet, 6–101. Cambridge: Cambridge University Press, 1999.
Hegel, Georg Wilhelm Friedrich. *Gesammelte Werke. In Verbindung mit der Deutschen Forschungsgemeinschaft herausgegeben von der Nordrhein-Westfälischen Akademie der Wissenschaften und der Künste*. Hamburg: Felix Meiner, 1968–2017.
Hegel, Georg Wilhelm Friedrich. *Über die Reichsverfassung*, edited by Hans Maier, text version Kurt Rainer Meist. Hamburg: Felix Meiner, 2004.
Hert, Johann Nicholas. 'Lectori'. In Ludolph Hugo, *Statu regionum germaniae liber unus*. Frankfurt: Zunerri, 1689.
Hobbes, Thomas. *Leviathan*, edited by Richard Tuck. Cambridge: Cambridge University Press, 1996.
Hobbes, Thomas. *On the Citizen*, translated and edited by Richard Tuck and Michael Silverthorne. Cambridge: Cambridge University Press, 1998.
Hoffmeister, Johannes, ed. *Briefe von und an Hegel. Band I* (1785–1812). Hamburg: Felix Meiner, 1969.
Hoffmeister, Johannes, ed. *Briefe von und an Hegel. Band II (1813–1822)*. Hamburg: Felix Meiner, 1969.
Hölderlin, Friedrich. *Hyperion: Or the Hermit in Greece*, translated by Howard Gaskill. Cambridge: Open Book, 2019.
Hugo, Ludolph. *Statu regionum germaniae liber unus*. Frankfurt: Zunerri, 1689.
Justi, Johann Heinrich Gottlieb. *Natur und Wesen der Staaten als die Quelle aller Regierungswissenschaften und Gesezze*. Mitau: Steidel, 1771.
Kant, Immanuel. *Metaphysical Foundations of Natural Science*, edited and translated by Michael Friedman. Cambridge: Cambridge University Press, 2012.
Kant, Immanuel. 'On the Common Saying: "This May Be True in Theory, but It Does Not Apply in Practice'. In *Political Writings*, edited by Hans Reiss and translated by H. B. Nisbet, 61–92. Cambridge: Cambridge University Press, 2006.
Kant, Immanuel. 'Perpetual Peace: A Philosophical Sketch', In *Political Writings*, edited by Hans Reiss and translated by H. B. Nisbet, 93–130. Cambridge: Cambridge University Press, 2006.
Kant, Immanuel. *The Critique of Pure Reason*, edited and translated by Paul Guyer and Allen W. Wood. Cambridge: Cambridge University Press, 1998.
Kant, Immanuel. *The Critique of the Power of Judgement*, edited and translated by Paul Guyer. Cambridge: Cambridge University Press, 2000.
Kant, Immanuel. *The Metaphysics of Morals*, translated and edited by Mary Gregor. Cambridge: Cambridge University Press, 1991.
Krause, Johann Christoph. *Abhandlungen aus dem deutschen Staatsrechte, mit beständiger Rücksicht auf das teutsche Herkommen. Band I*. Halle: Regnerische Buchhandlung, 1797.
Lapide, Hippolythus à. *Dissertatio de ratione status in imperio nostro Romano-Germanico*. Amsterdam, 1647.
Leibniz, Gottfried Wilhelm. *Monadology: A New Translation and Guide*, edited and translated by L. Strickland. Edinburgh: Edinburgh University Press, 2014.
Leibniz, Gottfried Wilhelm. *Political Writings*, edited by Patrick Riley. Cambridge: Cambridge University Press, 1988.
Leibniz, Gottfried Wilhelm. *The New Method of Learning and Teaching Jurisprudence*, translated by Carmelo Massimo de Iuliis. New Jersey: Talbot, 2017.

Limnaeus, Johannes. *Juris publici Imperii Romano-Germanici I*. Strasburg: Spoor, 1628.
Luden, Heinrich. *Hugo Grotius nach seinen Schicksalen und Schriften dargestellt*. Berlin: Unger, 1806.
Machiavelli, Niccolò. *Discourses on Livy*, translated by Harvey C. Mansfield and Nathan Tarcov. Chicago: University of Chicago Press, 1999.
Machiavelli, Niccolò. *Florentine Histories*, translated by Laura F. Banfield and Harvey C. Mansfield. Princeton, NJ: Princeton University Press, 1988.
Majer, Johann Christian von. *Allgemeine Einleitung in Privat-Fürstenrecht überhaupt*. Tübingen: Heerbrandt, 1783.
Majer, Johann Christian von. *Allgemeine Theorie der Staatskonstitution*. Hamburg: Bohn, 1799.
Majer, Johann Christian von. *Autonomie vornehmlich des Fürsten- und übrigen unmittelbaren Adelstandes im Römischen deutschen Reiche*. Tübingen: Herrbrandt, 1782.
Majer, Johann Christian von. 'Beyträge zur Geschichte der Menschheit aus den Annalen der Teutschen', *Teutsche Merkur* 2, no. 1 (1773): 30–44, 136–49; 3, no. 1 (1773), 39–63; 4, no. 2 (1773): 195–244; 6, no. 1 (1773): 76–112.
Majer, Johann Christian von. *Germaniens Urverfassung mit einer Vorrede über den akademischen Vortrag der teutschen Reichsgeschichte*. Hamburg: Bohn, 1798.
Majer, Johann Christian von. *System der Staatsregierung im Grundrisse*. Hof: G. A. Grau, 1803.
Majer, Johann Christian von. *Teutsche Staatskonstitution. Erster Band*. Hamburg: Bohn, 1800.
Majer, Johann Christian von. *Teutsche Staatskonstitution. Zweyter Band*. Hamburg: Bohn, 1800.
Majer, Johann Christian von. *Teutsches weltliches Staatsrecht abgetheilt in Reichs- und Landrecht. Erster Band*. Leipzig: Weygand, 1775.
Majer, Johann Christian von. *Teutsches weltliches Staatsrecht abgetheilt in Reichs- und Landrecht. Zweither Band*. Leipzig: Weygand, 1775.
Majer, Johann Christian von. *Teutsches weltliches Staatsrecht abgetheilt in Reichs- und Landrecht. Dritter Band*. Leipzig: Weygand, 1776.
Marx, Karl. *Capital. A Critique of Political Economy, Volume One*, translated by Ben Fowkes. London: Penguin Books, 1976.
Marx, Karl. *Critique of Hegel's Philosophy of Right*, translated by Joseph O'Malley. Cambridge: Cambridge University Press, 1970.
Marx, Karl. *Early Political Writings*, edited and translated by Joseph O'Malley. Cambridge: Cambridge University Press, 1994.
Melanchthon, Philipp. *Chronicon carionis latine ex positum et auctum multis et veteribus et recentibus Historiis, in narrationibus rerum Graecarum, Germanicarum et Eccleisiasticarum*. Frankfurt: Zepffelii, 1559.
Melanchthon, Philipp. *Commentarii in aliquot politicos libros Aristotelis*. Wittenberg, 1530.
Mommsen, Theodor, and Paul Kruger, ed. *Corpus iuris civilis. Institutiones et digesta*. Cambridge: Cambridge University Press, 1872.
Montesquieu, Charles de. *The Spirit of Laws*, translated and edited by Anne M. Cohler, Basia C. Miller and Harold S. Stone. Cambridge: Cambridge University Press, 1989.
Moser, Johann Jacob. *Compendium juris publici moderni regni germanici. Oder Grund-Riß der heutigen Staats-Verfassung des Teutschen Reichs*. Stuttgart: Cotta, 1742.
Moser, Johann Jacob. *Grundriss der heutigen Staatsverfassung des teutschen Reiche*. Cotta: Tübingen, 1754.

Moser, Johann Jacob. *Neueste Geschichte der Teutschen Staats-Rechts Lehre und deren Lehrer*. Frankfurt: Garbe, 1770.
Moser, Johann Jacob. *Praecognita Juris Publici Germanici Generalissima. Oder Tractat Von der Lehre der heutigen Staats-Verfassung von Teutschland überhaupt*. Frankfurt: Stein, 1732.
Moser, Johann Jacob. *Teutsches Staats-Recht. Zweither Theil*. Frankfurt: Stein, 1738.
Moser, Johann Jacob. *Von denen kayserlichen Regierungs-Rechten und Pflichten. Erster Theil*. Frankfurt am Main, 1772.
Moser, Johann Jacob. *Von der Landeshoheit derer Teutschen Reichsstände überhaupt*. Stuttgart: Metzler, 1773.
Moser, Johann Jacob. *Von der teutschen Justiz-Verfassung*. Frankfurt am Main: Metzler, 1774.
Moser, Johann Jacob. *Von der teutschen Reichs-Stände Landen*. Frankfurt am Main: Metzler, 1769.
Moser, Johann Jacob. *Von Teutschland und dessen Staats-Verfassung überhaupt*. Frankfurt am Main: Metzler, 1766.
Möser, Justus. *Osnabrückische Geschichte allgemeine Einleitung*. Osnabrück: Schmid, 1768.
Möser, Justus. *Sämtliche Werke, neu geordnet aus dem Nachlass*, edited by Bernhard R. Abeken. Berlin: Nicolai, 1842.
Müller, Johannes von. *Darstellung des Fürstenbunds*. Leipzig: Weidmanns, 1787.
Nietzsche, Friedrich. *The Gay Science: With a Prelude in Rhymes and an Appendix of Songs*, translated by Walter Kaufmann. New York: Vintage, 1974.
Pufendorf, Samuel von. *Bericht Vom Zustande des Teutschen Reichs*. Dresden, 1667.
Pufendorf, Samuel von. 'De systematibus civitatum'. In *Dissertationes academicae*, 226–83. Uppsala: Junghans, 1667.
Pufendorf, Samuel von. *The Divine Feudal Law: Or, Covenants with Mankind, Represented*, translated Theophilus Dorrington and edited by Simone Zurbuchen. Indianapolis: Liberty Fund, 2002.
Pufendorf, Samuel von. *The Present State of Germany*, translated Edmund Bohun and edited by Michael J. Seidler. Indianapolis: Liberty Fund, 2007.
Pütter, Johann Stephan. *An Historical Development of the Present Constitution of the Germanic Empire*, translated by Josiah Dornford. London: Payne and Son, 1790.
Pütter, Johann Stephan. *Beyträge zum teutschen Staats- und Fürsten-Rechte. Erster Theil*. Göttingen: Vandenhoeck, 1777.
Pütter, Johann Stephan. *Beyträge zum teutschen Staats- und Fürsten-Rechte. Zweyther Theil*. Göttingen: Vandenhoeck, 1779.
Pütter, Johann Stephan. *Elementa iuris publici Germanici*. Göttingen: Vandenhoeck, 1754.
Pütter, Johann Stephan. *Erörterungen und Beyspielen des teutschen Staats- und Fürstenrechts. Erstes Heft*. Göttingen: Vandenhoeck, 1790.
Pütter, Johann Stephan. *Institutiones juris publici Germanici*. Göttingen: Vandenhoeck, 1802.
Pütter, Johann Stephan. *Kurzer Begriff des teutschen Staatsrechts*. Göttingen: Vandenhoeck, 1764.
Pütter, Johann Stephan. *Litteratur des teutschen Staatsrechts. Erster Theil*. Göttingen: Vandenhoeck, 1776.
Pütter, Johann Stephan. *Litteratur des teutschen Staatsrechts. Zweyter Theil*. Göttingen: Vandenhoeck, 1781.

Rehburg, August Wilhelm. *Über die Staatsverwaltung in Monarchien und die Dienerschaft des Regenten*. Hannover: Hahn, 1807.

Reinkingk, Dietrich. *Tractatus de regimine seculari et ecclesiastico*, Gießen: Nicola Hempeli, 1618.

Rixner, Taddäus Anselm. *Handbuch der Geschichte der Philosophie. Dritter Band*. Sulzbach: Seidel, 1823.

Robespierre, Maximilien. *Oeuvres de Maximilien Robespierre*, edited by Albert Laponneraye and Armand Carrel. Paris: Faubourg Saint-Denis, 1840.

Schelling, Friedrich Wilhelm Joseph von. 'Darstellung meines Systems der Philosophie'. In *Sämtliche Werke, Erste Abtheilung, Vierter Band*, edited by K. F. A. Schelling, 105–212. Stuttgart: Cotta, 1859.

Schelling, Friedrich Wilhelm Joseph von. *Einleitung zu seinem Entwurf eines Systems der Naturphilosophie oder ueber den Begriff der speculativen Physik*. Jena: Christian Ernst Gabler, 1799.

Schelling, Friedrich Wilhelm Joseph von. 'Philosophische Briefe über Dogmatismus und Kritizismus', in *Werke 3*, edited by Hartmut Buchner, Wilhelm Jacobs and Annemarie Pieper, 1–113. Stuttgart: Frommann-Holzboog, 1982.

Schiller, Friedrich. 'Deutsche Größe. Zur Feier der Jahhundertwende'. Available online: www.normannia-winterberg.de/mediapool/56/565510/data/Schiller_-deutsche_Groesse.pdf (accessed 30 April 2025).

Schiller, Friedrich. 'Resignation'. Available online: http://www.michaelbryson.net/academic/schiller-resignation.pdf (accessed 27 May 2025).

Sieyès, Emmanuel. 'Views of the Executive Means Available to the Representatives of France in 1789'. In *Political Writings: Including the Debate between Sieyès and Tom Paine in 1791*, edited and translated by Michael Sonenscher, 1–67. Indianapolis: Hackett, 2003.

Sieyès, Emmanuel. 'What Is the Third Estate?'. In *Political Writings: Including the Debate between Sieyès and Tom Paine in 1791*, edited and translated by Michael Sonenscher, 92–162. Indianapolis: Hackett, 2003.

Spinoza, Baruch. 'Ethics'. In *Complete Works*, edited by Michael L. Morgan and translated by Samuel Shirley, 213–362. Indianapolis: Hackett, 2002.

Svarez, Carl Gottlieb. 'Kurze Nachricht von dem neuen Preussischen Gesetzbuche und von dem Verfahren bey der Ausarbeitung desselben'. *Annalen der Gesetzgebung und Rechtsgelehrsamkeit in den preussischen Staaten* 8 (1791): xii–xxxviii.

Tacitus. *Agricola and Germany*, translated by Anthony R. Birley. Oxford: Oxford University Press, 1999.

Tacitus. *The Annals*, translated with introduction and notes by Anthony J. Woodman. Indianapolis: Hackett, 2004.

Tacitus. *The Histories*, translated by Kenneth Wellesley and Rhiannon Ash. London: Penguin Classics, 2009.

Thomasius, Christian. *Institutes of Divine Jurisprudence with Selections from Foundations of the Law of Nature and Nations*, edited and translated by Thomas Ahnert. Indianapolis: Liberty Fund, 2011.

Unpartheyische Gedanken über die Anmerkungen des teutschen Hippolithus a Lapide. Cologne: Peter Marteau, 1762.

Verzeichniss der von dem Professor Herrn Dr. Hegel und Dr. Herrn Seebeck hinterlassene Bücher-Sammlungen. Berlin: C.F. Müller, 1832.

Virgil, *Eclogues, Georgics, Aeneid Books 1–6*, translated by H. R. Fairclough, revised by G. P. Goold. Cambridge, MA: Harvard University Press, 1999.

Vogt, Nicolaus. *Gustav Adolph König in Schweden als Nachtrag zur europäischen Republik*. Mainz: Varrentrapp and Wenner, 1790.

Voltaire. *Essai sur les moeurs*. Geneva: Cramer, 1756.

Watson, Alan, Theodor Mommsen and Paul Kruger. *The Digest of Justinian*. Pennsylvania: University of Pennsylvania Press, 1985.

Wolff, Christian. *Vernünftige Gedanken von dem gesellschaftlichen Leben der Menschen, und insonderheit dem gemeinen Wesen, 'Deutsche Politik'*, edited by Hasso Hoffmann. Munich: C.H. Beck, 2004.

Zachariae, Karl Salomo. *Der Geist der deutschen Territorialverfassung*. Leipzig: Gerhard Fleischer, 1800.

Secondary sources

Ahl, Ingmar Kurt. 'Möser, Justus'. In *Juristen. Ein biographisches Lexikon. Von der Antike bis zum 20. Jahrhundert*, ed. Michael Stolleis, 445–7. Munich: C.H. Beck, 2001.

Aretin, Karl Otmar von, and Notker Hammerstein. 'Reich'. In *Geschichtliche Grundbegriffe. Historisches Lexikon zur politisch-sozialen Sprache in Deutschland, Bd 5*, edited by Otto Brunner, Werner Conze and Reinhart Koselleck, 456–86. Stuttgart: Klett-Cotta, 2004.

Balibar, Étienne. *Identity and Difference: John Locke and the Invention of Consciousness*, edited by Stella Sanford and translated by Warren Montag. London: Verso, 2013.

Balibar, Étienne. *The Philosophy of Marx*, translated by Chris Turner. London: Verso, 2007.

Baum, Manfred and Kurt Rainer Meist. 'Politik und Philosophie in der Bamberger Zeitung: Dukumente zu Hegels Redacktionstätigkeit 1807–1808'. *Hegel-Studien* 10 (1975): 87–127.

Bazzan, Marco Rampazzo. 'Das Ephorat bei J. G. Fichte'. *Fichte-Studien* 27 (2006): 117–33.

Becchi, Paolo. 'German Legal Science: The Crisis of Natural Law Theory, the Historicisms, and "Conceptual Jurisprudence"'. In *A Treatise of Legal Philosophy and General Jurisprudence: Volume 9, A History of the Philosophy of Law in the Civil World, 1600–1900*, edited by Damiano Canale, Paolo Grossi and Hasso Hofmann, 185–224. Dordrecht: Springer, 2009.

Beiser, Frederick C. 'Fichte and the French Revolution'. In *The Cambridge Companion to Fichte*, edited by David James and Günter Zöller, 38–64. Cambridge: Cambridge University Press, 2017.

Beiser, Frederick C. 'Justus Möser and the Roots of Historicism'. In *The German Historicist Tradition*, edited by Frederick C. Beiser, 63–97. Oxford: Oxford University Press, 2011.

Benjamin, Walter. 'Theses on the Philosophy of History'. In *Illuminations: Essays and Reflections*, edited by Hannah Arendt and translated by Harry Zohn, 253–64. New York: Schocken, 1969.

Berdahl, Robert M. *The Politics of the Prussian Nobility: The Development of a Conservative Ideology 1770–1848*. Princeton, NJ: Princeton University Press, 1988.

Berman, Harold J. *Law and Revolution II: The Impact of the Protestant Reformations on the Western Legal Tradition*. Cambridge, MA: Belknap, 2003.

Bien, Günter, Ulrich Dierse and Johannes Winckelmann. 'Despotie, Despotismus'. In *Historisches Wörterbuch der Philosophie. Band 2*, edited by Joachim Ritter, Karlfried Gründer and Gottfried Gabriel, 132–46. Basel: Schwabe, 1971–2007.

Bienenstock, Myriam. 'Die "Ungeschicklichkeit, die wahrhaften Sitten in die Form von Gesetzen zu bringen", ist "das Zeichen der Barbarey": Hegels Kodifikationsforderung um 1802'. In *Verfassung und Revolution. Hegels Verfassungskonzeption und die Revolution der Neuzeit, Hegel-Studien Beiheft 42*, edited by Elizabeth Weisser-Lohmann and Dietmar Köhler, 85–104. Hamburg: Felix Meiner, 2000.

Blänkner, Reinhard. 'Der Absolutismus war ein Glück, der doch nicht zu den Absolutisten gehört. Eduard Gans und die hegelianischen Ursprünge der Absolutismusforschung in Deutschland'. *Historische Zeitschrift* 256, no. 1 (1993): 31–66.

Böckenförde, Ernst-Wolfgang. 'Bemerkung zum Verhältnis von Staat und Religion bei Hegel'. In *Staat, Recht, Freiheit. Studien zur Rechtsphilosophie, Staatstheorie und Verfassungsgeschichte. Erweiterte Ausgabe*, 115–42. Frankfurt am Main: Suhrkamp, 2016.

Böckenförde, Ernst-Wolfgang. 'Die Entstehung des Staates als Vorgang der Säkularisierung'. In *Staat, Recht, Freiheit. Studien zur Rechtsphilosophie, Staatstheorie und Verfassungsgeschichte. Erweiterte Ausgabe*, 92–114. Frankfurt am Main: Suhrkamp, 2016.

Böckenförde, Ernst-Wolfgang. *Der Staat als sittlicher Staat*. Berlin: Dunker & Humblot, 1978.

Böckenförde, Ernst-Wolfgang and Gerhard Dohrn-van Rossum. 'Organ, Organismus, Organization, politischer Körper'. In *Geschichtliche Grundbegriffe. Historisches Lexikon zur politisch-sozialen Sprache in Deutschland, Bd 4*, edited by Otto Brunner, Werner Conze and Reinhart Koselleck, 519–622. Stuttgart: Klett-Cotta, 2004.

Bogdandy, Armin von, Reinhard Mehring and Adeel Hussain, ed. *Carl Schmitt's European Jurisprudence*. Baden-Baden: Nomos, 2022.

Bourke, Richard. *Hegel's World Revolutions*. Princeton, NJ: Princeton University Press, 2023.

Boyd, Nathaniel. 'Erich Kaufmann et la théorie hégélienne du droit international'. In *Hegel et le droit*, edited and translated by Élodie Djordjevic, 147–70. Paris: Éditions Panthéon-Assas, 2023.

Boyd, Nathaniel. 'Hegel's Hobbes: From the Historical Context of the Constitution to Conscience and Consciousness'. *History of Political Thought* 40, no. 2 (2019): 327–56.

Boyd, Nathaniel. 'Pufendorf on Confessional Strife and Interstate Relations'. In *Pufendorf's International Political and Legal Thought*, edited by Peter Schröder, 23–40. Oxford: Oxford University Press, 2024.

Boyd, Nathaniel. 'The Constitution of Crisis: Politics, Decline and Decision in Hegel's Verfassungsschrift'. In *Crisis and Renewal in the History of European Political Thought*, edited by Cesare Cuttica and Lazlo Kontler, 280–302. Leiden: Brill, 2021.

Brady, Thomas. A. Jr. *German Histories in the Age of Reformations, 1400–1650*. Cambridge: Cambridge University Press, 2009.

Brecht, Martin and Jörg Sandberger. 'Hegels Begegnung mit der Theologie im Tübinger Stift. Eine neue Quelle für die Studienzeit Hegels'. *Hegel-Studien* 5 (1969): 47–81.

Burgdorf, Wolfgang. 'Imperial Reform and Visions of a European Constitution in Germany Around 1800', *History of European Ideas* 19 (1994): 401–8.

Burgdorf, Wolfgang. 'Proto-Constitutionalism: The Imperial Constitution in the Electoral Capitulations and Basic Law Guarantees'. *German History* 36, no. 3 (1994): 415–31.

Canale, Damiano. 'The Many Faces of the Codification of Law in Modern Continental Europe'. In *A Treatise of Legal Philosophy and General Jurisprudence: Volume 9,*

A History of the Philosophy of Law in the Civil World, 1600–1900, edited by Damiano Canale, Paolo Grossi and Hasso Hofmann, 135–84. Dordrecht: Springer, 2009.

Colliot-Thélène, Catherine. *Le Désenchantement de l'État. De Hegel à Max Weber*. Paris: Les éditions de minuit, 1992.

da Vela, Beatrice, and Benjamin Earley. 'Senatus and Sénat: the Reception of the Roman Senate during the Radical Stage of the French Revolution (1792–4)'. *Classical Receptions Journal* 7, no. 1 (2015): 46–63.

Denzer, Horst. 'Bodins Staatsformenlehre'. In *Verhandlungen der internationalen Bodin Tagung*, edited by Horst Denzer, 233–43. Munich: C.H. Beck, 1973.

Dilthey, Wilhelm. 'Die Jugendgeschichte Hegels'. In *Gesammelte Schriften. Band 4*, 5–180. Stuttgart: Teubner, 1990.

Dreitzel, Horst. *Absolutismus und ständische Verfassung in Deutschland. Ein Beitrag zu Kontinuität und Diskontinuität der politischen Theorie in der frühen Neuzeit*. Mainz: Philipp von Zabern, 1992.

Dreitzel, Horst. *Monarchiebegriffe in der Fürstengesellschaft: Semantik und Theorie der Einherrschaft in Deutschland von der Reformation bis zum Vormärz. Band 2*. Cologne: Böhlau, 1991.

Dreitzel, Horst. *Protestantischer Aristotelismus und absoluter Staat. Die 'Politica' des Henning Arnisaeus (ca.1575–1636)*. Wiesbaden: Franz Steiner, 1970.

Dreitzel, Horst. 'Reason of State and the Crisis of Political Aristotelianism: An Essay on the Development of 17th Century Political Philosophy'. *History of European Ideas* 28, no. 3 (2002): 163–87.

Dreitzel, Horst. 'Samuel Pufendorf'. In *Grundriss der Geschichte der Philosophie. Die Philosophie des 17. Jahrhunderts, Band 4: Das Heilige Römisches Reich Deutscher Nation*, edited by Helmut Holzey and Wilhelm Schmidt-Biggemann, 757–812. Basel: Schwab, 2001.

Duke, George. *Aristotle and Law: The Politics of Nomos*. Cambridge: Cambridge University Press, 2019.

Edelstein, Dan. *On the Spirit of Rights*. Chicago: University of Chicago Press, 2018.

Epstein, Klaus. *The Genesis of German Conservatism*. Princeton, NJ: Princeton University Press, 1966.

Eulau, Heinz. 'Theories of Federalism under the Holy Roman Empire'. *The American Political Science Review* 35, no. 4 (1941): 643–64.

Evans, Robert. J. *The Wechel Presses: Humanism and Calvinism in Central Europe 1572–1627*. Oxford: Past and Present Society, 1975.

Fasolt, Constantin. *The Limits of History*. Chicago: University of Chicago Press, 2004.

Finley, Moses. *The Ancient Economy*. London: Hogarth Press, 1985.

Förster, Wolfgang. 'Potenz, Potenzen', In *Historisches Wörterbuch der Philosophie. Band 7*, edited by Joachim Ritter, Karlfried Gründer and Gottfried Gabriel, 1167–9. Basel: Schwabe, 1971–2007.

Foster, Marc. 'The Edict of Restitution (1629) and the Failure of Catholic Restoration'. In *The Ashgate Research Companion to the Thirty Years' War*, edited by Olaf Asbach and Peter Schröder, 205–15. London: Routledge, 2014.

Franklin, Julien. H. 'Sovereignty and the Mixed Constitution: Bodin and His Critics'. In *The Cambridge History of Political Thought 1450–1700*, edited by James Henderson Burns, 298–328. Cambridge: Cambridge University Press, 2006.

Friedrich, Manfred. 'Majer, Johann Christian von (württembergischer Personaladel 1808)'. *Neue Deutsche Biographie* 15 (1987): 717–18.

Gajda, Alexandra. 'Tacitus and Political Thought in Early Modern Europe'. In *The Cambridge Companion to Tacitus*, edited by Anthony J. Woodman, 253–68. Cambridge: Cambridge University Press, 2009.

Glare, Peter W. *The Oxford Latin Dictionary. Second Edition*. Oxford: Clarendon, 2012.

Gonza, Takeshi. 'Reichsauflösung, Rheinbundreformen und das Problem der Staatssouveränität. Die Entstehung der Hegelschen Souveränitätstheorie und ihr geschichtlicher Hintergrund'. *Hegel-Studien* 41 (2006): 113–48.

Grimm, Dieter. *Constitutionalism: Past, Present, and Future*. Oxford: Oxford University Press, 2016.

Gross, Hanns. *Empire and Sovereignty: A History of the Public Law Literature in the Holy Roman Empire, 1599–1804*. Chicago: University of Chicago Press, 1973.

Haakonssen, Knud. 'German Natural Law'. In *The Cambridge History of Eighteenth-Century Political Thought*, edited Marc Goldie and Robert Wokler, 251–90. Cambridge: Cambridge University Press, 2006.

Hammerstein, Notker. *Jus und Historie. Ein Beitrag zur Geschichte des historischen Denkens an deutschen Universitäten im späten 17. und im 18. Jahrhundert*. Göttingen: Vandenhoeck, 1972.

Hammerstein, Notker. 'Das Römische in der Lehre der Reichs-Publicisten'. In *Res publica litteraria Ausgewählte Aufsätze zur frühneuzeitlichen Bildungs-, Wissenschafts- und Universitätsgeschichte*, edited by Ulrich Muhlack and Gerrit Walter, 139–59. Berlin: Dunker & Humblot, 2000.

Harris, H. S. *Hegel's Development: Towards the Sunlight 1770–1801*. Oxford: Clarendon, 1972.

Harris, H. S. *Hegel's Development: Night Thoughts (Jena 1801–1806)*. Oxford: Clarendon, 1983.

Harris, Ian. 'Hegel, Jesus, and Political Theory'. *Leicester University Discussion Papers in Politics* 92, no. 10 (1992): 1–21.

Hayase, Akira. 'Die Frage nach der Souveränität, die sich durch die Verfassungsschrift Hegels zieht: Bodin, Pufendorf und Hegel'. *Kenkyu-ronso* 85 (2015): 97–114.

Hayase, Akira. 'Hegel und das alte Reich – Kontinuität der politischen Tradition'. In *Logik und Realität: Wie systematisch ist Hegels System?*, edited by Yohichi Kubo and Christoph Jamme, 277–86. Leiden: Brill, 2019.

Heckel, Martin. *Deutschland im konfessionellen Zeitalter*. Göttingen: Vandenhoeck, 1983.

Heiman, George. 'The Sources and Significance of Hegel's Corporate Doctrine'. In *Hegel's Political Philosophy: Problems and Perspectives*, edited by Zbigniew Pelczynski, 111–35. Cambridge: Cambridge University Press, 1971.

Henrich, Dieter. 'Einleitung des Herausgebers: Vernunft in Verwirklichung'. In *Hegels Philosophie des Rechts. Die Vorlesung von 1819/20 in einer Nachschrift*, edited by Dieter Henrich, 9–38. Frankfurt: Suhrkamp, 1983.

Henrich, Dieter. 'Logical Form and Real Totality: The Authentic Conceptual Form of Hegel's Concept of the State'. In *Hegel on Ethics and Politics*, edited by Robert B. Pippen and Otfried Höffe, 241–67. Cambridge: Cambridge University Press, 2004.

Hintze, Otto. 'Military Organization and the Organization of the State'. In *The Historical Essays of Otto Hintze*, edited and translated by Felix Gilbert and Robert Berdahl, 180–215. New York: Oxford University Press, 1975.

Hintze, Otto. 'The Preconditions of Representative Government'. In *The Historical Essays of Otto Hintze*, edited and translated by Felix Gilbert and Robert Berdahl, 302–53. New York: Oxford University Press, 1975.

Hintze, Otto. *Staatsverfassung und Heeresverfassung. Vortrag gehalten in der Gehe-Stiftung zu Dresden am 17. Februar 1906*. Dresden: v. Zahn & Jaensch, 1906.
Hočevar, Rolf K. *Stände und Repräsentation beim jungen Hegel: Ein Beitrag zu seiner Staats- und Gesellschaftslehre sowie zur Theorie der Repräsentation*. Munich: C.H. Beck, 1968.
Hoffheimer, Michael H. *Eduard Gans and the Hegelian Philosophy of Law*. Dordrecht: Springer, 1995.
Hofmann, Hasso. *Repräsentation. Studien zur Wort- und Begriffsgeschichte von der Antike bis ins 19. Jahrhundert. 4. Auflage mit einer neuem Einleitung*. Berlin: Duncker & Humblot, 2003.
Hoke, Rudolf. 'Bodins Einfluss auf die Anfänge der Dogmatik des deutschen Reichsstaatsrechts'. In *Verhandlungen der internationalen Bodin Tagung*, edited by Horst Denzer, 315–32. Munich: C.H. Beck, 1973.
Hoke, Rudolf. 'Die Emanzipation der deutschen Staatsrechtswissenschaft von der Zivilistik im 17 Jahrhundert'. *Der Staat* 15, no. 2 (1976): 211–30.
Hoke, Rudolf. 'Hippolithus a Lapide'. In *Staatsdenker in der frühen Neuzeit*, edited by Michael Stolleis, 118–28. Munich: C.H. Beck, 1995.
Hoke, Rudolf. 'Johannes Limnaeus'. In *Staatsdenker in der frühen Neuzeit*, edited by Michael Stolleis, 100–17. Munich: C.H. Beck, 1995.
Hoke, Rudolf. 'Staatsräson und Reichsverfassung bei Hippolithus a Lapide'. In *Staatsräson: Studien zur Geschichte eines politischen Begriffs*, edited by Roman Schnur, 407–25. Berlin: Duncker and Humblot, 1975.
Holland, Ben. 'De Systematibus Civitatum: Pufendorf on Confederations and Composite Kingdoms'. In *Pufendorf's International Political and Legal Thought*, edited by Peter Schröder, 41–57. Oxford: Oxford University Press, 2024.
Hunter, Ian. 'Public Law and the Limits of Philosophy: German Idealism and the Religious Constitution'. *Critical Inquiry* 44, no. 3 (2019): 528–53.
Ilting, Karl-Heinz. 'Hegels Auseinandersetzung mit der Aristotelischen Politik'. *Philosophisches Jahrbuch* 71 (1963): 38–58.
Ingram, David. 'Hegel on Leibniz and Individuation'. *Kant-Studien* 76 (1985): 420–35.
Jaeschke, Walter. *Hegel-Handbuch: Leben-Werk-Schule*. Stuttgart: Metzler, 2016.
Kaser, Max. *Roman Private Law*, translated by Rolf Dannenbring. Pretoria: Gutenberg, 1984.
Kervégan, Jean-François. *The Actual and the Rational: Hegel and Objective Spirit*. Chicago: University of Chicago Press, 2018.
Kimmerle, Heinz. *Das Problem der Abgeschlossenheit des Denkens. Hegels 'System der Philosophie' in den Jahren 1800–1804*. Bonn: Herbert Grundmann, 1982.
Kimmerle, Heinz. 'Die Staatsverfassung als "Konstituierung der absoluten sittlichen Identität" in der Jenaer Konzeption des "Naturrechts". Der Spekulative Charakter von Hegels politischer Philosophie'. In *Hegels Rechtsphilosophie im Zusammenhang der europäischen Verfassungsgeschichte*, edited by in Hans-Christian Lucas and Otto Pöggeler, 129–47. Stuttgart: Frommann-Holzboog, 1986.
Kimmerle, Heinz. 'Zur Chronologie von Hegels Jenaer Schriften'. *Hegel-Studien* 4 (1967): 125–76.
Kletzer, Christoph. 'Custom and Positivity: An Examination of the Philosophic Ground of the Hegel–Savigny Controversy'. In *The Nature of Customary Law: Legal, Historical and Philosophical Perspectives*, edited by Amanda Perreau-Saussine and James B. Murphy, 125–48. Cambridge: Cambridge University Press, 2007.

Koselleck, Reinhart. 'Crisis', translated by Michaela Richter. *Journal of the History of Ideas* 67, no. 2 (2006): 357–400.

Koselleck, Reinhart. *Critique and Crisis: Enlightenment and the Pathogenesis of Society.* Cambridge, MA: MIT Press, 2000.

Koselleck, Reinhart. *Preußen zwischen Reform und Revolution. Allgemeines Landrecht, Verwaltung und soziale Bewegung von 1791 bis 1848.* 2nd edn. Stuttgart: Klett, 1975.

Koselleck, Reinhart. 'Staat und Gesellschaft in Preußen 1815–1848'. In *Staat und Gesellschaft im deutschen Vormärz 1815–1848*, edited by Werner Conze, 79–112. Stuttgart: Ernst Klett, 1962.

Koskenniemi, Martti. *To the Uttermost Parts of the Earth: Legal Imagination and International Power (1300–1870).* Cambridge: Cambridge University Press, 2021.

Kraus, Hans-Christoph. *Das Ende des alten Deutschlands. Krise und Auflösung des Heiligen Römisches Reiches Deutscher Nation 1806.* Berlin: Dunker & Humblot, 2007.

Krüger, Kersten. *Die Landständische Verfassung. Enzyklopädie deutscher Geschichte, Band 67.* Munich: Oldenbourg, 2003.

Landsberg, Ernst. *Geschichte der Deutschen Rechtswissenschaft. Dritte Abtheilung.* Munich: Oldenbourg, 1898.

Lee, Daniel. *The Right of Sovereignty: Jean Bodin on the Right of State and the Law of Nations.* Oxford: Oxford University Press, 2023.

Lesaffer, Randall. 'The Westphalian Peace Treaties and the Development of the Tradition of Great European Peace Settlements Prior to 1648'. *Grotiana* 18 (1997): 71–95.

Link, Christoph. 'Dietrich Reinkingk'. In *Staatsdenker in der frühen Neuzeit*, edited by Michael Stolleis, 78–99. Munich: C.H. Beck, 1995.

Link, Christoph. 'Johann Stephan Pütter'. In *Staatsdenker in der frühen Neuzeit*, edited by Michael Stolleis, 310–31. Munich: C.H. Beck, 1995.

Löwith, Karl. *Martin Heidegger and European Nihilism*, edited by Richard Wolin and translated by Gary Steiner. New York: Columbia University Press, 1995.

Löwith, Karl. *Meaning in History: The Theological Implications of the Philosophy of History.* Chicago: University of Chicago Press, 1957.

Lübbe-Wolff, Gertrude. 'Die Bedeutung der Lehre von der vier Weltreichen für das Staatsrecht des Römischen-Deutschen Reichs'. *Der Staat* 23, no. 3 (1984): 369–89.

Lübbe-Wolff, Gertrude. 'Über das Fehlen von Grundrechten in Hegels Rechtsphilosophie. Zugleich ein Beitrag zum Verständnis der historischen Grundlagen des Hegelschen Staatsbegriffs'. In *Hegels Rechtsphilosophie im Zusammenhang der europäischen Verfassungsgeschichte*, edited by Hans-Christian Lucas and Otto Pöggeler, 421–46. Stuttgart: Frommann-Holzboog, 1986.

Lukács, György. *History and Class Consciousness*, translated by Rodney Livingstone. London: Verso, 2023.

Maier, Hans. 'Hegels Schrift über die Reichsverfassung'. *Politische Vierteljahresschrift* 4, no. 4 (1963): 334–49.

Maier, Hans. 'Hegels Schrift über die Reichsverfassung'. In Georg Wilhelm Friedrich Hegel, *Über die Reichsverfassung*, 195–217. Hamburg: Felix Meiner, 2004.

Malcolm, Noel. 'Hobbes and the European Republic of Letters'. In *Aspects of Hobbes*, 457–545. Oxford: Oxford University Press, 2002.

Malcolm, Noel. *Reason of State, Propaganda, and the Thirty Years' War: An Unknown Translation by Thomas Hobbes.* Oxford: Oxford University Press, 2007.

Mandt, Hella. 'Tyrannis, Despotie'. In *Geschichtliche Grundbegriffe. Historisches Lexikon zur politisch-sozialen Sprache in Deutschland. Band 6*, edited by Otto Brunner, Werner Conze and Reinhart Koselleck, 651–706. Stuttgart: Klett-Cotta, 2004.

Martin, Ronald H. 'From Manuscript to Print'. In *The Cambridge Companion to Tacitus*, edited by Anthony J. Woodman, 241–52. Cambridge: Cambridge University Press, 2009.

Maurer, Reinhart. 'Hegels politischer Protestantismus'. *Der Staat* 10, no. 4 (1971): 455–79.

Medick, Hans. *Naturzustand und Naturgeschichte der bürgerlichen Gesellschaft: die Ursprünge der bürgerlichen Sozialtheorie als Geschichtsphilosophie und Sozialwissenschaft bei Samuel Pufendorf, John Locke und Adam Smith*. Göttingen: Vandenhoeck, 1967.

Mehring, Reinhart. 'Savigny or Hegel? History of Origin, Context, Motives and Impact'. In *Carl Schmitt's European Jurisprudence*, edited by Armin von Bogdandy, Reinhart Mehring and Adeel Hussain, 65–86. Baden-Baden: Nomos, 2022.

Meinecke, Friedrich. *Die Idee der Staatsräson in der neueren Geschichte*. Munich: Oldenbourg, 1929.

Meinecke, Friedrich. *Die Entstehung des Historismus*, edited Carl Hinrichs. Munich: Oldenburg, 1959.

Meist, Kurt Rainer. 'Altenstein und Gans. Eine Frühe politische Option für Hegels *Rechtsphilosophie*'. *Hegel-Studien* 14 (1979): 39–72.

Meist, Kurt Rainer. 'Editorischer Bericht'. In Georg Wilhelm Friedrich Hegel, *Gesammelte Werke. Band 5. Schriften und Entwürfen*, 549–745. Hamburg: Felix Meiner, 1998.

Meist, Kurt Rainer. 'Anmerkungen'. In Georg Wilhelm Friedrich Hegel, *Gesammelte Werke. Band 5. Schriften und Entwürfen*, 746–825. Hamburg: Felix Meiner, 1998.

Meist, Kurt Rainer. 'Zur Textedition der Verfassungsschrift'. In Georg Wilhelm Friedrich Hegel, *Über die Reichsverfassung*, vii–lxxxi. Hamburg: Felix Meiner, 2004.

Melamed, Yitzhak Y. '"Omnis determinatio est negatio" – Determination, Negation and Self-Negation in Spinoza, Kant, and Hegel'. In *Spinoza and German Idealism*, edited by Eckart Forster and Yitzhak Y. Melamed, 175–96. Cambridge: Cambridge University Press, 2012.

Moggach, Douglas. *What is the State For? Karl von Dalberg's Critique of Liberalism and the Defence of Enlightened Absolutism*. London: Athlone Press, 2026.

Mohl, Robert von. *Die Geschichte und Literatur der Staatswissenschaften in Monographieën dargestellt. Zweiter Band*. Erlangen: Enke, 1856.

Mohl, Robert von. *Enzyklopädie der Staatswissenschaft. Zweite umgearbeitete Auflage*. Tübingen: Laupp, 1872.

Mohnhaupt, Heinz. 'Pütter, Johann Stephan'. In *Juristen. Ein biographisches Lexikon. Von der Antike bis zum 20. Jahrhundert*, edited by Michael Stolleis, 518–20. Munich: C.H. Beck, 2001.

Mohnhaupt, Heinz. 'Verfassung I'. In *Geschichtliche Grundbegriffe. Historisches Lexikon zur politisch-sozialen Sprache in Deutschland. Band 6*, edited by Otto Brunner, Werner Conze and Reinhart Koselleck, 831–62. Stuttgart: Klett-Cotta, 2004.

Momigliano, Arnaldo. *Studies in Historiography*. London: Weidenfeld & Nicolson, 1966.

Neschke-Hentschke, Ada. 'Frankreich im Zeitalter der Religionskriege: Jean Bodin'. In *Politischer Aristotelismus. Die Rezeption der aristotelischen Politik von der Antike bis zum 19. Jahrhundert*, edited by Christoph Horn and Ada Neschke-Hentschke, 192–217. Stuttgart: Metzler, 2008.

Niermeyer, Jan Frederik. *Mediae Latinitatis Lexicon Minus: A Medieval Latin French/English Dictionary*. Leiden: Brill, 1954.

Ottmann, Henning. 'Ein philosophisches Finale: Hegels Verfassungsschrift (1799–1803)'. In *Geschichte des politischen Denkens. Band 3: Neuzeit. Teilband: Von Machiavelli bis zu den großen Revolutionen*, 395–7. Stuttgart: Metzler, 2006.

Otto, Martin. 'Pütter, Johann Stephan'. *Neue Deutsche Biographie* 21 (2003): 1–2.

Pape, Mathias. 'Revolution und Reichsverfassung – Die Verfassungsdiskussion zwischen Fürstenbund und Rheinbund'. In *Verfassung und Revolution. Hegels Verfassungskonzeption und die Revolution der Neuzeit, Hegel-Studien Beiheft 42*, edited by Elizabeth Weisser-Lohmann and Dietmar Köhler, 40–84. Hamburg: Felix Meiner, 2000.

Peters, Martin. *Altes Reich und Europa: der Historiker, Statistiker und Publizist August Ludwig (v.) Schlözer (1735–1809)*. Munich: LIT, 2003.

Peters, Martin. 'Das Verhältnis von Staat und Gesellschaft im Werk A. L. Schlözers'. In *Souveränitätskonzeptionen Beiträge zur Analyse politischer Ordnungsvorstellungen im 17. bis zum 20. Jahrhundert*, edited by Martin Peters and Peter Schröder, 109–30. Berlin: Duncker & Humblot, 2000.

Pieper, Annemarie. 'Editorischer Bericht'. In Friedrich Wilhelm Joseph von Schelling. *Werke 3*, edited by Hartmut Buchner, Wilhelm Jacobs, Annemarie Pieper, 1–44. Stuttgart: Frommann-Holzboog, 1982.

Pinkard, Terry. *Hegel: A Biography*. Cambridge: Cambridge University Press, 2000.

Pinkard, Terry. *Hegel's Phenomenology: The Sociality of Reason*. Cambridge: Cambridge University Press, 1994.

Pippin, Robert B. *Hegel's Practical Philosophy*. Cambridge: Cambridge University Press, 2008.

Planty-Bonjour, Guy. 'Du Régime représentatif selon Sieyès à la monarchie constitutionnelle selon Hegel'. In *Hegels Rechtsphilosophie im Zusammenhang der europäischen Verfassungsgeschichte*, edited by Hans-Christian Lucas and Otto Pöggeler, 13–35. Stuttgart: Frommann-Holzboog, 1986.

Quaritsch, Helmut. *Souveränität. Entstehung und Entwicklung des Begriffs in Frankreich und Deutschland vom 13. Jahrhundert bis 1806*. Berlin: Dunker & Humblot, 1986.

Riedel, Manfred. *Between Tradition and Revolution: The Hegelian Transformation of Political Philosophy*, translated by Walter Wright. Cambridge: Cambridge University Press, 2011.

Riedel, Manfred. 'Gesellschaft, bürgerliche'. In *Geschichtliche Grundbegriffe. Historisches Lexikon zur politisch-sozialen Sprache in Deutschland. Band 2*, edited by Otto Brunner, Werner Conze and Reinhart Koselleck, 719–800. Stuttgart: Klett-Cotta, 2004.

Riedel, Manfred. 'System, Struktur'. In *Geschichtliche Grundbegriffe. Historisches Lexikon zur politisch-sozialen Sprache in Deutschland. Band 6*, edited by Otto Brunner, Werner Conze and Reinhart Koselleck, 285–322. Stuttgart: Klett-Cotta, 2004.

Ritter, Joachim. *Hegel and the French Revolution*. Cambridge, MA: MIT Press, 1984.

Ritter, Joachim. '"Politik" und "Ethik" in der praktischen Philosophie des Aristoteles'. In *Metaphysik und Politik. Erweiterte Neuausgabe*, 106–32. Frankfurt am Main: Suhrkamp, 2018.

Rosenkranz, Karl. *Hegels Leben*. Berlin: Duncker & Humblot, 1844.

Rosenzweig, Franz. *Hegel and the State*, translated Josiah Simon and Jules Simon. New York: Routledge, 2024.

Ruda, Frank. *Hegel's Rabble: An Investigation into Hegel's Philosophy of Right*. London: Continuum, 2011.

Rüping, Hinrich. 'Thomasius und seine Schüler im brandenburgischen Staat'. In *Humanismus und Naturrecht in Berlin Brandenburg Preussen: Ein Tagungsbericht*, edited by Hans Thieme, 76–90. Berlin: de Gruyter, 1979.

Sandkaulen, Birgit. 'Die Ontologie der Substanz, der Begriff der Subjektivität und die Faktizität des Einzelnen. Hegels reflexionslogische "Widerlegung" der Spinozanischen Metaphysik'. In *Internationales Jahrbuch des Deutschen Idealismus*, edited by Karl Ameriks and Jürgen Stolzenberg, 234–75. Berlin: de Gruyter, 2008.

Scattola, Merio. 'Scientia Iuris and Ius Naturae: The Jurisprudence of the Holy Roman Empire in the Seventeenth and Eighteenth Centuries'. In *A Treatise of Legal Philosophy and General Jurisprudence: Volume 9, A History of the Philosophy of Law in the Civil World, 1600–1900*, edited by Damiano Canale, Paolo Grossi and Hasso Hofmann, 1–41. Dordrecht: Springer, 2009.

Scheel, Heinrich. *Süddeutsche Jakobiner. Klassenkämpfe und republikanische Bestrebungen im deutschen Süden Ende des 18. Jahrhunderts*. Berlin: Akademie Verlag, 1962.

Schellhase, Kenneth. C. *Tacitus in Renaissance Political Thought*. Chicago: University of Chicago Press, 1976.

Schiavone, Aldo. *Alle origini del dritto borghese. Hegel contro Savigny*. Rome: Laterza & Figli, 1984.

Schmitt, Carl. 'Die Lage der europäischen Rechtswissenschaft (1943/44)'. In *Verfassungsrechtliche Aufsätze aus den Jahren 1924–1954. Materialien zu einer Verfassungslehre*, 386–429. Berlin: Duncker & Humblot, 2003.

Schröder, Jan. 'Gottfried Achenwall, Johann Stephan Pütter und die "Elementa Iuris Naturae"'. In *Anfangsgründe des Naturrechts*, edited by Gottfried Achenwall and Johann Stephan Pütter, 331–51. Frankfurt am Main: Insel, 1995.

Schröder, Jan. 'Justus Möser'. In *Staatsdenker in der frühen Neuzeit*, edited by Michael Stolleis, 294–309. Munich: C.H. Beck, 1995.

Schröder, Peter, ed. *Der Staat als Genossenschaft. Zum rechtshistorischen und politischen Werk Otto von Gierkes*. Baden-Baden: Nomos, 2021.

Schröder, Peter. 'Reich versus Territorien? Zum Problem der Souveränität im Heiligen Römischen Reich nach dem Westfälischen Frieden'. In *Altes Reich, Frankreich und Europa Politische, philosophische und historische Aspekte des französischen Deutschlandbildes im 17. und 18. Jahrhundert*, edited by Olaf Asbach, Klaus Malettke and Sven Externbrink, 123–43. Berlin: Dunker & Humblot, 2001.

Schröder, Peter. 'The Constitution of the Holy Roman Empire after 1648: Samuel Pufendorf's Assessment in His Monzambano'. *Historical Journal* 42, no. 4 (1999): 961–83.

Schröder, Peter. *Trust in Early Modern International Thought, 1598–1713*. Cambridge: Cambridge University Press, 2017.

Sellin, Volker. 'Regierung, Regime, Obrigkeit'. In *Geschichtliche Grundbegriffe. Historisches Lexikon zur politisch-sozialen Sprache in Deutschland. Band 5*, edited by Otto Brunner, Werner Conze and Reinhart Koselleck, 361–421. Stuttgart: Klett-Cotta, 2004.

Senellart, Michel. *Machiavélisme et raison d'état: XIIe-XVIIIe siècle*. Paris: Presses Universitaires de France, 1989.

Siep, Ludwig. 'Deutscher Idealismus: G.W.F. Hegel'. In *Politischer Aristotelismus. Die Rezeption der aristotelischen Politik von der Antike bis zum 19. Jahrhundert*, edited by Chistoph Horn and Ada Neschke-Hentschke, 276–96. Stuttgart: Metzler, 2008.

Sirks, Adriaan. 'Public Law'. In *The Cambridge Companion to Roman Law*, edited by David Johnson, 332–52. Cambridge: Cambridge University Press, 2015.

Stein, Peter. *Roman Law in European History*. Cambridge: Cambridge University Press, 2004.

Stintzing, Roderich von. *Geschichte der Deutschen Rechtswissenschaft. Zweite Abteilung*. Munich: Oldenbourg, 1884.

Stollberg-Rilinger, Barbara. *Der Staat als Maschine. Zur politischen Metaphorik des absoluten Fürstenstaats*. Berlin: Dunker & Humblot, 1986.

Stollberg-Rilinger, Barbara. *The Emperor's Old Clothes: Constitutional History and the Symbolic Language of the Holy Roman Empire*, translated by Thomas Dunlap. Oxford: Berghahn, 2015.

Stollberg-Rilinger, Barbara. *Vormünder des Volkes? Konzepte landständischer Repräsentation in der Spätphase des Alten Reiches*. Berlin: Duncker & Humblot, 1999.

Stolleis, Michael. *Geschichte des öffentlichen Rechts in Deutschland. Erster Band: Reichspublizistik und Policeywissenschaft 1600–1800*. Munich: C. H. Beck, 1988.

Stolleis, Michael. *Public Law in Germany 1800–1914*. Oxford: Berghahn, 2001.

Suter, J. F. 'Burke, Hegel, and the French Revolution'. In *Hegel's Political Philosophy: Problems and Perspectives*, edited by Zbigniew Pelczynski, 52–72. Cambridge: Cambridge University Press, 1971.

Taubes, Jacob. *Occidental Eschatology*, translated by David Ratmoko. Stanford: California University Press, 2009.

Thomas, Richard F. 'The Germania as a Literary Text'. In *The Cambridge Companion to Tacitus*, edited by Anthony J. Woodman, 59–72. Cambridge: Cambridge University Press, 2009.

Toews, John Edward. *Hegelianism: The Path Toward a Dialectical Humanism (1805-1841)*. Cambridge: Cambridge University Press, 1980.

Tuck, Richard. *Philosophy and Government 1572-1651*. Cambridge: Cambridge University Press, 1993.

Villey, Michel. 'Das römische Recht in Hegels Rechtsphilosophie'. In *Materialien zu Hegels Rechtsphilosophie. Band 2*, edited by Manfred Riedel, 131–51. Frankfurt am Main: Suhrkamp, 1974.

Walker, Max. *Johann Jakob Moser and the Holy Roman Empire of the German Nation*. Chapel Hill: University of North Carolina Press, 1981.

Waszek, Norbert. 'Eduard Gans on Poverty and on the Constitutional Debate'. In *The New Hegelians: Politics and Philosophy in the Hegelian School*, edited by Douglas Moggach, 24–49. Cambridge: Cambridge University Press, 2006.

Weber, Max. *Economy and Society*, edited by Guenther Roth and Claus Wittich. Berkeley: University of California Press, 1978.

Weber, Max. 'The Profession and Vocation of Politics'. In *Political Writings*, edited by Peter Lassman and Ronald Spiers, 309–69. Cambridge: Cambridge University Press, 2010.

Whaley, Joachim. *Germany and the Holy Roman Empire. Vol. I: From Maximilian to the Peace of Westphalia 1493–1648*. Oxford: Oxford University Press, 2012.

Whaley, Joachim. *Germany and the Holy Roman Empire. Vol. II: The Peace of Westphalia to the Dissolution of the Reich 1648–1806*. Oxford: Oxford University Press, 2012.

Wieacker, Franz. *A History of Private Law in Europe: With Particular Reference to Germany*, translated by Tony Weir. Oxford: Clarendon, 1995.

Willoweit, Dietmar. 'Kaiser, Reich und Reichsstände bei Hermann Conring'. In *Hermann Conring (1606–1681): Beiträge zu Leben und Werk*, edited by Michael Stolleis, 321–34. Berlin: Duncker & Humblot, 1983.

Willoweit, Dietmar. 'Privatfürstenrecht'. In *Handwörterbuch zur deutschen Rechtsgeschichte. Band IV*, 791–4. Berlin: Erich Schmidt, 2008.

Wolff, Michael. 'Hegel's Organicist Theory of the State: On the Concept and Method of Hegel's "Science of the State"'. In *Hegel on Ethics and Politics: The German Philosophical Tradition*, edited by Robert B. Pippen and Ottfried Höffe and translated by Nicholas Walker, 291–322. Cambridge: Cambridge University Press, 2004.

Zabel, Benno. 'The Institutional Turn in Hegel's Philosophy of Right'. *Hegel Bulletin* 31 (2015): 80–104.

Zurbuchen, Simone. 'Samuel Pufendorf's Concept of Toleration'. In *Difference and Dissent: Theories of Toleration in Medieval and Early Modern Europe*, edited by Cary J. Nederman and John C. Laursen, 163–84. Maryland: Rowman and Littlefield, 1996.

Index

absolutism 45–6, 50, 60, 66, 139, 143, 147, 149, 215 n. 157; *see also* Gans
Achenwall, Gottfried (statistician, Pütter's colleague) 16, 43, 197 n. 52, 207 n. 3, 208 n. 4, 210 n. 50
adiaphora (indifferent matters) 57, 117–21, 164, 166, 172, 176–7, 189
administration / administrative 55, 94, 139, 141; *see also* government law
  office 51, 62, 187–8
  power and state 21, 30, 108–9, 114
administration of justice 102, 109, 141, 143, 146, 158, 206 n. 207, 235 n. 492
administrative law 27, 46, 62, 85–6, 109; *see also* government law
administrator 21, 27–8, 122, 151
agriculturalism 94–104, 105–6, 117, 129; *see also* Möser
Allgemeines Landrecht für die Preußischen Staaten
  artificial system of legislation 141, 147
  Fichte 151, 239 n. 105
  Hegel 140–1, 151, 184, 233 n. 419, 246 n. 282
  Marx 184, 250 n. 399
  Roman law 138, 140
Altenstein (Prussian minister of education) 46–7, 183–4, 188, 250 n. 387 and n. 397
Althusius, Johannes (Monarchomachism) 151, 240 n. 130
anarchy 34, 36–8, 82, 88, 90, 141, 218 n. 244, 223 n. 106, 224 n. 128
ancien régime 20, 24, 86, 147
aristocracy / aristocratic 28–9, 30, 32, 33, 36–7, 64
  Hippolythus 67, 87–8, 122
  imperial estates 67, 71
  manorial 36, 90, 114
  mixed 28, 122
  pure 201 n. 133, 214 n. 135
  worst *forma Reipublicae* 37, 64, 159–60
aristocratic despotism 2, 46, 62–72, 87–8, 90, 102, 108, 141, 144, 166
Aristotle 63, 90, 116, 153, 196 n. 21
  forma Reipublicae 9, 11, 14, 15, 17–18, 19–23, 39, 49, 86, 197 n. 37
  political pathology 32, 60, 68, 108
  practical philosophy 16, 168
  taxonomy of despotism 68, 72, 108, 204 n. 180, 206 n. 207, 214 n. 141
armed neutrality 12, 52, 190; *see also* balance / balance of powers
Article V (*I.P.O*) 77, 169, 171, 181, 248 n. 345; see also *itio in partes*
Article VIII (*I.P.O*) 125, 248 n. 345
Arumaeus, Dominicus (Dutch jurist, Jena publicist) 214 n. 135
Augsburg Confession 171, 237 n. 37, 246 n. 293; *see also* Melanchthon
Aulic Council (*Reichshofrat*) 11, 95, 102–3, 196 n. 17
Austro-Prussian dualism 11, 52, 190
authority 19–20, 25, 41, 50–2, 61–2, 69, 114, 188
  common 49, 52, 54
  despotic and tyrannical 147, 149, 204 n. 180
  emperor 91, 93
  imperial estates 54, 62, 92
  landlord / territorial lord 92, 96, 106–7, 108, 113
  legal 11, 188
  public (*Staatsgewalt / Staatsmacht*) 11, 22–5, 34, 41, 50, 55, 57–60, 86, 89, 95, 100, 106–7, 109, 114, 119–20, 140–2, 146
  state 100, 102–3, 157, 174, 191
  supreme 2, 13, 20, 64, 124, 127, 191

autocracy / autocratic 45, 66, 72, 214 n. 141, 216 n. 200, 242 n. 159

balance / balance of power 5, 12, 16, 20, 22, 24, 27, 52, 55, 88, 142, 190, 192, 212 n. 93, 224 n. 118
Baur, Ferdinand Christian (dialectical theologian) 240
blood feud 34, 206 n. 207
Böckenförde, Ernst-Wolfgang 170
Bodin, Jean 4, 26, 27–30, 40, 49, 59–60, 62, 73, 202 n. 146, 202–3 n. 164, 213 n. 130, 214 n. 135, 215 n. 157
body politic 11, 12–13, 22–3, 26–7, 33
  aristocratic 83, 87–91
  composite 47, 50–1, 73
  head and members 23, 26, 30, 40, 62, 73
  Hegel 11–12, 21, 32, 36, 49–50, 94, 122, 127, 159, 162, 189
  Hippolythus 30–1, 89
  Majer 76–7, 90–1, 122, 127, 224 n. 126
  Moser 12, 23, 26–7, 32
  Pütter 50–2, 58–9
  Roman 37
Böhmer, Justus Henning (Halle jurist and privy councillor) 106
bond (*nexum*) / objective legal connection 25, 35, 49, 51, 59, 61, 73, 141–2, 146, 190–1, 211 n. 59, 214 n. 131
bondage (*Leibeigenschaft / Hörigkeit*) 112, 114, 115, 124
bourgeois / bourgeoisie 56, 63, 65, 66, 139, 141, 143, 147, 149, 158
bureaucracy / bureaucratic rule 46, 65–6, 114, 185–8, 232 n. 367

Calvinism 169, 175
Cardinal Richelieu 212 n. 94
Carolingian 4, 103, 166, 181
Catholicism 70, 169, 174, 175, 178
centralization 5, 24, 46, 50, 65, 139, 141–2, 164; *see also* absolutism
Charlemagne 4, 36, 38, 166
Chemnitz, Bogislaw Philipp von 78, 198 n. 65, 223 n. 118; see also *Hippolythus*
Christianity 99, 168, 171, 174, 179–81, 217 n. 209, 220 n. 19, 249 n. 352
Chronicon Carionis 5, 38
cives imperii 47, 56, 59, 62–72, 107–8, 123–5, 148, 191, 216 n. 177
civil religion 154, 175, 177
civil rights 67, 111, 181; *see also* private law *under* Roman law
civil service 46, 62, 182, 184–7; *see also* bureaucracy / bureaucratic rule
civil society (*bürgerliche Gesellschaft*) 182–8, 199 n. 98, 214 n. 144, 217 n. 209, 230 n. 299, 235 n. 492
  legal order / legal constitution 2, 6, 114, 131, 143, 181
  political 110
  security and protection of private property 130–1
  separation from the state 185–6, 188, 197 n. 52
  state as guardian 158, 184
civitas 71, 107, 110, 148, 230 n. 296
civitas composita / composite state 50–5, 73, 86, 121–2, 153
  quasi-federal 53, 126
  speculative 55, 153, 159, 162, 189
Clapmar, Arnold 227 n. 219; see also *simulacrum / simulacra*
Clarendon, Earl of (Edward Hyde) 247 n. 306
classical German philosophy, *see* German Idealism
Clerical Reservation ('*Geistlicher Vorbehalt*') 220 n. 24
Code Civil 140, 182, 246 n. 282
Codex, see *Corpus iuris civilis*
Confederation of the Rhine (*Rheinbund*) 3, 24, 79–80, 165–6, 244 n. 252
confessional conflict 35, 70, 169, 175–7, 181
Congress of Rastatt 18, 120, 125
Conring, Hermann 2, 4, 38, 47, 68–71, 84, 123, 198 n. 65, 210 n. 50, 216 n. 177, 227 n. 225
conscience 172–7, 249 n. 362
  freedom 77, 168–72, 176, 180, 192, 223 n. 118
  inner being / inwardness 137–8, 163, 167–8, 171, 173–4, 177, 180–1
  ius internum 167–70, 176, 179
  political / internal monarchical space of the state 138, 179

politics 177
Protestant 167, 169, 177, 223 n. 118
public law 139, 169–70, 179, 192
religion 170, 172, 175, 177, 180
transformation 192
trials and heresy 175
consciousness 139, 167, 192
bureaucratic 182–6, 187
conscience 139
doctrine of law / public law 6, 159, 170, 172, 174, 182–3, 187, 192
ethical life / institutional 164, 167, 170, 172, 174, 177
higher conceptual unity 180
ius externum 167–70, 180
Protestant / right to reformation 178–9
revolution 186–8
self-consciousness 38, 137–8, 170
constituent power 151–3
constitution (*Verfassung / Konstitution*); see also *forma Reipublicae*
ancient 94–104, 113, 117, 123, 127–8, 146
Aristotelian typology 9, 11, 14, 19–23, 39, 86, 197 n. 37
crisis 4, 7, 12, 133–7
fiefs (*Lehensverfassung*) 33–6, 38, 79, 87, 115, 145–7, 149, 204 n. 188
legal 2, 6, 34, 131, 141, 143
Majer 76–7
modern / true 5, 76, 86, 149, 157–9, 162, 164
Moser and the empirical 11, 12–13, 15–16, 25, 50
private law 13, 102, 125, 137
constitutional development 23, 35, 100, 103, 124, 126, 145, 149
constitutional / public / state law 13, 17, 18, 23, 34, 44, 53–4, 75–6, 85–6, 88, 92–4, 111, 123–5, 153–67, 171–6, 179, 199 n. 98, 206 n. 207; see also *Staatsgesetze*
constitutional patriotism 170, 177
constitutional relativism 80, 82, 105–6, 129, 221
constitutional theory 61, 82–3
contest of the faculties 46, 182–8
contract 57–9; *see also* Roman law
association / social (*Gesellschaftsvertrag*) 58–9, 207 n. 3
capitulations 11, 21, 23, 57–9, 74, 162
constitutional law 23
foundation of the state 58, 73, 104–5, 113
fundamental law 59–61
Hegel's critique 47, 57–8, 140, 147–8, 191, 217 n. 209
historical-sociological transformation 105
house 11, 23
house community 67, 114, 217 n. 209
law 2, 21, 57–9, 191, 213 n. 120
lordship and bondage / nascent service society as 67, 147, 162
Möser 104
submission (*Unterwerfungsvertrag*) 45, 60, 207 n. 3
union 148
written 58
corporate / corporatism 24, 56–7, 62–5, 89, 97, 103, 110, 113, 139–52, 157–9, 162, 164–5, 192, 195 n. 28
Corpus iuris civilis 20, 36, 64, 67, 69, 72, 111, 154; *see also* Roman law
Count Palatine 30, 31, 202 n. 147
custom / customary 21–3, 34, 62, 64, 67, 69, 90, 94–5, 99–100, 142–6, 148, 153, 168
Hegelianism versus Savigny 182–6, 249 n. 374
law 68, 102, 111, 170, 177, 179, 182, 192
crime / criminal 116, 128, 151, 164, 170, 178, 246 n. 282
crisis 35, 38, 133–8, 175, 178, 191, 236 n. 2

Dalberg, Karl Theodor von (Archbishop of Mainz) 4, 46, 55, 166, 209 n. 31, 223–4 n. 118, 244–5 n. 252
death 56–7, 116, 134–7, 165, 178
democracy 113, 139, 150, 158, 160, 188, 204 n. 180, 232 n. 370
depoliticization 63, 105, 112, 143–4
despotism / despotic 6, 10, 25, 29, 31; *see also* aristocratic despotism
absolutism 45–6, 50, 60, 66, 137, 141, 151
corrupt form 39

democratic form 204 n. 180
distinguished from political rule 45, 68, 72, 204 n. 180
domestic order / *societas herilis* 33, 60–1, 109, 204 n. 180, 206 n. 207, 214 n. 141, 216 n. 186
Fichte 151
freedom 147–51, 166 (*see also* Robespierre)
Haller 108
Hobbes 173
imperial estates 56
Kant 151
legal form 60, 204 n. 180, 206 n. 207
liberal reform dictatorship 166–7
Majer's denunciation 107, 109, 190
Melanchthon's affirmation 214 n. 141
oriental 38, 204 n. 180
religious, Ferdinand II 71
slavery 66–7, 71, 147
De statu regionum Germaniae liber unus 84–5, 200 n. 107
Deutsche Größe 4, 40; *see also* Schiller
Digest, see *Corpus iuris civilis*
Dilthey, Wilhelm 165–6
Doge of Venice 29–30, 33, 87, 89, 90
dogmatism and idealism 156, 160, 241 n. 157; *see also* Schelling
dominium 47, 63–8, 70–2, 74, 107–11, 113, 118, 120, 123, 125, 190, 215 n. 141, 217 n. 209; see also *imperium*
dynastic inheritance 35, 64, 90, 101, 103, 111, 113, 127; *see also* law of succession

eclectic / eclecticism 12, 40–1, 49–50, 148, 163–4, 176, 237 n. 43
Edict of Nantes 176
Edict of Potsdam 175
Edict of Restitution 29
education of the human race 14, 39, 41
egalitarianism 63, 105–6, 139, 149, 192
Eichhorn, Karl Friedrich (constitutional historian) 44, 223 n. 99
electoral capitulations 9, 11, 23, 27, 41, 47, 57–9, 73–4, 191
electors 12, 21, 23, 28, 30–1
Elementa juris civilis, see Heineccius
enlightenment (*Aufklärung / Frühaufklärung*) 46–7, 61, 82, 101, 140–67, 169, 172–7, 184–5, 233 n. 419
equality
abstract, formal 6, 24, 63, 113, 140, 143, 147–8, 175, 206 n. 212
bourgeois legal culture 158, 138, 143–4, 149, 164
lawless state of nature 147, 173
membership in an estate 63, 97, 158, 164
natural law 113, 143
slavery 63, 112, 137, 144, 146, 150
erilis, see *societas herilis / herilis*
eschatology / eschatological 5–6, 38–9, 167–82, 187, 248 n. 350
estate of the free 56, 63, 116, 128, 147, 149; *see also under* Germanic
estate of the unfree 56, 116–17; *see also under* Germanic
estates parliament / parliamentarianism 5, 15, 39, 82, 187; *see also* representation
estates system, *see* system of estates
Eugen, Friedrich (Duke of Württemberg) 81
Eugen, Karl (Duke of Württemberg) 10, 219 n. 17
Europe / European 1, 4, 79, 142–3, 192, 212 n. 94, 223 n. 118
agricultural 103 (*see also* agriculturalism, Möser)
Christianity 167–82
constitutionalism and representation 5, 7, 38–9, 142, 187
freedom 143
monarch and estates 39, 55, 87–9, 95, 129
Rome 178
Spirit 178, 181
external / internal state law (*das äußere Staatsrecht / auswärtiges Staatsrecht / inneres Staatsrecht*) 75, 110, 118, 179

fanaticism 142, 147–9, 152, 153, 175
fate 143, 170
ethical independence (*see also* Schiller) 4, 15, 40, 41, 138
Hegel and Majer 90, 95, 100
Hegelianism 182, 186

Jewish and German peoples 134, 137, 138
reconciliation 137, 178–9
federal / federative (*see also* subsidiarity)
Hegel 121, 123, 140–1, 166
imperial state as quasi-federal 47, 53, 64, 68, 70, 85–6, 121
Ludolph Hugo 47, 64, 68, 70, 72, 85–6, 93, 123, 200 n. 107, 223 n. 99
Mevius's formula 91–4
opposed to territorial sovereignty 24, 85–6
systems 79, 85
transformation of unitary state 22–3, 35, 55–7, 89, 126, 226 n. 198
Ferdinand II (Emperor) 29, 35, 71, 175
feudal hierarchy 31, 90, 92–3
Fichte / Fichtean
concept or organism of the state 148, 150
dogmatism 155, 160, 241 n. 157
Ephorate 151–3, 240 n. 130
estates 149, 184, 239 n. 105
French Revolution 63, 142, 149, 151–3
Grundlage des Naturrechts 147, 152
Hobbes 173, 247 n. 305
idealism 138–9, 141, 154, 161, 189, 241 n. 157
natural law 43, 147, 148, 153, 156
organic central authority 63, 148, 152, 155, 191
rejection of the separation of powers 151–2
revolutionary nationalist 4–6
Roman law 71, 140, 147–9
supreme point of union 160 (*see also under* sovereignty)
System der Sittlichkeit 147, 239 n. 88
universal monarchy 241–2 n. 159
First Coalition War 4, 11, 12, 18, 36, 53, 81, 91
forma imperii
Beyträge zum teutschen Staats- und Fürsten-Rechte 59–60
forma Reipublicae 6, 50, 81, 85, 189, 195 n. 29
Germanici 50, 53
Kant 66
Majer 75–6, 78–9, 219 n. 11
Staatsverfassung 75–6, 88, 219 n. 11
subjective not objective 81, 118–20, 160
System der Sittlichkeit 76, 154, 157, 159, 162
Weber's *Herrschaftstypen* 129
forma regiminis (*see also* government law)
civil service / public office 62
government and constitution 27–8, 59, 61, 62, 66, 81, 85–6, 215 n. 157, 223 n. 99
Hegel's structured monism 76, 154, 157, 162–3, 164
Hugo's original division 85, 223 n. 99
Landeshoheit or rights of government 51, 62
forma Reipublicae
Bodin's aristocratic 28–9, 201 n. 133
body politic 17, 76, 87–91
forma imperii 6, 50, 81, 85, 189, 195 n. 29
formless form / formlessness 86–7, 122, 126, 131 (see also *Unformlichkeit under* Majer)
Hippolythus 28, 31, 78, 122, 125
limited monarchy 35, 52, 54, 65
Majer 78–81, 84–91, 118–20
Moser's rejection 10–11, 13, 16–19, 24, 31–2
philosophy of world history 37–40, 80
politeia 39, 72, 207 n. 228
Pütter's taxonomy 48–62, 72–3
System der Sittlichkeit 49, 157–61
Verfassungsschrift 12, 15, 18, 23, 32, 34, 37–9, 49
formality / formalism 36–8, 62–3, 79, 138, 152, 161, 170, 175, 179, 206 n. 212
forms of government 45, 51, 105, 118–19, 195 n. 29; see also *forma regiminis*
Forster, Georg (geographer, Mainz Jacobin) 82, 165
four empires / monarchies 4, 38, 69, 192
Fragmente einer Kritik der Verfassung Deutschlands (Verfassungsschrift)
'Begriff des Staats' 5, 117–28, 126, 191
'Der Nahme für die Staatsverfassung' 13, 18, 86, 196 n. 6, 196 n. 7, 210 n. 37, 224 n. 126
'Diese Form des deutschen Staatsrechts' 34, 207 n. 236
ecclesiastical and constitutional law 176

Fichte 150, 155, 160
German legal evolution 22, 68, 100, 102, 104, 130, 182–3, 199 n. 98, 237–8 n. 48, 246 n. 285
historical context 11, 18, 24, 35, 63–4, 80–2, 125, 133–5, 150, 155, 166–7, 209 n. 31
'Im Deutschen Reich' 212–13 n. 102
institutionalism 138–40, 142–3
'kan, wodurch die Freiheit' 169, 211 n. 77
Leibniz 165–6
Majer / concept of the state 5, 38, 76–8, 81, 87, 94, 102, 114, 116, 117–21, 125–6, 129–30, 159–60, 162, 189, 191, 209–10 n. 37
Moser 10, 13–16, 18, 23, 40, 209–10 n. 37
political Aristotelianism 15, 37–40, 49, 62, 80
public law as private law 11, 13, 17, 22, 62–72, 74, 99–101, 101–4, 109–10, 123–5, 191
Pütter 43–4, 52–3, 58–9, 63, 65, 138–9, 144–5, 192, 211 n. 67
Reinschrift 5, 14–15, 18, 34, 49, 56, 76–7, 80–1, 86, 118, 120, 144, 191, 194 n. 23
'Religion' 169, 248 n. 341
'Sollte das politische Resultat' 14, 18, 23, 31, 34, 35, 48–9, 76, 86, 197 n. 37, 203 n. 165
'über ihre Entstehung' 23–4, 77, 89
world history 4, 14–15, 38–40, 79–80, 137, 194 n. 17

France / French
absolutism 46, 144–7
artificial representation and legislation 66, 141, 144, 147, 149
destruction of ancient constitution 113, 146, 149
imperial wars against 12, 24, 41, 86, 87–8, 122, 125, 140, 165, 224 n. 126
revolutionary 24, 105, 129, 155, 165 (*see also* French Revolution)

Francis II (Emperor) 80

freedom (*see also under* conscience)
civic 77, 109, 141
contra despotism / Kant 147
history 187, 138
legal 2, 148, 166, 170, 188
loss 63, 65, 147, 151
negative 63, 105, 111–14
organized 6, 55, 80, 150–5, 162, 189
positive 111–14
property and state 117–21, 126, 128, 130–1
public law 60, 172, 174, 177, 180, 182, 185, 191
revolutionary 150, 151
subjective 38, 137, 167, 168–9, 179

French Republic 82, 140, 147, 150, 165, 192, 206 n. 212

French Revolution 5–6, 24, 63, 82–3, 113, 129, 140, 147–52, 164, 168, 175, 181, 189, 190, 221 n. 62, 229 n. 279, 237 n. 46, 238 n. 65, 249 n. 374

Friedrich II (medieval German Emperor) 96

Friedrich II (Frederick the Great) 52

Friedrich Wilhelm (Great Elector) 175

Friedrich Wilhelm IV (crown prince, Prussian monarch) 183, 186, 250 n. 387

fundamental laws (*leges fundamentales*) 11, 26, 57–62, 157, 213 n. 130

Fürstenbundpublizistik 52, 55, 88, 165, 212 n. 94, 223–4 n. 118

Gans, Eduard
absolutism 45–6
Altenstein 183, 250 n. 387, 250 n. 397
'Der Nahme für die Staatsverfassung' 196 n. 6
doctrine of opposition 185
estates 250 n. 402
Marx 250 n. 399
Savigny 46–7, 183–4, 250 n. 387

Gedankenstaat, *see* theoretical *under* state

German freedom
critical 95, 225 n. 186
customs 18, 90, 101
Hippolythus 31, 67, 71, 91, 125, 198 n. 65, 201 n. 131
imperial estates 65, 88, 89, 90–1
particularization / legalization 36, 125, 198 n. 65
positive 111–17, 123, 128, 158, 165
private land appropriation / manorial 79, 90, 97, 100, 111, 124

representative 24, 123, 127
system of estates 82, 166
Tacitus 97–100
Third Germany 66, 91, 190
Germania (Libellus de situ moribus et populis Germaniae) 98–101, 112, 116, 226 n. 194, 228 n. 232, 232 n. 376
German Idealism 3, 27, 71, 148, 183
Germanic freedom, *see* German freedom
Germanic
constitution 89, 100, 101, 114, 123, 227–8 n. 225
Empire 4, 20, 38–9, 67, 70–1, 79, 104, 178, 192, 227–8 n. 225
estate of the free 64, 103, 106, 113, 115–16, 164
free association 90, 103, 127
institution of warlike retinues 101, 116, 145
law 111–14, 114–17, 145
national association 101–2, 116
Nordic principle 137, 163
prehistory 34, 68, 93, 97–8, 100–2, 104, 113, 123, 182
system of assembly / election 90, 98, 100, 103, 123, 127
tribes 50, 68, 95, 98–100, 104, 112, 114, 115, 127, 228 n. 235
World 4, 6, 33–40, 66, 79–80, 95, 104, 125, 138–9, 146, 163, 166, 170, 177, 179–80, 187
Gibbon, Edward 36, 71, 205 n. 200
Gierke, Otto von 98, 195 n. 28
God
abstract 137, 175–6
government / kingdom 176, 178
heresy 175–6
Hobbes, passive obedience 173
Leibnizian / *monas monadum* 154, 156, 162, 163–4
Protestant conception 168, 178
self-revelation 180
Spinozistic 154, 156–7, 159, 241 n. 150
structured monism / absolute 159, 162, 185
Goethe, Johann Wolfgang von 121, 227 n. 210, 245 n. 270
Golden Bull 9, 30
Gönner, Nikolaus Thaddäus (jurist philosophical-legal school) 212 n. 93
Göttingen School (*mos Gottingensis*) 3, 76, 84, 151, 229
government law (*see also* administrative law)
Bodin 27, 62, 215 n. 157
composite state 64
differentiation from constitutional law 44, 53, 62, 86
Fürstenrecht 72
Hegel 76, 154, 157, 162–3, 164
Ludolph Hugo 65, 70, 85, 91–2, 223 n. 99
Majer 75, 92, 94
Pütter 44, 53
regalia 19–20, 54, 62, 215 n. 161
Griesheim, Karl Gustav Julius von (Prussian military strategist) 125, 234 n. 462
Gross, Hanns 7, 83
Grotius, Hugo 55, 153, 215 n. 176, 216 n. 184
Gutscher, Jakob Friedrich, *see* *Landtagspublizistik*

Haas, Damian Ferdinand 211–12 n. 81
Häberlin, Carl Friedrich (public lawyer and historian) 84, 222 n. 84, 234 n. 439
Habsburgs 21, 28, 31, 67, 198 n. 65; *see also* Ferdinand II
Haller, Ludwig von 98, 108–10, 130, 184, 230 n. 299, 230–1 n. 315
Hardenberg, Karl August von (Prussian State Chancellor) 46, 80, 184–5, 187, 209 n. 31
Hayase, Akira 118
Hegel, Georg Ludwig 10, 219 n. 17
Hegel, Georg Wilhelm Friedrich
the absolute 61, 76, 157–8, 160–4, 178–9, 181, 185 (*see also* God)
Altenstein 46, 183–4, 250 n. 387
Antigone interpretation 170
atom / atomism 139, 147, 155–6, 158, 161, 163
Aufhebung 4, 17, 39, 80, 118, 131, 179, 237 n. 42
Augsburg Confession (Melanchthon) 171, 246 n. 293
Bamberg 166, 244–5 n. 252
Berlin 3, 45–6, 181, 183
Bern 16, 134, 171, 205 n. 200, 238 n. 65

civil religion 175, 177
civil society, *see* civil society (*bürgerliche Gesellschaft*)
common good 166
dialectic 38, 78, 116, 154, 159, 160, 167–9, 181–2, 187–8, 243 n. 206
Differenzschrift 77, 154, 160–3, 169
estate, absolute 63, 149, 160, 164
ethical disposition (*Gesinnung*) 116, 167, 170, 174–6, 180–1
ethical life, absolute 12, 56–7, 116, 128, 156, 159, 162, 164, 167, 192
ethical life, modern 6, 130, 138, 167, 174–5, 177, 189
ethical whole / totality 57, 146, 191
ethos and *nomos* 6, 168, 179–80
formlessness 142–7, 152, 183
Frankfurt 3–5, 121, 134–5, 236 n. 2
Glauben und Wissen 155, 169, 171
Heidelberg 13–14, 37, 39, 167, 182
idealism, absolute 5, 12, 46, 55, 139, 141, 153–7, 160, 162–4, 167, 170, 176, 179, 189
institutionalism 5, 57, 62–5, 138–9, 140–6, 151, 157, 166, 177, 180 (*see also* corporate / corporatism)
Jena 3–4, 43, 55, 133–5, 186, 206 n. 216, 236 n. 2
law as doctrine 170, 172, 177, 182, 186–8
legal constitution 2, 34, 131, 141, 143
lordship and bondage (*Herrschaft und Knechtschaft*) 67, 114–17, 147
Mainz 4, 82, 165–6, 223 n. 118, 244 n. 246
monarchical principle 57, 73, 80, 145, 191–2
Moser 9–10, 13, 15, 17–18, 23, 40–1
multiplicity, absolute 154, 163
Naturrechtsaufsatz 56, 63, 65, 146, 149, 164, 182
need for philosophy 136, 161, 163, 169
people (*Volk*) 12, 21, 35, 90, 95, 102, 116, 118, 124, 156, 158–62, 164, 178–9, 185, 187–8, 196 n. 21, 206 n. 207
political Protestantism / public law and religion 170–2, 174–5
Prussian reform 3, 45–6, 80, 188
public law 73, 123, 143–5, 150, 170–2, 176–7, 188, 199 n. 98
Pütter's public law 59, 73, 191–2
Rechtsphilosophie 15, 37, 39, 58, 80, 112, 137–9, 143, 154, 157, 168, 170, 185, 209 n. 31
Roman law of persons 36–8, 112, 137, 175, 179, 206 n. 212
Ständeschrift (1798) 81–2, 134, 135, 137, 245 n. 257
Ständeschrift (1817) 13, 167, 205 n. 198
Stuttgart 3, 75, 219 n. 3, 219–20 n. 17
subjective spirit 4, 133, 168, 170, 172, 179
subordinate systems and bodies 6, 55, 138–9, 142–4, 151, 164, 166, 186
substance 135–8, 143, 154–6
System der Sittlichkeit, see *System der Sittlichkeit* (*Critik des Fichteschen Naturrechts*)
Tacitus 75, 226 n. 194
Tübingen 3, 9, 44, 75, 77–8, 80–1, 120, 208 n. 12, 219–20 n. 17
universal estate 116, 182–6
universal spirit 138, 169
Verfassungsschrift, see *Fragmente einer Kritik der Verfassung Deutschlands*
world spirit 38, 156
Hegel (née Fromm), Maria Magdalena Louisa 219 n. 17
Hegelianism 154, 182–8
Hegel und der Staat 2, 75–6, 133
Heineccius, Johann Gottlieb (natural lawyer, philosophical school) 110, 112
Herder, Johann Gottfried 227 n. 210, 240 n. 111
Hert, Johann Nicholas (jurist, philosophical school) 84–5, 200 n. 107, 223 n. 94, 227 n. 225
Hippolythus (Dissertatio de ratione status in imperio nostro Romano-Germanico) 19, 35, 36, 67–71, 77, 78, 83–9, 122, 124, 201 n. 133, 202 n. 156, 203 n. 175, 214 n. 135
Hegel 32–3, 40, 70, 89, 91, 121–5, 198 n. 65, 201 n. 131, 203 n. 172, 223–4 n. 118, 234 n. 462
Majer 77–8, 87–8, 91, 121–6, 223 n. 94
Moser 28, 30–2, 200 n. 110, 202 n. 156

Pütter 67, 126, 201 n 131
Historical School of Law 3, 45–6, 98, 182–4, 186, 188; *see also* Savigny
historical sociology 97–8, 103, 105, 117, 120, 229 n. 286; *see also* historiography *under* natural law
Hobbes, Thomas 49, 153, 172–4, 176, 247 n. 305
Hočevar, Rolf K. 118, 196 n. 7, 218 n. 1
Hölderlin, Friedrich 66, 81, 120–1, 208 n. 8, 236 n. 2, 239 n. 86
Holy Roman Empire of the German Nation (Holy Roman Empire)
crisis and dissolution / impact on Hegel 4, 12, 133–6
legal and political complexity 5, 12, 17, 19–22, 37, 50–2, 96, 111, 149–50
private law 62–72, 107, 124
public law 5, 25, 124, 180
religion 77, 175, 179
sublation 4, 15, 38–9, 178
translatio imperii (transfer of Empire) 36–9, 65, 68–70, 178
universality 55, 69–70, 100
Horn, Caspar Heinrich (Wittenberg publicist) 206 n. 222
Hotho, Heinrich Gustav (art historian, Hegelian) 125
household rule, *see* despotism, *societas herilis / herilis*
Hugo, Gustav 44, 46, 184–5, 199 n. 98, 208 n. 15, 250 n. 383, 251 n. 411
Hugo, Ludolph 2, 47, 200 n. 107, 223 n. 99
cives imperii 47, 64–5, 68, 70–2, 107–8, 216 n. 177
doctrine of parallel 83–5, 91–2, 130
dominium 65, 68, 70, 107, 123
interpretation of the *regalia* / government law 62, 64–5, 85, 92–4, 102, 215 n. 161, 223 n. 99
summae aemula Maiestatis 62, 92, 94
Imperial Cameral Court (*Reichskammergericht*) 11, 65, 95, 102–3, 226 n. 187, 196, n. 17
Imperial Diet (*Reichstag*) 11, 22–3, 34–5, 54–7, 69, 88–90, 122, 169, 227–8 n. 225
imperial estates 198 n. 76; see also *cives imperii*
Landeshoheit 10, 19–21, 24, 41, 92, 111, 113, 202 n. 156, 215 n. 161
possessing *maiestas realis* / increasingly independent 11, 14, 24, 30–2, 36, 58–9, 62, 87, 90–1, 95–6, 122, 125, 203 n. 172
private law in political relations 2, 11, 20, 36, 37, 49, 58–60, 62–72, 74, 88, 102, 123, 125, 127, 190, 216 n. 177, 226 n. 187
in public law 21, 54, 125–6, 176, 198 n. 176, 199 n. 100, 200–1 n. 120, 206–7 n. 222, 220 n. 24
subordinate to emperor 5, 29–30, 54, 59–60, 84, 202 n. 156
of the Third Germany 55, 91, 165–6
imperial history (*Reichshistorie / Reichsgeschichte*) 9, 45, 90–1, 94, 113, 122, 126, 130
imperial patriotism 10, 25, 52, 55–6, 82, 98, 164–7, 178, 190, 237 n. 48; *see also* patriotism
imperial publicism (*Reichspublizistik*) 3, 4, 38, 79–80, 140, 162, 166, 172
imperium 107–10, 111, 113, 118, 120, 123
individualism 5–6, 63, 105, 113, 116, 136–7, 142–4, 146, 148, 156, 158, 163, 165, 167, 192
individuals, absolute 145, 147, 153, 158–9, 162
Instrumentum Pacis Osnabrugensis (*I.P.O.*) 23, 58, 77, 125, 169, 171, 181, 199 n. 100; *see also* Peace of Westphalia
irregular / irregularity 48–9, 61, 86, 100, 119, 159
itio in partes 169, 176, 248 n. 341, 248 n. 345; *see also* Article V. (*I.P.O.*)
ius publicum universale, *see* universal public law

Jesus 134, 137, 175, 178
judgement crisis 29–31, 38, 134–5, 137, 138, 174, 176, 178, 180, 202 n. 147; *see also* crisis
Justi, Johann Heinrich von (cameralist) 202 n. 156, 240 n. 111
Justinian (Roman Emperor) 20, 69, 140; see also *Corpus iuris civilis*

Kant / Kantian
a priori / apriorism 148, 156, 163
despotism and republicanism 66, 68, 139, 147, 150–1
dogmatism 241 n. 157
Elementa iuris naturae 43, 46, 66–8, 139, 151
idea of organism 155–6
legal philosophy 5, 66, 157, 189, 217 n. 209, 223 n. 99
Metaphysik der Sitten 147
natural law 139, 148, 153, 174, 176
Roman law 71, 147
separation of powers 151–3, 191
transcendental idealism 139, 141, 155–7, 160–1, 241 n 157, 243 n. 206
Karl (Archduke, Imperial Field Marshall) 103, 165–6, 209 n. 31, 237 n. 48
Karl V (Emperor) 71
Katechon 177–82, 181
Kaufmann, Erich (Bismarck Hegelian) 118, 237 n. 48
kingship bound by laws 33, 35, 38, 60–1, 214 n. 141; see also *Staatsgesetze*
Koskenniemi, Martti 7, 83
Krause, Johann Christoph (Halle philosopher) 34, 69, 84, 107, 122–3, 204 n. 185

Länder, *see* territorial states
Landeshoheit / territorial supremacy 10, 19–25, 41, 47, 53–4, 60, 62, 64, 69, 73, 77, 79, 84–7, 89–96, 98, 100, 102, 109, 111, 113, 124–7, 191, 191 n. 89, 196 n. 4, 199 n. 89, 215 n. 161
landlord / landlordship 97–8, 101–2, 104, 109, 113, 116–17, 124, 127, 221–2 n. 74
landownership 90, 95, 97, 100, 101–4, 105, 123
Landsberg, Ernst (German-Jewish legal historian) 84, 85, 98
Landtag, *see* Territorial Diet
Landtagspublizistik 81–2, 221–2 n. 74, 229 n. 279
Lapide à, see *Hippolythus*, Chemnitz
Last Recess of the Empire 25
law of succession 107, 109, 111
League of Princes, *see Fürstenbundpublizistik*
Le Bret, Johann Friedrich (Tübingen theologian and historian) 44, 208 n. 8
legal code / codification 50, 67–8, 140, 164, 182–6, 246 n. 282, 249 n. 374
legal condition (*Rechtszustand*) 143, 146–7, 173, 220 n. 19
Leibniz, Gottfried Wilhelm 5, 47, 153–67, 173, 184, 201 n. 131, 218 n. 238, 241 n. 142
Leibnizian 154, 157, 158, 160, 161, 163, 243 n. 206
Monadology 157, 161, 163
pre-critical substance metaphysics 5, 139, 153–4, 157, 162
simple substances 157–60
Leopold (Emperor) 66, 87, 90
Lessing, Gotthold Ephraim 14, 39, 41
Leviathan 173, 247 n. 306; *see also* Hobbes
Libri Feudorum 69, 110–11
Limnaeus, Johannes (famous early modern publicist) 26, 32, 61, 73, 205 n. 202, 211 n. 70, 214–15 n. 151, 215 n. 155
Lothar II (III) (Emperor) 68–9; *see also* Conring
Louis XIV 66, 147
Lübbe-Wolff, Gertrude 157
Ludwigsburg Treaty 24
Lukács, György 187
Luther, Martin (magisterial reformer) 29, 33, 163, 168, 174–5, 180, 204 n. 180, 214 n. 141

Machiavelli, Niccolò 31–3, 38, 40, 203 n. 168, 203 n. 175, 203 n. 176, 205 n. 198, 218 n. 244
machine / mechanism 46, 82, 140–64, 189, 240 n. 112, 242–3 n. 159, 246 n. 282
Maier, Hans 4, 98, 128, 130, 134, 169
maiestas (*see also* sovereignty)
personalis 26, 32, 203 n. 172
realis 26, 36, 61, 122, 126, 203 n. 172
Mainz 4, 29, 54, 82, 165–6, 198 n. 76, 244 n. 245; *see also under* Hegel
Majer, Johann Christian von
Allgemeine Einleitung in Privat-Fürstenrecht überhaupt 106, 110

Allgemeine Theorie der Staatskonstitution 5, 38, 76–8, 81, 84–6, 88–90, 96, 108, 117–22
autocratic free people's state (French revolutionary state) 82, 105, 114, 129, 232 n. 367
common good / purpose of the state 106, 107, 109–10, 118–20
common private landownership 94–104
concept of the state 76–8, 82, 109–10, 117–28
doctrine of parallel 85, 91–4, 124, 130
dominium and *imperium* 107–110, 120, 123
freeholder state 101, 103–4, 104–6, 111, 121–2, 222 n. 75
Germaniens Urverfassung 75, 81, 83, 94–9, 102–3, 117, 226 n. 194
hierarchy / hierarchical / hierarchical form 77, 87, 89, 90, 92–3, 98, 124, 126–7, 224 n. 135
legal analogy 84–5, 92–4
manorial aristocracy 79, 90, 95, 97, 101, 103, 105, 114
manorial rule (*Grundherrlichkeit*) 101, 105, 107, 113, 120, 124, 127, 222 n. 75
Mevius 84–5, 91–4
nameless form 84–6, 93, 209–10 n. 37
national legal principle 105, 113, 222 n. 75
national representation 82, 104, 221–2 n. 74
patrimonial state 107–10, 113, 119–20, 130, 222 n. 75, 232 n. 369
predial principle (manorial property) 104, 107, 113–14, 117, 119, 124, 222 n. 75
private princely law 2, 107, 108, 110–11, 123, 124, 127, 131, 219 n. 8 (see also *Privatfürstenrecht*)
religious principle 77, 93, 124, 222 n. 75
Tacitus 75, 94–104, 112, 114–16, 123, 127, 128, 227–8 n. 225, 232 n. 376
Teutsche Staatskonstitution 5, 76, 78, 81, 86, 92, 94, 96, 117, 118, 122, 123
Unformlichkeit 79, 86–94, 126–7, 130 (*see also* formlessness *under* Hegel)
Martens, Georg Friedrich von (diplomat and jurist) 231 n. 334; *see also* external state law
Marx, Karl 180, 184, 186, 187, 188, 250 n. 399
mass democracy 113, 139, 150, 188
Maximilian I (Emperor) 65
Meinecke, Friedrich 98
Meist, Kurt Rainer 7, 10, 44, 78, 80, 95, 122–3, 198 n. 65, 203 n. 172, 209–10 n. 37, 250 n. 387
Melanchthon, Philipp (magisterial reformer) 4, 33, 38, 123, 204 n. 180, 214 n. 141, 216 n. 186, 237 n. 37, 246 n. 293
Mevius, David (early modern legal theorist), *see under* Majer
Middle Ages 34, 68–9, 96, 124, 179, 184–5, 215 n. 176, 226 n. 198
mixed constitution, see *status mixtus*
modernity 7, 75–7, 79, 90, 125, 140, 149–51, 170, 188
Mohl, Robert von (professor of *Staatswissenschaften*) 84
Mollat, Georg (Bismarck Hegelian, first editor of the *Verfassungsschrift*) 237 n. 48
monarchy / monarchical 87–91
absolute 45, 60, 80, 147–8, 214 n. 141
constitutional 14–15, 39, 41, 45–6, 60, 80, 88, 95, 104, 166–7, 177, 179–80, 237 n. 42
despotic 46, 60, 204 n. 180
electoral 52–62, 73–4
hereditary 21, 87, 89
limited 3, 33–6, 46, 53, 73–4, 87, 88–90, 190
mixed 50
personality 57, 73, 80, 145, 191
pure 50, 54, 214 n. 135
transformation into aristocracy 30, 36–7, 65, 87–9, 127
universal 35, 38, 224 n. 118, 241–2 n. 159
monism / monistic
Bodinian 27, 49
Hegelian 5, 136–8, 148, 153, 159–60, 164, 185, 189, 192
Pütterian 47, 51, 52, 73
Roman concept of property (*dominium*) 111

monstrosity 37, 48–9, 61, 137, 159, 209–10 n. 37; *see also* irregular / irregularity
Montesquieu 43, 50, 64, 66, 68, 71, 95, 102, 103, 147–9, 151, 153, 163, 225 n. 186, 226 n. 194
Monzambano (De statu imperii germanici liber unus) 38, 47–9, 51, 53, 61, 73, 78–9, 196 n. 23, 204 n. 183, 206 n. 222, 209–10 n. 37
Moreau, Jean Victor Marie (French general) 81
Moser, Johann Jacob
  compilative method 10, 17, 18, 23, 25, 28
  'Der Nahme für die Staatsverfassung' 17–18, 196 n. 6, 209–10 n. 37, 224 n. 126
  emperor and Empire 200–1 n. 120, 202 n. 156
  empirical body politic 11, 12, 13, 25–7, 30, 50, 200 n. 110
  empiricism 2, 9, 12, 13, 15–17, 18, 29, 39, 246 n. 285
  Hegel 13, 15–16, 18, 40–1, 100, 126, 191–2, 211–12 n. 81
  Hugo, Ludolph 25, 199 n. 77, 200 n. 107, 223 n. 99
  juxtaposed to Majer 84, 93–4, 100, 219 n. 11
  Landeshoheit (territorial supremacy) 18–25, 202 n. 156
  Neues teutsches Staats-Recht 9, 13, 14, 17, 20, 34, 41, 81, 100, 199 n. 89
  positivism 9, 41, 195 n. 2
  private law / *Corpus iuris civilis* 2, 20, 64
  relation to Pütter's systematic approach 45–6
  sovereignty and *politica* 18–19, 23, 24–5, 27–30, 31–2, 48
  statistics 15–17
Möser, Justus (jurist) 94–104, 112–13, 115, 117, 124, 128–30
Müller, Johannes von (Swiss historian and political publicist) 44, 88, 122, 212 n. 94, 223–4 n. 118
Müntzer, Thomas (radical reformer) 204 n. 180

Napoleon, Bonaparte 3–4, 6, 24, 86, 120–1, 142, 147, 150, 166–7, 180–1, 190–1, 209 n. 31, 244–5 n. 252
natural law
  formal (Kant and Fichte) 5, 147, 148, 153, 155–6, 174, 176
  Hegel 2, 43, 57, 74, 144, 153, 184, 188, 190, 233 n. 419, 239 n. 88
  historiography 43, 46–7, 60, 104–6, 120, 129, 139, 153, 172–4, 176, 182–3, 185, 229 n. 286, 237 n. 43
  Majer 80, 84, 97, 105, 113–14, 117, 120, 129
  Moser 196 n. 4, 246 n. 285
  Pütter 3, 43, 45–6, 59, 208 n. 18, 209 n. 30, 229 n. 286
Niethammer, Friedrich 245 n. 259
Nietzsche, Friedrich 180–1
Normaljahr (1624) 77, 171
notitia rerumpublicarum, *see* statistics

Oelsner, Konrad Engelbert (Sieyès's biographer) 238 n. 65
oligarchy / oligarchic / oligarchical 36–7, 39, 56, 64, 125, 134, 136–7, 186, 204 n. 180, 221 n. 74; *see also* aristocratic despotism
organ / organism / organization
  Fichte 149–50, 152, 161
  Hegel 5–6, 55, 57, 116, 136–7, 140, 141–6, 150, 153, 157–60, 162, 164, 170, 188, 189, 191–2, 243 n. 191
  Kant 151, 155, 156, 161, 191
  laws 152, 157
  Leibniz opposite Spinoza's system 155–6, 158, 162
  opposed to artificial or mechanical systems 12, 65, 141, 147, 149, 155, 156–7, 161, 164, 182, 184, 186, 190, 239 n. 105, 241–2 n. 159
Osnabrückische Geschichte 97, 99, 102, 227 n. 210
Ottoman Empire 204 n. 180

patrimonialism / patrimonial (*see also under* Majer)
  compared to the feudalism / Weber 113, 114
  corruption of 103

genesis in agricultural prehistory 104–5, 106
Haller 98, 108–10
indifferent to the structural organization of the state 120–1
Möser 103
proto-sociological 129
state and public legal order 71–2, 101, 103–4, 106, 107, 108, 109, 119–20
patriotism 4, 66, 116, 164–7, 170, 172, 177, 181, 190; *see also* imperial patriotism
Peace of Augsburg 9, 138, 167, 169, 179, 220 n. 24
Peace of Basel 12, 35–6, 52, 87–8, 91, 94, 122, 126–7, 131, 165
Peace of Lunéville 52
Peace of Westphalia 9, 25, 77, 89, 91, 169, 198 n. 65, 199 n. 100; see also *Instrumentum Pacis Osnabrugensis*
Pfeffinger, Johann Friedrich (jurist, public lawyer) 26
Plato / Platonic 57, 60, 63, 167–8, 242 n. 178
politeúein 63, 116
Politics (Aristotle) 17, 32, 33, 204 n. 180
political Aristotelianism 9–11, 16, 17–18, 19, 39, 156, 168, 170, 188, 190, 193 n. 10, 246 n. 293
political modernity 76, 149–51; *see also* modernity
positive law 29, 45–7, 54, 57, 58, 73, 183, 213 n. 130
power, *see* authority
primitive accumulation, *see* prehistory *under* Germanic
prince-electors, *see* electors 12, 21, 23, 28, 30–1
princeps legibus solutas 61, 73, 215 n. 155
Privatfürstenrecht 51, 62–5, 215 n. 176, 230 n. 294; *see also* private princely law *under* Majer
private warfare (*Faustrecht*), *see* blood feud
property
abolition / abrogation 56–7, 116, 118, 125, 128
common defence 119–20, 126
common private 101, 103, 104, 106
directum and *utile* 110–11
indivisible / monistic 111
manorial 79, 97, 116
preservation 125
Protestant Aristotelianism, *see* political Aristotelianism
Protestantism 87, 124, 167, 169, 174, 178
provincial estates, *see* territorial estates
Prussia / Prussian
absolutism 46, 66, 139–55, 165, 216 n. 200
independent state system 11–12, 35, 52–3, 87, 91, 138, 165, 190
reform 3, 45–6, 80, 175, 184–88
Second Empire 237 n. 48
Pufendorf, Samuel von (see also *Monzambano*)
German natural law 139, 153, 174
Hegel 49, 51, 53, 159, 172–6, 191, 209–10 n. 237
limited monarchy 53, 191
Reichspublizistik 4, 48–9, 51, 53, 96, 122, 173
religion and the state 172–6
Pütter, Johann Stephan (*see also* reform absolutism)
Beyträge zum teutschen Staats- und Fürsten-Rechte 48, 54, 60, 199 n. 89
Bodin 59–60, 213 n. 130, 215 n. 155
common good / purpose of the state 45, 60, 61, 109
Elementa iuris naturae 43, 45, 49, 59, 65–8, 207 n. 3
Elementa iuris publici Germanici 44, 153, 211 n. 67, 219 n. 5
Hegel 3, 5, 43–7, 60, 66, 72, 73, 139, 167, 184, 190, 191, 192
Historische Entwickelung der heutigen Staatsverfassung des Teutschen Reichs 44–5, 248 n. 341
impersonal legal connection 25, 50, 51, 53, 59–61, 73, 141–2, 145–6, 190, 211, n. 59, 214 n. 131 (*see also* bond (*nexum*) / objective legal connection)
iura reservata Imperatori (imperial reserve rights) 54, 62
ius publicum universale 46
Limnaeus 61, 73, 211 n. 70, 214–15 n. 151, 215 n. 155

Litteratur des teutschen Staatsrechts 113, 123
Moser 10, 45, 46, 246 n. 285
rational natural law 45, 207 n. 3, 208 n. 18
Realverbindung 47, 51, 52, 61, 73, 190, 191
Wolff's methodology 46, 208 n. 18
reason of state / *ratio status* 9, 16, 18–19, 31–2, 35, 127, 203 n. 168, 203 n. 175
Rechtsstaat 2, 13, 34, 60, 114, 130–1, 141, 143, 157–8; *see also* legal constitution *under* Hegel
reconciliation (*Versöhnung*) 38, 77–8, 136–8, 163, 168, 174, 178–9, 185
reform absolutism 3, 5–6, 45, 60–1, 66, 72, 139, 167, 184, 241–2 n. 159
Reformation / *ius reformandi* 6, 69–70, 77, 138, 163, 168–9, 173, 175, 190, 220 n. 24
regalia / kingly attributes 54, 62, 69, 92, 215 n. 161
Regierungsrecht, see government law
Reichshoheit, see imperial *under* sovereignty
Reichspublizistik, see imperial publicism
Reichstag, see under representation
Reign of Terror 4, 24, 46, 142, 143, 147–9, 152, 175, 238 n. 65
Reinkingk, Dietrich (imperial monarchist) 94, 214 n. 135
religious civil war 77, 171, 173–5, 246 n. 285
religious freedom 77, 170, 172
representation (*see also* estates parliament / parliamentarianism)
critique of Otto Brunner 230–1 n. 315
destruction 46, 147, 149–50, 153, 164, 184
estates 15, 164, 185, 186
German territorial states 232 n. 369
Hegel 66, 79, 104, 113, 141–2, 145, 149, 150, 166, 187
Kant 150–1
Landtagspublizistik 221–2 n. 74, 229 n. 279
Lehensverfassung 38, 39, 145, 149, 204–5 n. 188
Majer 81–2, 104, 106, 110–11, 114, 120
Pütter 55–7
Reichskreise (imperial circles or districts) 84–5, 87, 91, 101, 127, 211 n. 80, 224 n. 126
Reichstag and *Landtag* 34–5, 55–7, 166
Resignation (poem by Schiller) 14, 38, 134, 137–8, 206 n. 218
Revocation of the Edict of Nantes 174
revolution, *see* French Revolution
revolutionary fanaticism, *see* fanaticism
Rheinbund, see Confederation of the Rhine
Rheinbunds-Akte 223 n. 102, 244 n. 252
Riedel, Manfred 112
Riemer, Friedrich Wilhelm (Goethe's secretary) 245 n. 270
right of representation 110–11
right to reformation, *see* Reformation / *ius reformandi*
Ritter, Joachim 179
Rixner, Taddäus Anselm 172–4, 246 n. 299
Robespierre, Maximilian 136, 147–52, 166, 175, 176, 191, 206 n. 212; *see also* Reign of Terror
Roman Empire 35, 68, 69, 98–9, 123, 137, 177–8, 227 n. 225
Roman law
contract law 2, 57–9, 191, 213 n. 20
despotism 107, 109–10
dominium, domus, dominus 63, 70, 72, 74, 123
familia 110 (see also *societas herilis / herilis*)
freedman 112, 115
French Revolution 147–51
Fürstenrecht 190–1
German reception 2, 5, 6, 34, 36–7, 63, 65, 68–9, 72, 101–2, 213 n. 20
ius commune 65–6, 69, 226 n. 187
Hegel 2, 5–6, 62–71, 140–51
law of persons 112, 115, 128
lex regia 70
Majer 2, 101–2, 123, 131
Moser and Pütter 2, 20
paterfamilias (*Patresfamilias*) 64–5, 67–8, 70–2, 214 n. 141, 216 n. 186 (see also *cives imperii*)
patria potestas 71–2
private law 2, 5, 6, 63–4, 70, 72, 74, 107, 110, 123, 147, 190–1, 216 n. 177
public law 70, 107, 205 n. 201, 205 n. 202, 218 n. 244

servus 115–16 (*see also* slavery, slave)
Roman Republic / republican 30, 37, 89, 115, 149, 151, 218 n. 244
Roman World 65, 112, 137, 149–51, 175, 177–8, 206 n. 212
romanticism 3, 46, 171, 184, 209 n. 32
Rome, Ancient 4, 36–7, 68–9, 115, 147, 149
Rosenkranz, Karl 16
Rosenzweig, Franz 2, 4, 14, 18, 44, 51, 56, 75–6, 78, 96, 118, 123, 133–4, 140, 196 n. 7, 196–7 n. 30, 237–8 n. 48

Sattelzeit 184
Savigny, Carl Friedrich von 181–5, 188, 209 n. 32, 249 n. 374, 250 n. 387
Schelling, Friedrich Wilhelm Joseph
absolute indifference point 160
dogmatism and idealism 241 n. 157
Hegel 43, 52, 141, 157, 173
influence on Gierke 195 n. 28
Potenzen 238 n. 68
reactionary 185, 188, 250 n. 387
Schiller, Friedrich 4, 14–15, 38–40, 52, 138, 177–8
Schmitt, Carl 181
Schöpflin, Johann Daniel (professor of history, rhetoric and law Strasbourg) 79; see also *Unformlichkeit under* Majer
Second Coalition War 4, 12, 24, 91, 94, 125, 135
secularization 69, 124, 176, 179, 190
separation of church and state 138, 169, 171, 176–7, 179–80, 246 n. 285
separation of powers 147, 151–3, 164, 191
simple substances, *see under* Leibniz
simulacrum / simulacra 32, 35–6, 40, 89, 126, 190, 203 n. 172, 218 n. 244
servitude, *see* slave / slavery
Seven Years' War 11, 12, 20, 31, 35, 36, 52, 53, 87, 131, 198 n. 65, 203 n. 176
Sieyès, Emmanuel Joseph 143, 150, 152–3, 238 n. 65, 240 n. 108, 240 n. 112
Sinclair, Issac von 81, 120, 221 n. 62, 236 n. 2
slave / slavery
despotism / absolutism 62–3, 65–8, 71, 74, 144, 147, 150
distinction from the estates / Germanic law 62–3, 112, 114, 115, 145
formal equality / Hegel 63, 137, 144, 146–7, 150
household 216 n. 186
monarchical / Fichte 241–2 n. 159
Sleidanus, Johannes (historian of the Reformation) 29–30, 202 n. 146; *see also* Doge of Venice
societas herilis / herilis 60–1, 65, 67, 108, 214 n. 141, 217 n. 209
Socrates 167–8, 170
sovereignty 41, 45, 57, 107 (see also *maiestas*)
absolute indifference point 143, 160, 166, 172
appearances 32, 36, 40, 67, 73, 89, 126, 203 n. 172 (see also *simulacrum / simulacra*)
Bodinian 27, 60, 62, 215 n. 155, 215 n. 157
constitutional 26, 60, 80, 191–2
contractual 58–60, 105
doctrine 1, 11, 26, 29, 31, 72, 75, 81, 89, 93, 109, 110, 117, 125, 129, 141, 160, 207 n. 3, 215 n. 176
form of organization 74–5, 119, 142
Hegelian 22, 24, 57–8, 89, 119–21, 143, 160, 166, 172, 209–10 n. 37, 220 n. 35
Hobbesian 49, 173–4
imperial 19, 25, 50, 51, 54, 57–8, 62, 69, 71–3, 85–6, 89, 92–4, 124–5, 127
indivisible 7, 27, 49, 51, 52, 62
internal and external 36, 58
limited 53, 54, 60, 61, 65, 73
locus 10, 19, 24, 32, 190
logic 49, 117
Majer 78, 85, 119, 122, 127, 160, 221–2 n. 74
marks 58, 127, 165, 202 n. 156
monarchical 24, 54, 57, 73, 95, 190–1
Moser 9, 18–25, 27, 29
objective organization 57, 73, 81, 96, 114, 119–21, 158, 160, 189
objective principle 61–2, 73, 106, 119
personal, *see maiestas personalis*
popular 59, 114, 150, 158, 212 n. 93
Pufendorf 48–9, 53
Pütter 45, 50–62

quasi- 19, 35, 52–3, 58, 78
real, *see maiestas realis*
rights 1, 19, 24, 51, 59, 61, 92, 96, 117, 202 n. 156
shared 51, 61–2
subjective organization 96, 118–19, 142
subjective principle 119
supreme point of union 89, 120, 143, 160, 166, 172
territorial 11, 20, 24, 35, 51, 53, 58–9, 64, 80, 85–6, 87, 90, 93–4, 100, 125, 166, 198 n. 69, 202 n. 156
true 30, 41, 59, 114
Spinoza / Spinozistic 5, 139, 153–7, 158, 160, 161, 163, 241 n. 150
spirit, absolute 38–9, 41, 57, 141, 156, 163, 169, 177, 186; *see also* world history
Spittler, Ludwig Timotheus (Göttingen professor) 221–2 n. 74, 229 n. 279; see also *Landtagspublizistik*
Staatsgesetze 15, 73, 142, 145, 150, 188, 191
Staatsverfassung 5, 9–10, 75–6, 86, 88, 159, 162
Stahl, Friedrich Julius (post-Hegelian conservative legal philosopher) 185, 188, 250 n. 387
state
absolute / power state 46, 50, 61, 141, 146, 147–8, 150, 185, 189
autocratic 72, 82, 105, 114, 129, 214 n. 141, 216 n. 200
bourgeois 66, 139, 141, 143, 147, 149, 245 n. 257
composite, *see* civitas composita / composite state
concept 5, 76–8, 82, 110, 116, 117–21, 125–6, 128–30, 162, 189, 191–2, 197 n. 37
constitutional 45–6, 59–60, 74, 138, 157, 166, 180–1, 191–2
despotic 37, 46 (*see also* despotism / despotic)
existence 13, 15, 73, 119, 128
guardian of civil society 2–3, 130–1, 158, 166, 184
imperial 2, 9, 51, 57–9, 65, 71–2, 73, 85, 87, 90, 94–5, 98, 122, 125–7, 158, 167, 189, 191
irregular, *see* irregular / irregularity
machine 139, 141, 150, 155, 161, 246 n. 282 (*see also* machine / mechanism)
minimal concept 121, 126, 130, 140–2
monarchical 138, 187, 241–2 n. 159
monocratic 46, 54, 66, 87–8, 110, 141
moral person 109, 110, 122, 131
organic 82, 157, 185–6, 188
patrimonial and freeholder 72, 101, 103, 104–17, 119–21, 130, 232 n. 369
polyarchic 121
predial conception of 98
proto-sociological 82, 129
quasi-federal 47, 53, 64, 68, 70, 72, 74, 85, 93, 121, 123, 126, 200 n. 107
structured monism 153–60, 164, 185, 192 (*see also* Hegelian *under* monism / monistic)
territorial 5, 22, 47, 56, 63, 65, 71–2, 74, 82–3, 86, 88, 98, 104–6, 108, 110, 114–15, 131, 138, 142, 222 n. 75, 226 n. 198, 232 n. 369
theoretical (*Gedankenstaat*) 15, 73, 189, 190
tutelary 185
unitary 35–6, 87, 184, 206–7 n. 222, 242 n. 178
Weberian 65, 129
state of nature 46, 58, 105, 112, 117, 126, 129, 143, 146–8, 159, 173, 207 n. 3, 229 n. 286
statistics 15–16, 40, 49, 86, 210 n. 50
status mixtus 26–7, 49, 50, 52–62, 66, 73, 77, 159, 215 n. 157
Stein, Friedrich Karl Baron vom und zum (Prussian reformer) 46, 80, 98, 184
Stolleis, Michael 7, 80, 83
subsidiarity 5–6, 186, 192, 194–5 n. 27
Svarez, Carl Gottlieb 233 n. 419; see also *Allgemeines Landrecht für die Preußischen Staaten*
System der Sittlichkeit (*Critik des Fichteschen Naturrechts*)
absolute idealism 12, 116, 139, 144, 156, 168, 170, 174, 178–9, 192
absolute movement 76, 150, 159, 164, 178
absolute universal 144, 146
body politic / corporatism / organism 55, 62–3, 150, 155–7, 159, 162, 182, 185, 243 n. 191

civitas composita 55, 159, 162
Fichte 147, 239 n. 88, 247 n. 305
forma Reipublicae 37, 62, 130, 237 n. 42
French Revolution 63, 139, 147, 150, 158
legal evolution 68, 144–5, 157, 168, 170, 182, 249 n. 370
Majer 75–6, 157, 189
political programme 5, 56, 140, 164–7
pre-critical substance metaphysics 153–8, 161–4, 165–6
Prussia 139, 141, 147, 149, 246 n. 282
Pütter 157–8
subjectobjectivity 154, 160, 162, 167
system of estates 62–3, 67, 144–5, 150, 157–9, 164, 192
true constitution (government) 76, 86, 103, 149, 157–9, 162, 164
universal constitution of estates 138, 144, 146
system of estates 63, 67, 101, 113, 142–3, 153, 157–8, 161, 165, 189, 192, 204–5 n. 188, 239 n. 105
system of states (*systematibus civitatum*) 47–9, 52, 73, 96, 149

Tacitus, Publius Cornelius
Hegel 75, 95, 96, 100, 102, 104, 112, 225 n. 186, 226 n. 194
Majer 75, 94–104, 111–12, 114–16, 123, 127–8, 225 n. 184, 232 n. 376
Möser 97, 99–100, 103, 112, 115, 228 n. 235
reception 98–9, 203 n. 168, 227 n. 221, 227 n. 225
territorial estates 6, 10, 20–1, 46, 54, 65–7, 90–1, 98–9, 109, 115, 144–6, 166, 222–1 n. 74, 229 n. 279, 237 n. 48
territorial estates constitution (*landständische Verfassung*) 21, 66, 134
territorial law 51, 53, 62, 64–5, 84, 92–4, 97–8, 102, 144; *see also* governmental law
territorial right 9, 24–5, 41, 51, 92, 169
territorial state constitution (*Staatskonstitution*) 82, 123
territorial supremacy, see *Landeshoheit / territorial supremacy*
teutsche Libertät, see *Hippolythus*
theodicy 5, 177–82, 187
Thibaut, Anton Friedrich Justus (jurist, Hegel's Heidelberg colleague) 182
third estate 56, 153
Third Germany 55, 66, 91, 190, 223–4 n. 118
Thirty Years' War 10–11, 12, 17, 28, 30–1, 35, 69–70, 78, 122, 125, 131, 171, 174–5, 201 n. 131
Thomasius, Christian 26, 48, 139, 153, 172–6, 209–10 n. 37, 237 n. 43, 247 n. 310
toleration 77, 167–82, 246 n. 285
translatio imperii, *see under* Holy Roman Empire of the German Nation
Treuer, Gottlieb Samuel 26, 28
turning point, *see* crisis
tyranny 31, 33, 37, 39, 60, 147, 204 n. 180, 206 n. 207, 214 n. 141

Ulpian (Roman jurist) 61, 73, 106–7, 109, 199 n. 98
universal estate 56, 116, 145, 182–8, 192
universality
abstract and formal 62–3, 67, 137, 146, 175
corporate (estate) 142, 145–6, 159, 164, 186–7
imperial 69–70, 167
legal 100, 145, 150, 162, 172, 183–4, 191
unity of universality and particularity (Christianity) 170
universal public law (*ius publicum universale*)
capitulation theory and contract 2, 57–9
definition 1
German Idealism 3, 183
Hegel 3, 60, 94, 109, 139, 144, 153, 158–9, 171, 188, 192 (see also *Staatsgesetze*)
Majer 109
Moser's rejection 9, 16, 246 n. 285
Pütter (and Achenwall) 3, 45, 54, 61–2, 109, 207 n. 3, 209 n. 30, 246 n. 285
University of Berlin 46, 183–5, 188, 250 n. 387
University of Göttingen 43, 45
University of Tübingen 44, 75, 218–19 n. 1, 219–20 n. 17, 245 n. 259, 248 n. 352

Verfassungsrecht, see constitutional / public / state law
Villey, Michel 71–2, 147, 218 n. 244
Vogt, Nicolaus (political theorist and historian) 223 n. 118
Völkerrecht (international law) 5, 51, 54, 118, 122
Voltaire 37, 223 n. 106, 224 n. 128, 225 n. 186
Vormärz (period prior to the 1848 revolution) 6, 182, 186, 249 n. 364

Walker, Mack 15, 16
Weber, Max 2, 35, 65, 116, 129, 232 n. 367, 233 n. 389
Wieland, Christoph Martin 75
Wilhelm II (German Emperor) 237–8 n. 48
Wolff, Christian 45, 46, 110, 139, 153–4, 157, 174, 184, 208 n. 18, 237 n. 43, 241 n. 140
world history 4–6, 14, 37–40, 80, 95, 136–8, 166–82, 186–7, 191, 194 n. 17, 206 n. 218, 248 n. 352
Württemberg 5, 9–10, 24, 56, 66, 78, 81–2, 134, 166–7, 218–19 n. 1, 219–20 n. 17
Württemberg Constitution (1815) 13, 167

Zachariae, Karl Salomo (jurist) 106, 229–30 n. 291

www.ingramcontent.com/pod-product-compliance
Ingram Content Group UK Ltd.
Pitfield, Milton Keynes, MK11 3LW, UK
UKHW020243290926
15470UKWH00002B/717

9 781350 584174